From
Reverence
to Rape

MOLLY HASKELL

From Reverence to Rape

*The Treatment of
Women in the Movies*

Second Edition

THE UNIVERSITY OF CHICAGO PRESS
Chicago & London

To Andrew

The University of Chicago Press, Chicago, 60637
The University of Chicago Press, Ltd., London

03 02 01 00 99 98 97 96 95 94   6 7 8 9 10 11

From Reverence to Rape was first published by Holt, Rinehart
and Winston, Inc., New York, 1974. Portions of "The
Twenties" previously appeared in *The Columbia Forum*.
Portions of "The Big Lie" previously appeared in *American
Film Institute* magazine.

Library of Congress Cataloging in Publication Data

Haskell, Molly.
   From reverence to rape.

   1. Women in moving-pictures—History.   I. Title.
PN1995.9.W6H3   1987   791.43′09′09352042   87–14354
ISBN 0–226–31885–0 (pbk.)

⊛ The paper used in this publication meets the minimum
requirements of the American National Standard for Information
Sciences—Permanence of Paper for Printed Library Materials,
ANSI Z39.48-1984.

CONTENTS

PREFACE TO THE SECOND EDITION

Updating a book is a risky business, especially if it was written more than a decade earlier, in a different mood and social context. In 1972–73, the rhetoric of the women's movement, then peaking, was at its most romantically utopian, yet there were no signs of a corresponding influx of bold and defiantly up-to-date screen women. In fact, there were no women of any kind, a situation depressing for those of us who liked movies (and women), but convenient for purposes of polemical thrust.

The book, I hoped, was more than just a polemic. It was intended to offer a historical study of the images of women in film as mostly defined and elaborated by men but with many glorious challenges by the presumed female victims. The trajectory, though, was a simple one of decline, and the message was equally straightforward: Down with sexism, up with women!

But as I discovered in trying to make thematic sense of the diverse material and odd cross currents of the last 12 years, sometimes it's easier to curse the darkness than light a candle, especially when the candles proliferate and vary enormously in brilliance, beauty, and illuminative power. Women directors have increased tenfold, but some are a good deal more interesting than others. Some are more feminist than others. And there's no invariable correlation between the good, the true, and the feminist.

Nor do the images on the screen offer anything much in the way of "positive role models." There were more working women, from trucking company CEOs to Macy's shopgirls, in the movies of the thirties and forties than in those of the seventies and eighties, and certainly a great deal more of a sense of women's orderly participation in the male-female business of life. The evidence of the seismic shift in perspective and ideas wrought by feminism is more oblique. For it, one must look to the anarchic and unsettling "crazy woman" roles of the recent past. Or, as counterpoint, to the backlash represented by the various kinds of male potency movies, from the grunting Rambo–Reaganite revenge fantasies to male mothering sagas to the runny-nose coming-of-age teen-pics now (hopefully) derided into oblivion as "pimple movies." Or to the European and independent cinemas, which have moved in to fill the gap left by Hollywood's increasingly crass, bottom-line thinking, and become champions of the adult, the offbeat, the socially complex, and the sexually ambiguous. And for the more adventurous films, there's the small but increasingly sophisticated (and influential) group of viewers and reviewers for whom feminism is now no longer a debating point but a given.

In academe, where the gut-reaction moviegoing of the old-fashioned cinephile has been supplanted by the overly cerebral study of film in the laboratory, feminist film scholarship has gained a firm if somewhat rigidly ideological foothold, and expanded enough to spawn splinter groups and controversies within its shifting boundaries.

When *From Reverence to Rape* came out in 1974, I gave myself a tag line that was both convenient and comprehensible to the most illiterate talk show host that would have me: I was a film critic first and a feminist second. It stuck like flypaper, but I'll still hold to that designation. The danger in any kind of movement or ideology is that it ceases to consider formal and aesthetic questions and concentrates on political ones. I've never wanted to overpoliticize the situation; for instance, I'd rather see a male director expressing his vision through the treatment of women, even if his biases are the luridly disturbed misogynist fantasies of Brian De Palma, than have him subject to some sort of cultural commissar, a feminist interpreter on the set who would make sure that he expressed the correct "line." On the other hand, the artist cannot claim immunity from feminist criticism, not even in the more individual arts. In drama, to be unable to express another point of view, a female point of view, is a deficiency. If a poet or novelist is bigoted or narrowminded or unfair, critics have the right and obligation to say so. This is even more true in movies, since male and female are rendered more naturalistically; and they are not the complete creation of the artist because they are occupied by flesh and blood actors.

By temperament and as a reviewer of movies for mainstream publications, I've tried to bridge the two worlds, the popular and the scholarly, not always to either side's full satisfaction. But I've had faith that somewhere between two extremes lies hope not only for women's aspirations but for art generally.

April 1987

ACKNOWLEDGMENTS

I wish to thank the following people for their help in providing information, photographs, and insights: Tom Allen, John Belton, Eileen Bowser, Stuart Byron, Mary Corliss, Richard Corliss, Bill Everson, Cynthia Harris, Bill Kenly, Mike Moore, Bill Paul, Richard Roud, Andrew Sarris, Barbara Shapiro, Betty Suyker, and Liz Weis.

I am grateful, too, to the Museum of Modern Art and Cinemabilia for supplying the stills included in this book.

With a special note of gratitude to my editor, Marian Wood, for contributions to both the spirit and the letter of this book.

INTRODUCTION

If it weren't for selective memory, the consolation of the loser, our consciousnesses might have risen a long time ago. Like recollections of old love affairs, the images of stars that stay with us are the triumphs rather than the disappointments. We remember them not for the humiliations and compromises they endured in conforming to stereotypes, but for the incandescent moments in which their uniqueness made mockery of the stereotypes. And it was through these moments, glimpses, and intuitions that were different for each of us and that we may blush to remember today, that we transcended our own sexual limitations.

My first idol was Margaret O'Brien, not for any role in particular but for the twin privileges she claimed as a movie star and a tomboy. She was a few years older than I, with long, sleek pigtails that were the model for my own short, stubbornly vagrant ones. I was as interested in reading about her as in seeing her perform, almost the only star I ever felt that way about. One of my most vivid childhood memories—a veritable crossroads of happinesses—is of standing before the vast magazine rack at Broad Street Station in Richmond, Virginia, waiting for the train to go to Florida, and persuading my father to pay an exorbitant fifty cents for a magazine devoted exclusively to her offscreen activities. In my eyes, she had everything. She was independent, but not alone. She was spoiled and petted, but as a child rather than a woman; she had not yet entered the sexual arena or discovered the bondage of emotional dependency. For me, and without my realizing it, these were the years of presexual freedom, and Margaret O'Brien, with her dogs and horses and her doting entourage, symbolized this interval of self-determination between childhood and womanhood, my own rite of passage between identifying with heroes and identifying with heroines. All too soon I would join my sex wholeheartedly. Soon I would be making preferential ten-best lists of boys (as I later would of movies) and crying my eyes out over passion's first tragedy as I discovered the cruelty of love, the inequity of a situation in which one sex could only stand and wait while the other enjoyed the freedom to phone or not to phone. Soon I discovered the discrepancy between life and the movies. But before this awakening, and before movies themselves "awoke" to their artistic obligations as a self-conscious art form, I was, for a brief moment, at one with myself, my horses, the world, and the movies.

One of the definitions of the loss of innocence is perhaps the fragmenting of that unified self—a split that is different, and emblematic, not only for each sex, but also for each era. My own split, between the way I saw myself (as a free agent) and the way I was expected to behave (as a lady, deferential to authority), was reflected, as such things often are, in the movies and in the parallel split in movie heroines.

It was a split that brought up to date the age-old dualism between body and soul, virgin and whore.

When the time came to transfer my allegiance to romantic heroines, I chose Audrey Hepburn and Grace Kelly whose aristocratic cool seemed an extension of the tomboy freedom of Margaret O'Brien, and who were above the sexual profligacy and vulnerability of Marilyn Monroe, Elizabeth Taylor, and Jennifer Jones. The whore-virgin dichotomy took hold with a vengeance in the uptight fifties, in the dialectical carica-tures of the "sexpot" and the "nice girl." On the one hand, the tarts and tootsies played by Monroe, Taylor, Russell—even the demonesses played by Ava Gardner—were inca-pable of an intelligent thought or a lapse of sexual appetite; on the other, the gamines, golightlys, and virgins played by Hepburn, Kelly, Doris Day, and Debbie Reynolds were equally incapable of a base instinct or the hint of sexual appetite. And the split was internalized in the moral code we adopted out of fear as well as out of an instinct for self-preservation. The taboos against sex, encoded in the paralyz-ing edict that no man would marry a woman who was not a virgin (with the unexpressed corollary that untasted sex was a woman's prime attraction for a man) held fearful sway in the southern community where I grew up. It was a morality handed down by our parents, but eagerly embraced by my peer group. American morals, which had increasingly rigidified after the Jazz Age and the Depression—a tendency that was reflected in Hollywood films and reinforced by the Production Code—could retrench no farther. With smiles frozen on our faces, we had turned into blocks of ice. We were as terrified of being labeled "fast" as girls today are of being labeled "square" by *not* making love or taking grass. What the peer-group pressures of both decades—fifties' repression and sixties' license—have in common is an undue emphasis on sex; sex becomes not simply an appetite or a matter of individual taste, but the supreme, defining quality of the self. She "puts out" or she doesn't. She balls or she doesn't. Will she or won't she becomes the unspoken question when boys discuss girls, will you or won't you the underlying question of heterosexual dialogue. So my generation fell into the trap, internalizing the either/or as we thought of ourselves as "hot" or "cold" and falling victim, once again, to the terms by which our sex had been conveniently divided for so many years.

To the degree that sex was the equivalent of the self, surrender to sex was to lose oneself, whereas abstinence would insure its safeguarding, if not its salvation. Our instincts were substantiated by the movies: The "virgin" was a primal, positive figure, honored and exalted beyond any merits she possessed as a woman (and eventually made to pay for her "superiority" in the professional virgins and teases of the fifties), while the "whore," Americanized into the good-bad girl, was publicly castigated and cautioned against—and privately sought by men.

We felt, obscurely, that we were safe if we didn't "go all the way" and so, for fear of blighting in the bud that ego that would have little enough chance to survive, we cauterized our sexual responses before they could develop freely. Those of us who were ambitious would use our femininity like Scarlett O'Hara used hers: would flirt, tease, withhold sex, to get what we wanted. It would rarely occur to us to ask outright for a place on the starting line, to enter the ranks of competitive male activities and thereby lose our place on the pedestal and our "preferred" passive position in the game of love. We became "superfemales" rather than "superwomen." We lied and manipulated and pretended to be helpless and were guilty of conspiring in our own idealization—and our own oppression. For whatever else may have been our goals, we still assumed that the need men and women had for each other, and its satisfaction, was indissolubly linked to their roles as conquerer and conquered, and we accepted all the implications that followed from that first parsing of human nature into active and passive. We accepted the ground rules of the game and participated in its penalties and rewards: the inhibition and self-denial, the duplicity, resistance, agony, uncertainty, and ecstasy. Yes, ecstasy, because there was at least as much excitement as anxiety (and was not one part of the other?) in this business of falling in love, in the sudden mysterious twist of one's insides, the hint of reciprocation, the self-consciousness, the loss of appetite, the floating, the first kiss, the upward trajectory, and the inevitable decline.

The yins and yangs of heterosexual romance, the power differential between the "stronger" and the "weaker" sex, are not just tricks of movie propaganda; they have been articles of faith among writers through the ages, and among these are the most independent-minded women novelists and screenwriters. Their heroines, rarely unpleasing to the eye, appealed to men. If Anita Loos' flappers were more flagrantly flirtatious, and if movie heroines were more improbably beautiful than literary ones, marriage was no less absolute a goal to Jane Austen's sensible and sensitive middle-class heroines, or George Eliot's passionately moral, subservient ones, or Charlotte and Emily Brontë's neurasthenic ones, or even Virginia Woolf's torn, introspective ones. It was not often one would find, even in literature, a heroine like Charlotte Brontë's Lucy Snowe, or Dickens' Ada, or E. M. Forster's Margaret Schlegel, a woman who was neither beautiful nor especially charming, who did not abide by sex-role definitions, and who (more scandalously than having a child out of wedlock) pursued knowledge and truth for their own sake. But even these subversive heroines or "female heroes," were conceived within the prevailing romantic conventions, according to a status quo which still seemed immutable. Even in the twentieth century, most antiheroines —heroines that are motivated by fires of passion other than sexual—are, like the women of Doris Lessing, and of southern writers like Carson McCullers and Flannery O'Connor, freaks, oddballs, and loners; or they are consciously polemical heroines like Shaw's Joan and Ibsen's Rebecca West. And, although there are probably as many (or as few) truly challenging heroines in movies as in literature, movies, for most of their history, have remained rooted in the nineteenth-century romantic values that are now being called into question.

It is only recently that we have begun to examine the whole complex alliance of love and need and its primacy for women; and the questions are painful and difficult. For we are asking, in the books and movies by women who most honestly confront the subject, whether it is possible to disentangle the neurotic and imprisoning aspects of love from its positive and liberating ones. Whether a woman's propensity for "total" love is basic or conditioned. Whether insecurity and dependency are crucial or incidental factors in that love, and whether such liberating devices as the pill, in removing those factors, remove the conditions of love. Whether a woman's professional advancement and diversification will leave less room, and less need, for love. Which is to ask whether, in removing the props and crutches of love, we will remove love altogether.

Is the separatism advocated by the lesbians and the man-haters (and which serves, like much movement rhetoric, to exalt rather than diminish men's power) the answer? Or is it possible that after the current stalemate, men and women will come to each other on a basis of greater mutual understanding? Can women love more wisely and less well? Can men love women as their equals? Why, for instance, are admiration and respect so indispensable to a woman's love for a man, while they play so little a part in, and seem even inimical to, his love for her? The relationship between Katharine Hepburn and Spencer Tracy that is pictured in such movies as *Adam's Rib* and *Pat and Mike* as proceeding from deep, mutual respect is the rare exception.

These are only a few of the questions, and anyone who says she has the answers is a fool. Yet everyone is busy giving summation speeches, coldly outlining marriage-love-career-childbirth charts, drawing up marriage contracts—all as if emotions were tonsils and the past a useless impediment to the "new woman." Knowing the pressures of cultural consumerism, we can understand the desperation of the fellows in the media racket to get into the act before the show closes. Less understandable is a similar desperation on the part of movement spokeswomen who betray in their shock tactics a lack of faith in the justice and logic of the cause they are promoting and an insensitivity to the valid claims of the past. Anyone who feels that the cause of women's liberation is just and irreversible will feel justified, between spells of vertigo, in searching history for clues to the present and the future. What we are in the midst of is less suggestive of a revolution, which knows, at least ideally, where it is going, than of an earthquake, an upheaval whose end is nowhere in sight. At stake is nothing less than the hierarchy of Western civilization which posits God, Man, Woman, and Child in descending order of importance. Women, at the center of the upheaval, are in a unique position to look forward and backward, to decide how much of the past is worth salvaging as a foundation for the future. The present is bewildering, and the numbness, the catatonia of so many recent women's movies, from *Diary of a Mad Housewife* to *Play It As It Lays,* is perhaps the only appropriately expressive reaction to the present dilemma.

Movies are one of the clearest and most accessible of looking glasses into the past, being both cultural artifacts and mirrors. Most of the popular novels, plays, short stories of the twenties, thirties, forties, and fifties have all but disappeared, but the films based on them have survived to tell us more vividly than any new or old journalism what it was like, or what our dream life was like, and how we saw ourselves in the women of those times. And these are images to which we can respond without shame, images that radiate—perhaps because of obstacles overcome and ogres appeased—at a greater intensity than those we receive from women in movies today.

THE BIG LIE

The big lie perpetrated on Western society is the idea of women's inferiority, a lie so deeply ingrained in our social behavior that merely to recognize it is to risk unraveling the entire fabric of civilization. Alfred Adler, unique among his professional colleagues as well as among his sex in acknowledging that occasionally women had ambitions similar to men's, called attention to this "mistake"—the notion of women's inferiority and men's superiority—fifty years ago. At about the same time, Virginia Woolf wrote, "Women have served all these centuries as looking glasses possessing the magic and delicious power of reflecting the figure of man at twice its natural size." How ironic that it was in the security of this enlarged image of himself, an image provided by wives or, more often, mothers, that man went forth to fight, conquer, legislate, create. And woman stayed home without so much as "a room of her own," her only "fulfillment" the hope of bearing a son to whom she could pass on the notion of male superiority.

The prejudice against women is no less pernicious because it is based on a fallacy. Indeed, to have sanctioned by law and custom a judgment that goes against our instincts is the cornerstone of bad faith on which monuments of misunderstanding have been erected. We can see that women live longer than men, give birth, and endure pain bravely; yet they are the "weaker sex." They can read and write as well as men—are actually *more* verbal according to aptitude tests. And they are encouraged to pursue advanced education as long as they don't forget their paramount destiny to marry and become mothers, an injunction that effectively dilutes intellectual concentration and discourages ambition. Women are not "real women" unless they marry and bear children, and even those without the inclination are often pressured into motherhood and just as often make a mess of it. The inequity is perpetuated as women transmit their sense of incompleteness to their daughters. But men, too, are victimized by the lie. Secretly they must wonder how they came to be entitled to their sense of superiority if it is to these "inferior" creatures they owe the debt of their existence. And defensively, they may feel "emasculated" by any show of strength or word of criticism from their nominal dependents.

In the movie business we have had an industry dedicated for the most part to reinforcing the lie. As the propaganda arm of the American Dream machine, Hollywood promoted a romantic fantasy of marital roles and conjugal euphoria and chronically ignored the facts and fears arising from an awareness of The End—the winding down of love, change, divorce, depression, mutation, death itself. But like the latent content of any good dream, unconscious elements, often elaborately disguised, came to trouble our sleep and stick pins in our technicolored balloons. The very unwillingness of the narrative to pursue love into marriage (except in the "woman's film," where the degree of rationalization needed to justify the disappointments of marriage made its own subversive comment) betrayed a certain skepticism. Not only did unconscious elements obtrude in the films, but they were part of the very nature of the industry itself.

The anomaly that women are the majority of the human race, half of its brains, half of its procreative power, most of its nurturing power, and yet are its servants and romantic slaves was brought home with peculiar force in the Hollywood film. Through the myths of subjection and sacrifice that were its fictional currency and the machinations of its moguls in the front offices, the film industry maneuvered to keep women in their place; and yet these very myths and this machinery catapulted women into spheres of power beyond the wildest dreams of most of their sex.

This is the contradiction that runs through the history of film, a kink in the machine of sociologists' generalizations: We see the *June Bride* played by Bette Davis surrender her independence at the altar; the actress played by Margaret Sullavan in *The Moon's Our Home* submit to the straitjacket in which Henry Fonda enfolds and symbolically subjugates her; Katharine Hepburn's *Alice Adams* achieve her highest ambitions in the arms of Fred MacMurray; Rosalind Russell as an advertising executive in *Take a Letter, Darling* find happiness in the same arms; Joan Crawford as the head of a trucking firm in *They All Kissed the Bride* go weak in the knees at the sight of the labor leader played by Melvyn Douglas. And yet we remember Bette Davis not as the blushing bride but as the aggressive reporter and sometime-bitch; Margaret Sullavan leading Fonda on a wild-goose chase through the backwoods of Vermont; Katharine Hepburn standing on the "secretarial stairway" to independence; Rosalind Russell giving MacMurray the eye as her prospective secretary; and Joan Crawford looking about as wobbly as the Statue of Liberty.

This tension—between the spirited single girl and the whimpering bride, between the "star" and the "stereotype" —existed for good reason. Audiences for the most part were not interested in seeing, and Hollywood was not interested in sponsoring, a smart, ambitious woman as a popular heroine. A woman who could compete and conceivably win in a man's world would defy emotional gravity, would go against the grain of prevailing notions about the female sex. A woman's intelligence was the equivalent of a man's penis: something to be kept out of sight. Ambition in a woman had either to be deflected into the vicarious drives of her loved ones or to be mocked and belittled. A movie heroine could act on the same power and career drives as a man only if, at the climax, they took second place to the sacred love of a man. Otherwise she forfeited her right to that love.

According to society's accepted role definitions, which films have always reflected in microcosm, the interests of men and women are not only different, but actually opposed. A man is supposedly most himself when he is driving to achieve, to create, to conquer; he is least himself when reflecting or making love. A woman is supposedly most herself in the throes of emotion (the love of man or of children), and least herself, that is, least "womanly," in the pursuit of knowledge or success. The stigma becomes a self-fulfilling prophecy. By defying cultural expectations, by insisting on professional relationships with men who want only to flatter and flirt with her, a woman becomes "unfeminine" and undesirable, she becomes, in short, a monster. This may explain why there is something monstrous in all the great women stars and why we often like the "best friends" better than the heroines, or the actresses who never quite got to the top (Ann Dvorak, Geraldine Fitzgerald, Mary Astor) better than the ones who did (Joan Crawford, Bette Davis, Elizabeth Taylor). The arrogance, the toughness were not merely make-believe. In a woman's "unnatural" climb to success, she *did* have to step on toes, jangle nerves, antagonize men, and run the risk of not being loved.

In no more than one out of a thousand movies was a woman allowed to sacrifice love for career rather than the other way around. Yet, in real life, the stars did it all the time, either by choice or by default—the result of devoting so much time and energy to a career and of achieving such fame that marriage suffered and the home fell apart. Even with allowances made for the general instability of Hollywood, the nature and number of these breakups suggest that no man could stand being overshadowed by a successful wife. The male ego was sacred; the woman's was presumed to be nonexistent. And yet, what was the "star" but a woman supremely driven to survive, a barely clothed ego on display for all the world to see.

The personality of the star, the mere fact of being a star, was as important as the roles they played, and affected the very conception of those roles. In her original literary form —the long-forgotten 1920s novel by Olive Higgins Prouty —Stella Dallas was the prototypical lower-class "woman as martyr." As played by Belle Bennett in Henry King's silent-film version, she is a tasteful and remote figure of pity. But as played front and center, tacky, tactless, and bravura by Barbara Stanwyck in King Vidor's 1937 remake, she is something else again. Stanwyck, in what may be at once the most excruciating and exhilarating performance on film, takes Stella onto a plane where, no longer just Everywoman as victim, she is an outrageous creature who breaks our hearts even as she grates on our nerves. As the boozy, over-dressed, social-climbing mother, Stella/Stanwyck ignores the socially accepted "oughts" by which she could keep our

—and her daughter's—sympathy; she risks losing both by exposing in egregious detail the seedy and insensitive side of her nature, the unlovable side of her love. Stanwyck brings us to admire something that is both herself and the character; she gives us a Stella that exceeds in stupidity and beauty and daring the temperate limitations of her literary model and all the generalizations about the second sex.

Again, in *Woman of the Year,* screenwriters Ring Lardner, Jr., and Michael Kanin did everything possible to sabotage the career woman played by Katharine Hepburn. In their hands she becomes a Lady Macbeth of overweening ambition with so little of the "milk of human kindness" that she is guilty of criminal negligence toward the child she and her husband Spencer Tracy have adopted. Tracy, by contrast, is a doting father—though never to the neglect of his newspaper work, which seems to say that love and ambition can coexist in a man but not in a woman. Yet, because of the strength of character and integrity Hepburn brought to the screen, and the soft and sensual radiance with which director George Stevens illuminated her (thereby contradicting the screenplay), she transcended the meannesses of the plot without in any way excusing them.

There are many stories, some true, some apocryphal, all of them larger than life to fit the stars.

Jean Arthur's name was proposed by Frank Capra to Harry Cohn, the self-made oligarch of Columbia, for the lead in *Mr. Deeds Goes to Town.* "Jean Arthur? D'ja ever hear of her," Cohn asked the director, and when Capra said no, Cohn phoned his yes-men, who also said no. (This was in 1936, when her only significant performance had been in *The Whole Town's Talking,* which apparently neither of them had seen.) "See," Cohn said triumphantly, "no name." "But she's got a great voice, Harry," Capra pressed. "Great voice," snarled the producer. "D'ja see her *face*? Half of it's angel, and the other half horse."

Bette Davis carried through her whole career the gallant epithet bestowed by her first producer, Carl Laemmle, that she had "as much sex appeal as Slim Summerville" and the memory (according to her autobiography) of Michael Curtiz directing her in *Cabin in the Cotton* and muttering from behind the camera, "God-damned-nothing-no-good-sexless-son-of-a-bitch!"

Katharine Hepburn got it from both sides. She was a regular winner of the Sour Apple award, as the most uncooperative actress of the year, from the Hollywood Women's Press Club. And she, Dietrich, and Mae West were the actresses smeared by W. R. Hearst in collaboration with the Catholic Legion of Decency as "box-office poison."

Of Judy Holliday, Harry Cohn, a caricature of both shrewdness and stupidity to the end, is reported by Garson Kanin to have said, "Don't waste my money [on a screen test]. You don't seem to understand. On the stage you can get away with a broad who looks like that, because the audience sits far enough away, but with the camera movin' in, she'd drive people out."

They didn't fit the mold and yet they made it anyway, the proud ones, the unconventional ones, the uppity ones. They were bucking the tide in an industry that, like the human race generally, preferred its women malleable and pleasing to the eye; and that, like men the world over, felt deep down that women should be seen but not heard. Like animals, or silent comics (Harpo Marx, Keaton, the silent Chaplin), women are more lovable without the disputatious, ego-defining dimension of speech. The conception of woman as idol, art object, icon, and visual entity is, after all, the first principle of the aesthetic of film as a visual medium, and filmmakers as divergent as Harry Cohn and Michelangelo Antonioni have subscribed to it. Monica Vitti's *angst* is a function of her blonde beauty—she can be effectively "used." For Jules and Jim, Catherine existed first as a work of art, a statue, an ideal vision to which there was, luckily, a true woman to conform.

And yet, in nefarious old Hollywood, where the feminine ideal could be, and often was, seen and stated in its crudest form, such stars as Davis and Crawford, Katharine Hepburn and Marie Dressler, Dietrich and Mae West, and so many others who were nothing if not unconventional and often troublemakers to boot, managed to survive. Sure, they had to be punished every so often, particularly as women's real-life power in society and in the job market increased. In the forties, once they had filled men's positions left vacant by the war, they were not so easy to dislodge. As women represented real threats to male economic supremacy, movie heroines had to be brought down to fictional size, domesticated or defanged. But even so, and in the midst of mediocre material, they rose to the surface and projected, through sheer will and talent and charisma, images of emotional and intellectual power.

Women have figured more prominently in film than in any other art, industry, or profession (and film is all three) dominated by men. Although few have made it to the seignorial ranks of director and producer, women have succeeded in every other area where size or physical strength was not a factor: as screenwriters, particularly in the twenties and thirties; as editors; as production and costume designers; as critics; and of course, and most especially, as actresses—as the stars who not only invaded our dream lives but began shaping the way we thought about ourselves before we knew enough to close the door. In the roles of love goddesses, mothers, martyrs, spinsters, broads, virgins, vamps, prudes, adventuresses, she-devils, and sex kittens, they embodied stereotypes and, occasionally, transcended them.

Some, like Mae West, Greta Garbo, Katharine Hepburn, and Joan Crawford, were institutions: stars powerful, eccentric, or intimidating enough to choose their projects and determine their own images, for at least some of their careers. Others, like Lillian Gish, Marlene Dietrich, and Monica Vitti were Galateas, molded and magnificently served by their Pygmalions; or, like Marion Davies and Jean Simmons, ruined by their patrons. Having made it as a star on her own, Norma Shearer sustained her career by marrying M-G-M's boy-genius Irving Thalberg. But not all of David Selznick's more tasteful efforts on Jennifer Jones' behalf (*Carrie,* with Laurence Olivier, William Wyler directing; *We Were Strangers,* with John Garfield, John Huston directing) could turn her into a star, probably because women didn't like her. There were actresses like Bette Davis and Ida Lupino who got off on the wrong foot through miscasting or mismanagement, but eventually found themselves. (In the You-Can't-Win department, Davis tells the story of being sent onto the set of the first film of a prop man-turned-director named William Wyler, force-dressed in a low-cut cotton dress that made her feel common, only to have Wyler turn to an assistant and say, "What do you think of these girls who show their chests and think they can get jobs?") There were others—Patricia Neal, Geraldine Fitzgerald, Mary Astor—who were also-rans, actresses of promise who never became stars, but who were as vivid in one or two roles as others were in a lifetime.

Some, like Carole Lombard, were at the right studio at the wrong time, and others, like Marilyn Monroe, were at the wrong studio at the right time. If Lombard, a classy Paramount comedienne in a decade of oversupply, had been at the same studio in the forties instead, her wistfully zany style might have been turned to better advantage by directors like Preston Sturges and Billy Wilder. Conversely, with Monroe (who was nothing if not fifties), at a studio other than Fox and paired with leading men other than the sex-less freaks and mock-lotharios she was always being saddled with, her image might have taken on the spiritual contours of a real woman (as Harlow's did) instead of constricting into a joke.

There was always that danger, and temptation—as there is for every public figure—of freezing in a role, of repeating the public's favorite "act" until the free agent, the unpre-dictable human being, disappeared behind the image. To women, being more dependent on the love of their public and the good grace of their bosses, and anxious not to lose their "few good years," this course was even more irre-sistible. To survive, Monroe, Crawford, and others became "signs" or caricatures of themselves, yielded to the pressure of mediocrity that emanated from the American public as much as from the pulses of Harry Cohn and Darryl Zanuck. Audiences didn't want to see Monroe as a sensitive comedi-enne, but as a sexual monster; nor did they want to see Ingrid Bergman as the soulful middle-class heroine of Ros-sellini's spiritual pilgrimages. Crawford became imprisoned in a tough heroic image, a mask of nobility that was finally shattered by the sledgehammer caricature of *What Ever Happened to Baby Jane?*

The stars' images, like their careers, fluctuated, grew, evolved, and were often contradictory. The most independ-ent-minded heroines—Katharine Hepburn, Dietrich, Rosa-lind Russell—suggest a vulnerability that is the underside, even the guilt, of self-sufficiency, the vulnerability of women who dare to lay themselves on the line. Those who appear most defenseless are, by contrast, often the most durable. The ladylike fragility of Joan Fontaine or Lillian Gish be-lies, in the former, the deep obsessiveness of the masochist, and, in the latter, the stubbornness of the survivor. Refined ladylike types like Irene Dunne and Myrna Loy could be as spiny as cacti, while semisluts like Harlow and Mae Murray were marshmallow soft at the center. An insidious directorial trick was to play one off against the other, with the lady, usually the "wife," looking doubly priggish by comparison.

Some stars, once they had been launched into orbit, remained relatively fixed. Others, like Susan Hayward, Gloria Swanson, and Linda Darnell, changed considerably, crossing the moral spectrum from white to black. Many of the impressions we have inherited are false; they are images that have become oversimplified, or discolored, with age. Pola Negri, contrary to reputation, was a seductress of more warmth than heat, with a twinkling sense of humor. Gloria Swanson and Marion Davies were at one time plucky all-American types and comediennes of great versatility, while Myrna Loy began movie life as an Oriental vamp and ended as a clean-cut, refined, and wholesome leading lady. There were stars who were victimized and exploited—by producers, by directors, by other stars, by life. There were those who, manipulating here, being manipulated there, held to a middle course and exercised a certain amount of artistic freedom. And there were a few who licked up to everyone in sight and then swallowed them whole for hors d'oeuvres.

But whatever their roles, whether they inspired or intimidated, the women in the movies had a mystical, quasi-religious connection with the public. Theirs was a potency made irresistible by the twin authority of cinematic illusion and flesh-and-blood reality, of fable and photography, of art and sociology. Until the disintegration of the studio system in the fifties and sixties, they were real gods and goddesses, and we were the slumbering, intransigent clay, yearning for formal perfection.

And women, in the early and middle ages of film, dominated. It is only recently that men have come to monopolize the popularity polls, the credits, and the romantic spotlight by allocating to themselves not just the traditional male warrior and adventurer roles, but those of the sex object and glamour queen as well. Back in the twenties and thirties, and to a lesser extent the forties, women were at the center. This was amply reflected in the billings, which revealed the shifts in star dynamics from decade to decade. Women were often billed ahead of men, either singly, as in the silents, or as the pivotal member of a team, the dominant form of the thirties. In the forties, because of the shortage of male stars during the war, available leading men were treated as spear-carriers and made to follow women on the marquee.

Far more than men, women were the vessels of men's and women's fantasies and the barometers of changing fashion. Like two-way mirrors linking the immediate past with the immediate future, women in the movies reflected, perpetuated, and in some respects offered innovations on the roles of women in society. Shopgirls copied them, house-wives escaped through them. Through the documentary au-thenticity (new hair styles, fashions in dress, and even fads in physical beauty) that actresses brought to their roles and the familiar, simplified tales in which they played, movie heroines were viscerally immediate and accountable to audi-ences in a way that the heroines of literature, highbrow or popular, were not. Movie stars, as well as the women they played—Stella Dallas, Mrs. Miniver, Mildred Pierce, Jezebel —were not like the women in print or on canvas. They be-longed to us and spoke to each of us personally from what, until the sixties and seventies, was the heart and emotional center of film itself.

Yet, considering the importance of these women in our lives and their centrality to film history, it is astonishing how little attention has been paid them, how little serious analysis, or even tribute, beyond the palpitating prose of the old-time fan-magazine writers or the prying, lively, but no more serious approach of the "new interviewers." At one extreme are the coffee-table picture books, with their two-sentence captions; at the other, film histories that sweep along their predetermined courses, touching on actresses only as they substantiate whatever trends and developments are being promulgated by the author. The political, socially conscious school of criticism (for years the most influential) fathered by the Scots film historian John Grierson, established the line, perfectly consonant with Anglo-American sexual attitudes, that such matters as love, romance, and the loss of virginity were women's concerns and belonged, in a properly demeaned and trivialized fashion, to that untouchable of film categories, the "woman's film." The contempt for the "woman's film" is still a general cultural attitude, not only restricted to critics who mistake "important subjects" for great films (and what could be more important than love anyway?), but conveyed in the snickering response of the supermale, himself a more sophisticated version of the little boy who holds his nose and groans during the hugging and kissing scenes. Critic John Simon describes the dissection of the morality of love and the complex interplay of feeling and conscience in Eric Rohmer's *Claire's Knee* as "triviality" and the "height of inconsequence." Most men, even in New York art-film audiences, would rather see *The Dirty Dozen, Deliverance, The French Connection,* and *The Godfather* several times apiece than see *Petulia, Sunday, Bloody Sunday,* or *The Touch* once. It is said that many wives got their husbands to go to *A Man and a Woman* for the automobile-racing scenes.

Women critics have hardly been in the vanguard of the effort to dignify the lot of the female. Judith Crist, an astute woman with more national power than any other film critic, male or female, gravitates instinctively to men and male material, frequently dismissing certain stories as "soap opera" or "women's films," and often complaining that this or that actress is too old or overripe for a part. And surely this fundamental inequity—that women are considered "over the hill" at forty when, with any luck, they are just coming into their own, sexually and intellectually, while men of that age are "in their prime"—is symbolic of our prejudices as well as being one of the most profound injustices of our ego-*man*iacal society; it has everything to do with the sense of martyrdom and self-pity that pervades the woman's film. Time and again, young women are paired with men twenty years their senior and nobody thinks twice about it; yet, a man paired with a woman a mere five years older is something out of the ordinary, often a joke or a perversion. Every woman, whatever her class, background, or nationality, must live in dread of the day her husband will turn to a younger woman, and, if he is rich and powerful, like Onassis, divorce her—often, like Rockefeller, for a younger version of herself. Like the George C. Scott character in *Plaza Suite,* a man wants "to do it over again"; for this second chance he will put his old wife out to pasture, for she reminds him of his own mortality. This is conceivably the greatest single injustice done to women, the greatest source of that anxiety about aging which hangs like a cloud over most of their lives. And it is inflicted not by faceless men, by society, or by Hollywood, but by individual men, famous men, respected men (and by young women, for let us not forget the hordes that are seeking a surrogate father to worship and idealize them). And the defection of these men from their wives and the natural cycle of growing old is treated as a gesture of heroism rather than as vanity or treachery, while a woman's interest in a younger man— and his in her—is considered unhealthy. One doesn't have to be inclined to the conspiracy theory to feel an unconscious drive working to keep women in their place, a taboo that has arisen out of a fear, or awe, of woman's greater survival and sexual powers. For if custom were to follow the logic of the situation in which women outlive men, the pairing of older women and younger men would be commonplace.

The tip-off in the mythology of films and literature is the singling out of a situation (by treating it as a "problem") that, were the sexes reversed, would claim no such attention. It is the labeling itself that borders on absurdity. With a young man of twenty-one (or sixteen), a woman of twenty-five (or twenty-one) is defined, in all seriousness, as an "older woman." Even when she is treated sympathetically, as in *Devil in the Flesh, The Game of Love, Summer of '42,* she is never conceived of as being more than a passing interlude, a course in the hero's self-education. The older man–younger woman arrangement, on the other hand, is viewed as something solid and normal. This is truer today in movies, and presumably in life as well, than it was in the thirties and forties. Then, the young went with the young and the old with the old. The "older husband," the Molière character, was doomed to lose the girl to a man her own age. Sometimes, like Edward Arnold, he fought the idea, or like Edward G. Robinson in *Tiger Shark,* fought the younger man himself. But most often he bowed out gracefully, and usually at the age of forty or forty-five. Now everyone thinks John Wayne shows great maturity and wisdom in relinquishing his pursuit of women, in *Rio Lobo* for example, at the age of sixty (but if you saw him with a woman of that age, you can bet your life she would be playing his mother). Howard Hawks, who directed *Rio Lobo* and has given us (though not in this film) some of Hollywood's great women characters, made a casually damning remark in an interview once when he admitted that he liked to find pretty new girls for his movies but—and this is the revealing part—he liked them to *seem* older, experienced, mature, while *looking* young. The perfect impossible sexual dream! Hence the exercises to deepen the voice and suggest, in Lauren Bacall and Angie Dickinson, a sensuality beyond the years given as their fictional ages.

Through the years, actors, like the rest of their sex, have had an advantage over actresses. It was considered perfectly normal for Fred Astaire or Cary Grant to go on playing romantic leads from one generation to another, while their early partners were forced to play mothers or character parts, or go wilting into retirement. Fred Astaire was paired romantically with Ginger Rogers in the thirties, with Rita Hayworth in the forties, and with Cyd Charisse and Audrey Hepburn in the fifties, while Cary Grant went with Katharine Hepburn in the thirties, Ingrid Bergman in the forties, Grace Kelly in the fifties, and Sophia Loren in the sixties.

The Electra complex is natural, the Oedipal unnatural. But the primal situation which, when prolonged, makes it unnatural is the emotional and sexual privation of the mature woman. Denied the satisfaction of love or flirtation, she turns her energies to the male child, spoiling him, pushing him to excel, and possibly crippling him for love. If women, seeing these vices perpetuated, don't complain, who will?

Male critics fall into any one of several categories: the Grierson approach of lofty and puritanical indifference to women; the dandyish, epicene-and-gay mixed bag of adulation, gossip, camp, bitchery, empathy, and encyclopedic recall (with antennae particularly attuned to the grotesque— dark roots of light hair, exaggerated mannerisms), and the heterosexual reviewers of the valentine school, the ones who punctuate their reviews with mash notes to their personal favorites. Although these paeans have little to do with serious analysis, they at least acknowledge the male-female chemistry as the source of their commitment to the movies. Here is Otis Ferguson on Margaret Sullavan in a picture called *The Good Fairy*: "[She] is, most of the time, entirely lovely, and if she isn't an actress I wouldn't know it, that is the way things are between Margaret Sullavan and me." And again, with a trace of self-mockery, on her performance in *The Shopworn Angel*: "For if you said, writing for *The Saturday Evening Post,* that the girl was knowing and tired, pert with her small mouth, stem of a torso, and low whispering voice, yet fresh with some wonder of dew still held in the inner leaves—you would have just those words and no more. . . . Whereas in the moving shadows of the screen Margaret Sullavan is there to bring this poet's tracery of a girl into the motion of life." For James Agee, it was another croaky-voiced actress, June Allyson, who could turn routine movies into musicals and musicals into masterpieces—momentarily. To Ferguson's and Agee's crushes (which he shares), Andrew Sarris adds a passion for Vivien Leigh which led him to see *That Hamilton Woman* eighty-five times. Vincent Canby has been known to make considerable allowances for the performances of Candice Bergen; and Roger Greenspun, ever perverse, courts retribution by women's libbers daily with panegyrics to sex-exploitation starlets with bodies (particularly breasts) developed in inverse ratio to their brains. A theatrically oriented critic like Stanley Kauffmann has written perceptively of actresses' performances, but steadfastly resists the concept, and the magic, of "screen presence." Auteurist critics, on the other hand, are sensitive to "movie-movie stars" like Dorothy Malone and Gail Russell, but too often prefer the actresses who express their director's personality rather than their own. The younger critics of both the general and the specialized, the mass-circulation and the underground press devote very little space, and are singularly unresponsive, to actresses. Perhaps this is not really so unusual after all; perhaps it is but one of the more common and less endearing manifestations of the eternal adolescence that hangs on in the American male—who, by the time he is mature and confident enough to appreciate a woman, is almost ready to retire from the arena. There are a few good years in which he can both appreciate and operate, but not enough (particularly with the current defections from heterosexuality) to satisfy the female population, which may be why more and more women are turning to each other, or to themselves.

A related and disheartening trend of recent years, perhaps in backlash to women's lib, has been the partiality of both directors and critics to models—bland, young, fashion-plate girls with symmetrical features who can be shaped by the director or adapted to the critic's fantasies—over the kind of strongly individualized women who imparted their distinctive characters to the films in which they starred. Take the progressively less interesting women of just one director, Howard Hawks: Ann Dvorak, Jean Arthur, Katharine Hepburn, Rosalind Russell in the thirties; Barbara Stanwyck and Lauren Bacall in the forties; Ginger Rogers, Marilyn Monroe, and Jane Russell in the early fifties; Angie Dickinson as his last outstanding woman in *Rio Bravo* (1957); and from then on a group of nondescript, sometimes touchingly, often painfully, awkward actresses including Elsa Martinelli, Michele Girardon, Paula Prentiss, Laura Devon, Charlene Holt, Marianna Hill, and Jennifer O'Neill.

Critics down to a man will prefer the mortuary, zombie-like beauty of Dominique Sanda or Candice Bergen to the teasing, difficult, and vulnerable sluttishness of Dyan Cannon in *Such Good Friends,* or the less compliant zombiism of Barbara Loden in *Wanda.* And directors will choose from an endless supply of interchangeable leading ladies, reconceiving women's roles as girls' roles, rather than take on the risks of a strong female personality.

Essayists bent on proving the witlessness of mass-cult or middle America through the Hollywood film will find ample evidence to set their heads shaking into eternity or into print, whichever comes first. In 1962, Dwight Macdonald scored debating points by lumping together totally dissimilar types into what he loftily assumed was the American Dream mold. In reviewing a group of Doris Day comedies (*Pillow Talk*; *Lover, Come Back*; *That Touch of Mink*), he traced the decline of the "sex goddess" from Theda Bara through Betty Grable to Doris Day. If you're going to talk about "sex goddesses," why not Dietrich to Rita Hayworth to Marilyn Monroe? By any but the most eccentric erotograph, Theda Bara and Betty Grable are rather dubious choices for starting and midpoints. Though sex "symbols," neither was a "sex goddess," and poor Doris Day was just trying to make a living, have a few laughs, and preserve her integrity. She didn't ask to be compared to Jeanne Moreau. But perhaps her problem was not, as Macdonald suggested, that she was no threat to women, but that she was no flatterer of men.

Parker Tyler, who has considerably more empathy and historical perspective, can make a similar miscalculation in attributing the decline of the "sex goddess" to the elements of self-parody that crept in in the thirties (through Harlow and Mae West) even as he realizes that the firsts—Theda Bara and Nita Naldi—were not the greats. Like Ursula Andress, whom Tyler has cited as the recent low, they were humorless and they presented sex as a gimmick, in isolation from the all-important elements of mind and personality. If there has been a falling off in feminine eroticism on the screen, it is from the *loss* of humor, or that aspect of humor that gives distance and perspective, rather than from an excess of it. Even the term "sex goddess" is a misnomer, a contradiction in terms that could have been invented only by Americans to redeem sex from its own base nature. The appeal of Garbo, however provocatively she might array herself, was romantic rather than sexual, and that is the reason women liked her. Her spirit leaped first and her body, in total exquisite accord, leaped after. She yearned not for pleasure in bed but for love in eternity.

When we seek to discover what does, in fact, bind those women we call sex goddesses, we find that it is not sex at all in any specific, erogenic sense. The outlandish, comical lechery of Mae West is of a different taste and temperament from the European sophistication of Pola Negri and Marlene Dietrich. What they do have in common, and almost in secret, beneath the layers of male and female impersonation and masks of self-parody by which they confuse and finally confound the issue of sexual identity, is their moral and romantic integrity. They all have scenes in which they take moral positions against the prevailing moral wind: Mae West addressing the jury in *I'm No Angel*; Dietrich applying fresh lipstick as she faces the firing squad in *Dishonored*; Pola Negri confronting the town council with its hypocrisy in *Woman of the World*. These are the scenes, with their special kind of honesty proceeding from intelligence, that entitle these stars to be, simultaneously, the object of women's admiration and men's desire.

The other reason for the decline of the sex goddess is, of course, the current availability of sex at every street corner and candy store, at least until local smut scourges, empowered by the Supreme Court decision, decide otherwise. On the screen, sex has been demystified (the mystery, the "goddess," has been removed) without a compensating understanding, on the part of most directors, of how to deal with the new freedom, or with a woman's body—or her mind.

American eroticism has always been of a different provenance and complexion than the European variety, an enjoyment both furtive and bland that is closer to a blushing cartoon than a sensual celebration. There is titillation in the *faux-innocence* of Busby Berkeley's banana'd bathing beauties; or the exaggerated gestures of the sex queens who could laugh and pretend it was a joke if it didn't come off. A European like André Bazin appreciated what a Europhile like Parker Tyler didn't: that the sexually devious vocabulary of metaphor and substitution called into being by the Hays Office was the natural idiom of American eroticism, and that the lollipop-licking tease was America's indigenous *femme fatale*.

Far from being a straitjacket imposed from without, the Production Code expressed, and reinforced, the instincts latent in the American psyche at its most romantic, puritanical, immature, energetic, and self-deluding; and the fear, implied by the very zeal of its moralism, that without such restraints the precarious edifice of civilization would collapse. In its support of the holy institution of matrimony, the code was trying to keep the family together and (theoretically) protect the American female from the footloose American male who would obviously flee at the first opportunity, unless he was bound by the chains of the sacrament, which Hollywood took upon itself to keep polished and shining. Ironically, the situation, even in the early thirties, when the code was imposed, may have been the reverse of what everyone thought: The great popularity of the "woman's film," providing a regular outlet for self-pity, would seem to prove just how much rationalization was needed to reconcile women to marriage. In fact, recent studies have shown that of four categories—married men, married women, single men, single women—it is married men who are the happiest and single men the unhappiest. One could well conclude that men rather than women stand to gain the most from marriage, American style.

The current stand-off between the sexes, the mutual hostility and suspicion, seems more typical of love relations in America than the glimpses of unanimity we are given in the films of the twenties and thirties. Even in the romantic comedies, love ends with a kiss, a blackout, marriage. But marriage (next film, other genre) means children, sacrifice, humiliation, hell. There is no passageway between the two, between love and marriage. There is no sense of growth and progression, but rather a vicious circle that relegates woman to the home and to a consequent dissatisfaction with herself, a dissatisfaction from which man will be justified in wanting to escape. And where her escape is the consolation prize, and prison, of the woman's film, his is the exuberant and heroic adventure of the all-male genre films—the Western, the gangster film, the war and *policier* films. Nor is this world just the refuge of the tired businessman, the right-wing Babbitt, or the middle-American husband out on a spree. In one form or another, these men are willing members of the virility cult, that inclusive society, the *modus vivendi* of novelists and journalists who honor the cult, not only in their writings, but also in their life style, as they hang out together in Irish saloons, mesmerized by the sports events on television and by the bodies of athletes, downing beers and demolishing bad guys during half-time intermission; and, in general, worrying far more about assuring the world and one another of their masculinity than John Wayne ever felt called upon to do. Of course, John Wayne doesn't need to prove anything. He has already shown what he can do, and has only to saunter (not swagger) into town, and evil is disarmed. Intellectuals, of course, have had no arena, no longer even war, in which to test themselves physically, and their assertions of virility, like the allegorical settings—the swamps and sporting clubs and grand rapids in which they display them—strike a false note of stridency. In a book of reminiscences, Budd Schulberg struts out the memory of lugubrious lunches with Bill (Saroyan) and Irwin (Shaw). At appropriately manly troughs like Manny Wolf's, they compare notes of adventures in the war, in the Everglades, or in the presence of each other. Kerouac and his cross-country hitchhikers were in the same bag. Bar-hopping and literary name-dropping rank second only to roughing it in some remote wilderness like Canada or Maine (away from one's wife, of course) in order to replenish one's male juices. Male relationships are the ones that count, and even the city slickers are more comfortable with their daddies (even as enemies) and buddies than with their wives and mistresses. As Mailer, the malest of them all, pointed out, all the feeling and emotional detail in Arthur Miller's plays belong to the male characters.

The various mythologies of the American male—as tragic hero, antihero, homoerotic hero, and hero sandwich for the insatiable American woman—have been more than adequately explored, and subtly extolled, by the likes of Robert Warshow, Leslie Fiedler, Parker Tyler, and D. H. Lawrence. The buddy system that Fiedler uncovers in literature with obsessive (and depressing) regularity is just as prevalent in American film. Once the backbone of the genre film, the male friendship has become, in recent womanless melodramas (*The French Connection, The Godfather, Easy Rider, Midnight Cowboy, Deliverance, Scarecrow*), the overt and exclusive "love interest" as well. In the thirties, every gangster from Edward G. Robinson to George Raft had his sidekick who would lay down his life for him and who often resented the intrusion of the female. The theme of male camaraderie has cropped up with increasing self-consciousness and sentimentality in recent years: in the reflective old-gunfighter Westerns of the sixties and seventies (*Wild Rovers, Ride the High Country,* and *Two Rode Together*) and in the young-gunfighter ones (*The Hired Hand, Butch Cassidy and the Sundance Kid,* and *Bad Company*), or the *amitiés particulières* of prep school stories (*A Separate Peace*), or middle-aged boxing-buddy pictures (*Fat City*) or countless rodeo and round-up pictures.

Sexual desire is not the point, nor "homoeroticism" the term for these relationships or for men fighting together shoulder to shoulder at the front, or back to back in a Hawksian fraternity, or cubicle to cubicle in a Ben Hecht–Charles MacArthur play; rather, the point is love—love in which men understand and support each other, speak the same language, and risk their lives to gain each other's respect. But this is also a delusion; the difficulties of the adventure disguise the fact that this is the easiest of loves: a love that is adolescent, presexual, tacit, the love of one's *semblable,* one's mirror reflection.

The irony is that the greatest risks are not in riding the rapids or bearhunting or bullfighting, where the fight is clean and the results can be tabulated. For better or for worse, these belonged to an earlier, simpler world, and to reenact them now in the name of virility is to seek security and peace of mind by obsolete definitions. Men have been deprived of the physical grounds for the testing of their virility and those magical mirrors women held up to their egos. It is, still, a painful transitional period. And they haven't yet adjusted to a new definition of masculinity, one that would include courage and bravery in personal relationships, endurance as a kind of Hawksian professionalism transferred to other areas, courage to speak when one would be safer silent, to question the scruples of one's superiors (a quality that Watergate showed to be in short supply), guts, even, to admit weakness. By underrating these virtues, we fail, also, to see heroism when it appears. It is all around us, but in different guises. And so the real risks (and thus, the test of "masculinity" is the same as the test of "femininity"—it is the test of character) lie in rising to meet other challenges, the challenge of another human being, of someone different but equal, in a love that relishes separateness, grows stronger with resistance, and, in the maturity of admitting dependence, acknowledges its own mortality.

This love of equals is no more frequently to be found in films than in life. In both, one point of view—generally the man's—usually predominates, seeing the "other" as a creature of his own fantasies, as someone deprived, precisely, of otherness, who then comes to inherit the burden of his neuroses as well. Three glorious exceptions, films in which the two points of view are separate and equal, and finally inextricable, are Howard Hawks' *To Have and Have Not* with Lauren Bacall and Humphrey Bogart, and George Cukor's *Pat and Mike* and *Adam's Rib* with Katharine Hepburn and Spencer Tracy. In quite different ways, Hawks and Cukor were concerned throughout their careers with the tensions and possibilities of a heterosexual relationship between equals: Hawks from a male point of view, always tempted back into the enveloping womb of male camaraderie, but evolving and resisting; Cukor, from the female point of view, championing the most intelligent side of a woman's personality. But even with directors as sensitive to women as Hawks and Cukor, and screenwriters as sympathetic as Jules Furthman, or Ruth Gordon and Garson Kanin, it was the real-life relationship and chemistry of the two sets of stars, Bogey and Bacall, Tracy and Hepburn, that gave these films their constant electric and emotional charge and their final sense of true, proud equality. Interestingly, Bogey and

Bacall convey nothing like the same excitement when they are paired again in John Huston's *Key Largo*. Here a "more mature" Bacall is but a pale facsimile of her former self, the dazzlingly adult woman of her first film, *To Have and Have Not*.

The stagy, sour melodrama of *Key Largo* is not untypical of Huston. Despite the derisively modern, antiheroic stance of his work, he takes the conventions of the action genre seriously, using them, like Hemingway, to expose cowardice, to separate "the men from the boys." Hawks, on the other hand, plays around with plot like a cat with a ball of yarn (the narrative of *The Big Sleep* is all but indecipherable). Action becomes the means by which people indirectly express their feelings for one another, take steps in forging their characters, and, finally, reveal heroism in unexpected, offhand ways. With Hawks' characters, we watch people behave better, rather than worse, than we do, people who are still struggling with a superego; in the case of Huston and most modern filmmakers, we come out of the theater feeling we have a slight edge in grace and sanity over the characters in the movie. It is the difference between classical and modern filmmaking, between the classical couple and the modern "relationship." The best of the classical couples —Bacall–Bogey in *To Have and Have Not,* Hepburn–Tracy in *Adam's Rib*—bring to the screen the kind of morally and socially beneficial "pedagogic" relationship that Lionel Trilling finds in Jane Austen's characters, the "intelligent love" in which the two partners instruct, inform, educate, and influence each other in the continuous college of love. In the confidence of mutuality, individuals grow, expand, exchange sexual characteristics. Bacall initiates the affair, Bogey is passive. Hepburn defeats Tracy, Tracy only half-playfully cries. The beauty of the marriage of true minds is that it allows the man to expose the feminine side of his nature, and the woman to act on the masculine side of hers.

The implication behind both Huston's work and that of many other contemporary filmmakers is that we have been sold a bill of goods by the Hollywood film, a bill of goods that has led us to expect love to be more beautiful and people to be better than they actually are. In the antimythic love stories of the seventies—*Made for Each Other* and *Minnie and Moscowitz*—couples like Renee Taylor and Joseph Bologna (married in real life) and Gena Rowlands and Seymour Cassel purport to tell us the way it *really* is, as opposed to the glamorized Hollywood version. But one of the attributes of love, like art, is to bring harmony and order out of chaos, to introduce meaning and affect where before there was none, to give rhythmic variations, highs and lows to a landscape that was previously flat. The cult of improvisation ("sincerity"), of "letting it all hang out" is the aesthetic and moral dictum of our age, but it offers no substitute for the more demanding order and rewards, the old-fashioned "character" of the classical film. It is precisely the kind of discipline exacted by classical filmmaking (which nonetheless acknowledged an obligation to "entertain") that we lack in our efforts at self-realization and in the nuclear isolation and solipsism of our relationships. We are lost in our freedom, longing to feel urgency, necessity, the preciousness of time in love and in like, the irrevocableness of a decision; but when anything is possible, nothing is special. Taylor and Bologna, like so many modern couples, come together in their weakness rather than in their strength; they are mirror reflections of each other's neuroses. Life is one long group-therapy session, no longer a means for achieving adulthood, but a way of staying young together, a way of learning to live with childishness. Perhaps that is no mean accomplishment, but it is less the love story of two adults, of male and female charting a risky course of human contact, than of little brother–little sister, two peas nestling into their pod.

From the evidence on the screen, most people have given up trying to make movies about love. The tension and inhibitions, even the taboos, that created the necessary distance and resistance for attraction have relaxed in an atmosphere of permissiveness. We have succumbed to a kind of emotional laziness and passivity, a state in which only violence can rouse us, and we are inclined to choose as our partners those who are reflections of, rather than challenges to, the soul. The homophile impulse, like most decadent tropisms, like incest, is, or can be, a surrender, a sinking back into one's own nature.

Just as we have lost faith in narrative forms, we have lost our sexual confidence. (If it survives at all, its last vestiges are to be found in that throwback genre, the black film. There, romantic and heroic values still hold sway, along with a comical but real sexism, in which bunnies and playgirls pop up like ducks in a shooting gallery—and get shot down as fast.) In the past, sexual confidence enabled stars to reverse roles, exchange sexes, and come back to center, a center that was fixed and easily found, being the repository of sexual norms that no longer have authority. A sense of equality pervaded the scripts of the thirties (there were a huge number of women screenwriters), the dialogue, the casting, and, in fact, whole genres—the musical, the screwball comedy, the romantic melodrama. And yet these genres are the exceptions that prove the rule of the basic double standard, according to which it is acceptable for a woman to "give up everything" for love and unacceptable, even emasculating, for a man to do the same. Thus, the man always has his career, which is either more or equally important than the woman. If she is not the emotional center of the film (as she is in the "woman's film" and the films of certain women's directors, for example), there are two ways for her to recover parity: if he more or less ignores or places little importance on his profession (Bogey in *To Have and Have Not,* as well as the heroes of many of the romantic comedies), or if she has a real profession of her own (Katharine Hepburn in *Pat and Mike* and *Adam's Rib,* Doris Day in many of her movies). If the balance is tipped in her favor in the "woman's film," it is only so that she can gain a sense of importance denied her in most films.

The basest of a man's ambitions (crime, espionage) are often viewed with more respect than the highest (executive power, literary ambition) of a woman's, and generally her role is to make herself attractive enough for a man to come home to. When a man "goes too far"—becomes a criminal —as a result of the ambition society has encouraged in him, he becomes heroic; when a woman pursues to extreme the prerogatives of the beauty for which society crowns her, she becomes a figure of contempt, a laughingstock. People bow to Edward G. Robinson's tough little gunman; he is comical, but still a hero, and when he is brought low for his hubris, as he must be, it is in a way that subtracts nothing from his glory. Bette Davis, on the other hand, must pay heavily, in films like *Dangerous* and *Mr. Skeffington,* for her selfishness and vanity. Not only does she have to return to her milquetoast husband (in *Dangerous*) as penance and become a garishly made-up parody of herself (in *Mr. Skeffington*), with ringlets dropping from her wig at embarrassing moments, but all through both films she is constantly being rebuked for thinking and living only for herself —for doing, in fact, what Edward G. Robinson is doing and getting away with and gaining audience sympathy for.

If the American woman of the movies is anything like the American woman of fiction—the Hester Prynne that Lawrence saw as a quintessentially American she-devil—it is because her intelligence has been too long insulted and her hunger for life too long unsatisfied. If men had not insisted quite so vehemently on their supremacy, perhaps women would not have felt the need to counterattack so violently. Much of the totalitarian stridency of women's current demands for power stems not just from the image of their own dependency, reiterated in novel and film, but from man's insistence, in film after "macho" film, on his independence of women.

Women have grounds for protest, and film is a rich field for the mining of female stereotypes. At the same time, there is a danger in going too far the other way, of grafting a modern sensibility onto the past so that all film history becomes grist in the mills of outraged feminism. If we see stereotypes in film, it is because stereotypes existed in society. Too often we interpret the roles of the past in the light of liberated positions that have only recently become thinkable. We can, for example, deplore the fact that in every movie where a woman excelled as a professional she had to be brought to heel at the end, but only as long as we acknowledge the corollary: that at least women *worked* in the films of the thirties and forties, and, moreover, that early film heroines were not only proportionately more active than the women who saw them, but more active than the heroines of today's films. Here we are today, with an unparalleled freedom of expression and a record number of women performing, achieving, choosing to fulfill themselves, and we are insulted with the worst—the most abused, neglected, and dehumanized—screen heroines in film history.

Indeed, the Production Code, for all its evils, was probably at least as responsible as the Depression for getting women out of the bedroom and into the office. It was not just that audiences were tired of wayward aristocrats; the characters themselves changed. Under threat from the Hays Office, women were no longer able to languish in satin on a chaise longue and subsist on passion; they were forced to do something, and a whole generation of working women came into being. Sexual liberation has done little more than reimprison women in sexual roles, but at a lower and more debased level. Hardly the counterparts of such pre-code exotics as Pola Negri, Mae West, and Jean Harlow, the sex kittens of the sixties are closer to the *Playboy* bunny image; next to them, even a pneumatic fifties' type like Jayne Mansfield takes on the complexity of a Bergman heroine.

Whatever the endings that were forced on Bette Davis, Joan Crawford, Carole Lombard, Katharine Hepburn, Margaret Sullavan, or Rosalind Russell, the images we retain of them are not those of subjugation or humiliation; rather, we remember their intermediate victories, we retain images of intelligence and personal style and forcefulness. These women far surpass women in movies today, where the most heroic model that women can fasten upon is Jane Fonda's grubby prostitute in *Klute,* or Tuesday Weld's deadpan actress in *Play It As It Lays,* or the comatose housewives in Marguerite Duras' *Nathalie Granger.*

We would be better advised to resurrect the past with one eye open for the exceptions to the rule, the extraordinary women who are the foundation of present claims to independence. Wondrously, they are there—on the late show, in revivals—for all the world to see. They are not, like so many of the subjects of Virginia Woolf's *Collected Essays,* women born to blush unseen, their talents hidden in secret diaries or out-of-print novels, or their creative energies channeled, without credit, into the achievements of their more famous husbands and sons.

It would not hurt to acknowledge, for example, that occasionally it was men who preferred the spunky and intelligent heroines, while women, either out of bitterness about their own lives or out of a Mrs. Babbitt identification, preferred the acquiescent ones. Even today, it is not just men who thrill to the violent, male-chauvinist world of *The Godfather,* but women who, wishing women's lib would go away like a bad dream, secretly enjoy the Sicilian gangster denigration of women, of "putting them in their place."

We need more of a sense of film history, and of the context in which films were released and images were formed. Gloria Steinem can write an intelligent and sympathetic article on Marilyn Monroe, and yet miss the satirical point of Howard Hawks' *Gentlemen Prefer Blondes,* which consciously exposes Monroe's ooh-la-la image and the men who collaborate to maintain it. Betty Friedan can write a stolid appraisal of *Husbands* that, like most sociological criticism, takes no account of the film's failures and accomplishments qua film, but sees it only as a convenient substantiation of *The Feminine Mystique.* A soapbox feminist can excoriate Hitchcock in *The New York Times* for the rape in *Frenzy,* ignoring point of view, context, style, the complex interplay of misogyny and sympathy in Hitchcock, and the equally complex interplay of fear and desire by which women respond to the image of rape. Another critic can write a feminist critique of *Last Tango in Paris* as a male fantasy ignoring both the empirical fact that it is largely women, rather than men, who respond to the film, and the more subtle implication that our rearguard fantasies of rape, sadism, submission, liberation, and anonymous sex are as important a key to our emancipation, our self-understanding, as our more advanced and admirable efforts at self-definition. The same critic, offering a plot synopsis to substantiate her claim to the film's sexist point of view, reveals the irrelevancy of this technique, for *Last Tango* is about Brando, is Brando, and our reaction to the film will depend, directly and chemically, on our response to Brando. The plots in five movies may be identical, may all show women degraded and humiliated and chained to stereotype, and we will react differently to each one, depending on the woman, and the director's treatment of her.

For despite their impact on cinema, there have been few women in positions of creative authority that would have fostered the development of a woman's point of view. There have been shamefully few women directors (though no fewer, perhaps, than women orchestra conductors or prime ministers or reverends or stage directors), and fewer still in America than in Europe where the unions are less powerfully chauvinistic and the whole structure of filmmaking is looser. In an issue of *Film Comment,* historian Richard Henshaw compiled filmographies of the 150 women known to have directed films. Of the forty-five Americans, no more than five or six names are known to the general public (and of these, several—Lillian Gish, Ida Lupino, Barbara Loden —are known as actresses rather than as directors), and hardly more to film buffs.

The reason, aside from union prejudice, is obvious. Directing—giving orders, mastering not only people but machinery—is a typically masculine, even militaristic, activity. The existence of such a dominant authority figure—and in this respect, the great directors, the *auteurs,* impose their ideas more forcefully than the mere technicians—would seem to present an inherently sexist situation. Decrying such use of power, feminist film critics have hastened to disavow auteurism, but in the next breath they will raise a merely competent director like Ida Lupino to that category, by assuming she has enough artistic control of her projects and enough creative vision to invest her films with a subversive ideology. The attack on auteurism is less theoretical than emotional (and no less valid for that)—an expression of indignation that all the great directors have been men, rather than a soundly argued dismissal of these directors and the historical tool (auteurism) that embraces them. For there are certainly subversive elements, obtrusions of a woman's point of view, in the work of men directors, particularly in classical filmmaking, before the twin male cults (director as superstud and superstar) converged to demote women, once again, to chicks, chattels, and pure figures of fantasy.

Actually, until the current obsession with virility and violence, filmmaking, as an activity, may be seen to have provided an outlet for those quasi-athletic masculine impulses that were thwarted in the "arts," and whose strident confirmation discolored the work of so many American writers—particularly those who have felt uncomfortable with the feminine side of their minds. The director, half-artist, half-politician, battles the devils in the front office, wages war on the set, and engages in power politics whether he likes it or not. The writer battles the demons of the night, measures his solitariness and inefficacy against the American Dream of power and action. If these dreams, cherished by some of our most revered writers, can be fulfilled only in his prose, it is not surprising that his novels are more insistently masculine than the films of our "action" directors, and are little affected by the presence of the feminine sensibility, or good women characters. The professional *modus operandi* of the director —which is, after all, a metier of action as much as reflection, of aptitude as much as art—relieves him of the necessity of going to extreme lengths to prove his virility either extraneously (in a cock-of-the-walk life style) or in the compensatory distortions of art.

And yet to the extent that he is an artist, the director is driven to create by some maladjustment, however minor: by the wound, the stutter, the irritation, the limp that keeps him out of step with the world's drummer. Directors with the most lavish film fantasies, Ophuls, Sternberg, Lubitsch, Cukor, for example, were often short or unprepossessing men who were able, luckily for us, to live through and for magnificent women.

For an artist-director, the wound, the social and sexual malformation, becomes both cause and effect. Women will be made to reflect his puritanism, his obsessions, his hostility, just as the men created by a feminist novelist will be made to reflect her disenchantment and bitterness.

The terms "heterosexual" and "homosexual," "idealist" and "misogynist," are not enough to describe a director who defines his feelings about women through his actresses. There is a kind of reverence, expressed in the early films of John Ford, which transfixes and isolates woman as an icon of purity; and there is another kind of reverence, in Griffith for instance, that integrates woman into the flow of life. There are directors, like Robert Aldrich, who separate their men-movies from their women-movies (*The Dirty Dozen*; *What Ever Happened to Baby Jane?*); and others, like John Huston, who include women in a man's world, but as camp followers, whores, and lushes. There are heterosexuals who despise women and homosexuals who adore them. There are directors whose love distorts and degrades, and others, like Cukor, who realize that the best in woman is not too different from the best in man.

One of the reasons women's parts have deteriorated is the decline of film as a classical art, with a world, a plot, and autonomous characters outside the director's ego. Women are no longer the focus of a director's passion, but the satellites of his alter ego. Where once we watched Paul Henreid light Bette Davis' cigarette in *Now, Voyager* and lift her from smoldering spinsterhood into femininity and passion, or Elizabeth Taylor being given in marriage to Don Taylor by her father Spencer Tracy in *Father of the Bride,* we were, by the seventies, in *Summer of '42,* watching Oscie and Hermie and their dates watching Paul Henreid and

Bette Davis; and, in *The Last Picture Show,* we were watching Jeff Bridges and his date watching Elizabeth Taylor, etc. We were watching ourselves watching movies, but only from the man's point of view. In the coming-of-age story, the women figured only incidentally in the man's struggle to maturity. They represented the ugly girl, whom he abandoned as soon as possible; the "older woman," who helped him emerge from the cocoon; or the beautiful bitch, who wounded the wing of the butterfly.

But what about her point of view, this woman who exists only as a chapter heading, a way station? What about the anxiety of the plain Jane, or the struggles of the unwilling adolescent girl in the front seat of a broken-down jalopy. Or what about *her* feeling of small-town claustrophobia, her itch to escape, themes that since the late fifties and early sixties have rarely made it onto the screen?

The fifties were, by unanimous consent, a bland period, but deceptively so, and by no means the wasteland that some of its survivors would have us believe. It is fashionable to claim to have misspent one's adolescence in a movie theater, in escape from the horrors of dating-and-mating rituals, studies, and other impositions of an insensitive society. And one director has reconstructed his autobiography as a kid who knew "even then" the difference between a dolly and a tracking shot. But this reclamation of the fifties is not entirely the work of specious rationalization or staircase wit. For it was under the cover of the fifties that the seeds of disillusionment were germinating. Many of the divisive forces whose consequences we are only now beginning to feel took hold behind that impassive facade: the break in the historical continuity of film as a mass medium, in the graduated pace of social change, and in woman's acceptance of her traditional role.

Going once or twice a week to the movies, we responded

in the degree to which we identified with Elizabeth Taylor, Audrey Hepburn, Doris Day, Marilyn Monroe, Debbie Reynolds, and so on. But already movies were beginning to suffer a credibility gap, a gap between themselves and their mass audiences, between what the movie stars were and what we were. It was in the space of this gap that women began to take stock and stretch their wings, and the seeds of alienation that were sown in the fifties may account for the high preponderance of the fifties' veterans in women's lib generally.

The sheer diversity of stars and heroines—and the split between the two—as well as the fact that they are public property and familiar to everyone, makes them more difficult to write about than women in literature, or drama. We accept authorities in these fields, whereas every human being over ten is not only his own film critic, never quite accepting the idea that movies, much less movie critics, should be taken seriously, but is the self-appointed defender of a personal favorite. Each of us feels proprietary about certain stars; conversely, there is no star, however obscure or untalented, who hasn't a champion ready to risk life and laughter and rise to her defense. Almost all of them have something to tell us: the ones who played the game and the ones who refused; the glamorous ones and the smart ones; the sensualists and the comics; the lambs in she-wolves' clothing, the vamps in virginal vestments; and the freckle-faced puritans who are closer in spirit to the American psyche than we would collectively care to admit. How to choose, and what to emphasize? Their very multifariousness defies the easy rhetoric of trends and categories, or the blanket allocation of guilt to their "oppressors," and dictates that any selection will be personal. To say this is perhaps to state the obvious in the area of film criticism, where all responses are, to the everlasting dismay of theoreticians and methodologists, at least fractionally, and often fractiously, personal. But it needs restating. And the problem becomes even stickier in film criticism with a feminist point of view, where the delights of the specialist often collide with the despairs of the ideologue. The enthusiast in me—an intellectual neuter—has to apologize to the feminist in me for films like *Woman of the Year,* or Hawk's *Only Angels Have Wings* and King Vidor's *Duel in the Sun,* where Jean Arthur and Jennifer Jones throw themselves, respectively, at indifferent men. But then the feminist in me (an idiosyncratic feminist to be sure) gets her own back by rejecting *Carnal Knowledge, Juliet of the Spirits,* and *Cries and Whispers,* or a cult favorite like Nicholas Ray's *Bigger Than Life,* in all of which the misogyny is furtive, a hatred that dares not speak its name. Then, the critic and the feminist join hands to protect their respectability against the romantic, a slobbery atavistic soul ready to sabotage all their deliberations with a few convulsive sobs. For this character, the eyes are still the seat of both love and eroticism, tears the true test of value, and *Back Street* a film that is immune to the carpings of critic and feminist.

My selections reflect my own affinities, and these valences, in shifting positions and proportions. The fact that I consider myself a film critic first and a feminist second means that I feel an obligation to the wholeness and complexity of film history. It means that art will always take precedence over sociology, the unique over the general. Hence I have tried to suggest the films that deviate from, as well as those that conform to, the pattern: the dialectic between past and present that I see as the major theme of, and logical approach to, the treatment of women in the movies. From the woman-oriented "progressive" twenties, from the sexual confidence and equality of the thirties, to the suspicion and sense of betrayal of the forties (and a consequent portrayal of women as predators), films move, forward and backward, to the repressed and distorted sexuality of the fifties and, finally, to the "liberated" sixties and seventies and the current nadir in the presentation and representation of women in films. The traditional refuge, the "woman's film," with its own peaks and valleys, has gone the way of the double feature, *The Saturday Evening Post,* the five-cent pack of gum, and the train.

Hollywood does not lack for detractors from either sex. By contrast, our attitude toward European films, and the women in them, borders on the idolatrous. But it is an appreciation based on the few "quality" films of internationally known directors, and it ignores the mediocre output of national industries more cynical and sexist than our own. We are overfamiliar with the themes of directors like Bergman, Fellini, Truffaut; their attitudes toward women are, unlike those of most Hollywood directors, more self-consciously and explicitly on display. If there are fewer of the subterranean tremors that we can explore with fascination in the Hollywood film, there are still dark corners of ambivalence that escape partisan film critics. We hear them—usually the men—waxing lyrical over how much this or that director "loves women," a love that, on closer inspection, turns out to be more smothering than benign indifference. Or how a director "gets to the heart of women" by showing sexual humiliation or self-abuse that, if practiced by men (see *Portnoy's Complaint*), would be considered the disgrace, rather than the essence, of their sex.

Whether in the European or the American film, whether seen as sociological artifact or artistic creation, women, by the logistics of film production and the laws of Western society, generally emerge as the projections of male values. Whether as the product of one *auteur* or of the system (and if I gravitate, critically, to the former, it is because I see history and cinema and art in terms of individuals rather than groups), women are the vehicle of men's fantasies, the "anima" of the collective male unconscious, and the scapegoat of men's fears. And in the principle of compensation that seems so fundamental a link between our conscious and unconscious, one is never far from the other.

Woman is idealized as the "feminine principle incarnate" by sexual Victorians like Griffith and Chaplin—sometimes out of a hostility that, like Norman Bates' matricide in *Psycho,* masquerades as its opposite. Eventually misogyny will out, as it does, with a vengeance, in the seventies' malevolence of *Straw Dogs* and *A Clockwork Orange.*

Or woman is worshipped as "mother"—by Ford, Fellini, and other Catholic and crypto-Catholic directors—and thereby kept in her place, inoculated with sanctity against the disease of ambition.

Or she is venerated by European directors like Bergman and Renoir, but as an "earth goddess," as an emblem of the natural order; or, for Jean-Luc Godard, as an "enigma" who would as easily betray as love and whose amoral cruelty inheres in the very quality, the innocence, for which he loves her.

Or she is celebrated and feared as separate-but-equal by American directors like Keaton and Hawks. Or perceived, in some remarkable "women's films" of Max Ophuls and Douglas Sirk, as both heroine, capable of radical decisions and intense feelings, and victim, at the mercy of a system that militates against the free play of such choices and feelings. The "noble sacrifice" by which the "woman's film" traditionally rationalizes the housewife's life boomerangs in the films of Ophuls and Sirk, where children are not their mothers' pride and joys but their jailors, carriers of a disease called middle-class family life.

After all this, woman reaches, perhaps understandably,

a dead end of emotional apathy: first, as the heroines of the films of Rossellini and Antonioni; then as the heroines of the "neo-woman's films"—*Klute, Diary of a Mad Housewife, Something Different, Wanda.* The women of these films, torn between the negative and positive of the feminist consciousness—rage at the old order, hope for the new—have arrived, anesthetized, at an emotional and cultural "stasis," a death. But it is out of this death, out of the ashes of her sacrifice, that the new woman will be born.

THE TWENTIES

There are two cinemas: the films we have actually seen and the memories we have of them. The gap between the two widens over the years, and nowhere is this more apparent than in the chasm that separates us from the twenties—a time from which most of us have seen so little and "remember" so much. Our memories are not even firsthand, but instead are drawn from photographs and the reminiscences of others, facsimiles of a lost civilization whose perimeters have faded. They have faded because of the inaccessibility of the films themselves, the artifacts on which the nostalgia crazes for later decades have been nourished. Twenties' films are inaccessible in part because we are alienated from the conventions of silent film, and, in even larger part, because of the gap in film preservation. From a feverish and fertile period, only a few films survive. The problem that has always faced film historians—the industry's careless treatment of films as disposable products—was compounded by the official attitude that, once sound came in, silent movies were obsolete.

We have no hope, then, of seeing the stars across the sound barrier in the context of a succession of good and bad films, as they changed and evolved or glittered and went out. For the most part, we have only the crystallized images posterity has given them, a sense of archetypal forms without the variations. We see the "vamp" and the "virgin" in bold outline, and yet they were as interesting for the subtle modification of design each actress gave them, as each star subsumed the type. Theda Bara is one kind of vamp, formidable in her isolation and magnification of the sex principle. Of the same lineage, Gloria Swanson and Constance Talmadge are vamps too, but "virtuous vamps" as Irving Berlin called Talmadge. And how different they are from each other. Swanson is even different from herself, metamorphosing from spunky Sennett-type comedienne in her Allan Dwan films to soigné De Mille sophisticate in his marital melodramas to von Stroheim's Little Orphan Annie turned strumpet in *Queen Kelly*. There is almost as much difference between Norma Shearer and Joan Crawford as "party girls," or Janet Gaynor and Lillian Gish as Victorian "virgins," as there was between the types themselves.

Many of the most important stars of the period didn't survive the transition to sound, and our impressions of those who did are based primarily on their work in sound films. The proof of this is that for the longest time—until quite recently, in fact—such supremely talented silent stars as Marion Davies and the sublime Buster Keaton were completely discredited by their sound films, on which their reputations were based.

The twenties are largely a mystery, and even the memories of those who have been there are not to be trusted.

(So John Houseman suggests in his autobiography, when his recollection of the movies he saw in the summer of 1926 proves, upon his check with *Variety,* to be almost completely in error.) And yet, in the ferment over women's rights and the loosening of the cultural stays, the twenties seem closer to our time than any intervening decade. They seem, indeed, the antecedent to the current women's liberation movement and the "new morality" and, more, to anticipate the split between the two. Just as the serious and political "Apollonian" side of the current women's movement seems often opposed to the hedonistic and sexual "Dionysian" side, so the "emancipated woman" of the twenties was either a suffragette or a flapper, depending on what she wanted and how she chose to get it. In an interview not too long ago, Anita Loos, scoffing at the tactics of today's feminists, said that women always knew they were more intelligent than men, but that in the twenties they were smart enough not to let men know it. But it is precisely this kind of duplicity, the holy fallacy of women's inferiority that current feminists —and yesteryear's suffragettes—challenge. For the Anita Loos' flapper, who wanted social and sexual, rather than political and intellectual, power, this was a gold-plated philosophy. As long as she played dumb she could stay on her pedestal. But the suffragette (who rarely made her way into films) was more honest. She wanted direct, not indirect, power and authority, and her approach was uningratiatingly direct.

Women won suffrage in 1920 and were admitted to the nominating conventions of both major parties the same year. Even before suffrage, women had begun to enter the professions and, as the decade dawned, more were choosing to do so. By the twenties, plays and novels were increasingly focusing on the "new woman," some to encourage her, others to satirize her. But it was awhile before such a rebel, even in flapper form, penetrated film. Decades are artificial divisions, full of contradictions, particularly in film where there is always a partial lag. The spirit of anarchy and experimentation we associate with the twenties, with Fitzgerald and Stein and Hemingway and Paris and Freud and German Expressionism did not filter into film until a much later date. It was really in the early thirties that the revolutionary twenties' spirit, at least the questioning of marriage and conventional morality, took hold. But in the twenties, De Mille and even von Stroheim introduced intrigue and sexual excitement to marital drama without really challenging the basic sense and sanctity of the institution. For the most part, Victorian values prevailed in silent films and even as the "It" girl came sashaying into view, the rural sweetheart, for which Mary Pickford was the prototype, continued to claim the loyalty of a huge number of Americans. And even the "It" girl, who, with her inventor, the British novelist Elinor Glyn, became a naturalized Hollywood citizen, was not as naughty as she seemed, but rather a disturber of the peace, redeemable by marriage.

There was nevertheless a dialectic between the "new" and the "old-fashioned woman" (a power struggle that D. W. Griffith obviously felt when he began "modernizing" his heroines) that was reflected in the corresponding opposition between the city and the country as the real heart of America. The country was the repository of traditional values that, for Griffith and F. W. Murnau, Pickford and Gish, were pure, noble, and true; but for De Mille, or Lubitsch, or Clara Bow, these same values were narrow, repressive, and old hat. For both groups, the sense of strong contrasts and extremes that was aesthetically crucial to silent film became morally determining. Lacking speech, movies had to tell their stories through image and incident, and through characters with an instantly identifiable iconography.

The morality play names—"the Man," "the Wife," "the Woman from the City"—used by Murnau in *Sunrise* are indicative of the allegorical nature of silent film generally. (As a sidelight, it's worth noting the double standard unconsciously expressed in the labels "the Man" and "the Wife," the male being defined by gender only, the female by her marital status.)

In the identification of physical type with role, the films of Murnau and his colleagues bear a close resemblance to the "typage" method of Eisenstein—a director who in other ways was Murnau's antithesis. Developed from the Russian director's interest in Oriental drama and calligraphy, "typage" dictated that an actor be cast according to his physical resemblance to a part, to the "idea" of a workingman or an aristocrat. The American categories corresponding to Eisenstein's types differ less in kind than in shadings, being moral rather than political, implicitly, rather than explicitly, didactic. But such instantly recognizable types as the "virgin" (fair-haired and tiny), the "vamp" (dark and sultry, larger than the "virgin," but smaller than the "mother") and the "woman of the world" (a sophisticated blend of the "virgin's" soul and the "vamp's" facade) are as stylized within an American context as the ritualistic figures of Kabuki and Noh drama.

Moreover, just as silent film submits to the tyranny of type, so all of film submits to the tyranny of the visual. The camera is mercilessly and mysteriously selective in its criteria for photogeneity, which are not the criteria, necessarily, of conventional beauty. Not just the deformed and the ugly, the opaque or self-conscious, but the surpassingly beautiful may not photograph well, while some dwarfish male or delicate-featured girl may blow up into an extraordinary and sensual presence on the screen. And she, or he, will stand for the rest of us, her transparent complexion, his sea-blue eyes, perfectly expressing the pool of integrity that is our collectively clear soul. To the extent that it prefers surfaces to essences and types to individuals, all of cinema is allegorical, a preference in which silent film exceeds sound film by the same ratio that sound film exceeds (and is "broader" and more universal than) drama and literature.

Frances Marion, one of the most successful screenwriters of the twenties and thirties (*Little Lord Fauntleroy, Stella Dallas, Anna Christie, Min and Bill, Dinner at Eight,* and *Camille* among many others) writes amusingly in her autobiography, *Off with Their Heads,* of the idiotic pressures of typecasting. Clara Kimball Young, a lovely, high-spirited actress, had been lured from Vitagraph to the World Film Company by ex-jeweler Lewis J. Selznick. He forced her to conform to the Mona Lisa image he had created for her regardless of her natural disposition, reminding her constantly to be "mysterious and elusive." (She was neither.) He refused to let her go out at night, lest she destroy her melancholy image. "Poop to the public," she finally complained. "What's the good of making all this money if I can't have any fun?"

Frances Marion herself, through no fault of her own except physical attractiveness, enjoyed a brief career as an actress before becoming a screenwriter. After a short interview with director Lois Weber, to whom she applied for a job designing sets or costumes, she was placed on file as: "Frances Marion. Actress. Refined Type. Age 19 [five years younger than her real age]." She was transferred to the "vamp" category with her second film, and about that time decided to try her hand in another side of the business.

For the most part, even when a name director or big star had some kind of aesthetic control, the producer was the authority figure and, in the early days of studio satrapies, he had considerable power—wielding a wand of stardust magic, as he spoke in monosyllables. Naturally, it was beyond his understanding that any woman would resist his Svengalian efforts on her behalf. Frances Marion recounts an exchange with producer William Fox, to whom she had written for a job as screenwriter at the then-outrageous salary of $200 a week. Amused by her letter, he grants her an interview, but when he sees her he is mystified by her desire to write screenplays since she is good-looking enough to be an actress.

"Why does a pretty girl like you want to be a writer?" he asks incredulously, and goes on to tell her how she would look in "the most expensive outfits they got at Saks Fifth Avenue, earrings, bracelets—no phonies, all real stuff."

"Actresses—yes! they got glamour—" he says later, "but writers the poor schliemiels! Now if you're smart you'll gamble on yourself. Easy, just like tossing a coin."

"A coin, Mr. Fox, can only fall heads or tails," Frances Marion says she said, and even if it's staircase wit, it should go down in history as the true shooting script, "and I'll gamble on heads, they last longer."

In running to type, silent films exploited the tendency of American women to conform to type, to choose hair styles, dress, even personalities according to the models of "in-ness" or "it-ness" in any given period. The packaging of women is but another aspect of love-and-sex-object consumerism, a process in which they themselves have conspired, leaving themselves open to the risk of becoming passé as the style wears off. For a movie star, the risk is particularly high: She has not just her age, but her type, to undo her. A fey Audrey Hepburn, a busty Sophia Loren, a sun-speckled Doris Day all become obsolete, while sturdy John Wayne, wearing his beat-up basics, survives from decade to decade. (Theoretically, all this is changing as men become more fashion-and-plumage conscious, and women less. But Seventh Avenue being what it is, today's rebellion becomes to-morrow's merchandising cliché, and Parisian *haute couture* gives way to blue-jean *basse couture*.)

From the twenties' frizzy-haired flapper to the seventies' long-haired model, we are never quite as unique as we think we are. If the stars of the twenties look, to our unfamiliar eyes, like an old group photograph in which the distinguishing traits have disappeared and only the physical similarities remain, we too—and the stars who represent us—may look astonishingly alike to our grandchildren. It is one of the properties of perspective that from a distance of time or space everyone, like the Chinese, looks alike.

If the women stars of the twenties were more defined by type than the men—as women always are—they were also more colorful and more central to the myths of the period. The action heroes and the male comedians had a world to themselves, but most of the films of the twenties (a larger proportion than in other decades) were romances and melodramas dominated by a single star, billed above the title, and the women stars outnumbered their male counterparts. Different types coexisted. These were genuinely wild, experimental days in Hollywood, before sound, before the Crash, and before the social crusaders came in, in the form of the Legion of Decency in the early thirties, to legislate morals and arbitrate between good and evil in films. Stars were demoted by box-office failure rather than by social pressure. The falling star of Theda Bara, who reached the peak of her vampire's powers (and largely publicity-induced popularity) in 1915, met Mary Pickford's star going the other way the same year that Griffith's *Birth of a Nation* introduced Lillian Gish. Gish, in turn, would be succeeded by a long line of replica mirror-image virgins.

At this juncture of the Victorian moral world and the allegorical tendency of silent film, the virgin emerges in her purest form, fair-haired, delicate, and above all, tiny, in the time-honored tradition of the "weaker sex." (The symbolic importance of size suggests that women's increased height over the years has influenced their changing self-image.) But it is a true innocence—as if she, like the industry, like the country, had not yet been deflowered—an innocence that belongs not just to her, but to the way she is seen, to the eye of her beholder. For, in the nineteenth-century imagination of such directors as Griffith and Borzage, the vision of woman idealized and debased, above and below, was, as George Eliot suggested in *The Mill on the Floss*, metaphysically the same. By the romantic code, woman's chastity was a correlative of male honor, her Fall, of his concupiscence and guilt. The notion of the virgin ideal unfortunately outlived the romantic code which gave it plausibility. In film, subsequent virgins, like the medium itself, would be tainted by self-consciousness at best, at worst, depicted in venom, the underside of a chivalry gone sour and of sexual uncertainty in a world of fluctuating values.

But throughout the twenties, the virgin-heroine was still rooted in the romantic spirit of mutual reverence. As late as 1927 and 1928, in Janet Gaynor's sublimely sentimental heroines of *Seventh Heaven* and *Street Angel,* she is alive and well, her chastity imperiled but her purity intact.

Such glistening icons of femininity as Gaynor and Gish were often steely underneath but they belonged to the "women-rule-the-world-but-don't-tell-anybody" school and they made a point of concealing their strength. (We can be sure that when Gish directed her own film she gave orders —or made requests—like a lady, never raising her voice above a genteel chirp.)

The image of Gaynor as one of the most ethereal of the angel-heroines comes primarily from the two Borzage films, *Seventh Heaven* and *Street Angel.* As an expression of

Borzage's Italian-Catholic romantic sensibility, she is a kind of Madonna of the streets, an urban peasant sanctified by a vocation for love and sacrifice. She is the perfect example of the woman who, in the metaphysical, religious vision of Borzage, combines the virgin and the whore, as in *Street Angel* she literally, but only temporarily, takes to the streets. (In an exception that proves the rule, a Raoul Walsh thirties' movie called *The Man Who Came Back,* she would play a fallen woman to no avail.)

It is interesting to compare the way Borzage uses, and exalts, her with the way Murnau treats her in *Sunrise.* Just as she is paired with the towering Charles Farrell in *Seventh Heaven* and *Street Angel* to emphasize both her vulnerability and the miracle of her inner strength, she is paired in *Sunrise* with the enormous George O'Brien. But the emphasis here is on O'Brien's character—the Frankensteinish horror of a man possessed by the devil. The film focuses on his moral dilemma, and Gaynor, her hair pulled back in a severe bun, merges with the animals, the rustic simplicity of the home, the country, to become a symbol of the "good." She is a part of nature for Murnau, an element in a directorial style that in subordinating the actress to the overall vision, distinguishes the "art film" from the "star vehicle." As Borzage worships her like a Madonna, he treats her like a star. Framed in a halo of backlighting and soft focus, her eyes raised romantically and religiously to her man-god, she galvanizes attention in an ecstasy of feeling, a submissiveness that assures her of preeminence.

In both *Seventh Heaven,* where she agonizes in her garret flat for the return of her soldier-lover, and *Street Angel,* where she is a poverty-stricken Cinderella who sacrifices herself to save her artist-husband, she is seen as plain and ordinary, and yet transfigured by love. Where there is something naturally refined and aristocratic about Gish, Gaynor represents the common people, the peasant turned saint. She is round-faced, fluffy-haired, mincing, a "good girl" who by doing a supreme right is transfigured into a goddess; an ordinary actress who, through Borzage's direction, through a counterpointing of doll-like gestures and enormous, radiant close-ups, achieves an incredible emotional intensity.

Street Angel deals with that recurrent myth of the woman who prostitutes herself to save her husband, endures disgrace, and is finally forgiven—a transposition, perhaps, of the mother's "sin" of sleeping with the father to conceive the son. And thus does the son "forgive" and redeem his mother by sanctifying her as virgin. Gaynor embarks on a career as a prostitute—and here, Borzage is not without a sense of the humor of the situation—but, looking about as seductive as the brick wall against which she plants herself, she waits while one and another and another potential client pass her by.

She finally succeeds in "falling," and after a binge of suffering the indifference and hatred from her lover, is reconciled with him. In one of those scenes which to describe is to destroy, but to see is to succumb to completely, he collapses before an altar as she is superimposed on the painting of the Virgin Mary, a final image of romantic redemption.

If Gaynor was Borzage's Galatea, the fragile, powerful Gish was Griffith's—but not his only one. The director who dominated cinema from 1915 to 1925 was a notorious ladies' man, and expressed his tastes in both the actresses he molded and the women he loved. Alongside Lillian Gish, and expressing different registers of the idealized woman, Dorothy Gish, Mae Marsh, Blanche Sweet, and Bessie Love were all chiseled from the same stone—pure-white alabaster.

But for an overbearing, interfering father, Mary Astor might have found herself cast in the same mold. In *A Life on*

Film, she tells the story of doing a screen test for him at the kind arrangement of Lillian Gish. The two women were friends in the early days in New York, when Griffith's stock company in Mamaroneck was the dream of every serious movie actor. Accompanied by her mother and her crass, bullying German father ("I wish he had transmitted his energy and ambition to me genetically," Mary wrote, "instead of using me as a channel."), she took the test, and waited, in vain, for word. Finally she appealed to Gish, who reported that Griffith had been put off by Gish's zeal in pushing Mary—he liked to make his own discoveries. This had the ring of truth, and it was not until years later that Gish confessed what had really happened: Griffith had been horrified by Mary's father. "That man's a walking cash register," Gish quoted Griffith as saying. "I could never mold this child into an actress with him on my neck all the time."

It is fascinating to speculate on what might have happened had Mary Astor been taken on by Griffith at Biograph. At first glance, she seems a most unlikely candidate for his pedestal: The cheerfully lying Brigid in *The Maltese Falcon* is a far cry from the tearfully virtuous heroine of *Broken Blossoms.* But in photographs taken at the time, she has an innocent, Madonna-like beauty, her thick, wavy hair framing a pre-Raphaelite face. If Griffith had taken her in hand, he would have intensified her mythic beauty, and, undoubtedly, transfixed her at the sweet, surrogate-daughter stage of her career. Instead she remained financially—but not aesthetically—indentured to her father. He was concerned with getting every penny he could out of her career, not with shaping it artistically. When he released her, she was free to go her own way, but hadn't the confidence or know-how to make decisions. Repressed for so long, she was a classic example of the intelligent woman without the self-assurance to take responsibility for her own career. But eventually, by fits and starts, she evolved into the screen identity—very much her own woman—she seemed destined to assume: the adult adulteress, an unusual mixture of passion and sophistication, sensuality and irony, with a touch of matronliness that we think of as the mature Mary Astor. Needless to say, parts for such a woman were not plentiful, particularly in the Hollywood of her day. She was too adult and demanding for most men, or most movies, and she went —prematurely and unjustly—into sexless "mother" roles before she blossomed as a "woman" in the forties.

Delicate and chaste as they may have been, Griffith's heroines were never passive love objects or martyrs to male authority. The energy of sublimated sexuality fuels the indomitable pioneer spirit of the heroines of *True Heart Susie, Broken Blossoms,* and *Intolerance.* In *Intolerance,* the emphasis is on Mae Marsh and the fortitude with which she carries on alone as her husband spends long years in jail. The lack of that self-pity that makes unrequited love such anguish for women places Gish's spurned Susie squarely in the tradition of the gutsy American heroine. The disturbing force and depth of sexual-familial feeling in Griffith's films, and the erotic appeal of the women, is quite obviously generated by a dual relationship (father-daughter, lover-beloved) with his stars that is as powerful and creatively complex as Bergman's is today. The expression, of course, is quite different—in some ways richer, in all ways less direct. The quasi-incestuous feelings of Griffith's surrogate families are mediated by the fictions of Victorian melodrama, where they swirl and clash in a curious (and curiously American) mixture of excess, denial, and displacement. In *Orphans of the Storm,* sisters Lillian and Dorothy Gish kiss each other passionately on the lips, a gesture which transmutes sexuality into a social form that can be accepted as family affection, but that goes quite beyond it. However romantic the context in which he places his women, Griffith certainly takes them, and their emotions, as seriously as the great Swedish director.

His women, honored at the center of his imagined South, are totally, and traditionally, distinct from men and yet are integrated into the fiber of men's lives. In *The Battle of Elderbush Gulch,* Mae Marsh has come, with her dog, to stay with her big brothers, who are living on an army post fighting the Indians. One night her dog runs away into Indian territory, where she chases him and unwittingly causes an outbreak of war. Where most directors would treat this scathingly, making us wring our hands over the consequences of a "stupid female impulse," Griffith not only treasures its naturalness but finds a girl's love for her dog a good enough reason for men to go to war.

It is their emotional complexity and intensity that binds Griffith's women together and gives them their stature. As early as 1912, his actresses are breaking out of the genteel tradition and into a kind of heightened, emotional realism. In a two-reeler called *The Female of the Species,* three women (Claire McDowell, Mary Pickford, and Dorothy Bernard) set against one another while crossing the desert. Dorothy Bernard, supported by her sister (Pickford), has convinced herself that Claire McDowell encouraged the advances of her husband. (Actually, he was an inveterate lecher, and has now died for his sins.) They continue their trek, their furious hostility overwhelming even their hunger. It is only when they come upon an Indian woman with a baby whose husband has been killed, and Bernard sees McDowell's tender feelings for the baby, that they are reconciled. The revelation is not so much, or not merely, the resurgence of the maternal instinct, but the existence of deeper levels of feeling that are suddenly plumbed. By eliciting such emotionally intuitive performances, Griffith makes us realize that the difference between the supposedly "interesting" woman and the oppressed one is not a question of modern versus traditional roles necessarily, but of the richness and variety with which a woman is invested within the role. The range of emotions expressed by the trio in *The Female of the Species*—the sense of isolation, the jealousy, the ugly, building hatred, and finally the sudden rush of love—is quite extraordinary, not only for a film of its time, but for actresses who might wish only to be loved as America's sweethearts.

Lillian Gish, the least modern of Griffith's heroines, is in many ways the most emotionally resourceful and intense. She is flowerlike and naïve, delicate as a figurine but durable as an ox, and her fascination arises from a contradiction between the two, between her daintiness and the ferocity with which she maintains it. Her movements—her agitated gestures and flutteriness—can be more erotic than the explicit semaphore of the vamp, since they suggest the energy of pent-up sexuality engaged in its own suppression. And yet she is more often tragic than gay. As the miserable waif of *Broken Blossoms,* she must use her hands to force her lips into a smile. The images in *Way Down East* of a young mother cradling her dead baby in her arms and later seeking destruction on the ice-covered river are as primal as anything in our film consciousness; they are expressions of a life-and-death force that is both greater than man or womankind, yet altogether female.

Mae Marsh is already several degrees more sophisticated, more "grown up," more urban. She looks at the world with a candor and sense of humor lacking in the sublimely chaste Gish. She is closer to being a "working woman" and is the halfway heroine between Gish and Carol Dempster, the leading lady of Griffith's later films, done at a time when the vestal virgin was in box-office decline and he had to make his bid to keep up with the fashions.

Dempster, more modern and self-sufficient than Gish, is a heroine most people feel more comfortable with today. She is the driving force that keeps a poverty-stricken family alive in *Isn't Life Wonderful?* In *Sorrows of Satan,* she is actually an authoress, living in rags in a garret and writing away by candlelight. And yet, it is not always the "working" women who have, simply by definition, the greatest character and sense of self. Dempster is a working girl, but her vivacity and initiative seem willed into being—probably because Griffith himself isn't convinced. Gish's old-fashioned resilience, on the other hand, springs from a character more subtle and rounded, more complete within herself. Similarly, in the thirties, Loretta Young's and Ruth Chatterton's politicians and executives would be less genuinely forceful than stronger actresses in less exalted positions—Barbara Stanwyck's housewife or Jean Arthur's secretary or Carole Lombard's lowly but spirited manicurist. The mistake is, first, to assume that only in "male" roles can women fulfill themselves, and, second, to take labels and conventions at face value. Although professions and plot synopses are important, they convey little of the sense of identity transmitted through personality.

So often the artist who idealizes woman—whether he be filmmaker or poet—is re-creating her in an image that will do honor to him, to his exquisite sensibility. The focus, in Chaplin, or even Truffaut, is on the anguished worship of the protagonist, the artist or artist-surrogate. But with Griffith, the emphasis is on the woman herself. Yes, she is the Holy Grail, but not just as an abstract principle for which man journeys forth, but as a living being, with her own life, to whom he can return.

For all his vaunted Victorianism, Griffith dealt more

explicitly with sex than any other director of the period. Although the emphasis was on their suffering rather than on their sensuality, his women did become pregnant and have babies, even out of wedlock. The usual practice, even in the more rakish melodramas, was to redeem any indiscretion with the revelation that the straying couple had actually been married all along. Even in the heavy-breathing romances—the Valentino sagas, for example—the affair was consummated with no more than a kiss, and the audience was left to complete the picture in its own fantasies, or satisfy itself that the kiss was all there was to it. Griffith catered to no such fill-in-the-blank wish fulfillments. He created an artistically whole universe, where the impulse to degrade his Galateas was inseparable from the impulse to elevate them.

Implicit in the conventions of Victorian melodrama that appealed to both Griffith and Mary Pickford, but in different ways, are the fears and fantasies of a child's world: the violent vicissitudes of family relationships, the fear of being orphaned, or of being an adopted rather than a natural child, magnified into the nightmare of inheriting a wicked stepfather or stepmother; the drama of instant wealth or poverty; the impulse to run away from home and be on one's own, and the conflicting sense of dependency. Griffith projected these primitive feelings into an adult arena, where they acquired their peculiar erotic and universal dimension. With Mary Pickford, on the other hand, they remained in the asexual world of a child, in a little girl's self-glorifying daydreams.

If Lillian Gish was the prototype and most gifted incarnation of the diminutive child-woman created by Griffith, Mary Pickford, "America's Sweetheart," was the most beloved, as cheerful as a month of Sundays. Although there is more saccharine and fluorescence than sweetness and

light to her personality, she was neither as insufferably ingenuous nor as limited as the image held of her today, but
there has simply not been an adequate enough revival of
her films to allow for a reappraisal of that image.

She was employed by Griffith (who, according to some
reports, discovered her) from 1909 to 1913, and she learned
most of what she knew about acting, producing, and directing—which was considerable—at Biograph. She left for
Adolph Zukor's Famous Players (later Paramount) in 1913,
went from there to First National in 1919, and, in 1920,
she founded United Artists with her husband, Douglas Fairbanks, and Charlie Chaplin. Long before she became her own
producer, however, she was choosing her scripts and directing her directors. She was thus in a unique position among
American actresses: She played whatever roles she wished
and she shaped her own image. If the American public eventually refused to accept her as anything other than their
adored child image of themselves, it was, after all, the role
she had created and given them.

Her admirers insist that she was always trying to test
her talents and expand her repertory. In *Stella Maris,* for
example, she undertook the dramatic challenge of a double
role, playing both a wretched and ugly housekeeper called
Unity Blake (who ends by committing murder for her employer and then suicide) and the beautiful and bounteous
lady employer, Stella Maris. It is a surprisingly successful
tour de force, although Unity Blake, being the dark underside of the sunny Mary Pickford image, is in a sense not
a separate character at all. This dualism brings into focus
the convention of the double role and its particular appeal for
actresses. The Jekyll-and-Hyde vehicle was the perfect solution for the star who wanted to try something challenging
without tarnishing her popularity and the image on which
it was based. It was also an unconscious means, in the larger

mythological sense, for preserving the "good" (the beautiful, the virginal, the pure) by divorcing it from the "bad" (the ugly, the fallen, the tainted), for maintaining the ideal of woman by creating her mirror opposite. Pickford in *Stella Maris,* Norma Shearer as reform-school Molly and rich Florence in *Lady of the Night,* Bette Davis as both sisters in *A Stolen Life,* and Joan Crawford as the disfigured woman and the same woman transformed in *A Woman's Face,* all show the evil or unpleasant side of a woman's character not as one aspect of a complex, total personality, but as something disengaged, isolated, extreme, nonthreatening, and therefore acceptable to society. The she-devil—Theda Bara's vamp, Bette Davis' villainesses—is not a real woman but a *doppelgänger,* and as such a magnet that draws off the impurities of other women and disinfects them.

But even at her most arch-angelic, Pickford was no American Cinderella or Snow White whose only claim to consequence was a tiny foot or a pretty face. She was a rebel who, in the somewhat sentimental spirit of the prize puppy as underdog, championed the poor against the rich, the scruffy orphans against the prissy rich kids. She was a little girl with gumption and self-reliance who could get herself out of trouble as easily as into it. She was even capable of teasing her own image, as in *Pollyanna,* where the excessive cheerfulness of the "glad girl" becomes obnoxious and deflects sympathy to the wizened, misanthropic aunt. Pickford takes us by surprise when she acknowledges the cheerful-at-breakfast bore in herself because most of the time she gives us the sunshine unrefracted.

Her child roles, the delight of her fans and perhaps the first branch and chapter of the American Lolita cult (or certainly a tributary feeding into it) are the hardest to swallow, precisely because of those adult intuitions her admirers have praised, the knowingness with which she—a good ten years' older than most of the parts—invests the child's behavior. While Gish's agitation has sexual roots, Pickford's is an affectation of childish ebullience and masks a calculating spirit. As the little hands clap in glee, the little mind is contriving how to get what it wants, how to charm the little boy or the disagreeable old man. The fact that she came to these child roles late in her career, in her maturity, only confirms that unwillingness to grow up she shares with a huge portion of the American public, who flocked to these pictures in an orgy of misty-eyed infantilism.

The urge to return to childhood, to recover an innocence both historical and personal, is as deeply ingrained in the American psyche as the idealism that, corrupted, gives rise to it. It is the escape valve from the responsibilities and disillusionments—particularly the disillusionments—of marriage and family, of growing up and old. From dreary adult realities, a woman reverts to childhood, the spoiled state of daughterhood, or even to adolescence, when everything was still possible and ideal, not yet delimited by sexual or domestic submission. A man may travel back down the dusty road to childhood through the Huck Finn adventurer or Skippy and Sooky or the Dead End kids, but childhood contains bitter memories of helplessness and dependency. He is more likely to seek his El Dorado by escaping to a world of action or of comic defiance, that is, a world without, or subversive of, women.

The flight from women and the fight against them in their role as entrappers and civilizers is one of the major underlying themes of American cinema; it is the impetus behind such genres as the Western and the silent comedy. The comic spirit, particularly in the rambunctious, anarchic forms of silent comedy, or the debunking shafts of verbal wit, is basically masculine in gender and often antifeminine in intention. A woman can display humor in the diluted forms of sarcasm or "personality," but if she indulges in either the athletics of the clown or the epigrams of the wit, she risks losing the all-important status of "lady." Comedy as a personal style is the weapon of the outsider, the defense against the world of normal, happy people from whose ranks he, by reason of his ugliness, smallness, or clumsiness, is excluded. And yet the comic character, if it is a man, often becomes a romantic figure in his quixotic destiny. A woman doesn't have this option. If she is ugly or ungainly she is regarded more as a desecration to her sex than a holy fool. While a male comedian can have sex appeal—in fact, his humor may contribute to it—a female comedian (and how few there have been and, of these, how few have been "sexually attractive!") automatically disqualifies herself as an object of desire.

This is actually truer today than it was years ago. Joan Rivers makes a fetish out of her ugliness and Lily Tomlin twists her infinitely expressive features into grotesque characters to conceal her beauty. In the twenties and thirties, the definitions (of comedy and of ladies) were much looser. The smart, wisecracking dame was a hallmark of the thirties, and in the twenties, perhaps in defense of the assault on the "woman's domain" by silent comedy, there were a great many female comics of varying types. Although none ever had the sustaining artistic vision of a Keaton or a Chaplin, or even of a Harold Lloyd, there were such illustrious lady mimics, pranksters, and buffoons as Colleen Moore, Gloria Swanson, Bea Lillie, Marie Dressler, Mabel Normand, Bebe Daniels, Clara Bow, and Marion Davies. They had more space to breathe and be foolish in in the twenties. There was a tradition of the cutup or personality girl, or even the action heroine in the Pearl White tradition, who was more down to earth and (theoretically) less beautiful than the romantic heroine. They, too, were divided by sexual stereotyping into "good girls" and "gargoyles," but the categories were less hierarchical. Thus Marie Dressler, a "gargoyle," was not just a supporting character in other stars' pictures, but became her own genre in the successful thirties' *Min and Bill*. It was only when she came out of the gargoyle-type, as the elegantly faded actress in *Dinner at Eight,* that critics refused to accept her. Bea Lillie, an uproarious and inventive comedienne, fell flat on her beautiful horse face commercially in the one film, *Exit Smiling,* that might have made her a star. Recently revived to the delight of contemporary audiences, it sealed her doom in the film industry when it appeared in 1926, but whether this was because of poor promotion and distribution or audience disfavor it is impossible to say. Perhaps her vision of female lunacy on the rampage was too "unfeminine" and yet not grotesque enough. Along with such incomparable lady comics as Gertrude Lawrence and Fanny Brice, she fared better in the more detached and less looks-sensitive realm of theater.

Mabel Normand was also a physical comic, but one of more energy than wit. She was a star graduate, and teacher's pet, of the Mack Sennett school—not of the bathing-beauty line that produced Gloria Swanson, but of the custard-pie-throwing division. She seems to have made her reputation as much for her shenanigans offscreen as for those on film, which display her in an irritating blend of seductress and practical joker. But perhaps the prejudice is in us and our conditioning, in our inability to accept a woman who is both buffoon and sweetheart.

Swanson, like Crawford after her, was one of those emblematic (and aggressively adaptable) figures in whom we see reflected the changing tastes of a decade. Her image altered considerably until it became frozen for posterity as the imperious prima-donna-past-her-prime of *Sunset Boulevard*. In her earliest, and in some cases most interesting, films, she was just the opposite: a dippy, half-witted trouper who would rather hover in the wings than steal the spotlight.

Alternating with her woman-of-the-world roles, she often played unspoiled ingenues. In Allan Dwan's *Stage Struck,* she played a goofy, gracefully incompetent waitress in a greasy spoon who makes halfhearted attempts to efface herself while her boyfriend moons over the visiting actress— the posturing, arrogant prima donna, the whirlwind of conceited womanhood she herself would be playing some years later.

The rivalry between the good-sport–type and the glamour goddess (or between comic Swanson and her more artificial heroines) and the conflict between the values they represented was a recurrent theme of silent movies, providing a perfect vehicle for the "good girl" comedienne and at the same time reflecting Hollywood's self-directed ambivalence, its guilt and anxiety over the consequences of sudden wealth and fame. "Homely" actresses like Colleen Moore (in *Ella Cinders*) and Marion Davies (in *Show People*) would represent the true, back-home values that were being threatened by that symbol of false glamour, the Hollywood star. The "personality" girl, her hidden virtues suddenly discovered (Miss Moore's rolling eyes, Miss Davies' naturalness) would go to Hollywood. There she would be briefly mesmerized and turned into a "phony" (and here Hollywood could satirize its own pretensions). But eventually, by calling for her old boyfriend or some such thing, she would revert to her former self, and achieve a synthesis of Hollywood fame and hometown virtue. It was the Cinderella story but with a true American twist, as if Cinderella, once she married the prince and moved to the castle, had insisted on doing her own housekeeping.

In *The Patsy,* probably her best film, Marion Davies plays a girl who envies her older sister's sophistication, *savoir-faire* . . . and boyfriend. A comic and a cutup, she is convinced she doesn't have the personality to win a man, and to correct this she reads a book on developing poise and glamour. In real life, she had the reputation of being a great mimic at parties, and here she does impersonations of Mae Murray, Lillian Gish, and Pola Negri that are devastatingly funny. After "adopting" alien personalities, she discovers, naturally, that she had one all along, and with it, she wins her sister's boyfriend.

It is ironic that the prejudice against obstreperousness in ladies that King Vidor mocks in *The Patsy* and *Show People,* was a decisive factor in Marion Davies' career. She was probably more hampered than helped by her lover-benefactor W. R. Hearst, who planted himself on the set and refused to let his darling's hair be mussed. A hell-raiser who was adored by everyone, she was apparently forced into a more romantic mold than the one to which her inclinations, briefly sustained by Vidor, would have led her. Her thirties' films, which were probably the only ones seen by Herman Mankiewicz and Welles before they did *Citizen Kane,* were terrible. Thus the portrait of Hearst/Kane's protégé, the opera singer Susan Alexander, that is supposedly based on Davies has more to do with Hearst's promotion of her than with her real talent. But it has stood as the official estimation of her work for years, until revivals of the two Vidor comedies finally placed her in the rank of talented twenties' comediennes where she rightfully belongs.

Women comedians, even at their most rambunctious, are more accommodating to society, while their male counterparts, even at their most docile, are more heretical. The woman's need for a man (even Min had her Bill) takes precedence over unbridled self-expression or transgression of the rules that were thought to be created for her protection. To the extent that it flies in the face of these rules, most comedy is masculine (or to the extent that most comedy is masculine, it flies against these rules . . . and is antifeminine). It instinctively sets out to destroy, through ridicule or physical assault, the props of an orderly society over which woman presides. Comedy is a gust of fresh air, anarchic and disruptive; it spills the tea, shatters glass and conversation; it is a mad dog that shreds the napkins and the tablecloth, and along with them the last vestiges of romantic illusion.

Understandably, women audiences have never responded with great warmth to physical comedy, with its misogynous overtones. As film-buffs, women may appreciate the comedians intellectually, but women in general, responding at a more instinctive level, reject low comedy and knockabout farce. M-G-M forced the Marx Brothers to feature a romantic love story in *A Night at the Opera* to attract women audiences. To this day, many older women remember the film for the thrush-throated courting of Allan Jones and Kitty Carlisle rather than for the Marx Brothers' antics, which they found an irritating intrusion. Even among modern, liberated audiences, women seem to prefer Woody Allen's more conventionally romantic *Play It Again, Sam* to its nuttier predecessors, in which the romantic interest was only comical and incidental.

Of all the silent comedians, Laurel and Hardy are perhaps the most threatening to women, as they combine physical ruination with misogyny. One epicene and gross, the other emaciated, they are an aesthetic offense. With their disaster-prone bodies and their exclusive relationship that not only shuts out women but questions their very necessity, they constitute a two-man wrecking team of female—that is, civilized and bourgeois—society. The male duo, from Laurel and Hardy to Abbott and Costello, is almost by definition, or by metaphor, latently homosexual: a union of opposites (tall/short, thin/fat, straight/comic) who, like husband and wife, combine to make a whole. Practicing heterosexual (machismo twice over) partners like Martin and Lewis are likely, in real life, to clash at some point and "divorce."

By their absurd but compatible physiques, Laurel and Hardy are at one and the same time disqualified from the world of normal heterosexual activity and united against it, the misfits against the fits. Constantly expressing affection for each other, they form a parody male-female couple. In *Their First Mistake,* they "elope," adopt a baby, feign breast-feeding it, sleep together (as they did often in their movies), and try out various male-female roles. But the sexual implications are not so much hidden beneath, as arrested at, the innocently anal idiocy of child's play. In contrast, the Marx Brothers, who are heterosexually aggressive and, being natural brothers, don't need surrogate ones, show genuine, if not particularly genteel, warmth and love in their relations with women. However brutally they may treat poor Margaret Dumont in *A Day at the Races* and *A Night at the Opera,* they secretly adore her—the poise and unruffled splendor with which she graces their films is ample testimony to her place in their hearts and in film history. Laurel and Hardy—and to an even greater and unpleasanter extent, Abbott and Costello—ridicule older women and, by implication, all women. Laurel and Hardy's best films—like the exhilarating *Big Business* in which they start out selling Christmas trees and end by dismembering a car, destroying, piece by symbolic piece, this pride of the capitalist economy— escape the sexual bias in a splurge of irresistible anarchy. But most of their routines are unequivocally antifemale and make one appreciate the self-contained misogyny of a black-guard like W. C. Fields. Though no less a woman-hater, he expresses his antipathy in a language—verbal rather than physical—women can respond to, and his isolationist elegance is less threatening to the borders of female hegemony than the bull-in-a-china-shop antics of Laurel and Hardy.

The real surprise is that women have always seemed to react more adversely to physical aggression than to misogyny, have seemed to find the desecration of property and the home more threatening than the violation of their spiritual and sexual value. Actually, it is probably because women identify in spirit with certain male comedians and respond to the "feminine" side of their nature. Women project themselves into the place of the comic rather than into that of the women he ignores or rejects.

Ambivalence toward women, if not misogyny, was practically the stock in trade of silent comedy, whose activating force was a kind of compensation—physical or *spirituelle*—for the comic's social maladjustment. The social maladjustment in turn became the trophy, the hoop of fire, the chip on the shoulder of his comic act. The comedian had a vested interest in his social ineptitude, but as he became professionally more successful, the illusion of helplessness was more difficult to maintain.

The contradictions in all men—between arrogance and insecurity, between innocence and calculation, between idealism and misogyny—are more apparent in the comedian whose self-image is the substance of his art, but, with geniuses like Chaplin and Keaton, they achieve a brief reconciliation and illumination in comic relief.

Again, size was all important. Sharing with many comedians the small frame of the "weakling," the little man, Chaplin and Keaton developed wit and ingenuity the way other men develop muscles. In creating their comic personae, they used size as a metaphor for the outsider (Chaplin always more self-pityingly than Keaton). By placing themselves in competition with champion boxers or towering Confederate soldiers, they accentuated the incongruity and multiplied their disadvantages. And they felt their size most keenly when they competed with their rivals for the hand of a girl.

She, in turn, was never a "realistic" partner, with defects like their own, but the most beautiful and exquisite of creatures, a paragon suited, not to the ants of the earth, but to its giants, not to its poets, but to its athletes. Thus, they created a situation which could only lead to disappointment, and a woman who, in her blindness to the comedian's true values, could only reflect the shallowness and vanity of all women. Like the sadomasochist, the comic—or the idealist/misogynist—creates a woman who will quicken the pulse of his own self-hatred, who will, in her unapproachable perfection, justify his misogyny and, if he is an artist, simultaneously shape and fuel his art. But then, much of the animating spirit of misogyny (indeed, the male *anima*) is a self-fulfilling prophecy deriving from the particular image of the mother (or any other key female in early life) that predates, and in a sense predetermines, the women who will come to elicit it.

Beside such legendary misogynists as Strindberg and Swift the more gentle Chaplin and Keaton look mild indeed. Yet an excess of reverence for women, which leads, upon disappointment (and it must be disappointed) to profound misogyny, unites them all. Still, to dismiss them as misogynists would be too simple, for their attitude toward women is characterized by anything but undifferentiated hatred. The biographies of Swift, Strindberg, and Chaplin reveal that all were continuously attracted to, obsessed with, and even adored by, women. In the abuse he took from women in life, Chaplin seems more justified in his misogyny than Swift and Strindberg do in theirs, but Chaplin, like the others, and in a peculiar mixture of arrogance and obsequiousness, was driven to seek out the very woman, the "ideal," who would end by disappointing him and destroying his illusions.

In their films, built around a romantic female image, Chaplin and Keaton both illuminate the love-hate feelings that lie dormant in most men and show the progression from one to the other. For the idealist to turn misogynist, the princess must turn shrew, a metamorphosis that, for both Chaplin and Keaton, was conveniently represented by the transformation of a woman from sweetheart to wife. Misogyny was cloaked in the acceptably American and automatically comic form of misogamy, the hatred of marriage and, by extension, the wife. In Keaton's *College,* the happily-ever-after ending was ironically undercut by successive shots of the couple with children, the couple grown old, and the headstones of two graves—a startlingly corrosive ending for a romantic comedy. In *The Three Ages,* his spoof of Griffith's *Intolerance,* Keaton introduced the figure of the Amazon; she would crop up, in different forms, in several of his later films. One of the bitterest and funniest comedies on sexual relations ever made is Keaton's uxorious *Seven Chances.* In the first half, the hero endures the supreme social torture of having a marriage proposal whispered from one to another in a roomful of women, and then, when everyone has gotten the word, he is mocked in a chorus of laughter. The same kind of nightmare proliferation turns the second half from funhouse ingenuity into horror, with the beleaguered hero racing down Main Street pursued by a tribe of termagants, a thousand prospective dowager-brides who have responded to an ad for a wife he has placed in the paper. In that one masterstroke of a visual gag, Keaton runs the gamut of male fears—fears of female supremacy, of entrapment by marriage, and of woman as "wife," of the little man pitted against the big woman and dwarfed by her overriding competence, and, most of all, of castration.

There is a similar, if more gallant, awe of women in *Balloonatics,* a short film in which Keaton plays a lothario on a back-to-nature trip, living in the wilds and struggling unsuccessfully with fish, bears, the rapids; into his midst, a young woman materializes and overcomes all these difficulties with humiliating ease. The Amazon heroine is offset by the sweetheart, a hardy if foolhardy specimen, who can be counted on to do something enchantingly imbecilic at the crucial moment. In *The General* there is the scene (Andrew Sarris has rightly called it "one of the most glorious celebrations of heterosexual love in the history of cinema") in which Keaton turns to his girlfriend, who is busily stoking the engine of the train with pieces of wood the size of pencils, makes as if to strangle her, and suddenly changes his mind and kisses her. Keaton is not upset by woman's incompetence; on the contrary, he is alarmed by her competence. In this he perhaps reflects, not only his personal fears, but also those of a period in which women were taking the initiative and threatening the bastions of male supremacy. And yet Keaton was one of the few directors, or artists of any kind, to envision (and envision himself with) both kinds of women—the soft, feminine dodo, the towering Amazon, and even (in *Balloonatics*) a soft, feminine Amazon and (in *Seven Chances*) a towering dodo. Keaton's women (we can almost hear them, like the secret amplified into a roar) rise up in a glorious cacophony of mixed moods and emotions, a testimonial to the tolerance of their creator.

If Chaplin never achieved the sublime equanimity with women that Keaton did, it is perhaps because women were more traumatically crucial to his life and to the ego at the center of his art. Keaton was detached, almost complacent; for him, women, like the elements and the machines with which he achieved rapport, were part of the scheme of things, a technological-sociological-meteorological harmony of parts with which his own motions wondrously synchronized. We hardly know the names of Keaton's actresses, whereas Chaplin's, though not stars in their own right, enjoyed a one-to-one relationship with him and were psychologically central to his stories.

There is a discernible progression in Chaplin's heroines.

He begins with Edna Purviance, the frailest, the most idealized and otherworldly of his women, in the two-reelers *The
Kid* and *The Woman of Paris.* She is the model for what the
great French critic André Bazin, in his definitive essay on
Chaplin, called the Edna Purviance myth, the feminine ideal,
the inspiration for Chaplin's spasmodic attempts at moral
rehabilitation. She is succeeded by Georgia Hale, the dance-
hall demimondaine in *The Gold Rush* (and, incidentally, a
Sternberg discovery), who is a tougher version of the ideal
woman. Initially, she responds only to power; in the end,
she is reconciled with Chaplin, but in a union that seems
inspired less by her own feelings than by the obligatory
need for a happy ending. The two films made with Paulette
Goddard, *Modern Times* and *The Great Dictator,* reflect a
relationship of something like sexual equality with a normal
woman, although, as gamine and waif, soulmate to the Tramp
and streetfighter like him, she is normal only in the solipsistic
terms of Chaplin's world. Still, the last image of the two
trotting hand in hand down the road of life suggests a collaboration of equals, in contrast to the last shot of *City Lights*
—a close-up of Chaplin as the self-deprecating suppliant at
the altar of love. In the relationship between Chaplin and
Claire Bloom, the fading vaudevillian and the rising ballerina
of *Limelight,* it is the relationship rather than the woman
herself that is idealized, a fusion of personal love and love of
art that remains a perfect mystery.

But Chaplin's idealism is not softened, like Keaton's, by
tolerance, and when he reaches out to strangle, he does not
change his mind at the last minute. The virus, so long suppressed, has grown into a monster, the way Keaton's demons
multiplied. In *Monsieur Verdoux,* Chaplin cowers in the
back of a rowboat, a would-be murderer, drawing his legs
under him and his expression into that familiar wormy,
fastidious grin. In this, Chaplin's most scathing film, he

uses the Bluebeard tale not just to expose the absurdities of capitalism, but to express the final rage of his disillusionment with women, all poured into the quintessential shrew figure played by Martha Raye. She is the virago, the overblown slob, the distorted mirror image of all the women who took advantage of him and deceived him, the Lita Greys and the Mildred Harrises; but now the tables are turned and he is the philanderer, the thief, the murderer.

There are, as Bazin has indicated, two kinds of Chaplin women: The fragile, helpless wife, the Edna Purviance myth extended into matrimony, who is dependent on Chaplin and whom he kills because he can no longer protect her and no longer hopes to be reconciled to society through his love for her; and the shrew who, by the very abrasiveness Martha Raye imparts to her, vindicates Verdoux's crimes and turns him into a sympathetic victim. But these two types are closer to each other than is at first apparent. They share an alliance born of Chaplin's schizophrenia, prefigured in the split, in *The Great Dictator,* between Chaplin the Jewish barber and Chaplin the mad dictator. United by the word "wife," both women have to be killed. "Wife" is the loaded word which, like the blade of the guillotine that kills Verdoux, spells death to the ideal of woman. She dies so that the myth of the sweetheart can live. Chaplin/Verdoux kills her rather than revise his opinion of woman to include a more proportionate balance of good and evil. But, as if in retaliation, Verdoux is defeated by her ghost, her avenging spirit—Martha Raye as the negative, the evil he refused to recognize, refused to integrate into a total picture of an individual woman. She is Edna Purviance's opposite and twin, just as Verdoux is the Tramp's, the one a direct outgrowth of the other. The man who splits women in two splits himself in two, or vice versa. The wife must take the blame for the illusion of the sweetheart, must pay for the whore-birth of the son; woman must be raped, or murdered, because the lover was foolish enough to believe in a perfection she never promised.

If the preference expressed by directors like Chaplin and Griffith for the paragon of virtue, the old-fashioned girl, was significant, at one extreme, the heroines of the Jazz Age melodramas and the feminist and women's rights films were equally significant at the other. There were an unusually large number of women screenwriters in the teens and twenties, as well as a handful of women directors. Among the latter were Alice Guy Blache, who had her own production company (as did many of the actresses themselves—the Talmadge sisters, Mary Pickford, Alla Nazimova, Nell Shipman, and Helen Holmes), Vera McCord, and Gene Gauntier, who directed herself in, of all things, Westerns. These women, businesswomen and artists, were not "political," that is, they were less the expression of a feminist movement (except indirectly, as examples of successful women professionals) than a reflection of the general female orientation of the film industry and the specific popularity of women's themes as subjects.

There were slight political stirrings at the beginning of the decade but they remain mysteries or curiosities and even then were more written about than seen. Record has it that a few documentaries and lightly fictionalized films were produced on such subjects as sex education, abortion, and women's rights, but these do not seem to have gained any kind of real distribution. Producer-director Lois Weber was supposed to have made some feminist films (including one favorable to abortion), but none of these is extant. Her surviving, and presumably more commercially successful, films are conventional melodramas of the kind that were being turned out by the truckload in every studio. There is even evidence for supposing that her sympathies were at the very least mixed, if not blatantly opposed to feminism; in *The Rise of the American Film,* Lewis Jacobs mentions a Weber film, *Where Are My Children?,* that "rebuked 'married butterflies who shirked motherhood.' "

It is startling to discover, smack in the middle of a Victorian melodrama like *Hail the Woman,* a scene in which a young woman (Florence Vidor) is advised of her legal rights as an adoptive mother. And it was against the kind of straitlaced, rural puritanism of the men in *Hail the Woman* that the flapper stood in conscious rebellion. In that film, the country and the small town are synonymous with bigotry and provincialism, and it is only with the heroine's arrival in New York City that she becomes aware of her rights. In *Miss Lulu Bett,* the spinster heroine (Lois Wilson) is cruelly mistreated by the smalltown justice of the peace. In *A Woman of the World,* once again, the small town is associated with hypocrisy, this time that of the district attorney who is confronted by Pola Negri.

But the flapper's main objective was social, rather than intellectual, liberation. She was halfway between the suffragette and the demure, dewy-eyed "womanly woman," the epithet Shaw had hurled at the submissive heroine of Victorian drama. His disgust had been leveled not so much at her as at the playwrights who created her and the critics who promoted her. "But that's no woman!" cried the drama critics in response to Shaw, as they do to this day, revealing their own bias: "Whoever heard of a woman who thinks logically, speaks rationally, and trades in the currency of ideas rather than sentiments?" And so, rather than contend with the idea of a woman who could think, they dismissed the Shavian woman as unfeminine and therefore unnatural.

Still a few millionairesses and Major Barbaras, Heddas and Noras sneaked by on the boards. But there was little possibility of such a heroine emerging in silent film, where the very instrument of her emancipation—speech—was denied her. By definition, silent film is a medium in which women can be seen but not heard. The conversational nuances of an intelligent woman can hardly be conveyed in a one-sentence title; an emancipation proclamation cannot be delivered in pantomime. (Though they were hardly polemical, Anita Loos' wonderfully verbose titles were an exception to the rule.) When the "new woman" did announce herself in the vocally and sexually repressed idiom of silent movies, it had to be by posturing in satin and inhaling a cigarette, rather than by turning a phrase—or a trick.

Freedom meant "lingerie" parties on yachts, all-night fraternity parties, complete with hip flasks and mud baths. The trend was toward a more sophisticated view of the world, of marriage and divorce and desire, a view in tune with the accelerating pace and shifting patterns of the Jazz Age. And yet for the most part the "new morality" extolled in such films was more rhetorical than real, a vicarious splurge for women who wanted to look and feel daring without actually doing anything, who wanted to shock the world by coming home after midnight—but no later. *Why Girls Leave Home* was the title by which a 1921 film proudly announced itself. *Why Girls Go Back Home* was a sheepishly titled 1926 successor.

Even the De Mille domestic dramas of his most innovative period, the late teens and early twenties, did not actually question the validity of marriage but rather—and this was what was revolutionary—gave it sex appeal! He dared to suggest that the married woman was as desirable and exciting as the pubescent party girl. His films, sympathetic to the strapped or straying wife, started a vogue for sophisticated comedies and melodramas of marital intrigue. De Mille's *The Cheat* and *Don't Change Your Husband* describe women caught, respectively, in the binds of blackmail and of boring marriage. *Forbidden Fruit* and *Manslaughter* are "society melodramas" (both with screenplays by the same woman, Jeanie Macpherson) with women's roles ranging from sacrificial lambs to social lionesses to wanton murderesses. The films De Mille made with Gloria Swanson—*The Affairs of Anatol, Male and Female,* and *Why Change Your Wife?*—set her off amid the baroque ornaments of eroticism (furs, bubble baths in marble bathrooms, gigantic four-poster beds) that served as "intimate" sketches for the later orgy spectacles. Like those Sodom-and-Gomorrah epics, the domestic melodramas masqueraded as cautionary tales telling women that, as one title put it, *You Can't Have Everything,* while energetically rebutting the premise. De Mille was perhaps the first to understand, and to define, the nature of the Hollywood "woman's film," which was to indulge women, vicariously, in those peccancies which they were simultaneously made to feel noble in resisting.

Among these films of the most sophisticated earlytwenties' director, there is no record of a wife failing to be reconciled with her husband in the final reel. Hence, it is all the more surprising to find a *Doll's House*–ending in an unheralded 1926 movie called *Dancing Mothers,* in which Alice Joyce, the mother of a spoiled hellion (Clara Bow) and the wife of a straying husband (Conway Tearle), walks out on them and closes the door. Here the sympathy is entirely with the older woman, who is seen as quite attractive in her own right. There is an implied criticism of the flapper, the daughter played by Clara Bow, that is as characteristic of the age and of movie morality (and of a tendency to exploit what is being cautioned against) as the breathless promotion of the flapper. The one, of course, was an outgrowth of the other. The wildness produced a predictable counterreaction (Prohibition is one example), one that was excessive, and often repressive, in its disapproval. There was a good deal of moralistic ambivalence toward the feckless flapper, even among playwrights like Rachel Crothers, who helped to invent her. Plays reserved punitive or corrective endings for their more rebellious heroines, and the American public never really warmed to the most thoroughgoing libertine and free-swinging flapper of the age, Tallulah Bankhead.

The titles of the films suggest more succinctly than any plot synopsis could that marvelous, contradictory blend of Victorian prudery, Dickensian melodrama, and the "new morality" that were the ingredients of the jazz film: *The Careless Woman, The Little Snob, Foolish Wives, Strictly Unconventional, The Lure of the Night Club, Wickedness Preferred, Speed Crazed, The Good-Bad Wife, Souls for Sables, Lady of the Pavements, Madonna of the Streets, Rose of the Tenements, Why Change Your Wife?,* and *Why Bring That Up?* These were not lyrical love stories or mere escapist fantasies, but lurid melodramas in which infidelity, illegitimacy, blackmail, suicide, larceny, and murder figured, not only in the same film, but often within minutes of each other. The material came mostly from magazine stories and popular stage plays and ranged indiscriminately from high style to low life, from international intrigues to backwater scandal, covering the glories and penalties of both.

As often as not women were the authors and adapters of these screenplays and thus helped fashion the image of the flapper and woman of the world, but it was the actresses who gave them their final, quite different forms. Anita Loos' flapper is different from Elinor Glyn's; but the difference between Clara Bow and Norma Talmadge is the more striking. Bow, the "It" girl, was urban and lower, or lower-middle, class; Talmadge, even when she played working girls, suggested a more privileged, upper-middle-class background. But both brought these backgrounds (with their suggestion of family and moral pressure, and, ultimately, puritanism) with them, whereas Joan Crawford and Gloria Swanson, self-invented "stars" in the truest sense, came out of nowhere and were freer to follow the inclinations of the moment. The burden of conscience, and social context, that kept the flapper from going too far didn't cast its shadow of guilt over Swanson and Crawford; thus they enjoyed a freedom that is closer to the European *femme fatale*.

But generally the American flapper was, by definition, only superficially uninhibited. She was, after all, the middle-class (whether upper or lower) daughter of puritans, and she would pass this heritage on to her own daughters and granddaughters. As the flaming incarnation of the flapper spirit, Clara Bow suggests sensuality and wildness but doesn't stray any farther from the straight and narrow than the distance of a long cigarette holder or a midnight joy ride. She is the twentieth century pitted against the nineteenth, urban against rural society, the liberated working girl against the Victorian valentine, the boisterous flapper against Lillian Gish's whispering wild flower. But Clara Bow's recklessness is as deceptive as Lillian Gish's delicacy. In Victor Seastrom's *The Wind,* Gish is buffeted, literally, by more ill winds than Clara Bow will ever know. At her wickedest, Bow might flirt with a married man, but he would usually be superseded by an appropriate suitor in a relationship sanctified by marriage. Even her sensuality, the soft contours and roundness of her body, were babyish, schoolgirlish—a quality Dorothy Arzner caught in *The Wild Party.* An early sound film, this story of a college girl in love with her professor (Fredric March), is unremarkable except for the very sensual handling of Clara Bow and her pals in the girls' dormitory and for Bow's "male" code of loyalty and camaraderie. Her image —formed, really, by Elinor Glyn, who wrote *It* and *Three Week Ends*—is that of an innocent sybarite, and her films, like her morals, are more good-humored than heavy-breathing.

Sexual puritanism varied according to class, but, puritanism being a constant in America, the variations were in degree rather than in kind: Clara Bow's working-class flapper had less margin for error and therefore less appetite for sexual experimentation than society's more cushioned play-girls. And of course the middle class, concerned with upward mobility and respectability, is characteristically more strait-laced. In some cases, the "nice girl" image is more carefully maintained by the upper-middle classes: Clara Bow wanted to be thought wild, while to such well-brought-up ladies as the Talmadges, even to be thought indiscreet was to risk losing one's reputation.

Constance Talmadge is the epitome of the privileged flap-per. She is funny, beautiful, and bright, and in such movies as *Learning to Love* and the earlier *Woman's Place*, both written for her by Anita Loos and directed by Loos' husband John Emerson, she more than holds her own against the men who fall at her feet. (Significantly, in *Woman's Place*, more political in cast, she plays a mayoral candidate and in the other, a socialite.) She is unconventional and daring, but without "cutting herself off" from her roots or milieu, and her flouting of proprieties is a matter more of style than of substance.

In another Loos–Emerson film, *The Social Secretary* (made in 1916 and reissued in 1924), Norma Talmadge played a white-collar heroine, but one who landed in the Social Register. It is a typical Loos' blend of feminism and accommodation, with Norma as a pretty secretary whose jobs invariably end when her lecherous bosses expect the usual "after-hours" attention. Having eluded the clutches of her latest wolf-employer, she is about to despair when she reads an advertisement for a social secretary who "must be unattractive." The rich dowager, Norma's future employer, has tired of hiring pretty girls who immediately leave to get married. Norma is delighted at the chance to disguise herself as a mousy stenographer, especially when she sees the lady has a son with roving eyes.

And yet, with all the sense of social security they radiate, the upper-class flapper types, even when they are not concerned with reputation, are not all that abandoned either. They are bigger teases perhaps, and more arrogant heartbreakers than Clara Bow, but they are no more genuinely free with themselves. Like the aristocratic playgirls played by Katharine Hepburn in the thirties, their freedom is emotional rather than sexual.

The bluff of the flapper was not just Hollywood playing coy; it had its roots in the experience of real women, as anyone familiar with Zelda Fitzgerald's biography can testify. As Nancy Milford portrays her, she was a woman torn, not only between her social and creative impulses (the conditioning of the belle being antithetical to the commitment of the writer), but between Old World propriety and the new morality. As she consciously rejected, for her daughter and, by implication herself, the "career that calls for hard work, intellectual pessimism, and loneliness" for the careless existence of the flapper, so she unconsciously abided by the sexual puritanism instilled in her by her southern breeding.

Zelda's most uninhibited acts were grandstand public gestures: splashing around in the Plaza fountain in her clothes or staying up all night drinking champagne. She flew in the face of convention and her parents' morality to the point of notoriety, but without actually forsaking the safeguards and the protection of that morality. In her one piddling almost-affair with an aviator, an act of retaliation against Scott, she apparently experienced greater pangs of remorse than of sexual pleasure or desire. At the other extreme, but no more genuinely sensual, was Tallulah Bankhead, whose ravenous catholicity in sexual matters was geared, by all reports, to providing her with partners to relieve her loneliness rather than to give positive pleasure.

Both share, with the Talmadges, and even Clara Bow, a

sense of family and social context and deep inhibitions. The contradiction between the worldly woman and the breathless little girl, which comes through in the letters Zelda and Tallulah wrote and the expressions they used, suggests itself in the physical incongruities of the flapper screen-type: the round cherubic face, wide eyes, and tiny lips, and the slinky satins clinging suggestively to slender, boyish bodies.

In many ways, the vessels of purity played by Lillian Gish and Mae Marsh, Griffith's rearguard heroines, experienced more sexual mishap and took more sexual abuse (always of course rebounding in the end) than those brazen shockers, the flapper and the party girl. It is the sexual chastity of Bow rather than of Gish that we understand today, because it is hidden beneath the bravado of a woman of the world. It is the bravado, moreover, of a woman afraid of losing control, and there is not much difference between Clara Bow, who does it with no one, and the character Jane Fonda plays in *Klute,* who does it with everyone; both are women going about the business of saving their fragile egos and both are in danger of losing their souls.

While Americans responded to the alien exoticism of types like Theda Bara, Swanson, and Negri, Europeans grooved on the perverse innocence of Clara Bow. The attraction of opposites (the *esprit de contradiction*) and the dialectic between the American and the European woman has operated as both the theme and the source of underlying tension in films from the twenties to the seventies. A two-part dialectic, it is the conflict between the European woman's ease with her body and her relative enslavement to traditional social values and the American woman's anxiety over her body and relative social freedom.

An instinct for contrast, and the compensation factor, figure almost automatically in the work of directors who, like critics, find their erotic fancies tickled by women who are at opposite sides of the sexual-cultural pole from themselves. Thus for Josef von Sternberg, a launderer from Brooklyn with an acquired Viennese sensibility, Marlene Dietrich, a woman redolent of the demimonde and smoke-filled cabarets, became the vessel of his obsessions, while German director G. W. Pabst, in his search for the ideal Lulu for *Pandora's Box,* found Dietrich, his countrywoman, too "old" and too "knowing." Instead, and against the advice of those around him (and to the everlasting resentment of his compatriots), he opted for the gleaming unworldliness of Louise Brooks, a relatively unknown American actress. She had appeared, not greatly to her advantage, in Howard Hawks' *A Girl in Every Port,* where she was the third wheel in a male friendship. In *Love 'Em and Leave 'Em* she was charmingly uninhibited, but in the secondary role of Evelyn Brent's bad sister. It remained for Pabst to make her a star, exposing her animal sensuality and turning her into one of the most erotic figures on the screen—the bold, black-helmeted young girl who, with only a shy grin to acknowledge her "fall," becomes a prostitute in *Diary of a Lost Girl* and who, with no more sense of sin than a baby, drives men out of their minds in *Pandora's Box.*

One difference between the sophisticated comedies and melodramas of De Mille and those of Europeans like Stroheim, Lubitsch, and Sternberg, was that De Mille allotted his women less space—architectural and emotional—for the development and analysis of feelings. These expatriates in America automatically brought with them a sense of contrast, brought real wit and style to Hollywood, and, in the back lots of Paramount and Universal and M-G-M, created an imaginary continent of romantic intrigue, of innocents abroad and philandering royalty, translating their own obsessions into those of their characters. Most of Stroheim's women are American or American-type heroines, Daisy

Millers caught up in a European maelstrom of flattery, corruption, and sexual encounters both satiric and satyric. They are foolish and impressionable—Mae Murray in *The Merry Widow,* Miss du Pont in *Foolish Wives,* Gloria Swanson in *Queen Kelly*—but they are also sympathetic. They must undergo and inflict humiliations and inspire fetishisms that only Stroheim could have thought of (many of which did not get by the studio censors). But they are nonetheless women of stature and emotional dimension. Stroheim's lurid and bizarre tastes look somewhat fabricated today, but the women stand up well, running the gamut from the grotesquely beautiful (Swanson as the maiden turned madam in *Queen Kelly*) to the grotesquely pathetic (Zasu Pitts in *Greed,* a film Stroheim dedicated to his mother, and in *Hello Sister*). In *Hello Sister,* which, as a result of studio intervention and other problems, was remade without credit to Stroheim, Pitts gave an intense, unsettling performance as the ugly duckling of two sisters. She misinterprets a young man's attentions to her sister, thinking they are directed at her, and then, when she realizes the truth, determines to get the man anyway and at any cost. This film, with its brutal but compassionate portrait of an ugly woman, more than any other sustains Stroheim's claim to naturalism.

Josef von Sternberg was another Svengali with a bogus "von," but unlike Stroheim, he made no claim to anything resembling realism in his films. For Sternberg, obsessed as he is with women, it is man who is initially blind, who has separated style from content in the codes he lives by, and whose judgment is clouded by self-importance. The trappings of Sternbergian decor—the veils and fishnets, the smoke and chiaroscuro—conspire not to obscure, nor merely enhance, but to reveal, to expose, slowly and ironically, the nature of woman, in whom style and sensibility, role and reality, are one. The Sternbergian woman—Evelyn Brent in *Under-*

world, Betty Compson in *The Docks of New York,* Dietrich in everything—is neither idealized nor debased. Her chief quality is intelligence, an alert self-awareness within the loose-fitting costume of her sexuality. Vulnerable, but wide awake and responsible for her fate, she is the antithesis of what critic Parker Tyler calls the "somnambules," the sexual sleepwalkers whose personae are a denial and an evasion of their sexuality. Thus, in *The Docks of New York,* the first time we see Compson's face is not until she wakes up after being rescued unconscious from the river by George Bancroft. It is not a drugged and passive woman, a sleeping beauty, but a live and idiosyncratic one to whom we are introduced. She is a woman who has "been around," and when she lights a cigarette and makes a disparaging remark, she enters the world of the film fully clothed in her own earthy personality.

One of Sternberg's most beautiful films, *Docks* deals with the discovery of mutual trust and love between a cynical sailor and a prostitute, ending not just with the woman's redemption from her profession, but with the man's redemption from his moral arrogance. Instead of just the male "homophile" relationship that is standard for the genre (Bancroft's truculent sidekick who wants him to give up Compson), there is a parallel female "companion," a woman who has given up men and warns Compson to do the same. In overcoming equal temptations to inertia, the choice of heterosexual love is made more freely and with greater hope of success.

In *Underworld,* one of the earliest and least typical gangster films, Evelyn Brent is more than just the focus of the love and rivalry of two men. She grows, exerts a moral force, and is capable of changing the direction of her own and other people's lives. Although the situation resembles the one in Hawks' *A Girl in Every Port,* the sympathies in

Sternberg's film are entirely different. Not only is there no resentment of the woman but the feeling prevails, as in Griffith, that a woman, the right woman, is worth fighting and dying for. (Hawks' women would become stronger, more positive, and even sensual as time goes on. One of his most glorious heroines, Angie Dickinson in the 1957 *Rio Bravo,* shares a name—"Feathers"—and a screenwriter— Jules Furthman—with Sternberg's Evelyn Brent.)

Smoother and less Svengalian than either Sternberg or von Stroheim, Ernst Lubitsch was a rare combination of sophistication and savvy. He had made his reputation with two spectacles in Germany, *Anna Boleyn* and *Madame Du Barry,* the latter starring Pola Negri. Lubitsch brought with him a new kind of sexual champagne, dry and delicious, to an America parched with prohibitionist—and puritanical— thirst. This magician of visual innuendo would combine European immorality with American technological know- how to make Paramount the most elegant and interesting studio of the thirties. But even among the silents, Lubitsch's films—in their exposition of intricate plots and subtle pas- sions—were in a class all their own. His stories involved the extramarital pursuits of idle aristocrats: the gentle duplicity of a husband flirting, even sleeping with, another woman because she resembles his wife; or a bored wife, after failing to break up her best friend's marriage, riding off with another suitor. In *Three Women,* Lubitsch satirized, with as much compassion as wit, the desperate desire of a mature woman (Pauline Frederick) to stay young and keep up with the antics of her younger, but no less desperate, daughter. We see her anxiety as part of the youth obsession of an age not unlike our own. To his everlasting glory, Lubitsch's interest flows naturally and invariably to the "older woman," and, in *Lady Windermere's Fan,* his sympathy as well. In Lubitsch's brilliant silent version of the Wilde play, a worldly mother returns to America to collect payment from her son-in-law. She had agreed to live her disreputable life in Europe out of sight of her daughter (who believes her to be dead), in return for certain compensations on which the husband has apparently defaulted. When the young wife sees her husband hobnobbing with a strange woman, she becomes insanely jealous, and with good reason. As played by Irene Rich, the mother suggests depths of intelligence and sensuality that easily account for the wife's anxiety. We are a long way from the contemporary conception of the grotesque "older woman" as exemplified by the Anne Bancroft character in *The Graduate*. And we are also a long way from contemporary youth-centered films in which there are not only no attractive older women, but very few older women of any description.

As Lubitsch's power at Paramount increased, he was forced to become more "responsible" to the public and to the repressive drift of American screen morality. He was more likely to force upbeat endings and impose didactic messages on charmingly amoral characters. But if he never assumed the uncompromising-director stance of Stroheim and Sternberg, he did have more influence than they. If occasionally he stooped to the demands of official morality, more often he raised the level of film fable—and provincial eyes—to the possibility of life as a continuing adventure, a perpetuity of feeling, as opposed to a living death in marriage. He gave the American public brioche when they wanted bread, and he made them like it.

As in most other decades, two kinds of *auteurs* operated during the twenties: the directors and the stars. With the director, women reflected his tastes and took on the coloration of his fantasies. For better or worse, the women of Sternberg and von Stroheim, of Hawks and Ford, were direct expressions of their obsessions, and obeyed the laws of their universe. On the other hand, stars like Garbo and Pickford and, to a lesser extent, Negri and Bow were the *auteurs* of their films, the *raison d' être* and guiding spirit. Occasionally, director and star coincided, as with Lubitsch and Negri in *Forbidden Paradise* or, later, Garbo and Cukor in *Camille,* but more often they collided, like Lubitsch and Pickford, or never crossed paths at all. Pickford, who had bucked anti-German feeling to bring Lubitsch to America, quarreled with him over *Dorothy Vernon of Haddon Hall,* which she had hired him to direct. Lubitsch had his way with *Rosita* but the victory was pyrrhic, since Mary, as the sultry Spanish streetsinger-turned-countess, was not at her best.

Negri, who was badly handled in America, where her career foundered, made a great display of preferring her German films to her American ones, and the stills from the latter would seem to corroborate her preference. But she gave some lovely performances in films that deserve more than the abuse she and others have heaped on them. Her image was that of a worldly woman to which, in her best films, large measures of irony and understanding were added. As Catherine the Great in *Forbidden Paradise,* she suggests a subtle union of woman and queen, particularly in the scene in which she looks at her young idealistic lover with an expression of mixed regret, amusement, and self-awareness. We see in her eyes the passing of a love affair into memory, without bitterness and with the bloom of its first days as vivid as the deliquescence of its last.

In *A Woman of the World,* Negri played a countess who, at the end of an unhappy love affair on the Riviera, goes to visit her boorish relatives in a backwater town of the American Midwest. Just as their vulgarity is beginning to irritate us beyond repair, and we are dreading her own reaction of embarrassment and disdain, she arrives and, like a true queen, puts everyone at ease. Her humorous compassion for her relatives reconciles us to them, and the European-American dialectic is resolved by the mating of the former's (Negri's) sexual honesty with the romantic idealism of the latter (the uptight district attorney Negri "loosens" and marries). Here again, the woman represents the moral force, a voluptuous, cigarette-stained voice of integrity, a creature who knows who and what she is and cuts through the hypocrisy of American provincialism, salvaging what is best from the wreckage.

Garbo, her own inimitable *auteur* and sexual opposite, was able, of course, to survive not only good and bad directors and bad and awful leading men, but changing fashions of women, for she was timeless. More than Negri, Garbo was the woman who lived for love and, hence, was less free; enchained to the idea of absolute love, she was incapable of enjoying its intermittent savories and provisional pleasures. But her commitment carried a sense of fatalism present in many of the great twenties' films and in the tragic vision of life: a belief that certain choices are irrevocable. It is an idea no longer fashionable in today's postanalytic, group- and trip-therapy ambience and in our current free-floating narrative forms of film, where everything is revocable and nothing, least of all one's emotional commitments, is beyond revision. As Leonora, the opera singer in *The Torrent,* her first American film, she is visited one last time by her former lover (Ricardo Cortez), now gray-haired and defeated. The consequences of his choice—respectable marriage and family —can actually be seen in his appearance and felt in his air of weary resignation. They look at each other in mutually clear-eyed recognition of the fatal consequences of a missed opportunity.

Garbo's body may have belonged to the twenties, but her heart was already yearning for the thirties. She belonged, for better or worse, to the alchemies being wrought by changing tastes and by the Production Code—to the magic, or the hypocrisy, by which body would be converted into spirit, lust into love, sexuality into romance.

THE THIRTIES

Because of the initial difficulties in the transition from silent cinema to sound and the vested interest of most contemporary critics in the artistic glories of the former, the early thirties were for the longest time considered to be the Dark Ages of film history. Now, however, this period presents strong claims to being a Renaissance, having produced a wider variety and larger percentage of good-to-great American movies than any other three-year period. Many of the early efforts were awkward, as directors tried to modify stage elocution to the more naturalistic demands of movie dialogue and to recover visual fluidity, hampered by cumbersome sound equipment. But they adapted with amazing speed to the new technology and, en route, the experimentation brought with it a kind of freedom, an artistic and moral adventurousness, before discovery hardened into convention and cliché and before the erotic license of cinema's frankest period was revoked by the Legionnaires of Decency.

Until the Production Code went into full force, between 1933 and 1934, women were conceived of as having sexual desire without being freaks, villains, or even necessarily Europeans—an attitude surprising to those of us nurtured on the movies of any other period. Women were entitled to initiate sexual encounters, to pursue men, even to embody certain "male" characteristics without being stigmatized as "unfeminine" or "predatory." Nor was their sexuality thought of as cunning and destructive, in the manner of certain forties' heroines; rather, it was unabashedly front and center, and if a man allowed himself to be victimized by a woman's sex, it was probably through some long-standing misapprehension of his own nature. Sensualists without guilt, in one of the few truly "liberated" periods of cinema: such were the heroines of *Morocco, Trouble in Paradise, The Blue Angel, Shanghai Express, Dinner at Eight, Blonde Venus, Queen Christina, She Done Him Wrong, Design for Living,* and *Rain*—all made between 1930 and 1933. It's true that the same period gave us, with *Little Caesar, Public Enemy,* and *Scarface,* the most violently machismo, woman-bruising films in history. But there was a kind of naked directness to these gangsters and their ambivalence toward women, to Jimmy Cagney's shoving the grapefruit in Mae Clarke's face—surely a cleaner and less generalized expression of hostility than rape and the more insidious modern forms of misogyny in which women characters are drawn as bitches to be blotted out.

The demarcation line between films of the early thirties and those made afterward, between films with satin and Freudian slips and explicit sexuality and films in which sex took cover under veils of metaphor, is particularly important in its effect on women's roles. It is the difference between Ginger Rogers having sex without children—*Gold Diggers of 1933, Upper World* (1934)—and Ginger Rogers having children without sex—*Bachelor Mother* (1939). It is the difference in emphasis between two movie heroines based on the redoubtable Adela Rogers St. John: between Norma Shearer as the straying sybarite of *A Free Soul* (1931) and Rosalind Russell as the smartly tailored quick-witted reporter in *His Girl Friday* (1940), the difference, literally, between night and day.

The stars and the types change from one period to the other. Garbo, Dietrich, Mae West, and Harlow belong unmistakably to pre-code liberation; Katharine Hepburn, Jean Arthur, Rosalind Russell, and most of the professional and working-class heroines come after. The paradox is unavoidable: while the Hays Office, having assumed the mantle of our national superego, suppressed the salutary impulse of female sexuality, it was also largely responsible for the emergence of the driving, hyperactive woman, a heroine more congenial to current tastes than her sultrier sisters. The "working woman" (fulfilling also a demand, created by the Depression, for a more down-to-earth heroine) was more at ease pursuing a career, whether for its own sake or as a pretext for finding a husband, than languishing in a love nest.

Of all the locked rooms in the Gothic mansion of society, female sexuality is still the most tantalizing and mysterious. Women's sexual desires and fantasies are subject to the same social conditioning as are their emotional and social lives, and only a change of one will effect a change of the other. The prohibition against freely expressed sexuality is compounded by a double taboo: that of society as a whole (which affects men as well) and that of men individually in their relations with women. Along with the current questioning and reordering of roles, biological studies (such as Mary Jane Sherfey's *The Nature and Evolution of Female Sexuality,* which deals with the primacy of the female embryo and the extent of female orgasmic potential) suggest, rather frighteningly, that conventional male-dominated theories and sexual behavior are only temporary, a drop in the bucket of eternity, a thumb in the hole of the dike that may soon give way to the free expression of aggressive female sexuality.

Probably (and for our own protection), as women are "slow to arouse," it will take generations for this new era to be upon us. But at this juncture, women expect perhaps too much of themselves, and, likewise, of women on the screen—expect an image of driving, dynamic sexuality without the intervening stages of sensual awakening. Even among the young, sexual experience doesn't seem to carry with it a greater sense of freedom, or a more relaxed sensuality. A screening of Lubitsch's *Trouble in Paradise* for a college audience provoked a surprisingly puritanical response. Lubitsch capitalized on the virgin-whore opposition by making Herbert Marshall (a dapper society thief) the cause of contention between Miriam Hopkins (as his sporting accomplice) and Kay Francis (as a sensual millionairess for whom he briefly works as secretary). Despite Francis' allure, and she has never been more attractive, the young audience unanimously rooted for Hopkins, the romantic buddy figure. Disregarding other possible influences (the character's money or her position as boss), the audience picked the soulmate over the suitemate, and perhaps they were right. Sexual liberation has become oppressive. The braless or microskirted woman is a walking contradiction, a denial of the freedom she claims to express. In riveting the eyes of passersby from her face—the window of her soul, her uniqueness—to her figure, she turns herself into the object of lust she is theoretically trying to transcend. Moreover, her "dare" is false, it conceals a hostility to men and sex—the tease as an inverted rape. To flaunt one's sexuality and expect men not to look is like lovers kissing in public: They pretend to think that their own obliviousness makes them invisible, while all the time they are aggressing on the awareness, the privacy of those who pass.

In periods of sexual liberation, women have too often

found themselves imprisoned by their sexual identities, stuck in the bedroom when they would rather be at the barricades. The proscriptions of the Production Code that were catastrophic to sexually defined, negligee-wearing glamour goddesses were liberating for active or professional women, for girls with more brains than cleavage. (Not that a woman couldn't have both, but somehow, on the screen, she never did; in life, it is often not a want of equipment, but of *time*, that prevents a woman from excelling in both areas.) Nevertheless, there was something tremendously exciting in the moral latitude offered movie heroines of the early thirties. They occasionally had affairs that were consummated by more than a kiss; a married woman who lapsed was forgiven without inordinate breastbeating (although it would help if, like Loretta Young in *Employees' Entrance,* she tried to commit suicide); a woman might walk out on her husband and family (as Alice Joyce did in the twenties' film, *Dancing Mothers*); and, in the silents, who knows how many four-letter words were uttered that never made it into the titles. Even in a film like *Only Yesterday,* where Margaret Sullavan seemed to pay heavily for her two one-night stands with John Boles—the outcome of the first is pregnancy, of the second, her untimely death—there is more joy than anxiety in the first encounter with her lover, and more eroticism than recrimination in their ambiguous, "anonymous" (re)union ten years later.

It is not that the early thirties' films are unduly optimistic or utopian. If anything they are more tragic than later love stories and gangster films precisely because they were not subject to the rulings of the official code of morality, to the closed Pavlovian system of penalties and rewards wherein human freedom was diminished and the experience of pleasure hopelessly entwined with a sense of wrong. When, in *Employees' Entrance,* Loretta Young goes off to a hotel room with her boss and ex-lover to spite her husband, director Roy del Ruth not only treats the seduction scene matter-of-factly, but has Young gain forgiveness with what would be considered insufficient, and inadequately prolonged, suffering by subsequent movie standards. Nor does her husband assume the position of moral superiority that would later become obligatory for injured spouses of the male sex.

In this temporary abrogation of the double standard according to which women are condemned and penalized for what men are expected to do, sex queens like Pola Negri, Mae West, and Jean Harlow were not villainesses but heroines, and they possessed the kind of brains and wit that were later thought to be incompatible with sensuality. Generally the sex principle has had, for the protection of American audiences, to be isolated and distorted—into a deity (the "sex goddess"), a mamma (the mammary idols of the forties and fifties), a bunny. But for a brief period the more sophisticated influences of Europe and Broadway were assimilated without the usual cultural and sexual tension between "art" and "commerce," between class and mass taste.

Actually, it was in the cross-fertilization of these two worlds that some of the fullest women characters emerged, the product of the combined forces of Hollywood technology, pioneer energy, and the woman-promoting features of the studio system on the one hand, and, on the other, the amorous and amoral proclivities of a European world-view. With such emissaries from the Old World as Greta Garbo, Mauritz Stiller, Victor Sjostrom (soon to be Americanized as Seastrom), Pola Negri, F. W. Murnau, Fritz Lang, Marlene Dietrich, Josef von Sternberg, Erich von Stroheim, and Ernst Lubitsch, the Trojan horse was within the gates, and out of it poured Helens whose powers of sorcery it would take more than the forces of moral armament to extinguish. In the early years of the Depression, Hollywood was offering the public frivolous upper-class entertainments, and for once the time lag between the real world and Hollywood's apprehension of it was a blessing. Not only did the musicals and comedies provide the mass public with much needed relief, but these fictions confirmed that the good life was still thinkable, even possible, that the world might right itself again. While the bluestockings called for grim realism, the blue-collar workers, as usual, went to musical comedies.

The spirit of Lubitsch's world—a never-never land of smiling lieutenants and lonely princesses, lady robbers and philanderesses (a world in which sexual innuendo was not an evasion of the real thing but an engraved announcement of it)—was not so remote from Hollywood as we like to think. His style of comedy, ironic and irrepressible, set the tone of Paramount Studios, and was the David to the Depression's Goliath. Lubitsch's greatness was largely self-concealing: It lay in an ability to blend different elements—satire, musical comedy, and melodrama, for example—in a manner so effervescent that genius was mistaken for mere "touch." At the same time, he created women characters of depth and complexity whose originality was glossed over in the general designation of "Continental sophistication." But Lubitsch's worldliness was as deceptive as his touch. If anything, it was in going against the grain of the polished surface, in the hints of awkwardness with which he invested his men and women, that they—particularly the women—acquired complexity. By the unwritten code of even the pre-code thirties, the equation of sex and perdition did not apply to the "European woman." She was entitled, even expected, to devour life and commit indiscretions that would be unseemly, not to say immoral, for an American girl. At the same time, her power to excite and titillate rested firmly on the contrast, implicit or overt, with American women. Lubitsch not only explored this contrast; he often went one revolutionary step farther by uniting the poles of sense and sensuality in one heroine.

He brought with him his own milieu: an imaginary European *crème de la crème,* already cut with Lubitschian vinegar, to which he added American blood. By cross-breeding American and European types and by shifting expectations, he set up reverberations within the plot and within characters that went against the usual stereotypes: Jeanette MacDonald as a lonely princess or a Riviera gambler; Garbo as a stalwart Soviet functionary; Jennifer Jones as a Cockney plumber; Miriam Hopkins as an American semisophisticate on the Continental make; Dietrich as an upper-middle-class housewife. But as Dietrich is a housewife only to her husband (Herbert Marshall), and an angel to her lover (Melvyn Douglas) in the 1937 film *Angel,* so the other women are what they seem only intermittently and to certain people. Lubitsch's women benefit not just from the double exposure of the director's often-cited "keyhole" view of society, by which kings are reduced to the perspective of their valets, but from his sense of the multiplicity of a woman's roles as a primary condition of her being. Pola Negri as queen and mistress; Irene Rich as both delinquent mother and potential rival to her daughter; Gene Tierney as both aging companion to her husband (Don Ameche) and unchanged idol of his first love. For Lubitsch, women are as often in the driver's seat as men, and roles are oppressive only insofar as life, and love, are imperfect and no one person is wholly adequate to the needs of another. All emotional hunger tends toward an ideal resolution, one sublime, all-encompassing relationship, but until that infinite moment of eternal oneness, roles collide with and succeed one another. How better to elucidate, without explaining, such shifting impulses of the personality, than the triangle—a more eternal form of human geometry than the pair—that repeatedly appears as the structural basis of his films!

The triangle permits us to see a person being seen by

two different people, being interpreted, like the proverbial glass of water, as half-empty or half-full. From this we perceive that a person is less an active role-player than a passive receptacle, that he is not so much perpetrating an illusion as being selectively appreciated. In *Trouble in Paradise,* Herbert Marshall is seen as a schemer and scoundrel in his kooky partnership with Miriam Hopkins, but in proximity to the luscious plutocrat played by Kay Francis, he himself becomes languorously sybaritic. As the neglected wife in *Angel,* Dietrich is one thing to her husband and quite another to her occasional lover. But it is not just the difference between marriage and the taint of familiarity, and nonmarriage and the tickle of desire, but between one man's way of loving and another's. For when Douglas asks Marshall what an hour with the incomparable Angel would mean to him, Marshall, little guessing Angel's identity, replies with a practical and concrete "sixty minutes," while Douglas the lover translates, and protracts, the same time span into "three thousand six hundred seconds!" And thus is woman divided between the realist and the romantic, taking refuge from prose in poetry but wishing for the man, and the vision of herself, that could embrace the two. But *Angel* is also a brilliant reversal of the customary one man–two woman setup, with its implication that whereas a woman will be satisfied with one man, one *type* of man, only, a man needs a variety of women (or at least one from Column A and one from Colmun B) to satisfy his needs.

In the end, Marshall discovers that Angel is his wife and makes the choice that means he will take her back, forever—a gesture that would normally be read as her redemption through his forgiveness, but which is actually the contrary. For it is his acceptance of a side of her that he may not ever be able to fulfill that is *his* redemption and therefore, in its acceptance of her totality, hers; just as, in *Trouble in Paradise,* it is Hopkins' tacit acknowledgment of Marshall's carnal liaison with Kay Francis that enables their wholly different "marriage" to survive.

No one person is the complete complement to any other; the side of the person exposed by the triangle continues to exist, even when the triangle has been superseded by the pair. Sometimes, as in *Design for Living,* the triangle itself endures. In this adaptation of the Coward play, Lubitsch combines the daisy freshness of the new world with the orchid exoticism of the old, producing a rare, slightly scandalous hybrid flower with Miriam Hopkins at its center. For Hopkins, who often played the "wild-nice girl," the southern lady of breeding who would try anything once, this was her definitive role. (It is a relatively recent convention that southerners—particularly southern women—have to be shown as cretins and played by actresses with phony, honey-dripping, "dumb-female" accents.)

In *Design for Living,* Hopkins plays an American in Paris who gives herself—first professionally, and finally sexually—to two men, taking their hearts and careers in hand. The official consensus held that the film was a poor second to the play. It was blasted for Ben Hecht's piss-elegant screenplay, for Hollywood's toning down of the racy dialogue, for Lubitsch's casting of Hollywood types instead of the original stage cast (for and about whom the play had been written) of Coward and Alfred Lunt as the playwright and the painter, and Lynn Fontanne as the girl they both love. But it is precisely the casting of such unsuave Americans as Fredric March and Gary Cooper as the playwright and painter, and Miriam Hopkins as the girl they meet on a train, that makes the film iconoclastic and moving and disinfects it of the sexual innuendoes of the original cast that would have become more obvious on the screen.

While the triangle of the film is equilateral, the triangle

of the play is isosceles, with the characters based on Lunt and Fontanne—Otto the painter and Gilda (in the play, an interior decorator)—forming the central, quasi-marital relationship to which the Coward character, the "mercurial" Leo Mercure, is the outsider. Critic Richard Corliss has suggested that in adapting the play, Hecht may have shaped it to express the relationship between himself, Charles MacArthur, and Helen Hayes, MacArthur's wife, but if that had been the case, it is very likely (given Hecht's *esprit de* buddies) the woman would have gradually receded from view, with the Front Page–back-room boys taking over completely. And the relationship between the two men would probably have come full circle: from the perverse shadings of the Coward play to the male ethos of "love without pain or anger," which Hecht celebrated as his credo. The perfect balance of the triangle, three people in a state of permanent, breathless suspension, can only be the work of Lubitsch. Like the enchanting threesome in *Trouble in Paradise,* the March–Hopkins–Cooper relationship is rooted in the Lubitschian faith that while women may—indeed *must*—have the same moral (or immoral) disposition as men, sexually they are far from interchangeable. Perhaps the greatest and fullest relationships, like the greatest art, come from the imaginative, rather than physical, exchange of sexual characteristics, from a spiritual, rather than literal, identification of one sex with the other.

Hopkins is caught, in *Design for Living,* between the Puritan work ethic and antipuritanical Eros, between a gentleman's agreement and her own uncivilized impulses. Lubitsch's choice of Hopkins for the part was a masterstroke. Who could match the sly, saucy gentility of her innocent abroad, a woman who wants sex partly because she wants it, but mostly because she's never had it. Who could give quite the same earnestness to the complaint she makes that men are allowed to try on different women, like hats, until they find the right one, whereas women have to take the man that happens to fit at the right time. To remedy this inequity, and solve the problem of being in love with both men at the same time, she proposes a *ménage à trois,* substituting work for sex. The two artists will pursue their respective muses while she, having abandoned her own career as a commercial artist to invest in their more promising ones, enforces discipline. This unconventional arrangement is topped—and toppled—in the delicious moment when Hopkins breaks her own rules. March has taken his play to London leaving her alone with Cooper, whom she finds she can no longer resist. "It's true we have a gentleman's agreement," she says reflectively, then, flopping back on the bed, "but I'm no gentleman." Whether the scene implies, in the later words of the Production Code, that the "low forms of sex relationship are the accepted or common thing," it is surely one that wouldn't have passed the censor after 1934. The number of sacred cows gaily demolished by the film— premarital virginity, fidelity, monogamy, marriage, and, finally, the one article of even bohemian faith, the exclusive, one-to-one love relationship—is staggering. And though Hopkins gives up her own career to further those of the two men, she does it not as a housekeeper, bedmaker, and meal provider, but as an agent-manager and inspiration, to wheedle, discipline, criticize, and take an active part in their work. She doesn't put all her emotional—*or* professional—eggs in one basket, and each artist has the benefit of a full-time agent, half-time woman, and plenty of time for work.

The candor and innocence of the relationships, male-male and male-female, preclude any taint of perversion or coyness and enable the film to go beyond sex to its true spirit which is not carnal but romantic, the collusion of kindred souls, of blithe spirits in a working relationship that works.

Coward's characters suggest elegantly ambisexual cosmopolites, but Lubitsch takes the trio farther in feeling. His casting is gently and decisively heterosexual; far from indicating any inclination for the kind of closed and infantile buddy system found in so many American films, March and Cooper suggest two individuals who, without Hopkins, would probably get on each other's nerves after a while. At any rate, Lubitsch is the antithesis of the kind of puritan director or writer in whom sexual subthemes appear as the latent content of his work. It is out in the open as one of many possibilities in the human comedy, a spectacle in which fulfillment is neither a male nor a female value, neither exclusively a professional nor exclusively a private and personal matter. If Lubitsch's women are hard to grasp hold of and categorize, it is because they are busy turning in different directions and realizing the multiple sides of themselves.

Although for convenience' sake we think of American and European attitudes toward women as dialectically opposed, the range of feelings expressed by directors would be more accurately reflected in a spectrum (Lubitsch would be in the middle), itself composed of smaller spectrums. Taken in isolation and in extremis, the traditional European conception of women is no healthier or broader than our own and in many ways it is more binding. For if American directors at their most American (Hawks and Walsh) see women, on their individual spectrum, as analogous to men —enterprising, strong, smart, courageous, unmotherly—the Europeans see women as men's complements—Nature's handmaidens, exponents of the "eternal feminine," immanent rather than transcendent; to use another of Simone de Beauvoir's terms, the "other."

The "vamp" was an early example of an Americanization of the "enemy," a European archetype (the "other" as *femme fatale*), literalized and exaggerated into a freak by the puritanical impulse. Even the gravitation to sharply delineated iconography in the early silents can hardly account for the outrageously broad malevolence of such comical carnivores as Theda Bara and Nita Naldi. They are meant to represent demonic natural forces that, like a cyclone, threaten to uproot man from himself, but they are more like storm warnings than the storm itself. Sagging under the excess weight of makeup and jewels—the emblems of their wickedness—they are not likely to seduce anyone unawares, but, with *Caveat Emptor* written on their brow, are self-contained cautionary fables, like a De Mille orgy sequence. But as a crude prototype, Bara presented in the most stylized form certain traits that were modified in her more "normal" successors, the sex goddesses: the hypnotic glare of the bird of prey, eyes smoldering under half-closed lids, like shades partly lowered in a whorehouse. In one "fell swoop" of these lids she reveals the association of images, elaborated by de Beauvoir, by which woman became, for man, the personification of nature as the "other," whether in the benevolent guise of the nutrient-mother or her destructive, inverted counterpart, malefic natural force. In either case, woman, progenitor and life-giver or angel of death, is man's mysterious opposite and potential enemy, a force he must circumvent, dominate, or propitiate with his lifework. This is the (biological) view of woman, always framed from a male viewpoint, that Simone de Beauvoir takes as the starting point and principal opposition of *The Second Sex*. It is fundamentally a classical, European view, characterizing the work of directors as diverse as Bergman, Godard, Pabst, and Fellini, although, to the degree that they are related, by background or religion, to Europe, it has permeated the consciousness of American artists.

In European art and mythology, woman's alliance with nature, hence her "earthiness," is an absolute; her contingent form is dependent upon the artist or mythmaker, that is, whether she is enjoyed as the "whore," feared as the *femme fatale*, or revered as the "muse" or "earth mother." To the American male, whose popular mythology is constructed to forestall an acceptance of death, the very association of women and the life-death cycle is one of terror. With the term "sex goddess" he takes worship of the "mother"/"Madonna" one step farther by redeeming not just woman, but sex, itself. Sex, like dirt, disease, and death, is anathema to a country that treasures cleanliness above godliness and innocence above experience. To the number one producer of antiseptics it becomes a matter of both religious and professional honor to sanitize what it cannot dispense with. The terms "vamp" and "sex goddess," like the names of hurricanes or classical deities, are magical words, incantations invented by men to explain the inexplicable and, as in the custom of naming hurricanes after women, to locate the source of destruction within the "mysterious" sex. The Greeks and Romans, notorious chauvinists in real life, at least gave their goddesses such prestigious offices as "wisdom" and "the hunt" (it was, as Freud has pointed out, the tendency of monotheism, as a patriarchal, revolutionary religion, to drive out polytheistic matriarchy) ; but the Americans, in sanctifying sex, confine woman to a sexual role while simultaneously raising her above nature, above mortal life. While the European male artist or experiencer of life may want to bury himself in woman in order to brush shoulders with death and conquer his own fear, the American wishes to remove woman from the cycle of nature and its reminder of mortality, wishes to keep her young forever.

In this bizarre canonization, the "sex goddess" redeems sex from itself, from both the awkward, fumbling initiatory rites and the odor of death that the French glory in, and turns it into something separate, self-contained, ideal. Not always divine, however, for the title "sex goddess" has been held by many different kinds of women and some have won it for attributes less spiritual than Garbo's face. Amazonian might be a better word to describe the degree to which these stars, by virtue of some specialty or other (Hayworth's lips, Grable's legs, Jane Russell's and Marilyn Monroe's breasts) become overpowering. The inflated value of one feature over the others is an index to the collective male libido at any given time. (Dietrich's extraordinary legs were nevertheless but one part of a total picture of her, while Grable's were a substitute for a deficient whole. The mammary fixation is the most infantile—and most American—of the sex fetishes, and indeed the fifties, in which bosom power was supreme, was the least adult decade in movie, and national, history.)

Neither did the sex goddesses serve identical functions, nor were they the straight-faced, monolithic symbols of fan hagiography. More often than not, they were consciously playing a role, or "playing up" to a role. Like department store Santa Clauses, they wore a familiar costume, paraded themselves, played a game with the kids, catered to their fantasies, but not always with a straight face. The humor in Pola Negri's vamping, the mincing speech and wide-eyed wonder of Marilyn Monroe, have an element of self-parody. Like the nigger antics of Stepin Fetchit, like the schizophrenic's self-protective mask, they form a subtle, skin-fitting camouflage by which not the slave but the master, not the patient but the doctor, is slyly ridiculed. But it is a strategy that is played out on a tightrope: the tightrope of the "weaker" sex and the disempowered psyche. However much the schizophrenic may elude institutional manipulation, he is hardly in control of his mind. And the sex goddess treads a thin line of self-possession: If she becomes too masculine, she is dismissed as a woman; if she carries her parody too far, she mimics her own sex and falls into the hands of her "camp" followers who play up to the impersonation until it usurps the person underneath.*

At its best, the sex goddess's alienation is Brechtian, preserving a dramatic unity while suggesting a certain consciousness of effect: Beyond the pantomime of the regal presence—the seduction, the surrender, the posture of helplessness—we occasionally hear the actress chuckle, or see her peeking out from behind her lines. To attribute high seriousness to these performances is like seeing a silent movie projected at sound speed and mistaking the accelerated motion for the way people actually ran. In *The Princess Comes Across,* Carole Lombard played the entire film as a heavily accented Garbo-like impostor of a princess. And Garbo herself was not without traces of self-mockery. The raised eyebrow indicated infinite knowledge of the world including a playful regard for her own image. But unlike Dietrich, whose irony was a permanent fixture and a defense against disappointment, Garbo subordinated hers to the final certainty that love is more serious and more important, which meant that she herself, as love's embodiment, was beyond disappointment.

As actress, myth, and image of woman, Garbo, like any other star, was neither wholly unique nor wholly representative. She was not like the solitary and self-derived creation of the writer, on the one hand; nor was she a spontaneous eruption of the national "anima," an archetypal

* The camp reincarnations of forties' and fifties' glamour goddesses by the transvestite stars (Candy Darling, Jackie Curtis, and Holly Woodlawn) of the Warhol-Morissey studio are merely the latest and most extreme example of the appropriation of sex goddesses by their gay devotees. Irony and stylization create the margin for transsexual innuendoes. Dietrich was certified by some of her followers to be a female impersonator, by others to have undergone an operation. And gays insist the tag line, "There never was a woman like Gilda," should be taken at face, rather than figurative, value.

heroine as might emerge from a truly "collective" art like television. In *Mata Hari* or *Grand Hotel,* in *Camille* or *Conquest,* in *Ninotchka* or even *Two-Faced Woman,* she was different and yet the same, partly an expression of the collective unconscious, partly of her own inner light; partly of the shifting tension between the actress/star and the director, and between the director and the "system." Marlene Dietrich, as the feminine principle according to Josef von Sternberg, is even less a national archetype than Garbo. But she is also less of a sex object. She is Sternberg's creation, his anima, and yet she absorbs so much of him into her that she is not an "other" as object, on the far side of the sexual gulf, but an androgynous subject. Mae West, self-created, is both anima and animus, while Garbo as that other great androgyne, is the anima of no single *auteur* or even society, but is a natural force, a principle of beauty that, once set into motion, becomes autonomous.

Transcending mortality, her appeal was not specifically sexual; it was both greater and less than Dietrich's, more diffuse and therefore less erotic. She cast a wider net, catered to no specific sexual tastes, not even masculine or feminine, whereas Dietrich catered specifically to both but not to all tastes. Garbo asked for "eternal love," a fairy-tale phrase; Dietrich asked for something far more difficult: love now, today. Dietrich's irony kept men at a distance, posed questions, and signaled her intelligence; Garbo's was conspiratorial, secret—it darkened the room, excluded the world, and drew men, flattering them, deep into the womb of her mystery. And they emerged, dissatisfied with the rest of womankind, to write epigrams like Kenneth Tynan's: "What one sees in other women drunk, one sees in Garbo sober." Perhaps if men were less concerned with women's faces than with their souls and minds, they wouldn't have to drown their disappointment in drink, real or metaphorical. But then perhaps men's souls, as the focus of women's attraction to them, can no more sustain sober inspection than women's faces. And so women, too, have found occasion to get drunk on Garbo.

Whether as a nurse, a dying swan, or a repentant courtesan, Garbo is sex constantly transformed and spiritualized. She is the perfect metaphor for the Hollywood film, the high priestess at the holy communion of American romance, where sex is converted into love, body into spirit, and a transitory experience into an ultimate and permanent grace. Thus, nothing is quite what it seems. Suffering, when it is so exquisitely felt and expressed, is no longer suffering but an art, a symbol of suffering; the man she loves is of less importance than love itself. And it is no accident that her leading men were either weak to begin with, or became invisible, for as a figure who combined elements of both sexes, and the essence of love itself, she usurped the whole screen. Like Brando, who would be androgynous in the same way; rarely paired with an "equal" of the opposite sex, Garbo was also too much of a star to subordinate herself to a strong director; as a result, she made few good movies. And yet she is timeless because she understood instinctively the trick of being actively passive, of being all things to all people, and of carefully hiding the real person behind the image. (Katharine Hepburn was the opposite: Her cantankerous personality intruded on her image, to the point that moviegoers lost sight of just how beautiful she was.)

To the extent that the love she offers is maternal and self-sacrificial, Garbo appeals to men and adherents of male supremacy. As Marie Walewska, Napoleon's mistress in *Conquest,* she waits in his antechambers while he entertains Désirée and, like his mother, whose constant companion she is, seeks only Napoleon's happiness, whatever grief or deprivation it may cause her. In return for this willingness to sacrifice herself, her degraded position in life (for she is generally a mistress or courtesan) is redeemed, the innocence of Mary regained by the Virgin Birth. Hence whatever her peccancies or previous sins, she remains, from moment to redeemed moment, a spiritual virgin.

Dietrich, Harlow, and Mae West, on the other hand, are hedonists, unshackled sensualists who would rather go to hell than achieve salvation at the price of erasing all those moments of carnal bliss. They are the goddesses of sex and yet are not, being earthly rather than divine. In the resplendence of her beauty, Dietrich comes closest to being a goddess, but she refuses to be one, refuses to take on the generalized aspects of love and suffering with which a mass audience could identify, and refuses to pretend for the sake of a man's ego that love will not die or that she will love only him. Unlike Garbo, who holds out the hope of life everlasting in love, Dietrich is realistic, even fatalistic. She accepts and understands human weakness and poverty, folly, perversity, and the need for redemption. And yet she is vulnerable. The men she responds to (except for Gary Cooper in *Morocco*) are less often the young-man paragons of the earth than their defective elders. Dietrich and her lovers are not, like Garbo and Robert Taylor, et al., ideal, aesthetic matches, but more perverse pairings, culminating in the delirious sadomasochism of the Concha Perez–Don Pasqual (Lionel Atwill) relationship in *The Devil Is a Woman*. The age or infirmity or weakness of the man corresponds to her vulnerability as a woman.

Although she is a creature of myth—and not, in any sociological sense, a "real woman"—she is also demystifying. She was born "knowing" and Sternberg has trouble projecting her, in the opening scenes of *The Scarlet Empress,* as the innocent Princess Sophia. But her realism, her way of adjusting, without preconceptions, to each new situation, is not without ideals. It signifies death to old values and a rebirth, as when, in *The Blue Angel,* she causes Emil Jannings to extinguish the stale, respectable death-in-life career of the schoolmaster to become the no-less-ridiculous, but at least briefly alive, moth to Marlene's flame.

To Victor McLaglen in *Dishonored* and Lionel Atwill in *The Devil Is a Woman,* her presence is subversive: of conventional, partisan heroics and of romantic vanity, of the gentleman's code that has no place for obsession. Theirs are tremendous sacrifices. Having made such a sacrifice, most men would want guarantees. After they have abandoned the security of bourgeois society, risked ridicule, lost face, they want to hear the words "always" and "only"; Dietrich says only "here" and "now." She smiles a radiant, soft, cynical smile with a touch of cruelty that says, "You have given up all this and for what? For a moment, a moment that will bring you closer to death." And she laughs: not at man, but at death. It is for this alliance in Dietrich of death and the comic spirit that men cannot forgive her.

As the lady spy confronting the firing squad in *Dishonored* (after having spent her last night on earth playing a piano in her cell), she waits patiently while a young soldier in a burst of heroism shouts, "No more butchery!" Marlene, as sure that there will be more butchery as she is that her own death will follow, merely applies fresh lipstick. This is the ultimate vision of beauty as courage and the ultimate victory of style (Dietrich's and Sternberg's) over content; style has become content. For what man will not feel his claims to courage dwarfed by such a gesture of acceptance, and what director will not feel the pretentions of his socially conscious film reduced by such a shrug!

In *Blonde Venus* she sleeps openly with gambler Cary Grant to get money for an operation to save husband Herbert Marshall's life. His horror at the discovery, his threat to take their child from her, are rooted in the view of infidelity as a transgression, regardless of circumstances or emotional content, and he confers a culpability on her action it would not otherwise have had. Sternberg makes it clear that, in this context, it is Marshall who is "evil" and prurient, not Dietrich. Unlike Borzage, for whom a belief in the intrinsic wickedness of the wife-turned-prostitute is necessary to give sacrifice (and redemption) its value, Sternberg never sees the sexual act itself as immoral. And although Dietrich, in an epic journey into squalor, descends to the bottom before she rises again, her soul remains chaste, and it is Marshall's that must be redeemed.

However exotic her setting or sumptuous her costume, Dietrich was always of this world. Her profession, whether chanteuse or cigarette girl or queen (and in *The Scarlet Empress* she provides us with a royal definition of sexual politics), was rooted in the concreteness, the physicality of an environment represented by Sternberg's *mise en scène,* whereas Garbo's was always a pretext. Garbo's past, her "checkered career," was an abstraction, a gift to be laid at her lover's feet. But Dietrich's past, her biography, really existed. Her trappings, her veils, jewels, and the different system of lighting with which Sternberg illuminated each characterization, were more than cosmetic. They were the visual equivalent of words, of layers of self, of the autobiography she carried with her, partially revealed.

Some critics have complained that in his depiction of Marlene in masculine attire (top hat and tails in *Morocco* and *Blonde Venus*) Sternberg has not drawn a woman, but a pseudo-male, and that the opposition in the film is not male and female but male and nonmale. Yet, there is a corresponding "feminization" of the male, particularly Cooper with his rose in *Morocco,* but also Marshall and Grant in *Blonde Venus,* Atwill in *The Devil Is a Woman,* Jannings in *The*

Blue Angel, all of whom are modified, from a traditional male-sexist point of view, by their relationship with her. More importantly, the objection highlights the dilemma that plagues feminist critics in all the arts who come to argue against women who think or write or compose or paint "like men," demanding a uniquely feminine voice and experience. True, the assumption of male characteristics (sexual or intellectual) by a woman is an implicit confirmation of male superiority, of the advantages of being male in the contemporary world. But the basic problem is one of value rather than kind. Should women eschew careers in science or music or law because they demand qualities of intellect habitually associated with men? The revolution, one of sexual revaluation, is far more radical than the simple formation of a "woman's aesthetic." Until a woman's life, whatever it may consist of, is granted equal importance with a man's, those who emulate men will continue to be aggrandized by their efforts, just as male impersonation operates on a principle of aggrandizement (and is therefore not funny), while the adoption of female characteristics, and female impersonation, resting as they do on the principle of belittlement, will continue to be comical.

What is subversive in Sternberg's conception of Dietrich is that she cannot be enlisted into one sexual-ideological camp against another. She parodies conventional notions of male authority and sexual role-playing without destroying her credibility as a woman. Her toughness and realism are not, in the manner of certain demystifying heroines in later films, unattractive and antiromantic: On the contrary, they dispel love's blindness without destroying love. She assumes male attire, gains entry through male activities, not to discredit the male sex, but to challenge the system of values by which it puffs itself up with false pride and vainglory.

If there is an imbalance, a "Dietrich-centrism" to Sternberg's films with her, it is because all androgynous characters, whether film stars or literary protagonists (for example, Virginia Woolf's *Orlando*) are complete unto themselves. Sternberg understands this, understands that Dietrich's overwhelming beauty and sense of identity are a kind of extravagance that must be paired not with a comparable beauty but with other kinds of extravagance, or eccentricity. He never used her to show up other women, the way Hitchcock later did, with Jane Wyman in *Stage Fright,* or the way Billy Wilder played her off against Jean Arthur in *A Foreign Affair.* Her beauty and self-knowledge should not be seen as a judgment on the rest of her sex, but on the pretensions of the opposite sex. For as one of the politically and ideologically disenfranchised, she embraces all women and, with nothing to lose, cuts through the layers of false ego to the true self, whose dictates she follows, whether it is to light a cigarette in a nightclub or stagger off through a desert in the noon sun.

The tendency to divide women into mutually exclusive categories was largely a habit of puritanism, but it afflicted even the more tolerant thirties. Harlow, one of the screen's raunchiest inventions, was often used to put down other women. If Dietrich was the epitome of class-sophistication, Harlow was the epitome of the common, but her lack of pretension or position gave her the same freedom. Dietrich disdained conventional morality; Harlow barely knew what it was. For all her worldly experience, Harlow was a social innocent, incapable of duplicity and calculating only in the most obvious mercenary way.

In 1931, she was cast, or miscast, as a society dame in William Wellman's *Public Enemy* and, again, in Frank Capra's *Platinum Blonde* (thanks to Capra's deflating populism, she emerged there closer to her true, randy self). Two years later, she came rip-snorting into type in Cukor's *Din-*

ner at Eight, where she and Wallace Beery, as the tacky *nouveau riche* couple, wore diamonds and yelled like tenement troubadours. In most of her films, she was sluttish and smart, cracking gum and one-liners simultaneously: chewing up the scenery as the vulgar star of *Bombshell* (whose temporary bout with motherhood, under the pressure of fan-magazine idolatry, makes a joke of both institutions); or, in *Red Dust,* sidling up to Clark Gable when Mary Astor, as the frigid nice girl, wasn't looking. For Harlow, like most sex kittens, queens, and goddesses, was no friend to her own sex. Having nothing to lose, she is a threat to other women, and any woman who prizes her security, her position, or her husband (and what else does the "normal" woman have?), is justified in being afraid of her. It is a favorite ploy not just of male writers and directors, but of women as well (see Clare Boothe's *The Women*) to play one type off against the other, the predatory female against the retiring one, the party girl or tart against the uptight wife, the girl who "loves him only" against the wife whose life and affections are distributed among children, community, and the like. These comparisons are odious because in conforming to such extremes each woman will be half a person, while the man who alternates between the two is, by implication, a whole. (It was rare that an artist-observer would suggest, as Lubitsch did, that every triangle has its reverse image.)

This division of women has for some years been implicit in the rationale of the suburban businessman who divides his time between the country spouse and the city spice. The onus of this arrangement generally fell upon the wife, because she was not consumed with interest in her husband's work, while he was exempted from the tiniest curiosity about the "trivia" which occupied her daily routine. The "frigidity" of the wife is adduced in favor of the husband's infidelity; it never seems to occur either to the deceivers or to the dramatists who use the wife's sexual inadequacy as a motive for the husband's philandering that perhaps he has failed to bring her to an enjoyment of sex. But this would be inimical to her "spiritual" role as wife and mother.

From the wife-as-shrew, Harlow provides the perfect fantasy escape for the businessman, both in and out of the movies. In *Wife Versus Secretary,* Harlow, as Clark Gable's secretary, is involved in a series of innocent but misinterpretable events that arouse the suspicion of wife Myrna Loy. Loy is made to seem evil-minded and bitchy, and Gable, the charming innocent, ever impervious to the passions he arouses, emerges blameless and untainted. Once again, women become the scapegoats for men who refuse to grow up and accept responsibility for their decisions, who want to have their cake at home and eat it at the office, too. Through her own unfounded suspicions and Harlow's ingenuousness, Loy is made to seem a nag, and the audience is asked to resent *her* rather than a state of affairs weighted heavily in man's favor.

Through no fault of her own, Harlow's toughness and intelligence were used as a weapon to clobber other women. Mae West, who shared some of Harlow's low-down lasciviousness, could not be used in the same way, for with her, as with Dietrich, there was no room for any other member of the female sex. Indeed, so complete was West's androgyny, that one hardly knows into which sex she belongs, and by any sexual-ideological standards of film criticism, she is an anomaly—too masculine to be a female impersonator, too gay in her tastes to be a woman. She was a composite of sexual types: the female impersonator that Parker Tyler has discerned (in whom the mother and gay son are reconciled); a hypothetical, sexually aggressive woman; and woman as sex object turned subject. Her tastes in men—musclemen, cowboys, studs—the equivalent to literary gamekeepers and

Poles, are homosexual pinups rather than female fantasies.

A wholesome, daytime version of vampirism with both humor and honor, Mae West turned male lechery on its ear. When, in *I'm No Angel,* she exits suggestively from the stage saying "Am I making myself clear, boys?" she hesitates and then adds under her breath, "Suckers." Without wounding anyone in particular, she castigates men as a race of voyeurs, at the mercy of a lust they barely enjoy. She, on the other hand, enjoys, and she projects what it would be like if we could enjoy: if male lechery and appraisal were directed to specific, sexual communication instead of an arrogant expression of power and the will-to-possession; if women were freed of repressive conditioning; if there were no ulterior motives or dirty minds, or cyclical purges of the kind that were her undoing. In her size, her voice, her boisterous one-liners, and her swagger, there was something decidedly, if parodistically, masculine. But she was a woman, and she thus stretched the definition of her sex. Those who object that in her masculinity (and her maternalism) she reinforced the myth of male supremacy (phallic, imperialist, sexist) in the cinema fail to see that it is the valuation of the sex itself, male over female, rather than their inherent qualities, which is the basis of structural inequality. When "female qualities"—softness, sensitivity, passivity—were exalted in the post-Brando hero and in the rock/antiwar ethic of the counterculture, it did not bring about a corresponding exaltation of woman, but, on the contrary, a diminution of

Facing page: Theda Bara, Antony's "Egyptian dish," in the 1917 version of *Cleopatra.* As Theodosia Goodman of Chicago, Bara had been discovered, renamed, re"vamp"ed, and promoted into the American screen's first sizzling sex symbol. Her image of exotic, faintly malignant sexuality was far enough removed from real women not to be considered dangerous.

Mary Pickford, America's Sweetheart, in her double role in *Stella Maris*: (*top*) as the winsome, demure Stella, and (*bottom*) as Unity Blake, the ugly housekeeper and Stella's opposite.

Top left: Chaplin's tramp, the eternal outsider, looks up to a glittering and inaccessible idol, the dance-hall hostess played by Georgia Hale, who is the toast of the brawny miners in *The Gold Rush. Bottom left:* In *Monsieur Verdoux*, the wine of reverence has soured and the idolater has turned misogynist—or rather, misogamist. In his version of the Bluebeard tale, Chaplin as wife-murderer soothes a prospective victim with an expression of fastidious disdain. *Below:* In *The Three Ages,* Keaton's parody of Griffith's *Intolerance,* the caveman played by Keaton is taken in hand by his Amazon girl friend.

Top: Lillian and Dorothy Gish as passionately devoted sisters in Griffith's *Orphans of the Storm* (1921). *Bottom:* Clara Bow, the "It" girl (*right*), and roommate Marceline Day in Dorothy Arzner's *The Wild Party,* an early sound film about a girl who falls in love with her professor. The film is given added interest by Arzner's sensitive—and sensual—handling of the female relationships and their "masculine" code of loyalty and camaraderie.

Left: Dietrich in *Blonde Venus* sweeps Paris like a tidal wave after emerging from the dregs of degradation in a New Orleans flophouse. Her status may change according to the whims of social morality, but she is always the same: ironic, intelligent, and adult, as forgiving of men's weaknesses as she is contemptuous of their sexual pride.

Top right: In *A Woman of the World,* Pola Negri, a worldly European countess, comes to visit American relatives and arrives smoking just as the district attorney, an antivice crusader played by Charles Emmett Mack, has delivered a lecture against smoking and drinking. *Bottom right:* Robert Montgomery, in *Inspiration,* speaks to Garbo, and Garbo speaks only to Garbo. Her leading men dwindle into oblivion beside a love that, like mother love, asks nothing in return except an occasional glimpse of its own noble reflection.

Facing page (top left):
Women in groups—Ina
Claire, Joan Blondell, and
Madge Evans
shake on a not-so-silent
partnership in *The Greeks
Had a Word for Them,*
a film about gold diggers
made by Lowell Sherman
from the Zoë Akins play.
Top right: Lucille Ball,
Ginger Rogers, and Ann
Miller, three actress-
pensionnaires at an all-
woman boarding house
in Gregory la Cava's *Stage
Door,* offer one another
moral support and
camaraderie through good
times and bad. *Bottom:*
Women on display—
women are wrapped in
ribbons and welded to
harps in Busbey Berkeley's
unabashedly sexist, sexy,
and camp production num-
ber in *Fashions of 1934.*

Top right: Miriam Hopkins as the
fulcrum of a *ménage à trois* that
works, in Ernst Lubitsch's film of
the Coward play *Design for Living.*
Gary Cooper and Fredric March are
her two friends. *Above:* Mae West
in *She Done Him Wrong* betrays with
a sidelong glance her suspicion that it's
not a gift but a deal that is being
offered her and that diamonds, alas!,
like all best friends, involve obligations.
Left: One round of a marathon
marital squabble between Wallace
Beery and Jean Harlow in Cukor's
Dinner at Eight.

Top left: Ginger Rogers and Fred Astaire, one of the screen's most romantic couples, doing what they did best together, in *The Gay Divorcee. Bottom left:* Carole Lombard, a patron saint of screwball comedy, as the leopard-sly actress who drives her director, John Barrymore, crazy in Hawks' *Twentieth Century.*
Below: In *Alice Adams,* Katharine Hepburn asks Fred MacMurray what kind of girl he would like her to be.

her role as the new movie hero appropriated her qualities without losing his place at the center of the stage.

If anything, Mae West shows that certain qualities thought to be incompatible—"male" concupiscence and aggressiveness and "female" romanticism and monogamy—can coexist. But she did this not by demonstration but by allusion, for after all, her essence was not sexual but verbal. And it was the words—specifically her recording of "A Guy What Takes His Time" in *She Done Him Wrong*—that set Mary Pickford's corkscrew curls to shaking and, in ever-widening ripples of discontent, W. R. Hearst's presses to rolling, and the good Catholic prelates to moaning and groaning and finally galumphing into action over this invasion of Original Sin in the New World. For the purpose of its expulsion, the National Legion of Decency was formed and a bible, in the form of the Production Code, was drawn up. They coordinated with the Hays Office, which had previously been only window dressing, a self-protective move set up in 1922 by the industry to forestall intervention by government or civic groups outraged by the evils of Hollywood. Will Hays had gotten his orders from the head office like everybody else, and the famous scissors were largely a ploy of studio propaganda to keep the real censors at bay. His office was more concerned with keeping the lid on private orgies—a measure designed to prevent the eruption of another Fatty Arbuckle or William Desmond Taylor scandal—than with purging the silver screen.

But the Production Code was something else again. In specifying the no-no's of cinema, it covered, with meticulous prurience, every conceivable offense to God, mom, and man ; the words and actions it prohibited are only now making their way back into movies, with a vengeance all the greater for having been so long suppressed. Marriage was declared sacrosanct, display of passion was discouraged (double beds were verboten, twin beds de rigueur), exposure of the "sex organs," male or female, child or animal, real or stuffed, was forbidden. (Unquestionably the most ludicrous image was not Tarzan and Jane in their Cole of California jungle wraparounds, but Cheetah and his simian siblings in body stockings.) There were further proscriptions against perversion, miscegenation, the detailed rendering of crime, or its depiction in such a way as to imply success or to glorify its perpetrators. The futility of crime, both spiritually and financially, had to be demonstrated: The villain had to die or, if the hero or heroine had erred, their contrition and conversion had to be triumphantly shown. (This was the general rule; there were, however, a number of films, notably those considered "artistically worthwhile," that obtained the Purity Seal without conforming to the code.) But the emphasis of the code, like that of the Hays Office before it and the rating system of the Motion Picture Association after it, was on sex, an activity both sinful and, from the moral referees' point of view, contagious, since it could be transmitted by the image on a screen like sperm on a toilet seat. Even today, in the mass-murder and government-by-crime seventies, there is less official indignation over violence and bloodshed in American movies than over sex, not only homonymous but synonymous with "X."

Mae West was forced to clean up her image and her dialogue and thereby commit professional suicide. In *Klondike Annie,* as the converted hooker, she offered what amounted to a recantation. But there was an ironic twist to her words. Emerging from the stateroom of the dead evangelist whose identity and garb she has adopted, she speaks to her in heaven: "You were right about the wages of sin, Annie—I never thought I'd get caught."

Moral righteousness coupled with commercial muscle (W. R. Hearst took up the cudgel in his newspapers) had its effect. Not even Garbo and Dietrich were to be exempt from the rules and double standards governing the behavior of women. Instead, retroactively indicted and condemned, they too were obliged to conform to approved standards of motherhood, family responsibility, and child worship. The before-and-after values figure successively in *Desire,* a 1936 Lubitsch production directed by Frank Borzage. The promise of the beginning—a sparklingly comic collision between Dietrich's slippery jewel thief and Gary Cooper's credulous American tourist—degenerates into a swamp of sentimentality and moralism, as Dietrich is forced to make a public confession and apology and, worse still, set sail with Cooper for Detroit and her glorious future as a middle-class automobile manufacturer's wife.

Dietrich goes West and becomes virginized, or revirginized. Or she will, paradoxically, once she bears a child, for then, obliterating herself as "woman" or even "wife" (in the curious one-dimensional process of mythic regeneration), she will become "mother" and as such will qualify for the mantle of purity—chaste, an "ex-virgin" (with the emphasis on virgin rather than on "ex") from which all trace of the sin of copulation with the father has been erased by the son, as he recasts his mother in the image of the Virgin Mary. Mother's purity, the most sacred and crucial image of our culture, is entirely a wish fulfillment invented by man, an Oedipal attempt by the son to banish the hated image of sex with the father. In so doing he deprives the woman who is his mother of part of her nature, and all of her past. It is the son, far more than the daughter, who forces the exclusive mother role on the woman who has conceived him. And it is man as son, rather than man as husband or lover, who is most responsible for keeping mother locked in her chastity belt and most responsible for keeping her imprisoned in her biological role. As for woman herself, it is not in catering to men's needs as his secretary, mistress, wife that she is most subservient; it is in fulfilling her Oedipal role as son-worshipper that she most dangerously denies herself, her daughter, and her sex and perpetuates the notion of their inferiority.

The fusion of wife and mother into a character whose chief attributes, even with regard to her husband, are maternal is a reduction through sanctification, a delimiting of the woman's role by placing her on a pedestal. But this process does not always end in apotheosis. While the values the "mother" represents as a domestic, civilizing force are honored by some males and certain (European or Europeanized) societies, they are feared, and fought bitterly, by others, by the adolescent male, for example, and by large segments of American culture, for whom woman, the antimale, becomes the pushy and constricting voice of responsibility.

In his influential essay on the movie Western, the late Robert Warshow pointed out that it is the sweetheart-wife character who is constantly after the hero to stop killing and settle down. But he must first "do what he has to do," a mission she can never understand, while the whore, a solitary like him, has given up the dream of marriage and children and understands what he is after. Once again, the two types of women are played off against each other, with the whore pointing up the rigidity of the would-be wife. But in one sense, even the whore is domesticated, virginized. She is less often a temptress than a buddy, a weatherbeaten female version of the hero—but without his compelling ambition and drive. In the American Western, as Bazin sees, the fallen woman has come to her shame not—as in European mythology—through her innate wickedness, but through the concupiscence of men. This is an inversion, not merely of European mythology, but of American social conduct which holds that the virgin, and not the man, is responsible for her "fall," and it is she who sustains the burden of middle-class morality, and gleams with a whiteness to which the whore and the *femme fatale* contrast and, in contrasting, enhance. But the American Western version of the

Fall buttresses the myth of male supremacy, since it implies that a man can make or break a woman morally. It is not in her nature, or her power, to choose between good and evil; she is but a mechanical toy set by her Creator on the path of good, where she will quietly chug along unless man intercepts and deflects her.

The Western from which Bazin drew his example was *Stagecoach.* Made in 1939, it is a relatively early John Ford film in which Claire Trevor is the prototype of the "good whore," the good- and gold-hearted woman whose natural warmth contrasts with the pinched souls and morals of the townspeople to whom she is a bête noire. As a director, Ford is almost a case study of the Madonna complex at its most reverential. His attitude toward women, particularly in the early films—a compound of Irish Catholicism and American puritanism—makes it impossible for him to appreciate, and do justice by, the Barbara Stanwyck character in *The Plough and the Stars,* a sensual and self-interested young lady who wants her man for herself—alive and not out with the boys and the revolution. Gradually, Ford's perception of women will widen to include creatures with the spirits of mortals rather than just mothers. But until then, his women will wait without a murmur for his men to accomplish their task; in return for their patience and self-sacrifice, they will be honored. Indeed, the honor they inspire is inseparable from the urge to *return* home that figures so much more notably in Ford's heroes than in the protagonists of other Westerns. For Ford, as for almost no other American writer or director, the word "wife" is an honorific term. Although the men of his adventures are torn between the compulsion to roam (as in *The Searchers*) and the desire to settle down, they differ from the westerners described by Warshow in being less relentlessly phallic, less power-oriented, less compulsively driven to "prove themselves," and, therefore, more genuinely easy in their relationships with women, more sincere in their desire to live out life as one member of a heterosexual couple rather than as a lone ranger or one of a triumvirate of buddies. Because his men are settlers as well as adventurers, his women, to the extent that they share, rather than repudiate, male interests, are nobler and less nagging than their counterparts in other films.

The problem is that the woman is still not a protagonist, a human being in her own right, but an adjunct to man. For Ford and other Catholic directors, woman is not (as she is for the early Hawks, for example) a disrupting influence between one man and another, or between man and his destiny; rather, she is an intermediary, a half-human, half-divine go-between between man and God, or between whatever extremes present themselves. Thus, in Frank Capra's *Mr. Smith Goes to Washington,* Jean Arthur is the medium, a woman of both sense and integrity, halfway between Jimmy Stewart's fanatic idealist and the corruption of Washington politics. She manages to move through Washington effectively and pragmatically and yet remain untainted, and as such, she becomes the lightning rod for Stewart's dreams, translating them into practical action. This is a traditional view of woman's temperament: She is not at the extremes of madness and idealism, but always holding down the center, the sweet small voice of reason. Actually, Capra's women are closer to being visionaries than his men, by virtue of their holy function, their hot line to heaven, their "woman's intuition." Barbara Stanwyck plays a glowing, Aimee Semple MacPherson—type evangelist in *Miracle Woman,* a career in which she can fufill the role of intermediary between her audience and her Maker. The link between woman, religious miracle, and the efficacy of the "little people" acting in unison is at the heart of Capra's theology, as in *Lady for a Day,* made in 1933, and the 1961 remake, *A Pocketful of Miracles,* in which an old beggar-woman (May Robson and Bette Davis, respectively) is enabled, through the machination of her underworld pals, to act the lady for her visiting daughter, who believes her to be an aristocrat, ensconced in luxury. Their favor to the old woman is compensation for the good luck that has pursued them with each "lucky" apple she has sold them. She is their surrogate mother; they, the "apples" of her eye, are her true ideal children, knowing and accepting what she is.

In the surge of wholesomeness that succeeded the Depression and the Production Code, there was a general whitewashing of women characters that, like any repressive tendency, produced reactions and deviates in disguise. One of the great vessels of virgin worship in this period of sexual latency was Shirley Temple, the ringlet-haired moppet who made her debut in 1932 at age four. She was always a greater favorite with adult males than with children, although when Graham Greene alluded to this perversity, in his review of *Wee Willie Winkie,* he was sued for libel by the star and her studio. (The offending passages are omitted from his collected reviews.) Actually, that John Ford film was one of her more appealing and forthright vehicles, her least Lolita-ish. Generally, her flirtatiousness with her daddy figures was outdone, in precociousness, only by the patronizing way in which she treated contemporaries. She was not only a "little lady," advanced in social etiquette beyond her years, but a "little mother," assuming the maternal role with older men who played (along) with her. She was an ideal post-Production Code sex kitten, her attraction politely shrouded in the natural interplay of family feeling. Like the agitation of the Gish sisters, the intense activity, the sheer locomotion of thirties' heroines was an obvious outlet for suppressed sexuality. The personality of Betty Hutton and of Ann Sheridan, the "oomph girls," even the cascade of words, words, words in a medium fascinated with sound, and swimming with screenwriters, were effusions of sublimated energy.

The restrictions of the Production Code and the demands of a new technology gave birth to new forms and figures of speech: to romantic comedies in which love was disguised as antagonism and sexual readiness as repartee. In propagandizing so zealously for marriage and the family, the film industry was actually lending its support to the woman— to the "wife"—in a society without the social and religious safeguards of marriage common to older societies and without their institutionalized escape valves. Without either the pressure to preserve marriage or the sanctioned opportunity for extramarital affairs, divorce has always been more prevalent, and family ties more tenuous, in America, and the blindly romantic approach to marriage only increases the odds of divorce. By tradition—largely supported by the Hollywood film—most marriages have been founded on nothing more than an initial attraction (too often of "opposites") of two people with no vision of themselves beyond the altar and no plan for future growth beyond a numerical one.

The forced enthusiasm and the neat evasions of so many happy endings have only increased the suspicion that darkness and despair follow marriage, a suspicion the "woman's film" confirmed by carefully pretending otherwise. Marriage was tacitly acknowledged by the Hollywood ethic to be a woman's only protection, since its initial impetus was based on nothing more lasting than a man's desire and a woman's denial of its fulfillment. A man, in the heat of passion (and at the peak of his sexual yearning) would pay for satisfaction with marriage, as a woman (years behind in her own sexual responsiveness) would pay with her body for the marriage that was her life's goal. But obviously, if a man could satisfy his lust without encumbering himself with marriage, why— since he had formed no spiritual ties with the woman, and enjoyed greater rapport with his men friends—why would he ever marry? It was Hollywood's duty to see that he did, to make the conventions that required it attractive, to prolong the thought of the first ecstatic kiss by postponing it as long as possible, and to project it into the infinity of marriage by closing the curtain on it.

A woman's only job was to withhold her favors, to be the eternal virgin—not all that difficult, really, since her repressive conditioning had so buried the urge in the first place. In this respect, Scarlett O'Hara is the thirties' antebellum version of the flapper, the woman who defies all conventions *except* the sexual ones. Scarlett has been unfairly lambasted for her wily flirtatiousness and waist-pinching femininity, but she was, in many ways, a forerunner of the career woman, with her profession-obsession (the land), her business acumen, her energy that accumulated steam from sexual repression.

Our heritage of sexual repression—one that the Hollywood film does not so much create as imitate—is double edged indeed, giving rise to the need to elevate (spiritualize) on the one hand, and to standardize (explain, debase) on the other. Our sexual emancipators and evangelists sometimes miss half of the truth: that if puritanism is the source of our greatest hypocrisies and most crippling illusions it is, as the primal anxiety whose therapy is civilization itself, the source of much, perhaps most, of our achievement. In movies, as in individuals, the sublimation of the sexual drive can be for some a poisoning influence while for others, it is the source, in compensating energy and action, of creative achievement. That the early suffragettes should not have been perfect homebodies, or that there is a strong puritanical streak in the women's movement, should come as no surprise.

For a woman like Scarlett, a driving woman as romantic heroine, sex was something she could easily do without, but it is also, she has been forced to realize, her most valuable commodity. In a world ruled by romantic conventions, a woman senses, with some justice, that she has no power over a man once the attraction wears off; she leads him on a merry chase to whet his appetite and simultaneously deny its fulfillment; in so doing she fills the stereotype as tease or castrator, while he becomes a madman or a misogynist, and both circle mindlessly on the treadmill of bad faith and role-playing so common to the American mating ritual. And yet, the effect, perhaps the very foundation, is not always the same. If it were, we could dismiss all the musicals, the romances, the screwball comedies of the thirties because they were constructed on the same principles of denial and delay, postponement and frustration, antagonism and accord, and a sizable share of contrivances along the way. But story-telling formulae, including the happy ending, are not intrinsically bad; plots, like romantic conventions, can be useful, allowing for the subtle, gradual revelation of feelings through stylistic conventions and metaphor.

What, then, makes some thirties' comedies and musicals coy and unbearable, and others sublime? Once again, it is all the definable and indefinable elements of style: director, screenwriters, casting, plus something chemical, combining to create an equilibrium in which no one is victimized, neither hero nor heroine gets more than his share of misery, and their attraction seems to arise from something more compelling than sheer frustration or the dictates of the code. Despite the conformist impulse underlying the code, some of the great comedies, movies like *The Awful Truth* and *His Girl Friday,* celebrate difficult and anarchic love rather than security and the suburban dream, a preference that is wedded into the very conventions of the thirties, favoring movement over stasis, and speech and argument over silent compliance. In the screwball comedies where love is consummated in gags, in the Rogers–Astaire musicals, where it is consummated in dance (or in other musicals, in song), there is an equalization of obstacles and a matching of temperaments. A man and a woman seem to prickle and blossom at each other's touch, seem to rub each other with and against the grain simultaneously, and, in the friction, in the light in the other's eyes, to know themselves for the first time.

In the comedy-romances that fail, through an imbalance of casting or direction (the kind of overdependence on reaction shots, for example, or on subsidiary character actors that makes *Top Hat* bottom-heavy), there is a lopsidedness. Plot artifices leap to the fore. Between the lovers the sense of tension and attraction is attenuated. Instead of awkwardness followed by a progressive intimacy, the "love situation" remains a skeleton, polished and unfulfilled. Thus, in one of Lubitsch's less felicitous projects, *Bluebeard's Eighth Wife,* Claudette Colbert withholds bedroom privileges from her lothario husband in order to hang on to him. But the casting is all wrong. Because as the husband, Gary Cooper is impossible to accept as a philanderer, and because Colbert can't give the heroine the note of sexual irresistibility that might salvage the part, the narrative is thrown off side, and she becomes the heavy in a comedy that, under the best circumstances, would have been distasteful.

Sometimes a star or director will throw such magic dust in our faces that we hardly perceive the moral inconsistencies or cruelties of the plot. George Stevens had a way of taking projects or scenarios that in themselves were savage commentaries on the American Dream and directing them as if they were the dream fulfilled. The combination of Stevens with a Katharine Hepburn who radiated under his touch made Alice Adams' social ambitiousness almost attractive and Tess Harding's Woman of the Year less excruciating than the self-absorbed, inhuman career woman of the Lardner-Kanin screenplay. In Stevens' *Penny Serenade,* Irene

Dunne and Cary Grant make both bearable and absurd their roles as an economically strapped, child-obsessed lower-middle-class couple. This is a perfect example of the split-level operation of the Hollywood film, a built-in duplicity between what is said and what, decoded, is meant, that became more exacerbated as social and sexual dissatisfaction increased and the need for disguise became greater. The truth is there, but in disguise; the neurosis presents itself as a virtue. The Irene Dunne character is defined by her obsession to have a child, a desire that quite clearly precedes, and culminates in, her marriage to Grant, and that finally wrecks his career and emotional stability. We are seduced into accepting this sick premise as the noblest of philosophies simply because Dunne and Grant, profiting from Stevens' instinct for human chemistry, generate star power at an unbelievable voltage.

In *Made for Each Other,* a domestic drama directed by John Cromwell, we are asked to believe in Jimmy Stewart as the struggling husband who asks the boss to dinner and Carole Lombard as his pathetically maladroit wife. The credibility gap—the contradiction between actress and part—would widen with the growing sentimentality and fondness for "little people" subject matter that characterized forties' films. Money became an object of shame rather than pleasure, ambition a quality to be avenged in a woman, and stardom a status to be concealed beneath proletarian rags.

In the forties, the threads of romance would begin to wear thin under the gnawing erosion of male paranoia, and the precise balance of romantic antagonism would capitulate to subjective distortion. One side or the other—sentimentality or cruelty—would dominate. In the 1944 film *Together Again,* Irene Dunne's strength as the mayor of a small town alternates with her love for artist Charles Boyer, without the two elements either conflicting dramatically or coalescing.

As mayor, she is effective and obviously happy, but Charles Coburn, playing the father of her dead husband, fears that she will lose her femininity in so authoritative a position, and with it her chances of remarriage. When he advises her to quit, she scoffs at his male egocentricity. "You're one of a dying race," she tells him. "Women can live perfectly well without men. But you're terrified of the idea that they can. If you lose your emotional power over women, you're lost." But it is to precisely that emotional power that she surrenders when, in the end, she forsakes her mayoralty to go off with Boyer.

In the comedies of the later forties, the underside—the bitterness, the sense of victimization of one partner by the other (usually husband by the wife)—begins to show through. In *The Bachelor and the Bobby-Soxer* Cary Grant is reduced to a teen-ager, not, as in *Monkey Business*, through his own infantilism, but through his courtship of Myrna Loy. Hawks' most "man"-like and emasculating heroine is the army officer played by Ann Sheridan in *I Was a Male War Bride*, an efficient strategist who shows up Grant professionally, eludes him sexually, and takes him in tow, in drag. And yet it is interesting that both of these films, in which men are the sympathetic, if ridiculous, figures and women the villains, make men rather than women uncomfortable, suggesting that men, in their manhood, have more to lose than women, in their womanhood. (An illustration, in another form, of the double standard inherent in the principles underlying male, and female, impersonation.)

But in the thirties and early forties the equilibrium was still holding fast. The movies seemed to be saying that because men are secure, women can outsmart them without unsexing them, and because women are secure, they can act smart without fearing reprisals, or the loss of femininity. The security was largely mythic—in real life, things were bleak—but the breezy confidence was a compensation for a powerlessness that afflicted society as a whole. It was not a male impotence for which they would have had to compensate by reducing the status of women. Thus Joan Blondell, a synthesis of snappy-smart and gentle, can form a partnership with Jimmy Cagney (in *Blonde Crazy*) in which she occasionally gets the best of him without humiliating or emasculating him and without appearing overbearing. Their easy rapport as buddies, like Hopkins' and Marshall's in *Trouble in Paradise,* is based on a similarity of interests and the unspoken understanding that a woman is every bit the "gentleman"—or nongentleman—a man is and can match him in wits and guts and maybe even surpass him. The battle of the sexes is a battle of equals, and the language of sexual antagonism—in Hawks' *Bringing Up Baby* or *His Girl Friday* or *Twentieth Century* or in Frank Capra's *It Happened One Night* or in Leo McCarey's *The Awful Truth*—tells as passionate a love story as Jerome Kern's music and Rogers' and Astaire's dancing in *Swing Time*. The postponements and conflicts are not arbitrary but integral: Grant's stuffy paleontologist (in *Baby*) resisting Hepburn's assault on the ossified shell of his dignity; Rosalind Russell's wavering between the rat she loves and her profession, and the mouse she's engaged to and security; Astaire's engagement to the "woman back home," which keeps him from being able to court Ginger Rogers, which in turn leads into the glorious song, "A Fine Romance, with No Kisses." The postponements, representing the social conventions that create a distance between man and woman and that have been internalized as inhibitions are nothing less than a metaphorical rendering of the essential ingredient of romantic love, creating the sense of strangeness and unfamiliarity, the curiosity whose business it is Eros' to awaken and love's to satisfy.

And so we accept, on the level of plot, character, and metaphor, the difficulties overcome before the final union of Katharine Hepburn and Cary Grant in *Holiday,* Grant and Ginger Rogers in *Once Upon a Honeymoon,* Charles Boyer and Jean Arthur in *History Is Made at Night,* Boyer and Irene Dunne in *Love Affair,* Maurice Chevalier and Jeanette MacDonald in *The Merry Widow,* Colbert and Clark Gable in *It Happened One Night,* Gable and Vivien Leigh in *Gone with the Wind,* Dietrich and Gary Cooper in *Morocco,* Garbo and Melvyn Douglas in *Ninotchka,* and many more.

The equalization of difficulties in these films is part of a larger equilibrium, a world in which male authority, or sexual imperialism, is reduced or in abeyance, while the feminine spirit is either dominant or equal. In *Holiday,* Grant embraces the spirit of foolishness and freedom that Katharine Hepburn represents, and in so doing, defects from the business world and the patriarchal order presided over by his prospective father-in-law and dutifully observed by his fiancée (the Electra daughter who, in reinforcing male superiority to the detriment of her own sex, is the treacherous equivalent of the Oedipal mother). In many of these films a deception is practiced in order that the hero and heroine may meet on an equal footing, a concealment of money or profession or a disability that would place one or the other at a disadvantage. The games they play are an attempt to discover the truth while taking the time to adjust to, or establish, a new balance, a bond of spiritual affinity that redeems the former, less important, discrepancies. The period of game-playing is a period of grace, of experimentation and discovery under the cover of conventions, of rules they are supposed to enact and which protect them until they are ready to act without them.

Only Scarlett and Rhett never reach an equilibrium, as

she uses games to extend her control and, placing herself eternally on the defensive, never comes to understand herself or Rhett. Afraid that if she yields an inch, she will lose herself completely, she is, contrary to appearances, the least secure of heroines. The rest, the other thirties' heroines who surrender their preeminence to regain it, are so immensely secure in their sexual identities and in the aura of mutual attractiveness that they can afford to play with their roles, reverse them, stray, with the confidence of being able to return to home base. Hence, the flourish of male impersonators: Dietrich in white tie and white tails, Garbo as the lesbian Queen Christina (although with a "cover" romance), Eleanor Powell in top hat and tails for her tap numbers, and Katharine Hepburn as the Peter Pan-like Sylvia Scarlett: all introduced tantalizing notes of sexual ambiguity that became permanent accretions to their screen identities. The conceit of role exchange was also popular in both the thirties and forties, but in the thirties, the questioning of roles was rooted in the security of the sexual and social framework at large, in the equal importance of a "man's function" and a "woman's function" and in the emphasis on a collectivity of interests in which men and women were united, rather than divided, by their sex. (It is possible to see the movie myths and the attitudes toward women expressed by the movies not as an actual reflection of social and economic conditions but an inversion of them, and an inversion—to make matters more complicated—not of conditions obtaining at the time of the film, but either prior or subsequent to it. As Freud points out, in *Moses and Monotheism*, maternal deities were at their most powerful when the matriarchy was about to be toppled, and the same principle of compensation may account for the rise and fall of goddesses in cinema.) Certainly as the forties wore on, the balance tipped first one way, then the other, as women became a more serious threat to the economic hegemony of men. The questioning was for real, and the films took on nasty, antifeminine overtones.

Mitchell Leisen's *Take a Letter, Darling* belongs, in spirit, to the evenly matched sex skirmishes characteristic of Paramount in the thirties. Rosalind Russell plays an advertising executive to whom Fred MacMurray applies for a position, not realizing until she begins to look him over and appraise his physique that he is to be her personal secretary, to escort her on social occasions, perform "personal duties," and suffer the winks and nods and knowing glances of subordinates and tradespeople. His ambiguous position, his demeaning duties, and the reactions they arouse would gladden the collective heart of female secretaries everywhere. And when, falling in love with Russell, he tries to tell her she is all business and no "pulse," she tells him, and we believe her, that she is "more woman than [he'll] ever know."

Russell was not a favorite with men. Like Dietrich, the combination of comic intelligence (and she had the best timing in the business) and femininity was overwhelming. Men preferred, like Fred MacMurray, to believe that her femininity was either absent or fake. But her tears at the end of *His Girl Friday* not only were in keeping with previous signs of "womanliness," but expressed most eloquently the confusion a woman feels when her two natures, feminine and professional, collide. The anomaly of the woman professional and the bewildering state in which she is torn between the impulse (the need? the unavoidable social necessity?) to relate to men sexually and to defer to their authority, and the contrary impulse to assert herself and forfeit her rights as a woman. The tears that are taken as a sign of woman's helplessness are indeed that, but of a different kind of helplessness than is usually assumed: not a physical but an emotional impotence, an inability to express anger at a male authority figure, to whom one is conditioned to defer. The anger and its frustration, turning in on itself, comes out as tears.

The title Hawks gives to his version of *The Front Page* is ironic because Russell, far from being a Girl Friday, is a star reporter whose return to the paper ex-husband and editor Cary Grant is determined to bring about. Hawks' stroke of intuitive genius was in sensing that the Hecht–MacArthur play was a love story (between the publisher and the reporter, between the reporter and the boys in the back room), and thence casting the reporter as a woman.

In her introduction to *The Citizen Kane Book,* Pauline Kael makes the point that the female reporters of the newspaper films were all based on Hearst's star woman reporter, Adela Rogers St. John (just as the cynical editor was based on Walter Howey); that the triangular pattern of *His Girl Friday* also occurs in Raoul Walsh's *Wedding Present* (with Cary Grant, Joan Bennett, and Conrad Nagel); and that Rosalind Russell's striped suit was even a copy of the St. John girl-reporter outfit. These links explain the derivation, but not the differences between one film and another—the superiority of the Hawks to the Walsh, or of the Russell character to the Bennett reporter. The opening scene between Russell and Grant, as he alternately bullies and pleads with her, as she alternately squelches him and squirms in her new lady-of-leisure role, is brilliantly directed, its breakneck pace at first disguising its emotional complexity. The tension, the thrust and parry, are both psychological and physical, as Hawks maintains a perfectly balanced rhythm between the comic medium shot and the emotional close-up, between Russell's womanliness and Grant's wiles, between her strength of character (and thus "manliness") and his deviousness (and thus "femininity"). In addition to this empathetic exchange of sexual characteristics, they share a passion for the newspaper business, so that it is almost impossible to tell where love of work leaves off and love of one another begins. But Grant's passion is unscrupulous: It is to get the story at any cost, regardless of the human consequences, whereas Russell's commitment is to the individuals involved, and to an emotional truth.

For Grant, work comes first. He has asserted the male prerogative of placing work above marriage and inflicted the ultimate heterosexual wound by leaving Russell on their wedding night to cover a fire (this event is reported rather than shown, and thus accrues, comically, to Grant's discredit rather than, unpleasantly, to Russell's humiliation). Having divorced him, Russell must now deal with the conflict between the pale alternative offered by her suitor (Ralph Bellamy) and her persistent attraction to Grant and work. If Bellamy is too sappily attentive, Grant, at the other extreme, is monstrous in his cruelty, in his willingness to exploit even her. But it is as a foil to Grant's (and the other reporters') opportunism that Russell's humanity gains in value, and she is the happy medium, not as dull compromise, but as heroic necessity. It is Grant who, in "going too far," shakes her into the realization of her true nature (as Hepburn does *him* in *Bringing Up Baby*). Russell does not become an imitation male; she remains true to the two sides—feminine and professional—of her nature, and as such promises to exercise a healthy influence on the hard-boiled, all-male world of criminal reporting. It is as a newspaper reporter, rather than as wife and mother, that she discovers her true "womanliness," which is to say, simply, herself.

Paradoxically, she is more womanly in the context of the newspaper office, under the direction of Howard Hawks, than as the "housewife supreme" in *Craig's Wife,* directed by Dorothy Arzner. This adaptation of the George Kelly play (with a screenplay by Mary C. McCall) might be taken as the flip side of *His Girl Friday*: what might have happened if Russell had married Ralph Bellamy and taken an obsessive interest in "the home" to fill the gap in her life. The Bellamy surrogate is John Boles, whom she has married not for love but for security, the material security of the home. In a sense she is Shaw's "womanly woman" taken to her monstrous extreme, or as Mary McCarthy suggested in her review of the Kelly play, a Jonsonian humor (a woman "who lives through her furniture") carried to the "point of inhumanity." Her consuming interest in decorating and preserving that home has displaced everything else in her life, finally driving everyone from her, including her husband. Arzner does grant Russell a kind of heroic stature, with a low-angle final shot that reveals her as awesome in her loneliness, but Arzner more or less accepts Russell's monstrosity, and its punishment, at face value. There is one Arzner-like scene in which Russell explains to her niece that she married for "emancipation" rather than love, which creates a certain sympathy for the heroine. But neither Kelly nor Arzner seems to grasp the full implications of the material, the meaning this particular obsession has both for the woman as drawn and for other housewives. Although the justification given for her behavior is that "a woman can lose a husband but not a home," Russell's near-psychotic distrust of the emotions probably has its roots in childhood. Early in the film, she and her niece are visiting the niece's mother at the hospital, and Russell wrests the niece away, on the peculiar grounds that emotional demonstrativeness is bad for the sick woman. Her overreaction is startling, and suggests a wide range of interpretations. One that is never confirmed by subsequent information, but that this situation would be likely to trigger, is that the mother—Russell's sister—had been their mother's favorite, and that Russell's emotional hardening has been a defensive action to avoid asking for the love she never expects to get, while, as an unconscious counteroffensive, the compulsive housekeeping is a bid for the affections of the mother through actions she would approve, actions which—most importantly—are utterly alien to Russell's nature. Adler once described just such a case and concluded that his patient was not unique in finding the occupation of housewife an inadequate outlet for real drive and talent, reminding us that perfectionism—the attribute most proudly claimed for housewife—is often an expression not of enthusiasm but of hostility.

Hawks' women, whatever their shortcomings from a female point of view, are never housekeepers and rarely just sensualists on the sideline; rather, they are admitted as (almost) full-fledged citizens to the male world, which then becomes a hyphenated one. Hawks glories in male heroics because he senses that flying a suicide mission is easier than trying to work things out with the opposite sex, but he keeps returning to women and to the tensions that exist on the most instinctive level. Whether they are male-imitators or men's bêtes noires, they don't really have the upper hand. They are on the same level of professional competence and social awkwardness, and, though the advantage may shift one way or the other, it adds up to a love match. In *Bringing Up Baby,* Katharine Hepburn makes Grant suffer for the cruelty he will inflict on Russell and for the indifference to which he will treat Jean Arthur in *Only Angels Have Wings.* Nothing can avail John Barrymore against the unpredictable assaults of Carole Lombard's charmingly mad actress in *Twentieth Century.* Lombard and Hepburn go too far, break the rules, but their unscrupulousness is more justified than Grant's as the newspaper editor, for it is the assault of powerlessness on power, the attempt by anarchy to unseat complacency. For all the hilarity of Hawks' comedies, a great deal is at stake, as the very momentum suggests. The characters dance the screwball dance on a precipice as steep as the Cliffs of Dover in *King Lear*; their fall is but a pratfall, but from the moment of humiliation—their metaphorical nudity—they work their way back to salvation.

Although genre works automatically to broaden milieu, one feels behind Hawks' world the influence of a specific social context: American W.A.S.P. upper-middle class, clean-cut, genuinely athletic. Just as any American male who has ever been in a fraternity responds instinctively to the buddy ethos of his films, so any woman who has been a tomboy, or traded insults with the boys after school, knows his women, knows that beneath Katharine Hepburn's breezy social security is a sexual, and emotional, insecurity. The unruliness of Lombard and Hepburn is not, as some French critics have suggested, just a sign of their alliance with nature and the threat of chaos, but an expression of a desire to dominate, to assert themselves as human beings, as strong as any man's. His women change and alter, but the heroines of the thirties' comedies are largely heroes, female heroes, bachelor girls, superwomen rather than superfemales. They are, like the men, puritanical, and they share with them the same impulses and longings and the vocation for what French critic-filmmaker Jacques Rivette once described as the "adventure of the intellect." The women are not sensualists: In keeping with a certain American tradition, they are more at ease with their bodies when the bodies are in motion, doing things. They do not cultivate seductive poses (even Lauren Bacall's undulating introduction in *To Have and Have Not* is half-teasing) or wear slinky clothes. Significantly, the one time Hepburn does, wearing a low-cut satin evening dress in *Bringing Up Baby*, she has it ripped from top to bottom. Extensions of the virgin-type with her sublimated sexuality, Hawks' women have a passion to do, to accomplish, to hold their own. At their best they embrace both the drive and ambition (with its potential for evil) of men, but are not wholly "manthropormorphic," since they are closer to their instincts and to nature.

This instinct (and this "nature") is not a voluptuous passivity but an instinct for self-preservation translated into the motion of the mind, into verbal wit. Intelligence was a salient feature of the Hawksian heroine, and as a director who worked closely with his screenwriters, he was a pacesetter in the tradition of smart, crackling dialogue that characterized films of the thirties. It was a tradition that worked particularly to women's advantage: The more a heroine could talk, the more autonomous and idiosyncratic she became, and the more she seemed to define herself by her own lights. Conversation was an index not only of intelligence, but of confidence, of self-possession. The silent woman was more often a projection of the director's fantasies, an object manipulated into a desired setting, whereas the talking woman might take off on her own.

Just as the articulate heroine arose partly in response to a technological development—sound—the "working woman" arose in response to the prohibitions legislated by the Production Code and the new crop of Depression-related films. The Crash had brought on a collective and somewhat retarded *crise de conscience* and Hollywood, in penance for its indifference to life's harsh realities, went proletarian.

Warner Brothers, the "workingman's" studio, led the way as the toughest and the softest, the studio most likely to advance the cause of woman as a working member of society and most likely to pull the rug out from under her with a sentimental ending. The typical Warners' product, as exemplified in the films of Michael Curtiz (and others), was an efficient amalgam of breathless, staccato dialogue that zipped along with all the human inflection and variation of an electric typewriter; an elaborate, pseudo-Expressionist visual style that explained with atmospheric shadows and silhouettes what the dialogue didn't have time to register and the plot didn't have time to spell out; a cast of wise-cracking reporters, gangsters, big-city cynics, swashbucklers, dames; and a heart as squishy as the center of Mildred Pierce's homemade pies.

Studios, tremendously powerful all through the thirties and forties, shifted the gears of feminine fashions (M-G-M got Norma Shearer out of satin and into tailored suits), and were largely responsible for the creation, and propagation, of types. They developed stars like thoroughbreds, for certain courses, only to discover they had a sprinter in a two-mile race. There was a hierarchy in each studio, with room only for one or two of each type, and if an actress was a duplicate, no matter how good she was, she often got lost in the shuffle. Norma Shearer, Thalberg's wife, was the top-positioned "refined lady" at Metro. Myrna Loy, who began her career as an Oriental vamp, was suddenly transferred to a new category and a higher status with *The Thin Man*. She became third in line of succession for "romantic lead" after Shearer and Garbo. Under such an arbitrary and nepotistic system, it was astonishing that stars ever found their appropriate niches. Joan Crawford, who had been a go-go "party-girl" type in the twenties, was overshadowed in the thirties at Metro by the leading ladies ahead of her, and only came fully into her own at Warners in the forties. Bette Davis was mostly wasted in her early days at Warners, playing the breezy, good-sport pal, and it was not until the late thirties and forties that her vast neurotic potential was uncovered—an expression not just of the roles themselves, but of her militant campaign against the Warners' oligarchy to get them. (With both Crawford and Davis, the change in role-types significantly reflects the hardening of purpose and ambition that was necessary to secure the roles, to stay in the game.)

At Warners, there were whole genres of working-woman films, and if they look unusual today, it is only because there is nothing comparable in contemporary films. There was, for example, a series of films like the one with Bette Davis called *Marked Woman,* in which prostitutes turn state's witnesses to convict the heads of organized crime. There, or in horror films like *Mystery of the Wax Museum* in which a girl reporter (Glenda Farrell) is instrumental in uncovering the villain, women are seen as partners to men, as their equals in initiative and courage. In *Marked Woman,* examined in extensive detail by Karyn Kay in *The Velvet Light Trap,* a group of women "nightclub hostesses" (Production Code-word for prostitutes) are induced to give testimony against their racketeer boss. The impetus comes to Mary (Davis) not from a noble desire for self-reformation, but because her innocent young sister has been killed. (A recurrent, and justified, theme in such movies is that the law was not made for women, particularly this kind of woman, so why should they go out of their way to uphold it.) The testimony of the five women serves not only to accomplish the conviction of the Vanning–Luciano character, but to launch the political career of the district attorney played by Humphrey Bogart. He is applauded as the hero but, as Ms. Kay points out, it is on the five women, the true heroines, that Lloyd Bacon's camera focuses in the final shot. Such realism—an acceptance of the "separate worlds" of the women and the man, whose liberal good intentions are not quite up to bridging the gap— is unusual, and if the movie had been a star vehicle rather than a crime melodrama (that is, if it had been made a few years later, when Davis and Bogart were top bananas), the union of the two would have been almost mandatory. Generally, the "working woman" and leading man were closer in class and mutual interest—secretary/lawyer; gangster/ gangster's moll; newspaperman/newspaperwoman—so that a happy ending could be effectuated more plausibly. The actual professions related more to the demand for certain genres—crime, suspense, melodrama, for example—than to sociological probability. But even if they were nothing more than economical means of having a "love interest" without slowing down the action, they at least gave women a healthy piece of that action in the process.

The films of the thirties supply invaluable information in the most casual manner, providing details about working women and jobs—salaries, what goes on in offices—that you never see in films today. In *Big Business Girl,* Loretta Young comes straight from college to New York to become a career girl, and the trajectory of fallen hopes is traced in the two ads she places in the paper, the first by a "recent college graduate" who wants an "interesting job," the next by a college grad who will "work at anything."

Her frustrated attempts, when she finally gets a job at an advertising agency, to rise from the typing pool to writing copy, are dismayingly close to what one hears about today. When she does submit an outstanding proposal to her boss (Ricardo Cortez), his asides to the addled senior partner reveal that he knows he has a winner and is going to get her cheap. The movie makes it quite clear that her salary is probably a fourth of what a man in the same position would be making.

A woman's work is almost always seen as provisional, and almost never as a lifelong commitment, or as part of her definition as a woman. A subspecies of the "working woman," or rather of archetypal woman transposed into the business world, is the mediator, the woman who brings her feminine intuition to bear in the world of male bureaucracy or villainy. Her task is to arbitrate between good and evil, labor and management, law and outlaw. Her job is more than a pretext for catching a man, but less than a vocation. In Fritz Lang's *You and Me,* Sylvia Sidney, an ex-jailbird working in a department store, manages to dissuade husband George Raft and his gang from robbing the store. Just as the sophisticated romances and social comedies of the early thirties seemed to take place invariably in luxury apartments, with at least one New Year's Eve party in which social barriers were crossed and old lovers reunited, so films of the later thirties centered remarkably often on that multilevel institution, the department store, with a once-a-year mingling of the "classes" at a Christmas party. Department store employment, moreover, was a natural for the working woman: being a salesgirl capitalized on her feminine charms and gave her a chance to meet, and flatter, Mr. Right, while at the same time she was integrated into the collective spirit. Sylvia Sidney in *You and Me,* Ginger Rogers in *Bachelor Mother,* Jean Arthur in *The Devil and Miss Jones,* and Loretta Young in at least three or four movies, were department store heroines whose charms got them into trouble and whose intelligence, sometimes, got them out of it. In *The Devil and Miss Jones,* Jean Arthur is the unofficial representative of the striking store employees who brings about a reconciliation with owner Charles Coburn over the heads of the management. (Frequently the father-daughter relationship, with such gentle elders as Coburn and Thomas Mitchell paired with girls on their own like Arthur and Ginger Rogers, takes precedence over the romantic interest, in a brief, platonic, mutually advantageous relationship: The older man feels needed and protective, and the young woman is more at ease in a friendship without sexual tension and misunderstanding.) The white-collar heroine can play an important part in the action—as long as it draws on her womanliness. At an office party celebrating the settlement (the substitute for the Christmas party), Arthur speaks to each salesclerk by first name, an accomplishment typical of both her and the thirties' ethic. Because of her subordinate and subservient position, the salesgirl posed no threat to male supremacy, although as class differences once again eroded the spirit of togetherness, she might (see Joan Crawford in *The Women*) be a snake in the grass to her own sex.

There were, in the middle range, certain uniquely "feminine" jobs such as fashion editors or executives, that a woman could hold without endangering the status quo.

But the upper-echelon woman professional in the movies —the doctor or administrator—immediately assumed, to the detriment of her femininity and desirability, the masculine qualities associated with the job (even more so in the forties when women were a real economic threat). Ginger Rogers' suits and strident manner in *Lady in the Dark* signaled her difference from other women and her lack of all those things —love, sex, husband-master—that make a woman happy. More balanced but nevertheless "masculinized," psychiatrists Claudette Colbert in *Private Worlds* and Ingrid Bergman in *Spellbound* were drawn as brisk and efficient, with the implication that they arrived at their level of competence only by suppressing their female natures. Despite the "hole in the center of their lives" that only love can fill, they emerge as rounded and effective characters. But then in the maternal aspect of their ministrations, they are playing a more acceptable role than the female business executive, the head of a trucking firm (to take an extreme example, which films made a point of doing), portrayed in no uncertain terms as no job for a lady. In *Female* and *They All Kissed the Bride,* Ruth Chatterton and Joan Crawford, as the respective heads of such firms, had first of all to be outfitted in heavily masculine mannerisms, and then humiliated for being both too masculine to be "real women," and too feminine to fill their positions with complete efficiency. Though both films focus vindictively on female sexuality, *Female* seems a little freer in its outright exploitation of sex, *They All Kissed the Bride* more covert and coy. The forties, as we will see, is the danger zone, the river of no return, when women, lured into jobs because of the war, didn't want to leave them when it was over.

The gold digger tales constituted one of the happiest of working-woman genres, although they, too, were often soft at the center. As drawn in comedies (with screenplays by women like Zoë Akins and Faith Baldwin) and in musicals like the *Gold Digger* series, the gold diggers usually came in twos and threes, were played by smart, snappy actresses like Joan Blondell, Kay Francis, Ina Claire, and Aline Mac-Mahon, set out to make their way in a man's world but on their own terms, and, after preliminary success, usually abandoned these terms when the right man came along. They were often models (a euphemism for their "real" profession that the stage play, but not the movie, could disclose) or showgirls out of work, if it was felt that some legitimate profession had to be ascribed to them or if the film was a musical and called for a show within a show. With more zeal than self-pity, in contrast to the "fallen-woman" confessional films of the thirties, the gold digger didn't hesitate to use her assets to get ahead and to assert some control over her life. Not for her the nine-to-five hours of the salesgirl or the longer ones of the executive. Largely through the support of her pals, the "female community" established to outwit men rather than to compete with each other, she has the backing and confidence to do her number. This is one of the few genres and occasions where there is a real feeling of solidarity among women. Although theoretically in competition, they also realize that the cards are stacked against them, that they have this in common, and that they stand a much greater chance of succeeding if they unite.

A companion piece, or element in, the gold digger film was the show-biz saga, the "backstage" film, which afforded the dual opportunity of a vocation that allowed a woman to preserve her femininity and a role that allowed an actress to display her wares. The "exploitational," girly-merchandising aspect of the Ziegfeld production numbers or the Busby Berkeley ballets was usually balanced by the serious ambitions of at least one or two of the actresses, or an anchor-girl of substance and personality like Joan Blondell to counter the froth. (Even the frothmakers generally had to undergo the chastening *peripeteia*: the feckless tenor, played by Dick Powell, who must learn "character," the serious secretary, played by Ruby Keeler, who removes her glasses and becomes a star, proving beyond the fiction of the screenplay, that "anyone can do it.") The Busby Berkeley numbers, which are not only more spectacular and indigenous to Hollywood than the imported follies of Ziegfeld, are also more celebratory and less degrading of the female image. Maintaining a careful balance between abstraction and personalization, between the symmetrical and the erotic, Berkeley pays tribute to both the whole and the parts of a woman in a way that none of the fetishists of later decades and decadence have seemed able to do. His was a vision of women as sex objects raised to a kind of comic sublimity, a state of formal grace, and at the same time reduced, through the antics of the skulking child-dwarf, to the most primitive level of Peeping Tom voyeurism. Although not in a particularly critical way, Berkeley does implicate male lechery in his fascination with the female torso.

Far more critical is *Dance, Girl, Dance,* Dorothy Arzner's most explicitly feminist film, which counterposes the suffering and indignities of a serious ballerina (Maureen O'Hara) before an audience of lecherous males who show their preference, in no uncertain terms, for the broadly provocative gestures of a burlesque queen played by Lucille Ball. O'Hara, trying in vain to elevate the taste of the dirty old men, gets booed off the stage, while Ball—a symbol, no doubt, of the vulgarities of Hollywood as well as the female sellout to sexism—is a hit with the men whose leering fixation on women as sex objects she confirms with every bump and grind. It could be objected that O'Hara is a little out of her element in a vaudeville house, not exactly the temple of high art, and that there is something healthy in Ball's (and Hollywood's) vulgarity. Still, the contrivance helps to make the point, and once again Ms. Arzner captures with peculiar force the emotional reality of the women, independently and in their relationship as roommates and rivals. Most beautiful is the final exchange of looks between the two women in a courtroom where they have been arraigned for disturbing the peace. In a moment of instant communciation, Ball realizes that O'Hara fought with her not over a man, like most women, but over her art and her convictions.

Meanwhile, as production numbers were being planned and scratched in the show-biz sagas, and as understudies were replacing stars, back at the all-girl boardinghouse, decisions of equal importance were being made. One of the loveliest of these films, Gregory la Cava's *Stage Door,* portrayed a half-dozen women, all with different viewpoints and life patterns. In most of these films, including Arzner's *Dance, Girl, Dance,* one, and only one, girl was dead serious about her career. In *Stage Door* there were two, Andrea Leeds and Katharine Hepburn, but only one great role. (Hepburn was one of the few women of whom it was not just permitted but expected that she would seek to find herself—see *Little Women* and *Morning Glory*—outside the wife-mother roles reserved for her sisters. But for her arrogance, she, too, would pay—see *Woman of the Year* and *The Philadelphia Story.*) Leeds is the actress of phenomenal talent, Hepburn the brash and thoughtless upstart, but neither, contrary to the usual convention, is pictured as neurotic simply because of her determination. Nor do the life choices of the others—marriage, an affair, return home, den mother—appear as compromises but rather logical steps in each girl's evolution. Their feeling for, and enjoyment of, each other is intensely real (thus Hepburn's insensitivity, rather than her ambition, is resented), and one senses that the strong ties they have established with one another, in a kind of protective consciousness-raising sorority within the New York jungle, have enabled them to arrive at emotional maturity and self-knowledge.

It is ironic that this glowing representation of female solidarity—one that makes current claims look weak indeed —should come from a male director, and that this group should surpass, in rapport and mutual concern, the groups drawn by Mary McCarthy and Clare Boothe. (There is also more attention given the women as a group than in the Ferber-Kaufman play from which the film was made.) Clare Boothe's gang of Park Avenue parasites in *The Women* makes men, by omission, look like paragons indeed. In *Stage Door* there is only one important male character— Adolphe Menjou as the lascivious producer—but were he omitted, we would hardly notice the absence of men; in *The Women,* despite George Cukor's stylish direction and the excellent performances of Rosalind Russell, Joan Crawford, and Paulette Goddard particularly, we cry out for the intrusion of a male, any male, even a delivery boy. The women are such—vain, shallow, desperate, materialistic, conniving —that the men become, by implication, everything they are not: honorable, forthright, virtuous. Still, for all its inadequacies—and the major one is that the women are patronized rather than satirized, drawn too often with cattiness rather than insight or wit—it is exciting and unusual enough to have an all-woman film, one which tries to see what women are like in the absence of those men who define them. The segregation is merely an extension of the American sexist philosophy, embodied in the "woman's film," that love is women's department, while all the central—that is, money-making or villain-slaying—activities of life will be handled by men. Here we see women managing and mismanaging the business of love, and we feel once again, as with Russell in *Craig's Wife,* that if other avenues and opportunities were open to women, their energies would not be so often turned in on themselves in malice and destruction.

Even so, we can't help but prefer Russell's bitchiness to Norma Shearer's injured virtue, and we can't help but wish that Shearer would not only take her mother's advice to ignore her husband's affair, but go ahead and have one of her own. The film ends with a conventional marriage-saving message, but perhaps, for women like this, with no training and at their age, marriage is their only option. In a society that revolves around men and abhors single women ("of a certain age"), marriage is a woman's status, her security and, as Russell says in *Craig's Wife,* her emancipation.

Even a woman with a career, particularly one like acting that is at least partly associated with beauty and youth, will be expected to forsake it for the permanent security of a husband. The actress who clung to her career, as in *A Star Is Born* and *What Price Hollywood?* could be expected to ruin her husband's. Although in actual fact and among adults, marriages would seem to stand a better chance of surviving if the two partners are respectively engaged in stimulating activities, can feel self-reliant, and share a sense of mutual growth, the myth—and perhaps all too often the fact—is that marriage is based on the elevation of one ego at the expense of the other, on the superiority of the male over the female. In both pre- and post-Freudian philosophies, the mission of the wife, like that of the mother, is to pour herself, her essence, into her husband and strengthen his powers. This is so axiomatic that in the case of a competitive (that is, emasculating) wife, we are led with no effort whatsoever to sympathize with the man, with the Tolstoys and Fitzgeralds, rather than with the jealous, stifled souls and wasted talents of the Sophies and Zeldas. But with these writers their own testament has, until recently, served as fact, whereas in the movies, with a director like Cukor, we occasionally get a more balanced view, our sympathies divided, in *What Price Hollywood?*, between Lowell Sherman's drunken director going into decline as Constance Bennett's career advances, or the later parallel situation in *A Star Is Born*.

Aside from women like Joan Blondell and Jean Arthur, whom we associate with certain kinds of employment, there were leading ladies like Margaret Sullavan, Carole Lombard, Barbara Stanwyck, Claudette Colbert, Rosalind Russell, Kay Francis, and Katharine Hepburn who were always doing something, whether it was running a business or running just to keep from standing still. But their mythic destiny, like that of all women, was to find love and cast off the "veneer" of independence. In *The Moon's Our Home*, the minute Henry Fonda and Margaret Sullavan stop pretending they are a poor farm boy and a simple country girl and admit they are a New York social scion and a Hollywood actress, he insists that she give up her career. She refuses and goes to catch a plane to Hollywood. He runs after her, abducts her, and in the back seat of an ambulance, wraps her in a straitjacket. In the final shot of this film (on which Dorothy Parker, according to Pauline Kael, worked as screenwriter), she is made to look delighted at being so conclusively overpowered, but after the spirit she has shown throughout, the ending leaves a bad taste.

Generally, however, there was a reciprocity, a sense that man's highest destiny, like woman's, was love. Although he was allowed to keep his job (and was forced to get one, as part of the thirties' work ethic, if he was a playboy), it was incidental to his main adventure, wherein the scales of smugness and superiority fell from his eyes and he recognized love. If he was "driven," it was because he was misguided, or hadn't met his sexual match. Or, as in *Jimmy the Gent*, his energy is devoted to succeeding in terms that will impress the woman.

In the thrust and parry of romantic dialogue, the woman's point of view was often expressed through women screenwriters, who were more numerous in the thirties than during any other period. At Metro alone, were Anita Loos, Frances Marion, Dorothy Farnum, Bess Meredyth, Lorna Moon, Salka Viertel. The screenwriting credits of almost all of George Cukor's films of the thirties included women: on *Grumpy*, Doris Anderson; *The Royal Family of Broadway*, Gertrude Purcell; *What Price Hollywood?*, Jane Murfin (from an adaptation of an original story by Adela Rogers St. John); *Girls About Town*, from a Zoë Akins' story; *Rockabye*, Jane Murfin (from the play by Lucia Bronder); *Our Betters*, Jane Murfin; *Dinner at Eight*, Frances Marion; *Little Women*, Sarah Y. Mason; *Sylvia Scarlett*, Gladys Unger (adapted from a novel by Compton Mackenzie); *Camille*, Zoë Akins and Frances Marion; *The Women*, Anita Loos and Jane Murfin (from the play by Clare Boothe); *Susan and God*, Anita Loos (from the play by Rachel Crothers); and *Zaza*, Zoë Akins. If the point of view was not particularly feminist, neither was it slavishly submissive to a male ethic, as it is today. It was a reflection of, perhaps a slight improvement on, what women wanted to see. After all, most women were housewives and they didn't want to be made to feel that there was a whole world of possibilities they had forsaken through marriage or inertia; rather, they wanted confirmation of the choice they had made.

Love was a woman's career, and there was an entire

genre devoted to her exploits in this arena, a genre that, like the Gothic romance, could rise to the heights of art, or indulge in endless self-pity, could confirm woman's choice, or challenge the entire social foundation on which it was based. Which brings us to that pause in the day's occupation, and film history, that is known as the "woman's film."

THE WOMAN'S FILM

What more damning comment on the relations between men and women in America than the very notion of something called the "woman's film"? And what more telling sign of critical and sexual priorities than the low caste it has among the highbrows? Held at arm's length, it is, indeed, the untouchable of film genres. The concept of a "woman's film" and "women's fiction" as a separate category of art (and/or kitsch), implying a generically shared world of misery and masochism the individual work is designed to indulge, does not exist in Europe. There, affairs of the heart are of importance to both men and women and are the stuff of literature. In England, the woman's film occupies a place somewhere between its positions in France and in America; *Brief Encounter* and *The Seventh Veil* are not without soap opera elements, but they are on a slightly higher plane than their American counterparts.

Among the Anglo-American critical brotherhood (and a few of their sisters as well), the term "woman's film" is used disparagingly to conjure up the image of the pinched-virgin or little-old-lady writer, spilling out her secret longings in wish fulfillment or glorious martyrdom, and transmitting these fantasies to the frustrated housewife. The final image is one of wet, wasted afternoons. And if strong men have also cried their share of tears over the weepies, that is all the more reason (goes the argument) we should be suspicious, be on our guard against the flood of "unearned" feelings released by these assaults, unerringly accurate, on our emotional soft spots.

As a term of critical opprobrium, "woman's film" carries the implication that women, and therefore women's emotional problems, are of minor significance. A film that focuses on male relationships is not pejoratively dubbed a "man's film" (indeed, this term, when it is used, confers—like "a man's man"—an image of brute strength), but a "psychological drama." European films, too, are automatically exempted from the "woman's film" caste; thus, the critical status of *Mayerling* over *Love Affair, Le Carnet du Bal* over *Angel, Jules and Jim* over *Design for Living, My Night at Maud's* over *Petulia,* and *The Passion of Anna* over Bergman's English-language *The Touch*. Also exempted are films with literary prestige, like *Carrie* or *Sunday, Bloody Sunday.*

In the thirties and forties, the heyday of the "woman's film," it was as regular an item in studio production as the crime melodrama or the Western. Like any routine genre, it was subject to its highs and lows, and ranged from films that adhered safely to the formulae of escapist fantasy, films that were subversive only "between the lines" and in retrospect, and the rare few that used the conventions to undermine them. At the lowest level, as soap opera, the "woman's film" fills a masturbatory need, it is soft-core emotional porn for the frustrated housewife. The weepies are founded on a mock-Aristotelian and politically conservative aesthetic whereby women spectators are moved, not by pity and fear but by self-pity and tears, to accept, rather than reject, their lot. That there should be a need and an audience for such an opiate suggests an unholy amount of real misery. And that a term like "woman's film" can be summarily used to dismiss certain films, with no further need on the part of the critic to make distinctions and explore the genre, suggests some of the reasons for this misery.

In the woman's film, the woman—*a* woman—is at the center of the universe. Best friends and suitors, like Bette Davis' satellites (Geraldine Fitzgerald and George Brent) in *Dark Victory,* live only for her pleasure, talk about her constantly, and cease to exist when she dies. In the rare case where a man's point of view creeps in, as screenwriter Howard Koch's did in *No Sad Songs for Me,* it is generally reconciled with the woman's point of view. Thus, after Margaret Sullavan dies, the husband (Wendell Corey) will marry the woman (Viveca Lindfors) he almost had an affair with. But it is with the dead wife's blessing (she has actually chosen the woman who will replace her as wife and mother), and with the knowledge that when the chips were down, he preferred the wife to the "other woman." The result is the same as that of *Dark Victory*: The two loved ones —the remainders—may unite out of loneliness, but always with the shadow and memory of the "great woman" (vivid and in her prime) between them. If woman hogs this universe unrelentingly, it is perhaps her compensation for all the male-dominated universes from which she has been excluded: the gangster film, the Western, the war film, the *policier,* the rodeo film, the adventure film. Basically, the woman's film is no more maudlin and self-pitying than the male adventure film (what British critic Raymond Durgnat calls the "male weepies"), particularly in the male film's recent mood of bronco-busting buddies and bleary-eyed nostalgia. The well of self-pity in both types of films, though only hinted at, is bottomless, and in their sublimation or evasion of adult reality, they reveal, almost by accident, real attitudes toward marriage—disillusionment, frustration, and contempt—beneath the sunny-side-up philosophy congealed in the happy ending.

The underlying mystique of the man's film is that these are (or were) the best of times, roaming the plains, or prowling the city, in old clothes and unshaven, the days before settling down or going home, days spent battling nature or the enemy. In such films, the woman becomes a kind of urban or frontier Xantippe with rather limited options. She can be a meddling moralist who wants the hero to leave off his wandering; or a last resort for him, after his buddies have died or departed; or an uptight socialite to whom the hero can never confess his criminal, or even just shadowy, past; or a nagging nice-girl wife, who pesters the hero to spend more time with her, instead of always working, working, working or killing, killing, killing. The most common pattern is probably the wife competing with her husband's other life—business, crime, or crime detection; and since these activities are the dramatic focus and lifeblood of the film, the wife becomes a killjoy, distracting not only the hero but the audience from the fun and danger.

Marriage becomes the heavy. The implication is clear: All the excitment of life—the passion, the risk—occurs outside marriage rather than within it. Marriage is a deadly bore, made to play the role of the spoilsport, the ugly cousin one has to dance with at the ball. An excruciating example, and they abound, occurs in *The Big Clock,* in the husband-wife relationship of Ray Milland and Maureen O'Sullivan.

Milland, an advertising executive, has been framed for murder; he is in life-or-death danger as he tries to track down the real culprit. Meanwhile O'Sullivan—naturally, as the wife, the last to be informed—keeps complaining of Milland's long hours at the office and his failure to take her on a promised wedding trip. Indeed, the murderer (Charles Laughton) is by far a more sympathetic character than the wife. By intruding on and sometimes interfering with the melodrama, such women become harpies even when they aren't meant to—*The Big Clock,* after all, was directed by Maureen O'Sullivan's husband, John Farrow.

That love is woman's stuff is a hoary Anglo-Saxon idea, devolving from the (American) tough guy and (British) public school etiquette that to show emotion is bad form, a sign of effeminacy, and that being tender in love is the equivalent of doing the dishes or darning socks. The association takes. For the housewife, betrayed by her romantic ideals, the path of love leads to, becomes, the dead end of household drudgery. The domestic and the romantic are entwined, one redeeming the other, in the theme of self-sacrifice, which is the mainstay and oceanic force, high tide and low ebb, of the woman's film. The equation of time and Tide is not so risible as it seems, just as the emphasis in the women's movement on domestic arrangements is not a trivializing of "larger issues." Rather, it is an intuitive recognition that the essence of salvation is not in the single leap of the soul, but in the day-to-day struggle to keep the best of oneself afloat—the discovery that perdition is not the moment of Faustian sellout, but the gradual dribbling of self-esteem, and self, down the drain of meaningless activity.

To the view that women's concerns, and the films that depict them, are of minor significance in the drama of life and art, women themselves have acquiesced, and critics have led the way. James Agee was almost alone among critics in not dismissing the woman's film summarily. In a favorable review of *Brief Encounter,* he wrote that when he associated the film with the best of women's magazine fiction, he did not intend a backhand compliment. "For it seems to me that few writers of supposedly more serious talent even undertake themes as simple and important any more: so that, relatively dinky and sentimental as it is—a sort of vanity-sized *Anna Karenina*—*Brief Encounter* is to be thoroughly respected."

But for every Agee, there have been critics whose voices dripped sarcasm and whose pens went lax when they came to review a woman's film. In his 1946 book *On Documentary,* the late John Grierson, the father of the "serious subject" critics, interrupted his anti-Hollywood and prosocial-realism diatribe to deplore Anthony Asquith's waste of time and talent on *Dance, Pretty Lady.* Grierson, admitting the film was "a delight to the eye," nonetheless deplored its subject: "This is it, bless you. Claptrap about a virginity. Why the entire sentiment that makes a plot like that possible went into discard with the good, prosperous, complacent Victoria. It was, relatively, an important matter then. But it is mere infant fodder now when you consider the new problems we carry in our bellies, and think of the new emphases we must in mercy to ourselves create out of our different world." Apparently the way to a socially conscious critic's heart is through his stomach. A woman's virginity (infant fodder, indeed!), and where and how she lost it, is at least as important as the high and mighty manly themes of the films Grierson approved of.

The deprecation of women's films takes a different form among critics who are not socially conscious—the aesthetically open, "movie-movie critics" represented, in the thirties and forties, by Agee, Otis Ferguson, Robert Warshow, and Manny Farber. There, the prejudice is more subtle: It is not that they love women less, but that they admire men more.

Even Ferguson and Agee, who were enraptured with certain female presences on the screen, reserved their highest accolades for the films that showed men doing things and that captured the look and feel of down-at-heel losers, criminals, or soldiers, men battling nature or big-city odds. Agee never avoided the emotional or sentimental side of film (in the forties, who could?), but like the others, he had a slight case of Hemingwayitis. This infatuation with the masculine mystique was the pale-face New York intellectual's compensation for life in a cubicle, a *nostalgie de la boue* for the real grit and grime, as opposed to synthetic smudge—the kind that rubs off on your hands from typewriter erasures or newspapers.

There has been a corollary blindness on the part of most film critics to the achievements of the "woman's director," to the mixture of seriousness and high style that Europeans like Max Ophuls, Douglas Sirk, Otto Preminger, and Lubitsch bring to women's subjects, not just enhancing but transforming them; or to the commitment of a John Stahl or Edmund Goulding to material from which other directors withdraw in tasteful disdain (as did Wyler and Stevens, "graduating" as soon as they got the opportunity from the woman's film subjects of their early and best work to the bloated seriousness of their later work); or to the complete identification of a director like George Cukor with the woman's point of view, so that the attitude expressed is not his so much as hers.

Central to the woman's film is the notion of middle-classness, not just as an economic status, but as a state of mind and a relatively rigid moral code. The circumscribed world of the housewife corresponds to the state of woman in general, confronted by a range of options so limited she might as well inhabit a cell. The persistent irony is that she is dependent for her well-being and "fulfillment" on institutions—marriage, motherhood—that by translating the word "woman" into "wife" and "mother," end her independent identity. She then feels bound to adhere to a morality which demands that she stifle her own "illicit" creative or sexual urges in support of a social code that tolerates considerably more deviation on the part of her husband. She is encouraged to follow the lead of her romantic dreams, but when they expire she is stuck.

Beyond this common plight of a generic nature, there are as many kinds of woman's film as there are kinds of women. One division, providing the greatest tension with conventions of the genre, is between the upper-middle-class elite and the rest of the world, between women as models and women as victims. There are the "extraordinary" women —actresses like Marlene Dietrich, Katharine Hepburn, Rosalind Russell, Bette Davis, and characters like Scarlett O'Hara and Jezebel—who are the exceptions to the rule, the aristocrats of their sex. Their point of view is singular, and in calling the shots they transcend the limitations of their sexual identities. But their status as emancipated women, based as it is on the very quality of being exceptional, weakens their political value as demonstration-model victims and makes them, in their independence, unpopular with a majority of men and women.

Then there are the "ordinary" women—women whose options have been foreclosed by marriage or income, by children or age, who are, properly speaking, the subject of women's films at their lowest and largest common denominator. As audience surrogates, their heroines are defined negatively and collectively by their mutual limitations rather than by their talents or aspirations. Their point of view is not singular but plural, political rather than personal. They embrace the audience as victims, through the common myths of rejection and self-sacrifice and martyrdom as purveyed by the mass media. These—the media—have changed over the years, from magazines like *Good Housekeeping, Cosmopolitan, The Saturday Evening Post,* and from novels like those of Fannie Hurst, Edna Ferber, and Kathleen Norris, through the movies of the twenties, thirties, and forties, to television soap opera today. But the myths have not changed, nor has the underlying assumption: that these women are stuck, and would rather be stuck than sorry. The purpose of these fables is not to encourage "woman" to rebel or question her role, but to reconcile her to it, and thus preserve the status quo. The fictions are her defense not only against "man," but against the "extraordinary woman." For the average housewife, who has not quite gotten around to sex therapy or sensitivity training or group grope, prostitution, drugs, or even drink, these matinee myths are her alcoholic afternoons.

Between these two, there is a third category, one to which the better women's films aspire: It is the fiction of the "ordinary woman who becomes extraordinary," the woman who begins as a victim of discriminatory circumstances and rises, through pain, obsession, or defiance, to become mistress of her fate. Between the suds of soap opera we watch her scale the heights of Stendhalian romance. Her ascent is given stature and conviction not through a discreet contempt for the female sensibility, but through an all-out belief in it, through the faith, expressed in directorial sympathy and style, that the swirling river of a woman's emotions is as important as anything on earth. The difference between the soap opera palliative and the great woman's film (*Angel, Letter from an Unknown Woman*) is like the difference between masturbatory relief and mutually demanding love.

All women begin as victims. Anna Karenina is a victim of the double standard no less than is Laura in *Brief Encounter*; Emma Bovary is as much a casualty of middle-class morality as is Ruby Gentry. Anna and Emma cease to be victims, cease to be easy identification figures, as they become increasingly complex and cruel, as they take fate into their own hands. As with all his characters, Tolstoy kept Anna at arm's length, in "middle shot," finding external correlatives to suggest her inner state. But movie heroines are in close-up; they have a narrower context in which to operate, and they must achieve stature in a different way. They cannot afford to alienate us (if the movie *Madame Bovary* had ended like the novel it would have been more catastrophic than courageous), because there is no wider field of vision, no social context or alternate major characters to claim our attention and absorb the shock. The movie of *Anna Karenina* is not, like the novel, about [Anna + Vronsky + Karenin + Levin + Kitty; country + city; society + art + religion] but about Garbo—or, in the later version, Vivien Leigh. (Sometimes the producers' reluctance to have a star alienate or disappoint the audience goes too far; in the first, silent version of *Anna Karenina* which was called *Love,* and starred Garbo, an alternate happy ending was provided with the print sent to theaters; in it, according to a synopsis, "Anna and Vronsky are happily reunited three years later, after her husband's opportune death.") The movie *Madame Bovary* is not about [Emma + French provincial society + the art form itself] but about Jennifer Jones' rapt romanticism as envisioned by Vincente Minnelli. But in the distinguished women's films, the combination of director and star serve the same function as the complex perspective of the novelist: They take the woman out of the plural into the singular, out of defeat and passivity and collective identity into the radical adventure of the solitary soul, out of the contrivances of puritanical thinking into enlightened self-interest.

It is this unique combination of actress plus director that makes, for example, one version of *Back Street* better or worse than another, even when the plot is identical. There are stars like Garbo and Marie Dressler and Joan Crawford who are their own genres. There are also distinctions to be made between one decade and another. Still, the bare bones remain remarkably similar, like grammatical models from which linguistical examples are formed. The themes of the woman's film can themselves be reduced to four categories, often found overlapping or in combination: sacrifice, affliction, choice, competition.

In the first, the woman must "sacrifice" (1) herself for her children—e.g., *Madame X, The Sin of Madelon Claudet*; (2) her children for their own welfare—e.g., *The Old Maid, Stella Dallas, To Each His Own*; (3) marriage for her lover—e.g., *Back Street*; (4) her lover for marriage or for his own welfare—e.g., *Kitty Foyle* and *Intermezzo*, respectively; (5) her career for love—e.g., *Lady in the Dark, Together Again*; or (6) love for her career—e.g., *The Royal Family of Broadway, Morning Glory*. The sacrifice film may end happily, with the wife/mother reclaiming her husband/child when her rival dies, or tragically, as mother watches daughter's happiness from afar, or sees son or lover only to lose him once again. In either case, the purgative sensations—the joy of suffering, the pain of joy—are very close. But not identical. Indeed, most of the thirties' and forties' woman's films ended tragically, an indication perhaps of the vision women had of themselves.

In the second category, the heroine is struck by some "affliction" which she keeps a secret and eventually either dies unblemished (*Dark Victory*), despite the efforts of her doctor-turned-lover, or is cured (*The Magnificent Obsession*) by the efforts of her lover-turned-doctor.

The third category, "choice," has the heroine pursued by at least two suitors who wait, with undivided attention, her decision; on it, their future happiness depends (*The Seventh Veil, Daisy Kenyon, Lydia*).

In the final category, "competition," the heroine meets

and does battle with the woman whose husband (fiancé, lover) she loves (*The Great Lie, When Ladies Meet, Love Story*—the forties' English version; *Old Acquaintance*). While deciding the man's fate, the women will discover, without explicitly acknowledging it, that they prefer each other's company to his. The obtuseness of men generally is implied by their inability to perceive love or (in the case of the second category) disease.*

As patently idiotic as these themes sound, how is one to explain the degree to which some of them enthrall us: the mesmerized absorption, the choking, the welling up of tears over some lugubrious rendition of a famous piano concerto that will haunt us forever afterward with the memory of James Mason rapping Ann Todd's knuckles or Margaret Lockwood banging away in Albert Hall?

The Mason-Todd scene comes, of course, from *The Seventh Veil,* coauthored by the husband-and-wife team of Muriel and Sydney Box, and directed by Compton Bennett. The title refers, in the pseudo-psychoanalytical idiom of the film, to that last "wall" between a woman and her innermost thoughts. Along with *Daisy Kenyon,* this is a model of the "choice" category, one of the most likable and yet most spurious, the pretense of suffering in a totally pleasurable situation being the height of hypocrisy. It is woman's understandable revenge, and reversal, of the state of affairs in which, as Byron said, "Man's love is of man's life a thing apart/ 'Tis woman's whole existence." The pattern of such films is to open with a period in which the heroine is spoiled and petted (metaphorically, of course) by several devoted males whose infatuation she either does not notice or is aggrieved by, after which she is given an ultimatum. She has to make

* Sometimes the categories overlap, as in *No Sad Songs for Me,* in which a dying Margaret Sullavan prepares to turn her husband over to another woman.

a decision. At this point, a pretext will be found whereby the suitors are assembled, like characters in an Agatha Christie mystery—preferably at the bottom of a large staircase—to hear the "solution." This is, staircase and all, the arrangement that concludes *The Seventh Veil*. Ann Todd, resting upstairs, having been cured of her traumatic paralysis by psychiatrist Herbert Lom, will shortly descend and select either Hugh McDermott, the boorish American jazz musician whose wife has just divorced him, leaving him free to return to his first love; Albert Lieven, the world-weary Viennese artist who thought no woman could rekindle his dying passion; or James Mason, the witheringly sardonic guardian who trained and tyrannized her, poured his own pent-up talent into her, and couldn't let her go. (Although Lom, too, is undoubtedly in love with her, we can discount him as a contender, this being the modest era before mutual Oedipal transference and doctor-participation therapy.)

It isn't the list of players that tips us off—this is practically James Mason's first noteworthy movie. Nor is it the dime-store Freudianism that attaches to Mason's character (think of the penis envy potential in Todd's fingers and Mason's sadism). Nor is it just that he retains his dignity while those about him begin to fall apart. The choice has to be Mason, as any Anglo-American woman knows instinctively, because he, with his cultivated, misogynous manner, is the paragon of the English lover, the type most irresistible to the puritan woman. Father figure and mentor, Professor Higgins and Pygmalion, he exacts the best from her artistically, intellectually, spiritually, but makes no sexual demands. He never imposes on her; on the contrary, his indifference is the spur to her attraction. He is for most American women, the male ideal—cultured, genteel, refined, repressed, with a slight antagonism toward women that is not congenital but the result of an earlier wound or disillusionment, and therefore curable. But it is curable only by her. About all other women he continues to be cynical and disbelieving, and thus his fidelity is assured. He is, like the celibate clergyman or "confirmed bachelor," a challenge to a woman, and a relief from the sexually aggressive male.

The delicate, well-bred British hero (Mason, Herbert Marshall, the Howards—Trevor and Leslie) has had far more appeal than such matinee idol stock figures as John Boles, John Lund, George Brent, and all the other pretty profiles. Women's preference for the English gentleman—witty, overrefined, unsexual or apparently misogynous, paternal—is rooted in an instinct for self-preservation that expresses itself in the romantic drive. There is a split in a woman's sensibility, revealed over and over again in literature that expresses a woman's point of view, between her romantic interest—elevated, "total" (that is, not total, but psychological, spiritual)—focusing on a hero who will look into her eyes and embrace her soul and demand nothing sexually, and her sexual drive, brute and impersonal, demanding to be ravished "anonymously," that is, taken without asking, almost unawares, so that she will neither be responsible for her surrender nor bound by it afterward. (Even today, studies show that an amazing number of modern women neglect to prepare themselves for intercourse with contraception, indicating that women still prefer to think of sex as a seduction rather than a partnership. The reluctance of women to take responsibility for sex would seem a prime factor in perpetuating the stereotypes of the dominant, active male and the submissive, passive female.) Hence Scarlett's bliss the morning after her "rape" by Rhett Butler, although—and because—she will never love him the way she loves the unavailable, the undemanding Ashley. Her love for Ashley is passionate, but it is that of a tigress for a kitten; and his resistance and general effeteness assure us that even if he were to succumb she would have the upper hand. She is a diabolically strong woman—deceptively so, in the manner of the southern belle —and she fears the loss of her strength and selfhood that a total, "animal" relationship with Rhett would entail.

The "Ashley" figure, the sexually unthreatening male, whether as romantic lover or friend, crops up repeatedly in fiction written by women. The character of Waldo Lydecker, the acid-tongued columnist in Otto Preminger's *Laura,* is a perfect example. In Preminger's coolly perverse melodrama, made from a novel by Vera Caspary, the beautiful, self-possessed heroine has evaded marriage largely through the ritual savaging of her beaux by Clifton Webb's brilliant Lydecker. They make a dazzling team—Gene Tierney's career woman and the epicene, knife-blade-lean New York intellectual who launched her. Lydecker has a hold on Laura that cannot be explained merely by her indebtedness to him, and he is able to influence her further in the way that she is already predisposed. Not wanting to lose her, and expressing his own ambivalent attraction and repulsion, he ridicules her sexually demanding suitors, of whom Dana Andrews' detective is the crudest and therefore the least vulnerable. By making no claims to the chic and cultivation of the Laura–Lydecker world (by entering the battle of wits without a weapon), he emerges unscathed by Lydecker's sword and proves himself Laura's true knight.

Another Preminger gem and quintessential "choice" film is *Daisy Kenyon,* in which Joan Crawford, as a successful dress designer, has to choose between Dana Andrews, the married man who is her lover, and Henry Fonda, her boat-designing beau. Adapted from a novel by Elizabeth Janeway, it is a movie filled with typical "woman's film" scenes: the jangling telephone; the scene in the bar, when the rivals fruitlessly try to bypass Daisy and reach some sort of agreement on their own; or the climactic image of Joan Crawford, having left the two men at her country cabin to await her decision, driving eighty miles an hour through the woods, her chin jutting, her eyes glaring ahead not at the road but into the middle distance of her own self-absorption, in a narcissistic trance that can only be broken (since she can't change expression) by the crash when she drives off the road.

Strictly speaking, the "sacrifice" film constitutes a separate category, but in a broader sense it is, like the idea of "middle-classness," synonymous with the woman's film. The sacrifice film offers relief in, indeed thrives on, a contravention of its own morality: that "you can't have your cake and eat it too." The narrative impetus is based on an either/or ethic, on the universally accepted existence of fixed, life-and-death, in-or-out social rules which it is the film's precise purpose to circumvent. Doomed heroines, by not dying until the last moment, do not (as far as the experience of the film is concerned) really die. Women with fatal diseases receive all the attention and sympathy of an invalid without actually acting or looking sick. A heroine gets moral credit for not telling anyone of her illness . . . while only divulging it to an audience of millions.

Because the woman's film was designed for and tailored to a certain market, its recurrent themes represent the closest thing to an expression of the collective drives, conscious and unconscious, of American women, of their avowed obligations and their unconscious resistance. Children are an obsession in American movies—sacrifice of and for children, the use of children as justification for all manner of sacrifice—in marked contrast to European films about love and romantic intrigue, where children rarely appear at all and are almost never the instruments of judgment they are in American films. (To compare films made from almost-identical stories, Max Ophuls' *Letter from an Unknown Woman* introduces the illegitimate child only to kill him off shortly thereafter, while John Stahl's *Only Yesterday* makes his "legitimization" the culmination of the film and the redemption of the mother.)

But in true having-your-cake-and-eating-it-too fashion, the underlying resentment will have its say. In films where the unmarried or poverty-stricken mother sacrifices her children for their advancement, the children are usually such little monsters that their departure provides secret relief. Where a mother holds on to the kids and sacrifices herself for them, they are even more thankless (*Mildred Pierce* is a good example).

The sacrifice of and for children—two sides of the same coin—is a disease passing for a national virtue, and a constant theme in films that preach one thing and, for anyone who is listening, say another. Whether the totem is challenged, as in the woman's films of European directors like Ophuls and Sirk (*Reckless Moment, There's Always Tomorrow, All That Heaven Allows*), or played straight and heartwarmingly, as in *Penny Serenade, Mildred Pierce, To Each His Own,* all three versions of *Madame X, The Old Maid,* and *That Certain Woman,* the spectacle of a woman owned by her children or consumed by her maternal zeal is as much the mainstay of the woman's film as it is of American culture and middle-class marriage.

Like all obsessions, this one betrays a fear of its opposite, of a hatred so intense it must be disguised as love. The obsession is composed of various related elements: a conviction that children are the reason for getting married (*Penny Serenade*) or the only thing holding marriage together (*The Great Lie, The Marrying Kind*), or woman's ultimate *raison d'être,* her only worth-confirming "career." The chain becomes a vicious circle. The woman without a job, without interests, without an absorbing marriage, invests her whole life, her erotic and emotional energy, in the child, who then becomes a divining rod, further drawing off the energy and electricity that should provide a constant current between husband and wife. The child that is seen as the means of shoring up a marriage becomes the wedge that drives a couple apart. But to admit this, to admit any reservations about having children or toward the children themselves, is to commit heresy. The only way to express this hostility is through a noble inversion: the act of sacrifice, of giving them up. Thus, the surrender of the children for their welfare (*Stella Dallas* and *The Old Maid*) is a maneuver for circumventing the sacred taboo, for getting rid of the children in the guise of advancing their welfare. (The sacrifice of oneself for one's children is a more subtle and metaphorical means to the same end: of venting hostility on the children through approved channels.) Both of these transactions represent beautifully masked wish fulfillments, suggesting that the myth of obsession—the love lavished, the attention paid to children, their constant inclusion in narratives where their presence is not required—is compensation for women's guilt, for the deep, inadmissible feelings of not wanting children, or not wanting them unreservedly, in the first place.

This goes some way toward explaining the plot contrivances and emotional excesses to be found in the "sacrifice" film: Martyrdom must be proportionate to guilt, and the greater the aversion to having a child, the greater the sacrifices called for. The inconveniences the child will cause (to an unwed mother, for example) and which are the source of her aversion, become trials actively sought as tests of her mother-love. In *To Each His Own,* Olivia de Havilland has become pregnant as the result of a one-night affair with an aviator who has been killed in the war. She goes to New York to have the child, but instead of staying there, where she could live with the child unquestioned, she returns to the provincial hamlet and gives the baby up to a neighbor, asking only for the privilege of spending one day a week with him. In one sense she "rejects" the child, as her lover, in dying, had "rejected" her; in another sense, the child becomes the object of all her pent-up emotions, a surrogate lover. When an old beau reappears and tries to persuade her to marry him and go away, he mistakes her refusal—and the light in her eyes—for commitment to another. And indeed it is. But it is to her own son, not a suitor, and the misinterpretation which follows revealingly suggests the degree to which an American woman's feelings for son and lover are identical. The loveliest part of the film concerns neither of these passions, but the very touching, adult encounter—the flirtation between two middle-aged air wardens (de Havilland and Roland Culver) in London—that begins and ends the film.

The mother's excessive and covertly erotic attachment to her children leads to a sense of bereavement, of the mistress "spurned," when they grow up and away from her. Once again the "woman's film" provides her with myths to support her sense of betrayal, to give her the sweet taste of revenge. Her sacrifice has spoiled them: When they leave home or "outgrow" their parents, it is not from a child's natural desire to be on his or her own, but because they have adopted "false values." In the materialism with which mothers like Stella Dallas and Mildred Pierce smother their children (a figurative rendering of the cultural advantages, higher education, and "quality" friends, in which the children go beyond their parents), in pushing them to want "more," they are creating monsters who will reject and be "ashamed" of them; simultaneously, the children's heartlessness will vindicate and earn audience sympathy for the mothers.

Less riddled with ambivalence is the "sacrifice-for-lover" film, although it carries a similar sense of pessimism and doom regarding marriage. Love is not lasting under the best of circumstances, such films suggest philosophically, but the best circumstances are not to be found in marriage. Hence the numerous stories of impossible, imaginary, or extra-marital love. In the latter category, *Back Street* is perhaps the most familiar, and offers, in its various remakes, a reflection of changing values.

The woman's film underwent a change between the thirties and forties, affecting—and affected by—the change in the image of women themselves. The forties were more emotional and neurotic, alternating between the self-denying passivity of the waiting war wife and the brittle aggressiveness of heroines like Davis and Crawford; thirties' heroines were spunkier and more stoical than their forties' sisters, the difference perhaps between a stiff and a quivering upper lip. Thirties' films unfolded against a normal society, whose set of standards the heroine automatically accepted. The social structure wavered in the forties, with women moving up the employment ladder and down from the pedestal, paying for one with their fall from the other. There is, as a result, a constant ambivalence in forties' films, a sensibility that is alternately hard and squishy, scathing and sentimental.

In the thirties, most heroines were still content with white-collar jobs or life at home. In the 1932 version of *Back Street,* with John Boles and Irene Dunne, Dunne is merely and merrily the town beauty. Even when she transfers to New York, following a missed rendezvous and Boles' marriage to another woman, her job is vague. The emphasis is on her reunion with Boles, who becomes her lover, and the tiny apartment where she waits and suffers. The supreme suffering, which he inflicts on her, is his refusal to let her have a baby. (Naturally she, who wants a baby and has plenty of occasion to conceive, never becomes pregnant, while Olivia de Havilland, like most movie heroines, gets pregnant from a one-night fling. But even the one-night-stand pregnancy, the seemingly silliest of movie conventions, has a source in real life: indifference on the part of women seems practically to insure pregnancy, while desperate longing seems invariably to forestall it.) In the 1941 remake (with Charles Boyer in the Boles role), Margaret Sullavan is an enterprising woman working in the family dry goods store, a buyer who knows her stuff and trades quips with the men. It is, in fact, her sharp tongue that gets her into trouble and precipitates the missed appointment. But the fact that Sullavan is more independent and self-sufficient than Dunne makes her sacrifice for love that much more humiliating; in Dunne's case, that sacrifice gives point and nobility to a life that would have been at best ordinary and conventional. Love *is* Dunne's career, and obsession is its own justification. This is one of the paradoxes basic to the woman's film, a paradox which is promptly undermined by another: The idea of a woman "giving up all" for Charles Boyer is a lot easier on the pride than the idea of "giving up all" for John Boles. But then, Boyer's delicacy and intelligence make it impossible to believe him capable of the insensitive behavior toward a woman that one can believe of Boles. It is part of the double bind of masochistic rationalization triggering the woman's film that what adds to its conviction on one level subtracts from it on another. The intelligence and chemistry of Sullavan–Boyer make them a more exciting and romantic couple than Dunne–Boles, but the ending (in their separate deaths) seems a waste and a letdown, which the fantasy happy ending—in which they meet instead of missing each other at the dock—does nothing to dispel. On the other hand, John Stahl's direction, and the script, of the earlier version become sublime at just this point. In a stunning final sequence, the appointment at the gazebo (a more felicitous location than the dock) is kept, the lovers are united, and in death they gain a beauty they never had in life.

The third version, an inane, jet-setting remake, stars

John Gavin as the contemporary answer to Boles (plastic replacing plastic) and Susan Hayward as a globe-trotting fashion executive. Of all, she is the most exalted professionally and the least convincing emotionally, because her success and mobility (and here paradox dissolves in mere contradiction) undercut the closed system of decisions and consequences on which middle-class tragedy depends.

Women's films, particularly those of the thirties, have a stronger sense of social reality than their glossy-magazine or vacuum-sealed television equivalents. Aside from the portrait of American society they give as a matter of course, there are unconscious reflections of misery "in passing," like the image of a drunk or a prostitute reflected on the shiny surface of a parked limousine. The spectacle of perverted child-love is one such image, as are the American obsession with money, status, social climbing and its epiphenomenon, the *faux pas.* Who can forget the horror, and terrible humor, of the birthday party scene in King Vidor's *Stella Dallas,* when Stanwyck and daughter Anne Shirley wait at the place-marked and overdecorated table as first one, then another and another note of regret arrives.

A growing ambivalence and coyness in films began in the thirties and ran into the forties. (Sometimes it wasn't so ambivalent; for example, a strong antifeminist and philistine sentiment runs through Lubitsch's *That Uncertain Feeling,* with its derisive attitude toward the "cultural evening" that opens the film.) Part of the silliness arose from the fact that sexual passion and desire could not be shown: compare the 1929 version of *The Letter,* in which Jeanne Eagels seems to disintegrate before our eyes with the force of her passion, and the 1941 remake, in which Bette Davis has to give a suppressed and largely psychological performance in conformance with code decorum. There was also a retrenchment from the feminism of the twenties and thirties. Women might have better jobs, largely as a result of the war and a shortage of male personnel, but they would pay more heavily for them in the movies. Naturally. They were more of a threat. Men were nervous not so much about women taking their jobs—the firing of women directly after the war and the reinstatement of protective legislation that had been temporarily suspended would take care of that—but about women leaving the home "untended" as they crept back to work. For it was a fact that once women had savored the taste of work and independence, many didn't want to go back to being "just housewives." And so in films working women (who were statistically older than their prewar counterparts) were given a pseudo-toughness, a facade of steel wool that at a man's touch would turn into cotton candy.

As fixed point of Hollywood and lodestar of the woman's film, managing always to be where it was or vice versa, Joan Crawford provides a running commentary of changing attitudes. In *Susan and God,* her multiple-cause crusading woman, patterned on Eleanor Roosevelt, is subtly mocked for neglecting the home. Professionally, Crawford's roles reflected the American woman's rise up the wage scale: a perfume salesgirl in *The Women,* a chain-restaurateuse in *Mildred Pierce,* a designer in *Daisy Kenyon*; in *The Damned Don't Cry* she goes from being the smalltown wife of a pinchpenny hardhat, to being a "model," to being the rich and powerful "socialite" Lorna Hansen Forbes, and she does it by having more guts than any man ("I wouldn't have had the nerve," says her male protégé; "You don't need it," Crawford snaps back, "I got enough for both of us"). Then as the woman's film began to die, she moved into the neurotic women's roles of off-center *auteurs* like Nicholas Ray and Robert Aldrich. If her move from Mildred of Mildred's franchise to the single saloon-owner, Vienna, of Ray's *Johnny*

Guitar was a step down economically, it was something of a leap forward iconographically. Whatever satisfaction Mildred got from Jack Carson's doglike self-abasement, Vienna's prestige was multiplied by that of her employee, Sterling Hayden, as a guitar-playing gunfighter. Vienna's final showdown with malevolent Mercedes McCambridge not only puts Mildred's altercation with her daughter to shame, it rivals such climactic mortal combats as that between Gary Cooper and Walter Huston in *The Virginian*. As the outrageous gun-toting Vienna (a more respectful *reductio ad absurdum* of her persona than Aldrich's *What Ever Happened to Baby Jane?*), Crawford alternates between the masculine and feminine elements of her personality with a bravura that is grand and funny without ever being ludicrous or demeaning.

The all-out perversity and outrageousness of *Johnny Guitar* and *What Ever Happened to Baby Jane?* are to be preferred to the sly, hidden nastiness of a film like *They All Kissed the Bride*. There, Crawford played the head of a trucking firm in conflict with Melvyn Douglas' labor leader. To suggest—leeringly, not openly—that all male-female conflict is sexual and that Crawford is really "just a girl," she goes, literally, weak in the knees every time she sees Douglas and must grab on to something or fall. It would be more humiliating if one believed for a moment that Joan Crawford could really go weak in the knees. But she can't and one doesn't. Her appeal is that she is not "just a girl" underneath; in fact, there is nothing underneath. Her hard-as-nails exterior conceals no heart of gold, or even steel. That's all there is—a sheet-metal facade, intense and glittering.

The unselfconscious luster of the early Joan Crawford hardens into the carefully polished sheen of the star. That she was a woman of many faces and uncommon adaptability is not surprising, perhaps, for a girl who had four names before she was twenty-one. She was christened Billie Cassin by her mother and adoptive father (who, in a curious parallel to Bette Davis' biography, abandoned the family when Joan was seven); she took the name (Lucille) LeSueur from her real father when she learned of his existence; she was rechristened Joan Arden by the M-G-M publicity department when she first got to Hollywood; and finally, when it was discovered that the name Joan Arden had already been assigned, she became Joan Crawford.

Even the leading men she chose to share her life with reflect the evolution of her career. She was the dancing lady of the silents whose marriage to Douglas Fairbanks, Jr., confirmed her as a symbol of flaming youth; the aspiring actress of the thirties whose marriage to Franchot Tone confirmed her seriousness; the businesswoman of the forties whose marriage to Pepsi-Cola chairman Alfred Nu Steele cemented her power and gave her security as a lifetime executive of Pepsi-Cola. The obsessively responsible heroine of *Mildred Pierce* (1945) is a long way from the feckless secretary of *Grand Hotel* (1932), the flapper of the silents, or the beautiful degenerate of *Rain*. Indeed, her performance in *Rain* is one of her loveliest and most appealing, although the 1932 film was poorly received by the press and public, and Crawford herself dislikes it. In her autobiography, she blushes an un-Crawford-like blush over her portrayal of Sadie Thompson, insisting that the critics were indeed right (just this once, is the implication) in accusing her of overacting. But her twisted relationship with the zealous reformer played by Walter Huston—her spiritual conversion, his guilty surrender to the lust against which his whole life's work has been a fortress—is one of those heady, erotic encounters that only the pre-code thirties could produce.

In her transition from the wanton, overly made-up, fluffy-haired Sadie to the severe, self-sacrificing hollow-eyed convert of *Rain,* Crawford curiously prefigured the transition in her own career from the go-go flapper to the glazed icon, from the natural party girl to the star, conscious of the importance of her fan club, of her religious commitment. But in *Rain,* even at her most pious, she has a prodigal luster, the radiance of a woman not yet aware of her powers, or of the fingernail-digging strength she will need to survive.

As she became more of a star, she was less inclined to do anything unpleasant, anything that might antagonize her audience; she thus compounded a weakness already inherent in the woman's film. But it was a paradoxical progression: If she was always morally righteous at the expense of libertine recklessness, it was also a form of security, of self-possession in which she no longer felt the need to flirt with and flatter men. The message behind the progression is not reassuring, for it tells us that a woman can't be both feminine and successful. As Crawford ceases to use her charms, she becomes less "attractive" to men; she becomes tougher and professionally driven. She becomes a "woman's woman," but as such she transgresses the etiquette and basic social laws of woman's dependency; and so her toughness is exaggerated as if to punish her and, in a vicious circle, she becomes even less sexually appealing.

Crawford, in the transition from glamour girl to self-reliant woman, reveals not just what a woman must do once her sexual commodities are no longer in demand, but suggests that a terrible loss is sustained in the process. For a woman trading on her looks, survival and adaptability are gained at a price, the price of the inner self, the core, the continuum that exists in most men unaltered by phases or changes of life. It is something men are born with, or given a sense of almost at birth; it is the bedrock sense of self on which they build. But women, when they gear their lives to men and neglect their own inner resources, are caught short by the aging process and must suddenly develop in ways that could not have been foreseen. Thus the fragmentation of a woman's character, given symbolical and perhaps not altogether witting expression in Crawford's performance in *Possessed*. As a woman obsessed by her love for a callous architect (Van Heflin), a conscientious nurse to a rich man's wife, wife to that man (Raymond Massey) when the wife dies, suspect in the murder of the wife, mistrusted stepmother of Massey's wild daughter (Geraldine Brooks), and finally distraught murderer of Van Heflin, she encompasses vastly more facets than are strictly required by the "split personality" that is the subject of the film, one of the clinically oriented movies about psychoanalysis that were so popular in the forties. For reasons that are partly the fault of script and direction, but not entirely, we begin to wonder which, if any, is the real Crawford, so perfectly does she become each successive role. There finally seems to be no connecting link, and the madwoman roaming the streets in the film's first sequence becomes a perfect expression of the end of the line, the total confusion and centerlessness for a woman in whom existence has replaced essence.

In *Mildred Pierce,* the lower-middle-class, greasy spoon, California milieu of the James Cain novel was upgraded and much of the point was lost. By refusing to muss herself up, physically and psychologically, Crawford took the guts out of the character and the class crunch out of the mother-daughter conflict. She became a dulcifluous housewife, whose only fault, if it could be so designated, was loving her daughter too much. The obsession with the daughter (Ann Blyth), with its erotic implications, is the most fascinating aspect in the movie, since it is a veiled expression of self-love, and takes on the aspect of narcissism that is the ultimate Crawford posture.

Even Mildred's competence in the business world, radical enough, perhaps, for its time, is not a sign of independence sought for its own sake, but of initiative in the service of family (or of self-love pervertedly disguised). Mildred's ambitions are for some "higher purpose" than self-fulfillment. Her words to Pierce, her first husband, elided into one sesquipedalian word, might stand as the motto of the woman's film: "I'lldoanythingforthosekidsdoyouunderstandanything," she says, packing another homemade pie into a box for delivery.

Eve Arden's role in *Mildred Pierce* also tells us much. In the film she plays her characteristic role of the smart, cheerfully bitter woman, sidekick to the heroine and running commentator on the cruelties and stupidity of men. In many ways, her character is the most treacherously and heartbreakingly sexist of all. Independent, witty, intelligent, a true friend to her own sex and of all women the most apparently "complete" within herself, she is made to talk constantly and longingly of men, to deprecate her own powers of attraction, to place greater emphasis on sex than all the silly ninny sex objects who have nothing else to live for, in short, constantly to bemoan her "incompleteness." She thus becomes the greatest feather in the cap of male vanity. In what is an obvious contradiction of her true nature—for her relationship with Crawford is close, generous, and satisfying—she confirms the male (and, derivatively, female) idea that a bunch of women together are at best incomplete, if not downright silly.

Even more insidious is her portrayal as being "out of the running" romantically and sexually, while she is the most

Facing page: Jean Arthur commands the attention of the Senate in Capra's *Mr. Smith Goes to Washington* (this master shot does not appear in the film).

Rosalind Russell, in Howard Hawks' *His Girl Friday,* holding her own with her cynical "ex"-editor and "ex"-husband played by Cary Grant, whose unscrupulousness knows no bounds when confronted with the prospect of losing not just a wife but his star reporter.

Beautiful, independent women like Scarlett O'Hara (Vivien Leigh) and Laura (Gene Tierney) gravitate to men like Ashley (Leslie Howard, *top left*) and Waldo Lydecker (Clifton Webb, *top right*), romantic and sexually neutral figures whom they can "manage"; afraid of losing the thin thread of control, they resist the sexual appeal of Clark Gable's Rhett Butler (*bottom left*) and Dana Andrews' Brooklyn cop (*bottom right*).

Right: A devastating scene near the end of Max Ophuls' *Letter from an Unknown Woman* as Joan Fontaine, arriving at the apartment of the man she has loved all her life, finds he doesn't even remember her.

Top left: Back Street, one of the staples of the "woman's film," wa made three times, in 1932, 1941, and 1961. In the 1941 version, Margaret Sullavan is a career woman who sacrifices herself to Charles Boyer. *Bottom left:* Joan Crawford in Otto Preminger's *Dais Kenyon* (a shining example, in the "woman's film," of the "choice" genre). The happiness of Dana Andrews' lawyer and Henry Fonda's bo designer hangs by a thread as they await Daisy's decision, and Daisy looks off into the distance and thinks "What fools these mortals be!"

outspoken and least puritanical of women. There is, by implication, something "improper" in the woman (Aline MacMahon often plays the same type) who actually expresses sexual desire, and an ability to handle it, and a light touch, so that she must be denied getting the man, while the coy, hard-to-get virgin wins the prize. There is something as disheartening as it is brave in her acceptance of the status quo, for she is using her brains to deprecate their importance and downgrading her friendships with women as second-best arrangements.

Generally—and typically—the only films that allowed dignity to working women were those based on historical figures, real-life women, the singularity (and therefore non-applicability) of whose achievement would not make them a threat to men. Or to other women. Mme Curie and Amelia Earhart would hardly start a rush on women scientists and aviatrixes, or, being dead, intimidate the living with their accomplishments. In *Blossoms in the Dust,* Greer Garson's dedicated woman battling to erase the stigma of illegitimacy from birth certificates (based on a historical case) is no problem. Yet, despite the safety of the nineteenth-century milieu, Katharine Hepburn's feminist in *A Woman Rebels* was too threatening. The film flopped and ushered in her period of "box-office poison."

Hepburn was one of the few, if not the only, actresses allowed to sacrifice love for career, rather than the other way around. The explanation usually offered is that her arrogance and eccentricity exempted her: She was neither a "regular guy" (in fact, she never won any popularity prizes in Hollywood) nor a representative of the American woman. Even in *Morning Glory,* where she gave up love for her theatrical career, the implication was that she would turn into a dried-up, defeminized old lady. And even in the hands of a sympathetic director like George Stevens or Cukor or Hawks, there was a cutting edge to her parts as written, a kind of ruthless, upper-class eccentricity, that was more a revenge on, than an expression of, her personality. In *Woman of the Year,* her cosmopolitan political reporter is pitted against Spencer Tracy's no-nonsense, boys-in-the-back-room sports reporter. Their enchanting interplay (this was their first film together) creates a sense of complementary natures and equality which is gradually eroded, then cruelly and dishonestly shattered, as Hepburn's "weaknesses"—her drive, her lack of interest in creating a home and family—are belabored and blackened while Tracy's faults —his philistinism, his "old-fashioned" American values— are softened and colored as virtues by comparison. In *The Philadelphia Story,* she is attacked from all sides for her supposed coldness (for real coldness, see Grace Kelly in the fifties' musical version, *High Society*), of which there is not a shred of evidence. This is the furtive revenge of mediocrity on excellence; she is being convicted merely for being a superior creature. In *Alice Adams,* she is bitten by the most antipathetic and unattractive bug of them all, social climbing, and she manages to make it seem like the most charming of aspirations. In *Bringing Up Baby,* she is impervious to the havoc she wreaks on poor Cary Grant. But through all these films, she refuses to be humiliated or look ugly. Her combined integrity, intelligence, and proud, frank beauty rise to the surface, making us feel, with her, the difficulty and joy of being such a woman. A scene which is consummate Hepburn in its mingling of pride and vulnerability and the young, still-searching-for-herself woman, occurs during the courtship on the porch in *Alice Adams,* when she asks Fred MacMurray what his impression of her is, what he would like her to be. At this moment, as she looks into his eyes, she would willingly become what he wants, just as every girl is always shaping and reshaping her image according to her reflection in a man's eyes. Here she reveals the terrible, chameleon aspect of a woman's life, the necessity

of adapting to others' needs, in constant, cosmetic metamorphosis, rather than finding and remaining true to the
hard-core changeless being of the inner self. This is the
trembling, smiling readiness Hepburn expresses (the terrified eagerness of a woman for psychological rape, as for her
first sexual experience), and yet her entire life and persona
suggest exactly the opposite and are a victory over this.
She evolved, developed, played different parts, and in remaining true to her intractable self, made some enemies.
And she made life difficult for those who believed that a
woman could not be brilliant and beautiful, and ambitious
and feminine at the same time.

Women have been caught between Scylla and Charybdis.
Just as Hepburn was ridiculed in *Woman of the Year* for
not paying enough attention to the home, Rosalind Russell,
the heroine of *Craig's Wife,* was criticized for devoting too
much attention to the home, valuing its contents more than
people. In *Roughly Speaking,* the Rosalind Russell wife is
more ambiguous—a demoness of energy (childbearing and
otherwise) beside whom even her second husband (her first,
feeling superfluous, left), an indefatigable entrepreneur,
pales.

At the other end of the spouse spectrum, no less monstrous in her way, is Dorothy McGuire as *Claudia,* the helpless and adorably incompetent child-wife. Made from the
successful Broadway play by Rose Franken, the film, directed
by Edmund Goulding, was a hit and inspired a sequel,
Claudia and David, also starring Dorothy McGuire and
Robert Young. McGuire is the neurotic housewife whose
arsenal of charms and eccentricities seems an unconscious
device to postpone direct contact with her husband, and
whose fixation on her mother is transferred, after the
mother's death, to her own son. It is impossible to imagine
the husband and wife having any real communion, verbal or
sexual, "offstage," and the dynamics of both films spring

from the relationship between the women: Dorothy McGuire and Ina Claire in the first, Dorothy McGuire and Mary Astor in the second. Claudia's total and loving dependence on her mother, played by Ina Claire, becomes, like child obsession for other "woman's film" heroines, the relationship which takes all the emotional energy from her marital responsibilities (both sexual and spiritual) and from her own, indefinitely postponed growing up. Dorothy McGuire is irresistible in the part. One hears, in her slightly cracked, desperately pleading voice, the admission, for so many American women, of a complete unpreparedness for married life. And, with the fear of sex that has been inculcated in her, and the pressure to be a perfectionist housekeeper, who can blame her for reverting to a state of childlike helplessness in which she will not have to perform sexually or domestically? But these subterfuges only increase her self-contempt. Seeing that she cannot even perform these trivial chores (while her husband has his interesting work and masters "important" challenges), she is quite ready to believe that he could be lured by another, more interesting woman.

With McGuire, as with so many women's film heroines, what moves—even convulses—us is not her self-pity but, on the contrary, her absolute refusal to feel sorry for herself. We supply what these heroines hold back. Who can help weeping all the tears refused by the laughing-on-the-outside bravura of Bette Davis in *Dark Victory* or Margaret Sullavan in everything; the cheerfully stoical Irene Dunne in *Love Affair* or Susan Hayward in *My Foolish Heart*.

Given the fictional necessity of woman's self-sacrifice— a premise we rightly challenge today—the heroine's attitude was often resolute and brave, an act of strength rather than helplessness. Nor did she deal in the eternal hope and the endless postponements of tragedy provided by soap opera. Rather, hers was a more exacting and fatalistic form of "escape," in which certain steps or nonsteps were decisive and irrevocable. In *When Tomorrow Comes,* Irene Dunne plays a waitress to Charles Boyer's concert pianist. For their last dinner together, wearing a dress on which she has spent six months' wages, she sits conversing cheerfully, knowing she will never see him again. In *Only Yesterday,* John Boles has an affair with Margaret Sullavan and, unbeknownst to him, gets her pregnant. He goes off to war, she brings up the child, and that is the last she hears of him . . . until one day years later, she runs into him at a New Year's Eve party and he doesn't remember her at all. The ultimate nightmare of a man's (husband's, lover's) "forgetfulness." She goes and spends the night with him without reminding him.

A similar situation occurs in *Letter from an Unknown Woman,* Max Ophuls' 1949 masterpiece, in which Joan Fontaine loses her head and heart, first as a young girl, then as an adult, over concert pianist Louis Jourdan. The film, adapted by Howard Koch from a novel by Stefan Zweig, is framed by the letter in which a dying Fontaine informs Jourdan of her love for him, and, in awakening his honor, seals his death. They had an affair—one of many for him—but were separated. She has his child and in order to provide the boy with security, makes a comfortable marriage; Jourdan meanwhile continues his life of women and dissipation. One night a long time later, she encounters him after an opera; he asks her to come to his apartment the following night, and she accepts, knowing that if she goes, she will never be able to return to her husband. She arrives at the appointed time, begins talking to him, and, waiting tremulously for the reconciliation, suddenly realizes that he doesn't recognize her, that she is just another pretty woman and he hasn't the faintest idea who she is.

The exquisite pain of this scene, of her humiliating surrender to a love that is so unreciprocated, is balanced, in Ophuls' vision and sublimely sensitive direction, by the sense of Jourdan's general depletion and decline, but mainly by the counterweight of Fontaine's obsessiveness, the stubbornness of her will to love this one man against all reason and logic, her certainty that she can "save" him; by that total defiance of social rules, she becomes not only the architect of her fate, but the precipitator of her downfall, and thus a tragic heroine. She is radical in her refusal to follow the "normal" path of a woman's destiny—to stop dreaming once she has married the proper man and settled down. Similarly the Danielle Darrieux character in Ophuls' great French film, *Madame de* (note the anonymity of the women in both titles, their exemption from names and social identities) forgoes the duties and pleasures of a normal wife, first out of vanity and lovelessness, finally out of the love for which she dies. In their abrogation of ordinary responsibilities, both women become outlaws, militarists of love, heroic and cruel. From the opening of *Madame de,* when Darrieux is examining her clothes and jewels to determine which she will pawn, to the end in which the earrings are consecrated to God and her soul symbolically redeemed, she undergoes the tortures of love and, through the consequences of her habitual frivolity, the loss of that love, finally to attain the stature of a saint, as the movie attains the stature of great art.

What Ophuls shows is that he, like the ceremonial Boyer–Darrieux marriage, like the woman's film itself, is only superficially superficial. For what greater conflict can there be within woman than that between what she conceives of as a biologically rooted duty and her spiritual wish to be free? And, like the greatest directors, Ophuls reveals this deep conflict through surfaces: through the endless movements of camera, and characters within a fixed society, he captures the inner movement of the soul in its rare, solitary passage to tragedy and grace.

The woman's film reaches its apotheosis under Ophuls

and Douglas Sirk in the late forties and fifties, at a time when the genre was losing its mass audience to television soap opera. Eventually women-oriented films, like the women-oriented plays from which many of them were adapted, disappeared from the cultural scene. The derisive attitude of the eastern critical establishment won the day and drove them out of business. But at one time the "matinee audience" had considerable influence on movie production and on the popularity of certain stars. This influence has waned to the point that the only films being made for women are the afternoon soaps, and there is very little attempt to appeal to women in either regular films or nighttime television.

Where are the romantic idols who made their reputations on their appeal to women, the John Barrymores and Leslie Howards to whom women offered themselves in marriage? To Robert Redford and Paul Newman, who might conceivably be thought of as their successors, women, when they bother, send only billet-doux. But like most of their colleagues, Redford and Newman would rather be "real people" than actors, and would rather be "real actors" than romantic leads. So instead of playing opposite beautiful women in love stories of civilized narratives, they play opposite each other in *Butch Cassidy and the Sundance Kid* and romance takes on a whole new twist. They are on their way to becoming the Myrna Loy–William Powell of the seventies.

Women respond to them perhaps because they represent the wine of the old romance in a new bottle. It is the rapport between Newman and Redford in *Butch Cassidy* rather than between either one of them and Katharine Ross, that has all the staples—the love and loyalty, the yearning and spirituality, the eroticism sublimated in action and banter, the futility and fatalism, the willingness to die for someone—

of women's fantasies as traditionally celebrated by the woman's film.

The woman's film, its themes appropriated by the man's film, has died out, and with it a whole area of heterosexual feeling and fantasy. For the woman's film, like other art forms, pays tribute at its best (and at its worst) to the power of the imagination, to the mind's ability to picture a perfect love triumphing over the mortal and conditional. Fontaine's and Darrieux's obsessions become leaps into immortality. The lovers in *Back Street* are finally united—in the resurrection of filmed time. In *Peter Ibbetson,* Ann Harding and Gary Cooper, separated by prison walls, live their love in their dreams and in the bowery radiance of Lee Garmes' cinematography. They are transfixed at the sublime moment of their love (denying yet improving on reality) by the power of the imagination, by the screen, and by their permanence in our memories.

THE FORTIES

In the dark melodramas of the forties, woman came down from her pedestal and she didn't stop when she reached the ground. She kept going—down, down, like Eurydice, to the depths of the criminal world, the *enfer* of the *film noir*— and then compelled her lover to glance back and betray himself. Sometimes she sucked him down with her, like Rita Hayworth in *The Lady from Shanghai,* or Jane Greer in *Out of the Past,* or Barbara Stanwyck in *Double Indemnity.* Sometimes she used him and laughed in his face, like Joan Bennett in *Scarlet Street.* Sometimes, like Ava Gardner in *The Killers,* she let him take the rap for her and then, to show her gratitude, double-crossed him not once but twice. Sometimes she lied and lied and lied, like Mary Astor in *The Maltese Falcon,* or sold him out, like Maureen O'Hara in *Fallen Sparrow,* or Janis Carter in *Framed,* and, like Humphrey Bogart and John Garfield and Glenn Ford, he forgot he was a gentleman and sent her up. Sometimes she wasn't crooked, just a little out of line, like Lauren Bacall in *The Big Sleep,* or Rita Hayworth in *Gilda.* Sometimes she was a murderess and tried to bluff her way through, like Bette Davis in *The Letter* or Alida Valli in *The Paradine Case.* Sometimes she was a *femme fatale* like Rita Hayworth in *Blood and Sand,* who lured Tyrone Power away from Linda Darnell; or like Linda Darnell—getting her revenge and a bad-girl part to boot—in *Fallen Angel,* luring Dana Andrews *into* a marriage with Alice Faye, to get Faye's money. Sometimes she was a cool, enigmatic career girl, like Gene Tierney in *Laura,* who could tease the life out of some poor Dodgers' fan of a cop, or just psychotic, like Tierney in *Whirlpool.* Sometimes she was crazy in love enough to kill herself and her lover, like Jennifer Jones in *Duel in the Sun.* Sometimes she was possessed by an evil spirit, like Simone Simon in *The Cat People* and Edith Barrett in *I Walked with a Zombie.* Later (under the moralistic force of the fifties) she sometimes crossed over to good, like Gloria Grahame in *The Big Heat*; or, like Jean Peters in *Pickup on South Street,* diverted her man from evil. But even then she knew where she had come from and where she belonged.

She had sensual lips, or long hair that, passing over her face like Veronica Lake's, cast a shadow of moral ambiguity. Angel or devil, good-bad or bad-good girl, she was a change from the either/or—heroine or villainess—of the twenties and thirties. But for all her guts and valor, and for all her unredeemable venality (and she is especially refreshing after the goody-goody heroines who persuaded the wrongdoing man to go to jail and "pay his debt to society"), she hadn't a soul she could call her own. She was, in fact, a male fantasy. She was playing a man's game in a man's world of crime and carnal innuendo, where her long hair was the equivalent of a gun, where sex was the equivalent of evil. And where her power to destroy was a projection of man's feeling of impotence. Only this could never be spelled out; hence the subterfuge and melodrama. She is to her thirties' counterpart as night—or dusk—is to day. And the difference between their worlds, between the drawing room of romantic comedy and the underground of melodrama, is the difference between flirtation and fornication . . . or rape.

Under the heading of the "treacherous woman," one of the most striking phenomena of the forties, were actresses like Hayworth, Darnell, Jean Peters, Eve Arden, Ann Sothern, Lana Turner, Dorothy Malone. Filmwriter Ian Cameron has dubbed them "dames," but whatever the name, they played women of dubious ethics or unconventional femininity who were as likely to be found on the wrong side of the law as not. Or they were women like Lizabeth Scott, a kind of blonde Joan Crawford, who weren't necessarily evil themselves, but whose very presence seemed to invite evil. Every time she appeared, the atmosphere became heavy, and we knew that trouble, big trouble, was ahead.

If the treacherous woman is the most interesting, she is not the only female figure of the forties. The demarcation line between decades is never distinct. The Indian Summer of the thirties lasted into the forties as, conversely, there had been an advance chill of the forties in the thirties. The usual Hollywood time lag accounts for Depression-related comedies and melodramas being produced well into the late thirties, just as World War II films continued to be released into the late forties. In many films, the collective spirit of the thirties met the war camaraderie of the forties and the screen sagged with the combined sentimentality.

The spirit of screwball comedy took a darker turn but it

did not go flat with the last bubbles of thirties' champagne. Howard Hawks and Leo McCarey continued in their inimitable vein, and with romantic comedies like *Café Society, Take a Letter, Darling,* and *Remember the Night,* Mitchell Leisen provided the transitional link between the Paramount of the thirties and the more mordant Paramount of the forties—that of Preston Sturges and Billy Wilder. But beneath the cynicism and through the sensationalism, there was a layer of sentiment soggier than anything seen in the thirties. Often the optimism was false: Superimposed, it created a kind of neurotic tension. Films like *Mr. Skeffington* oscillate wildly in mood, from high to low comedy to pseudo-tragedy. Woman's films were more lachrymose than ever, drawing on that reservoir of tears, always close to the surface, created by the war. War wives and waiting women (Claudette Colbert and family in *Since You Went Away*) were stock figures, inspirational characters from whom no gesture of courage or patience or undying fidelity was considered excessive. This was the war that everyone believed in.

The waiting women were matched in fortitude only by the fighting women—Claudette Colbert, once again, with Paulette Goddard and Veronica Lake in *So Proudly We Hail.* As nurses living, loving, and dying behind enemy lines, they didn't all survive to tell the tale, but their heroism was enough to awe their male confederates. The large number of woman's films, war and otherwise, was a practical way of handling the shortage of men in Hollywood and the nation at large during the war. And they were given positions of authority, in the war and at home, in films and out, that they would be unwilling to relinquish.

A few "leading-man" types had to service the whole galaxy of women stars. In the pictures they were in, they rarely emerged from the shadows. In *So Proudly We Hail,* the appearances of Colbert's boyfriend, played by George Reeves, are kept to a minimum (he no sooner returns to the base for a reunion than he is dispatched on another mission); in one nighttime scene, as she is bidding him farewell in a dugout, his face is barely visible in the darkness while her profile (the left, as always) is bathed in light from the single source.

For every hard-boiled dame there was a soft-boiled sweetheart, and for every tarnished angel an untarnished one. June Allyson is every bit as characteristic of the forties as Joan Crawford. Indeed, the smiling, quavering blonde and the stony-faced brunette were sisters under the skin. The emotional hysteria of the one and the mercenary calculation of the other were both preludes to the great sacrificial gesture: One leans, one is leaned upon; one is surrounded by real invalids and cripples, one by emotional invalids and cripples. Both, in playing nursemaid to the world, were at least as neurotic as their patients.

Often, one seemed to express elements of the other. June Allyson, Olivia de Havilland, Judy Garland, Dorothy McGuire, Margaret Sullavan, Greer Garson were the sunny side of a decade whose underside included Davis, Hayworth, Lake, et al. But beneath the optimistic smiles and cheerful philosophy of the sweet heroines was a note of fatalism, betrayed in their voices—those tearful, supplicating, heartbreaking wails just this side of convulsion. The sense of living on the emotional edge, and the precarious control just beneath the (excessive) effervescence, created a feeling of peril more disquieting than the open malevolence of the bad girls. There were a few actresses—Vivien Leigh, Jennifer Jones—who crossed back and forth, who were sweetness and light one minute and devils incarnate the next, suggesting that their innocence was sheer hypocrisy. Or that their sensuality was.

A note of pessimism, whether explicit in the *films noirs* or suggested in the suppressed hysteria and emotional disproportion of the sentimental films, colors the forties. Toward the latter half of the decade, we are no longer steering our feet to the sunny side of the street, but are pulled irresistibly to the other, where the sidewalk ends. There is a feeling of social disaffection, a glimpse of criminal tracks running parallel to ordinary society not, as in the thirties, with the option of jumping back into the mainline, but continuing forever alongside and outside.

The image of woman, like the (more multifarious) image of man, takes its shadings from the general *Zeitgeist*: in this case, the alternating optimism/pessimism, and even boredom, over the war, the paranoia of the postwar anti-Communist furor, and, from the standpoint of sexual politics, the influx of women into the job market (and their obvious success). The latter surely contributed to that sense of instability, of dis-ease and even impotence that lurked beneath the surface of male characters and charged the atmosphere with a tension not entirely accounted for by plot. Meanwhile, in that odd way that the spirit of an age and its technology have of converging into an "aesthetic," German Expressionism was being assimilated, somewhat belatedly but still in time to express the *angst* of the age. *Citizen Kane* was but the first and most influential film to employ stylized lighting and strained camera angles to create a brooding, Gothic ambience, a subjective world of distrust that enveloped women as well as men.

In the thirties, the sense of equality and mutuality between romantic leads seemingly grew out of (or found perfect expression in) classical style and editing, symmetrical two-shot compositions, the contribution of women coscenarists, and the peculiarities of the star system. In the forties, the male-female equilibrium wavers without quite collapsing.

New and unexpected pairings, triplings, quadruplings take the place of the star duets. The chemistry, which begins to weaken in the fifties and sixties, is still there, but in different proportions and compounds, less romantic and less innocent, sexier and more perverse.

In the thirties, it was Boyer and Dunne, or Grant and Hepburn, who were the luminous couples destined to hook up. Other people—friends, rivals—were mere satellites, invisible, unimportant, or even ridiculous (like the fiancées in *Bringing Up Baby, Swing Time, Holiday, The Awful Truth*). Poor Ralph Bellamy: As the supererogatory whose dullness provided the foil for stars to shine, and as the alternative whereby women learned that their original choice wasn't so bad, he could have started a one-man liberation movement.

In the forties, the scorecard becomes muddled, and the third party may pose a threat or a real alternative. The intimidating ghost of *Rebecca*; the photo-finish race of the rivals, Cary Grant and Jimmy Stewart, in *The Philadelphia Story*; Paul Henreid's stature as Ingrid Bergman's husband in *Casablanca*; Claude Rains' even greater stature as her husband in *Notorious*; Joan Crawford's men in *Mildred Pierce* and *Daisy Kenyon*; Humphrey Bogart's girls in *High Sierra*. There are a number of films where there are no women at all, and others, like the *films noirs,* that are chockfull of them. In movies like *Johnny O'Clock, The Big Sleep,* and *Out of the Past,* women come out of the woodwork—tough women, good women, bad women—to haunt the detective or hero.

Even when the movies are adaptations of plays or novels written earlier, it is significant that, having been made in the forties, they take on its peculiar colorations. The trust that accompanied attraction is a thing of the past. Instead, relationships are rooted in fear and suspicion, impotence and

inadequacy: Charles Boyer driving Ingrid Bergman mad
in *Gaslight*; Joan Fontaine misunderstanding Laurence
Olivier's brooding in *Rebecca* and Cary Grant's deviousness
in *Suspicion*. In each of these films we find, in the ease with
which the men intimidate the women, an identification on the
part of the director (Cukor in *Gaslight* and Hitchcock in
Suspicion and *Rebecca*) with the woman's point of view,
with the peculiar susceptibility of women who have so little
self-confidence that they are only too ready to accept the most
sinister designs, ill-will, or indifference from their husbands.
The directors suggest, moreover, that cruelty and coldness
are indispensable elements in the fascination these men hold
for these particular women. Bergman remains under Boyer's
spell—indeed, most completely surrenders to its sexual implications—*after* she has discovered his true nature. Fontaine,
as the "ugly duckling" in *Suspicion,* is masochism incarnate.
Her tremulous insecurity invites rejection; she can never
believe that Grant would really love her. In emphasizing
Fontaine's tendency to voluptuous masochism, Hitchcock
gives ominous overtones to casual incidents and suggests the
kinship of fear and desire, emotions that are always closely
allied in Hitchcock but nowhere more inextricably than in
this abject woman, at zero degree of self-esteem. She fears
(or desires?) murder (or rape?) by her husband, whose
every move not only acquires a double meaning, but awakens
in us conflicting emotions of horror and desire. Other films
of the forties are less sexual in their implications: Fritz
Lang's *Ministry of Fear,* in which Ray Milland suspects his
girlfriend of being a Nazi spy. But they all might stand as
parables of the paranoid forties. Even when the suspicion
proves unfounded, a doubt lingers which the happy ending
fails to dispel. The very fact that such fears could attach to
the beloved taints the relationship with a stain as difficult
to remove as blood (an analogy that is intrinsic to the visual

Top: Barbara Stanwyck's nightclub dancer/gangster's moll in Hawks' *Ball of Fire*, infusing life into a group of lexicographers with a conga line through the mausoleum where they have been working in all-male solitude to compile a dictionary. She also contributes a few words to their lexicon, under the heading "slang." *Bottom:* Women are central in a Hawks Western, even if they are there just to "break up" the boys and, as in *Rio Bravo*, wean one of them away. Angie Dickinson's Feathers chides John Wayne's Sheriff, as Bacall chided Bogart, for not having the brains or the guts to admit that, every once in a while, he needs help.

Top: Veronica Lake, one of the quintessential forties bad girls, in *This Gun for Hire* (1941), the first of several films she made with Alan Ladd in which she seduced, soothed, and sometimes betrayed him. *Bottom:* Jane Greer, in *Out of the Past,* as one of the most unforgettably rotten women of the forties who lures Mitchum into a plot thicker and more viscous than a swamp by night, and betrays both him and Kirk Douglas without so much as the flicker of an eyelash.

Facing page (top): The first meeting on screen of Lauren Bacall and Humphrey Bogart in Hawks' *To Have and Have Not.* Bogey has come into the room with Marcel Dalio to get something out of his desk when he is startled by a voice at the door: "Anybody got a light?" *Bottom:* Spencer Tracy keeping pace with his two jogging "properties"— Aldo Ray and Katharine Hepburn— in the Cukor-Gordon-Kanin *Pat and Mike.*

Above: Bette Davis as the terrible Rosa
Moline and Dona Drake as a dark-skinned
mirror image of her in Vidor's *Beyond
the Forest.* Davis has no use for the "dump"
she presides over with her mealy-mouthed
doctor-husband (Joseph Cotten), but yearns
to go to Chicago, to which end she risks
not only the spite and ridicule of the
townspeople, but those of the audience as
well. *Right:* June Allyson, clear-eyed and
tremulous, as the "waiting woman," the
other characteristically forties heroine, here
waiting wistfully for her baseball-playing,
amputee husband Jimmy Stewart, in *The
Stratton Story.* They also serve . . .

vocabulary of Hitchcock, to his feeling for the similarity between sexual and homicidal impulses).

Where once sexual antagonism was a game, a pretext, a holding action until the underlying affinity could emerge, attraction is now the illusion, the decoy, the duplicitous facade. Billy Wilder's *Double Indemnity* (vastly altered in the Chandler screenplay from the Cain novel) takes this convention to its lurid and logical conclusion with Barbara Stanwyck's black widow and Fred MacMurray's hooked insurance agent shooting each other in a final embrace. In most of her shady-lady roles, Stanwyck was a rare blend of toughness and femininity, lawlessness and virtue. She was a grownup, she knew who she was and what she wanted by the time she fell in love. In *Ball of Fire* she was a nightclub dancer and gangster's moll, in Preston Sturges' *The Lady Eve,* a card shark and classy adventuress who hooks an innocent Fonda. But nothing prepared us for the blonde wig and black heart of Phyllis Dietrichson, a dame with no redeeming qualities by Hollywood moral standards, but by aesthetic standards, quite sizable ones: intelligence, humor, and even an eleventh-hour reflex to love. She is a Southern California *femme fatale.* Just as Lillian Gish is an adaptation of the Victorian virgin to American soil, Stanwyck is a "corruption" of the European *femme fatale*: She is allied not with the dark forces of nature, but with the green forces of the capitalist economy. But her attraction to MacMurray's Neff is genuinely sexual, or sexual-homicidal (sex being the equivalent of evil, evil the metaphor for sex)—until the moment when, having just shot him in the shoulder, she drops the gun, acknowledging that her attraction has turned into love.

The impotence that, in a sharp and rather ingenious essay, Parker Tyler offered as explanation for Neff's character and which accounts for certain under-the-surface tensions (in both the relationship with Stanwyck and that with Edward G. Robinson as his boss) can be seen, in a wider and less narrowly sexual way to be at the source of the fear and paranoia, the misogyny and mistrust, of forties' melodrama. The intensely sexual suspicions of the forties obviously have some correlation—whether as cause or effect—in actual sexual apprehension, in a vision of the opposite sex as treacherous and intimidating. But *Double Indemnity,* like most of Wilder's films, is a crisscross of credulousness and cynicism, and a compound of homosexual and heterosexual feelings that culminate in the emblematic figure of Stanwyck as glorious monster.

Heterosexual attraction, whatever its neurotically Freudian roots, still exists in films like *Suspicion, Gaslight, Notorious, Double Indemnity,* but on different terms than attractions of thirties' romances. Suspicion is its own magnet, exerting as strong and sublimated a pull as ever the frustrations and obstacles of the screwball comedies did. A kill is just a kiss. But the difference is that the terms are no longer equal and bisexual but masculine, violent, and phallic. The rites of love are enacted not through the civilized art of verbal exchange (unless it is a verbal exchange that is a sexual duel, like the first encounter between Stanwyck and MacMurray in *Double Indemnity* and the "Officer" dialogue that ends with "that tears it"), but mutely, at gunpoint. With the increasing restrictiveness of the Production Code and the rise of sentimentality, those romantic comedies that did get by were smothered in coyness and prudery. Only violent melodramas could preserve a feeling for the low-down language of sex, disguised, as it was, in plot conventions of mystery and betrayal. The guilt for sexual initiative, and faithlessness, was projected onto woman; she became the aggressor by male design and in male terms, and as seen by the male in highly subjective narratives, often recounted in the first person and using interior monologue, by which she was deprived of her point of view.

Partly, this was a reaction against the boy-meets-girl glibness of the thirties, a realization that relations weren't always easy. With the collapse of the binary system, actors and actresses were more defined by sexual identity, standing apart as "men's men," "women's women," and as "men's women." Ida Lupino, Jennifer Jones, Linda Darnell were men's women, though not all "dames" were: Mary Astor and Eve Arden were women's women, and Barbara Stanwyck was both. Nor were all romantic heroines men's women. Vivien Leigh was, but Margaret Sullavan was both a man's woman and a woman's woman. Men's women share certain characteristics, one of which is that they share nothing with other women. Their long hair, like "bedroom eyes," gives the right signal, that they are enigmatic and available. The *film noir* is a French term, and the dark women of the forties are closer in their redolent sensuality to European models than the women of any other decade. These actresses generally have one salient feature, or sign (like, but aside from, the long hair) signifying sexual promise: lips, hips, legs, or breasts. Rita Hayworth's lips, Jennifer Jones' cheeks, Lauren Bacall's wide mouth and sideways-looking eyes.

They are nobody's fools, these women, but their smarts are devoted to getting what they can out of life—men and money (or more men and more money)—rather than to any high purpose or ideal. They compete for, rather than with, men, and when they pose a threat it is to a man's life rather than to his ego. The admiration we feel for the bold woman is often mitigated by our sense of her unscrupulousness. Whatever she does, she does not from conviction but from love, and in her ruthlessness she leaves the villains trailing in the dust.

It is not the evil in women, but the mutual exclusiveness of good and evil that we resent, since it is a way of converting women from their ambiguous reality into metaphors, visitations of an angel or a devil. If only the good woman and the bad woman weren't, in the extremes they represent, such mirror images of each other. If only men would understand, as Barbara Stanwyck explains it to Henry Fonda in *The Lady Eve* (knowing, by the note of resignation in her voice, that they never will), "that the best ones aren't as good as you think they are, and the bad ones aren't as bad . . . not nearly as bad."

If Vivien Leigh was the ultimate romantic bad-girl fantasy, Jennifer Jones was the ultimate sexual one—not as dear Bernadette or as the daughter in *Since You Went Away,* but in her King Vidor phase: as the tartish, hip-swinging, bosom-heaving, smudge-faced "Daisy Mae" of *Duel in the Sun* and *Ruby Gentry.* Like her modern counterpart Susan George in Sam Peckinpah's *Straw Dogs,* she exuded sex like a dog in heat, suggesting not so much a woman as a walking libido, a *machine à plaisir,* an orgone box with a woman's features. She represented for Vidor the sexual freedom of the lower classes or the dark-skinned races, not as they are in any cross section of life, but as they were in his own feverishly physical imagination; she stood as a reproach not to man's timidity, but to woman's. Unlike the Susan George character who, in a state of constant libidinous excitation, makes any man less than a sex fiend look like a fairy, Jennifer Jones' devotion is soul and body to her man, a devotion which makes the loves and compromises of the social folk around her look extremely pallid. She is unreal, even embarrassing, except in those outrageous moments when, like Stella Dallas, she explodes sexual stereotype, as in the magnificent erotic and romantic midnight ride on the beach with Charlton Heston in *Ruby Gentry* and the *liebestod* shoot-out on the cliff with Gregory Peck in *Duel in the Sun.* She rises to a wild magnificence as she gets her revenge on the two men who were "too good" for her. But in between these peaks her characteristic tagalong tigress is a confirmation of women's worst fears of men's most lubricious fantasies. That she doesn't get very far with the men she wants—Peck in *Duel,* Heston in *Ruby Gentry*—only makes her groveling more embarrassing, especially as Peck's bad boy and Heston's social climber are such low specimens. For the woman viewer, there is a special humiliation, a spiritual castration, tied to the spectacle of a woman clinging to a man who doesn't love her.

There are occasional exceptions to the everything-for-love bad girl: Ida Lupino, for instance, particularly in some of her Raoul Walsh movies. Lupino was tougher as an actress than as a director: the movies she made (*Hard, Fast, and Beautiful, The Bigamist, The Hitchhiker*) are conventional, even sexist; and in her interviews, like so many women who have nothing to complain about, she purrs like a contented kitten, arches her back at the mention of women's lib, and quotes Noël Coward to the effect that women should be struck regularly like gongs. But there is quite another side to her in her roles, an emotional, intuitively female, and yet tough side. In Walsh's *They Drive by Night* (a remake of *Border Town,* which had starred Bette Davis and Paul Muni) she plays the neurotic society woman who murders her husband because she is in love with a truck driver (George Raft). In *Ladies in Retirement,* she kills the old woman she works for to help out her two crazy sisters (Lupino is great on family feeling). In *The Hard Way,* directed by Vincent Sherman, she ruthlessly maneuvers to get her sister (Joan Leslie) out of the coal town in which they live. In *The Man I Love,* she goes to California to visit her sisters and brother, and ends by solving not only their problems but those of their next-door neighbors as well. And why not? She has more physical and emotional guts than any of the men around her.

But if Lupino came across in such films, some of the

credit must go to the director Raoul Walsh. Walsh's men, even his action heroes, are not swaggerers and have very little machismo. Because the men don't have to prove themselves, the women can take the initiative without emasculating them, can be tough and soft at the same time. Walsh plays one kind of woman off against the other, but without diminishing either. In *Strawberry Blonde* Jimmy Cagney falls in love with the town belle (Rita Hayworth), the archetypal adolescent sweetheart who appears once in every group, in every high school class, in every generation: a peaches-and-cream beauty, the queen of the prom who has every boy at her heels, the girl who makes the rest of us despair at how dumb boys are that they don't see through her. In her shadow, with her eye on Cagney, is Olivia de Havilland, the "free thinker" who doesn't believe in marriage and who states defensively that the penalty of having such ideas is "that you don't have many dates." The "right-ons" that are about to explode for de Havilland must be modified: Her progressive philosophy is but a veneer, a defense mechanism to avoid being hurt by her low grade in the popularity contest. She wants only to get married and have children. But even in this, in the proud vulnerability of the homely woman (although de Havilland never seems really vulnerable), her anguish strikes close to the pain of adolescence, illuminating the fearful conformity of American youth. And perhaps if there weren't that soul-destroying pressure for a girl to get married, her thinking might *really* be free, and her intellectualism a viable alternative.

Throughout the history of films, and the forties were no exception, women generally have been subsidiary to the action, to the profession, to the struggle between conscience and crime, between good and evil, with which a man's soul is engaged. And this has been true even of those films in which they have been romantically central. We can understand that the range of action open to women is limited, reflecting their limited operations in real life. But why have they so rarely experienced the moral dilemmas of real women? There have been very few heroines in literature who defined their lives morally rather than romantically, and likewise but a handful in film: Dreyer's women, Katharine Hepburn in *Adam's Rib*, Rosalind Russell in *His Girl Friday*, Liv Ullmann in *Persona*. There have been some (including Hepburn) who, in many of their films and without always realizing it, have had an instinctive moral appetite: Jean Arthur, Dietrich, Barbara Stanwyck, Mae West. But, below this level, actresses have played what might be called typically female roles, although with widely divergent results even within the same kind of role, so that disagreements abound. It may finally come down to personal taste—one may prefer Joan Fontaine, however masochistic, to Olivia de Havilland, however enterprising. Or one may prefer Mary Astor's "other woman" to the kinds of wives often played by Myrna Loy and Ruth Chatterton. What leads one to admire and respond to women, or to feel ashamed or humiliated by them, is not the situation—women have found themselves demeaned and degraded often enough in life —but the intrinsic dignity and autonomy accorded them. Our approval has everything to do with the degree to which a woman, however small her part, is seen to have an interior life: a continuum which precedes and succeeds her relationship with men and by which she, too, defeats time temporarily and transcends her biological fate.

Most characters, conceptually, are in that in-between area —neither degraded stereotypes nor striking originals—to which actresses bring their own personality (or lack of it) and directors their own prejudices. There is a subtle difference, for example, between a virago who seems to be one small, perhaps fascinating, slice of womanhood and one who, through exaggeration or the director's hidden hostility, seems to represent all women, and in whom we feel all women degraded.

Unfortunately, in recent times the most widely disseminated images of women have been those fashioned by directors who dislike women, nastiness being a more fashionable attitude than generosity. Orson Welles, John Huston, or, in the sixties, Stanley Kubrick, are in the mainstream of American misogyny: They are indifferent or hostile to women, get along better with men, whom they understand instinctively, and therefore devote more attention to in their films. Thus the Shakespeare plays—in fact all the plays—that Welles has directed in the theater or on film, have been "male" plays, plays with large male casts and male concerns: *Julius Caesar, Macbeth, Othello, Falstaff.* In *Citizen Kane,* the women are insignificant and no great credit to their sex. The most interesting and best-developed relationships in *Kane* are those between the men, along the shifting lines of power and loyalty; likewise in *Touch of Evil, The Trial,* and *Mr. Arkadin.*

In Welles' only two films that deal centrally with women, *The Magnificent Ambersons* and *The Lady from Shanghai,* women are responsible, either through too much love or too little, for the hero's tragic end. In *The Lady from Shanghai,* Rita Hayworth sings the siren song of gold, or compromise, or Hollywood success, and Welles' romantic fool follows. In *The Magnificent Ambersons,* young George (Tim Holt) is caught in the crossfire between Dolores Costello's beautiful, smothering mother, Agnes Moorehead's hysterical aunt, and Anne Baxter's ingenue. Monsters yes, but uninteresting no, although they must squeeze in after Welles' ego or alter ego has taken its place. The Dolores Costello character in *Ambersons* represents the enchanting mother figure at her most destructive, a woman not unlike the mother in D. H. Lawrence's *Sons and Lovers* (Mother of the Artist as a young

Oedipus) who in her youth and beauty and preference for her son to all other men reciprocally occupies a place in his heart which no other woman can fill and beside whose image they will all be judged lacking. This Freudian relationship, so significant in the male's subsequent attitude toward and emotional failure with women (as it was in Freud's case), and instrumental in the artist's vision of women, so often an impetus behind "genius" (from such a mother, Freud wrote, the son emerges with the "confidence of a conqueror"—but unable, he neglected to say, to envision women in any other role), is of obvious importance in so many women's roles in literature and cinema. Welles gives a subjective, brooding, more darkly Freudian reading to Booth Tarkington's 1918 novel, and makes the character of the mother and the son his own—to the point of having Tim Holt, an actor less attractive and more Wellesian than one imagines the protagonist of the novel, play him. Welles' rivalry with his father, also an inventor, which John Houseman claims to have been Welles' major unconscious drive, may explain the further weakening of the Oedipally important character, Eugene Morgan (the original lover of Isabel Amberson), by casting an unthreatening Joseph Cotten in the part.

Like *Sons and Lovers, Ambersons* emerges as a tribute to a mother who beneath a gracious, loving exterior is a demon of possessiveness and whose loveless marriage has driven her into a barely disguised erotic relationship with her son. The work of art and the woman become not just an autobiographical annotation, but a reliving of, even an improvement on, life, as the beautiful mother, idealized, banishes all competition and enters into an exclusive relationship with the son. Because she is the mother, she is sacred, beyond the reach of the younger woman who loves her son, whose jealousy will seem ridiculous and whose love will seem only selfish and mortal by comparison.

Far better, nevertheless, to play Jocasta in Welles' repertory than one of the Furies in John Huston's menagerie of grotesques. Horses are another matter, and to them go the choice parts and the superior sensibilities. Were it possible for a woman to metapsychose into a horse, the way Jane Fonda did in Roger Vadim's *Metzengerstein,* then she would be assured a place of honor in Huston's films. As it is, not only is she left with the crumbs, she has to sing for them. One of the most degrading scenes in cinema occurs in *Key Largo,* when Edward G. Robinson makes Claire Trevor, his boozy mistress and an ex-singer, suffer (and the audience suffer with her) through a torch song to get a drink. In a way meant to remind us of her better days, she gets through all the verses and then he tells her, "It wasn't good enough." With Huston's women—hard-drinking, hard-talking whores and barflies who are second cousins to the human shipwrecks of Tennessee Williams—we never do see the shadow of the former self; with his men we do. In however contrived a manner, the men are provided with a sense of the height from which they have fallen and thus with the prospect of redemption. None of this resonance attaches to his women, who are invented on the spot and as readily abandoned, like one-night stands in a strange city.

Huston's ethic, in all its rugged puerility, can be succinctly conveyed in a scene from *White Hunter, Black Heart,* a thinly fictionalized story about Huston by Peter Viertel, who wrote the screenplay of *The African Queen.* In London, before leaving on the African venture, the book's Huston-like hero expounds on his criterion of friendship: A friend is the person who would help you escape if you went to him after having committed a cold-blooded, premeditated murder; and he offers his own list, which includes a Sunset Boulevard madam, jockeys, playboys, and other glamorous misfits. The rest of the world, those who would try to confront and come to terms with what you had done, were, by implication, hopelessly square or, even worse, unsportsman-like. Most of Huston's women are not even in this despised category; they would rather betray than help. Even as betrayers, they are given little depth. Mary Astor as the mendacious Brigid in *The Maltese Falcon* radiates elegance and self-esteem, and is the noblest of Huston's ignoble swine, but even she is defined totally by her wickedness, as if the word "liar" exhausted all other possibilities, as if there were nothing further to be said. Huston's men, even when they are on a treadmill—where they prefer to be, rather than risk the precarious highs and lows of life with women—have several different gears. The women have only one—as can be seen in the gravel-voiced, lunging pathos of Jean Hagen's hanger-on (*The Asphalt Jungle*) or Claire Trevor's lush, or Susan Tyrrell's (Huston's latest dipsomaniac darling) in *Fat City*.

The preoccupation of most movies of the forties, par-ticularly the "masculine" genres, is with man's soul and sal-vation, rather than with woman's. It is man's prerogative to follow the path from blindness to discovery, which is the principal movement of fiction. In the bad-girl films like *Gilda* and *Out of the Past,* it is the man who is being cor-rupted, his soul which is in jeopardy. Women are not fit to be the battleground for Lucifer and the angels; they are something already decided, simple, of a piece. Donna Reed finally refused to make any more movies with Alan Ladd because he always had a scene (it was in his contract) in which he would leave the little woman in the outer office, or some equivalent, while he went off to deal with the Big Problem that only a man could handle. Even the musicals of the forties—the Donen–Kelly collaborations—concentrate on man's quest, on his rather than her story.

In the penumbral world of the detective story, based on the virile and existentially skeptical work of writers like Ham-mett, Chandler, Cain, and David Goodis (which found its way into crime films like *Dark Passage, The Blue Dahlia, Farewell My Lovely, Double Indemnity, I Wake Up Screaming,* and *The Big Sleep*), the proliferation of women— broads, dames, and ladies in as many shapes and flavors, hard and soft centers as a Whitman's sampler—was a way of not having to concentrate on a single woman, and again, of reducing woman's stature by siphoning her qualities off into separate women.

Although Howard Hawks would seem to fall into this tradition with *The Big Sleep,* in which he actually increases the number of women from the Chandler novel, there is something in the women and in Hawks' conception of them that suggests a real, if not entirely articulated, sense of a woman's point of view (or at least an antisexist point of view) that will become increasingly apparent in the work of this supposed "man's director." In contrast to most crime melodramas, where plot and its unraveling are all, the plot of *The Big Sleep* is next to incomprehensible, and the women are what it is all about: Lauren Bacall's sleek feline lead, Martha Vickers' spoiled, strung-out younger sister, Dorothy Malone's deceptively dignified bookstore clerk, Peggy Knudsen's petulant gangster's moll, and an unbilled woman taxi driver. Their lechery is as playful as the plot, and they are not stock figures of good and evil but surprisingly mixed and vivid, some of them in roles lasting only a few moments.

By including women in traditionally male settings (the newspaper office in *His Girl Friday,* the trapping party in *The Big Sky,* the big-game hunters in *Hatari!*), Hawks reveals the tension that other directors conceal or avoid by omitting women or by relegating them to the home. Many of Ford's thirties' and forties' films have no women in them at all, whereas even in Hawks' most rough-and-tumble, male-oriented films, the men are generally seen in relation to women, and women are the point of reference and exposition.

Hawks is both a product of sexual puritanism and male supremacy, and, in the evolution of his films and the alternation-compensation between tragedy and comedy, a critic of it. In the group experience of filmmaking, he lives out the homoerotic themes of American life, literature, and his own films. Thus, the John Wayne older-man figure in *Rio Bravo* and its companion Westerns seems finally to have developed into a "complete" man, to the point where he is able to go it alone, to find his self-esteem within himself rather than from the admiration of his friends, and to greet a "complete" woman on her own terms. Like most American men, Hawks and Ford and their protagonists become more at ease with women as they grow older. In his early adventure films, in which the women repeatedly break up male friendships and the men do little to resist what filmwriter Robin Wood has called the "lure of irresponsibility," Hawks betrays the sensibility of an arrested adolescent. His fear of woman is twofold: (1) as the emotional and "unmanly" side of human nature, and (2) as its progenitor. He is like the young boy who, in recoiling from his mother's kiss, refuses to acknowledge his debt of birth to her and who simultaneously fears revealing his own feelings of love and dependency.

In *Only Angels Have Wings,* Jean Arthur provides an alternative to the all-male world of stoical camaraderie on the one hand, and to the destructive femininity represented by Rita Hayworth on the other, but what an alternative! A man dies trying to land a plane in a storm in time for a date with her, she breaks down in defiance of the prevailing stiff-upper-lip ethic, and thereafter she hangs around like a puppy dog waiting for Cary Grant to fall in love with her. For female Hawksians, this is the film most difficult to accept, more difficult than the early films in which women figure only as devils *ex machina*. Although the relationship Jean Arthur offers Grant seems to have been conceived as something "different but equal," women feel it (as Hawks seems to have felt it) as second best. In the all-male community of civil aviators Grant heads up, the central relationship is the tacit, mutual devotion between Grant and Thomas Mitchell. In a milieu of constant, physical danger and sublimated feelings, Arthur's emotionalism is a threat—but it is also, or it is meant to be, a release. The trouble is that Arthur, deprived of the pepperiness and sense of purpose she has in her other thirties' and forties' films (or the sweetly misplaced glamour of *Easy Living*), becomes a sobbing stone around the collective neck of civil aviation; and she doesn't have the easy come–easy go sexual confidence with which Lauren Bacall and Angie Dickinson invest Slim and Feathers, Hawks' most sensually aggressive, European-style heroines. Still, technically, *Only Angels Have Wings* is a transition film. When Mitchell dies, Arthur takes his place, marking the progression of woman from second to first string.

Ball of Fire is a perfect fusion of Hawks' dialectics and those of Leigh, Brackett, and Wilder, who wrote the screenplay. When Barbara Stanwyck as a fast-talking gangster's moll invades the sanctuary of a group of lexicographers headed by Gary Cooper, it is as if Hawks had recognized the sclerotic danger of male camaraderie—and was resisting it. But Sugarpuss O'Shea is as much a Wilder–Brackett creation, a worldly, romantic sensualist who shakes up a group of typically American fuddy-duddies and "regenerates" them. Stanwyck is as emotionally responsive as Jean Arthur, but tougher; she brings her own world of jive and street talk with her, and manages to "corrupt" the ivory-tower purity of the scholars—and expand their vision. Her humanizing influence paves the way for the rapprochement of the sexes that occurs in Hawks' subsequent films, particularly in the Bogart–Bacall melodramas, and in the John Wayne–Angie Dickinson relationship in *Rio Bravo*. If the highest tribute

Hawks can pay a woman is to tell her she has performed like a man (Bogey's "You're good, you're awful good"), isn't that, at least partly, what the American woman has always wanted to be told? Hasn't she always wanted to join the action, to be appreciated for her achievements rather than for her sex? But one often seems to have been gained at the expense of the other, the performing excellence at the cost of the "womanly" awareness. Hawks' sensitivity to the American girl's anxiety, to her shame at "being a girl," expresses itself later in such fifties' characters as Charlene Holt in *Red Line 7,000,* and Paula Prentiss in *Man's Favorite Sport?* As actresses, and as characters, they lack the usual coordinates of "sex appeal"; both their athletic ability and their anxiety bespeak a lack of sexual confidence that is disturbingly real. In *Man's Favorite Sport?* it is Paula Prentiss who makes Rock Hudson take the plunge into the sport (fishing, or, on an allegorical level, sex) on which he is supposed to be an authority. He was written a "how to" book without ever having gotten his feet wet.

In Hawks' best films, there is a sense of playacting for real, of men and women thrusting themselves ironically at each other, auditioning for acceptance but finding out in the process who they really are. In *To Have and Have Not,* Bacall combines intelligence and sensuality, pride and submission. She holds her own. She is a singer and is as surrounded by her "musical world" as Bogart is by his underground one, and she combines with him to create one of the great perfectly balanced couples, as highly defined by fantasy and wit as Millamant and Mirabell in *The Way of the World,* or as Emma Woodhouse and Mr. Knightley in *Emma.* For the Hawks' heroine, the vocal quality, the facial and bodily gestures are the equivalent of the literary heroine's words, and with these she engages in a thrust-and-parry as highly inflected and intricate as the great love duels of literature.

The fable of *To Have and Have Not,* like so many of the action melodramas during the forties (for example, *Casablanca*) is that of the tough guy who "doesn't believe in" patriotic action or sticking his neck out, and who eventually sticks his neck out farther and more heroically than anyone else. In *To Have and Have Not,* it is Bogart's willingness to risk death, pshawing all the while, to bring a French Resistance fighter into Martinique, under the eyes of the Vichy government. But there is an additional, and even more important, meaning to the idea of involvement in Hawks, the involvement of a man with a woman, a scarier and deeper risk of oneself, perhaps, than death.

Typically, a man (in *Only Angels Have Wings, To Have and Have Not,* and *Rio Bravo*) is avoiding women like the plague. He has been badly burned and he doesn't want to get involved. But he, we are entitled to think, doth protest too much. Like the woman's child obsession in the woman's film, which conceals a secret desire to be rid of her offspring, the single man's retreat from marriage conceals a contrary desire. Otherwise, why would he leave so many strings for her to seize upon? (There are very few such "strings," and little sense of heterosexual need, in the action films of the sixties and seventies, which is one of the differences between then and now, and between Hawks and his colleagues and successors.) But it is the woman who has to bring the man around to seeing and claiming the invisible ties (in *To Have and Have Not,* Bacall asks Bogey to walk around her, and then says, "See? No strings," while he is tripping over them without realizing it). The man backs off, using as a pretext or real motive his disapproval of the woman's past. They exchange roles: The woman "proves herself" by playing it his way, by showing her physical courage or competence. And through a respect for her, first on his own terms, then on hers, he is brought around to a more "feminine" point of view.

Because proving themselves to each other is so fundamentally important for the action hero, and for Hawks' men, a woman who is (behaves, thinks) like a man is the transitional step to heterosexual love. In some ways this tribute to love means more coming from a "man's director" than if it had come from a "woman's director." *To Have and Have Not* is so far from the machismo mold of the Hemingway original that the Resistance Frenchman's courage is not in being willing to die, but in having brought along the woman whose presence "weakened" him, by making him concerned for her safety. His heroism, for which he will win no medals, is to have accepted the consequences of heterosexual love. And she, as a spoiled, destructive girl, redeems herself when she understands this. *To Have and Have Not* ultimately contradicts the mystique of those forties' films that, in pretending to deprecate heroics, are most infatuated with them as judged by and performed for men themselves. In the end of *Casablanca,* it is with Claude Rains that Bogart walks off into the Moroccan mist, the equivalent of the lovers' sunset; in *To Have and Have Not,* it is with Lauren Bacall. *Casablanca* reaps the conventional glory for an act—rejection—that is easiest; *To Have and Have Not,* opting for the love that is least honored in the virility ethic, is more truly glorious.

Under Hawks' supervision (being forced, the story goes, to yell at the top of her lungs on a mountaintop, to deepen her voice), Lauren Bacall's Slim is one of film's richly superior heroines and a rare example of a woman holding her own in a man's world. Her characters in *The Big Sleep* and *To Have and Have Not* are romantic paragons, women who have been conceived in what remains, essentially, a "man's world." But in the forties, certain movie stars emerged with distinctive, highly intelligent points of view (strong women like Davis, Crawford, Hepburn, and Russell), which they imposed openly or surreptitiously on the films they made. In this, either as stars or in the parts they played, they corresponded to certain kinds of women that literature had abstracted, over the years, from life. Because society dictated the proper, and severely restricted, domain for women, those who didn't "fit"—the "extraordinary women"—were tortured and frustrated; hence, the "neurotic woman." Finding no outlet for her brains or talent except as wife and mother, she dissipates her energies, diverts them, or goes outside society. Of such women, literature gives us two basic types, one European, the other Anglo-Saxon.

The first, and basically European model, is the "superfemale"—a woman who, while exceedingly "feminine" and flirtatious, is too ambitious and intelligent for the docile role society has decreed she play. She is uncomfortable, but not uncomfortable enough to rebel completely; her circumstances are too pleasurable. She remains within traditional society, but having no worthwhile project for her creative energies, turns them onto the only available material—the people around her—with demonic results. Hedda Gabler, Emma Bovary, and Emma Woodhouse are literary superfemales of the first order.

The other type is the "superwoman"—a woman who, like the "superfemale," has a high degree of intelligence or imagination, but instead of exploiting her femininity, adopts male characteristics in order to enjoy male prerogatives, or merely to survive. In this category are the transsexual impersonators (Shakespeare's Rosalind and Viola) who arrogate male freedoms along with their clothes, as well as the Shavian heroines who assume "male logic" and ideology to influence people—and who lose friends and, most triumphantly, make enemies in the process.

Scarlett and Jezebel, Vivien Leigh and Bette Davis are superfemales. Sylvia Scarlett and Vienna, Joan Crawford and (often) Katharine Hepburn are superwomen. The southern heroine, because of her conditioning and background, is a natural superfemale. Like the European woman, she is treated by men and her society with something close to veneration, a position she is not entirely willing to abandon for the barricades. Rather than rebel and lose her status, she plays on her assets, becomes a self-exploiter, uses her sex (without ever surrendering it) to gain power over men. Romantically attractive, even magnetic, she is not sexual (though more so than her northern counterpart, hence the incongruity, even neurosis, in the New England Davis' southern belle performances); she is repressed more from Victorianism than puritanism, and instinctively resists any situation in which she might lose her self-control. (The distinction between North and South obtains in the literary "superfemales" as well; the "Northern European" types, Hedda Gabler and Emma Woodhouse, suggest respectively sexual frigidity and apathy; Mme Bovary, being more Mediterranean, is more likely to have found sexual satisfaction.)

Bette Davis, superfemale and sometime southern belle, was not born in the South at all, but in Lowell, Massachusetts, of an old, respectable Protestant family. The only clue in her background to the seething polarities of toughness and vulnerability expressed in her roles was the trauma (glossed over in her autobiography) of her father's desertion of the family when she was only a child. She was supported in her theatrical career by her mother, Ruthie, who was also her lifelong friend, even as she progressed (or regressed) from the guardian of her struggling daughter to the spoiled charge of her successful one. All this might or might not explain the conflicting impulses of the Davis persona (in tandem or from film to film): the quicksilver shifts between distrust and loyalty, the darting, fearful eyes, and the bravura, the quick wit of the abruptly terminated sentences, the defensiveness and the throttled passion.

She was the wicked girl who sometimes was, sometimes

wasn't, so bad underneath, while Crawford was the self-made gracious lady with ice water for blood. At some point (Crawford in *Rain* and *A Woman's Face*) each of them was bisected by the puritan ethic into two mutually exclusive extremes of good and evil. But even in her double role in *A Stolen Life,* when she played Katy, the sweet-and-passive sister and her bitch twin Pat, Davis did not really draw a radical distinction between the two (as de Havilland did in *The Dark Mirror*), thus suggesting the interdependence of the two halves.

In the beginning of her career, Davis was just plain Katy ("the cake," as Glenn Ford describes her, in contrast to Pat, "without the frosting"). In her first picture, *Bad Sister,* reportedly one of the worst films ever made, Davis was not the eponymous hellion (that was Zasu Pitts) but her simpering, virtuous sibling. "Embarrassment always made me have a one-sided smile," she recounts in her autobiography, "and since I was constantly embarrassed in front of a camera, I constantly smiled in a one-sided manner."

She was universally considered unsexy, not to say unusable; still, when her contract expired she managed to hang on until she was taken up by Warners. Her lack of success or star status became an asset, as she was able to take parts—like Mildred in *Of Human Bondage*—that nobody else would touch. This was her first villainess, and her enthusiasm extended to the makeup, which she persuaded director John Cromwell to let her apply herself. In so doing, she thus gained the upper hand, which she would use whenever she could (and not always to her own advantage), and demonstrated that feeling for greasepaint grotesque that only she could get away with, and sometimes even she could not.

She determined to make it very clear "that Mildred was not going to die of a dread disease looking as if a deb had missed her noon nap. The last stages of consumption, poverty and neglect are not pretty and I intended to be convincing-looking. We pulled no punches and Mildred emerged as a reality—as immediate as a newsreel and as starkly real as a pestilence." (Actually, Davis' notions of feminine vanity and excesses, daring as they often are, have led her into those parodies of womanhood that are closer to Grand Guignol than newsreel, and that have surrounded her with camp followers whose image of her obliterates her real strengths.)

From then on, she was one of the few actresses willing—even eager—to play against audience sympathy. In her southern belle phase, she managed to combine the vanity of the "deb" with the venality of Mildred. Even in her superfemale roles, the charm has a cutting edge—the taunting Julie Marsden of *Jezebel* (the consolation role for missing out on Scarlett); the "jinx" actress, Joyce Heath, patterned on Jeanne Eagels, in *Dangerous* (for which she won the consolation Academy Award denied her for *Of Human Bondage*); the mortally ill socialite, Judith Traherne, in *Dark Victory*); and the frivolous Fanny Trellis of *Mr. Skeffington.*

The superfemale is an actress by nature; what is flirtation, after all, but role-playing? Coquetry is an art, and Davis exulted in the artistry. In *Jezebel,* she captivates her beaux but with less natural effervescence than Scarlett. Davis is more neurotic than Vivien Leigh, less cool. When coolness is called for, Davis gives us a cold chill; when warmth, a barely suppressed passion. Her charm, like her beauty, is something willed into being. It is not a question of whether she is inside or outside the part (for curiously she is both) but of the intensity of her conviction, a sense of character in the old-fashioned sense of "moral fiber." Through sheer, driving guts she turns herself into a flower of the Old South, and in that one determined gesture reveals the bedrock toughness of the superfemale that we discover only by degrees in Scarlett.

Davis' reputation is based on a career composed of equal parts art, three-star trash, and garbage, sometimes all in the same film—which makes fine critical distinctions difficult. Warners gave her a hard time, and she reciprocated. (She even brought a lawsuit against them once, which she lost, but in so doing, she paved the way for future action on actors' behalf.) William Wyler was her toughest and best director—on *Jezebel, The Letter,* and *The Little Foxes*—but she broke with him over *The Little Foxes*. She was in an invisible competition with Tallulah Bankhead, who had played Regina brilliantly on Broadway, and from whom she also inherited (and probably improved upon) *Jezebel* and *Dark Victory*. Surely none of these films was a "betrayal" of the original stage play, and as to who outshone whom, only those who have witnessed both can decide—and even they, given the fierce, partisan loyalties these two women inspire, are not entirely trustworthy.

For all her enmities, Davis really was a friend to other actresses, content to take the back seat and let them run with the showy parts. (Actually, some of her "back-seat" parts—the sweet-tempered but strong girl in *The Great Lie*—are some of her most appealing and underrated roles.) Mary Astor tells the story of how she and Davis built her—Mary's—part in *The Great Lie* into an Academy Award-winning performance. Every day before shooting they added material to the screenplay, to make Mary look good as well as to enliven the movie, and between them (and with the sympathetic direction of Edmund Goulding) they created one of the most complex women's relationships in a woman's film. They are cast as stereotypes: Astor, the sophisticated and selfish concert pianist who wants George Brent more than his baby; Davis, Brent's Baltimore bride, who makes a deal with Astor for the baby when they think Brent is dead. Their relationship during Astor's delivery alternates between tenderness and spite, love and hate, as Davis plays the "father" (in jodhpurs, pacing the floor) to Astor's mother.

Part of Davis' greatness lies in the sheer, galvanic force she brought to the most outrageous and unlikely roles, giving an intensity that saved them, usually, from camp. Even when she is "outside" a part (through its, or her, unsuitability), she is dynamic. As the harridan housewife of *Beyond the Forest*, she surveys her despised domestic kingdom and says "What a dump!" and we are with her. By the time Martha in *Who's Afraid of Virginia Woolf?* says the same line, it has already been consecrated as camp. In spite of the fact that the only way we can think of Davis as a *femme fatale* is if she contemplates murder or literally kills somebody (*The Letter, The Little Foxes*), she makes us accept her as a girl men fight duels over and die for. She is constantly being cast against type as a heartbreaker, and then made to pick up the pieces when foolish hearts shatter. As the actress "witch" (*Dangerous*) whose stage presence has caused suicides and inspired epiphanies, she is made to do penance, for the rest of her life, with her milquetoast husband. But if we look closely, here and elsewhere, it is not she but others who insist on her supernatural evil, who throw up a smoke screen of illusions, who invoke mystical catchwords to explain her "magic" or her "jinx," why she is "different" from other women.

In her film career, Davis casts a cold eye, and not a few dampening remarks, on sentimentality. When Claude Rains, as the doting Mr. Skeffington, tells her "A woman is beautiful only when she is loved," Davis, miserable over the discovery of her pregnancy, replies, "A woman is beautiful if she has eight hours of sleep and goes to the beauty parlor every day. And bone structure has a lot to do with it."

In King Vidor's *Beyond the Forest*, her wildest and most uncompromising film, one she herself dislikes, she plays the

FROM REVERENCE TO RAPE

evil Rosa Moline, married to Joseph Cotton's small-town doctor. He is seen as "good" because he goes without, and makes his wife go without, so his impecunious patients won't have to pay their bills—and will "love" the good doctor. His "virtue" succeeds in driving his wife into further malice. One of the earliest discontented housewives on record, Rosa sashays around wearing a long black wig, like her surly housekeeper, Dona Drake, who is a dark-skinned lower-class parody of her. Davis' obsession is to go to Chicago, and to this end she wrecks everyone's lives. In one of the film's most modern, *angst*-ridden scenes, she wanders the back streets of Chicago, staggering through the rain (having been turned out of a bar where women "without escorts" are not allowed), looking like another star who would later claim her influence— Jeanne Moreau in *La Notte*.

"I don't want people to love me," Rosa says—one of the most difficult things for a woman to bring herself to say, ever, and one of the most important. It is something Davis the actress must have said. Thus, does the superfemale become the superwoman, by taking life into her own hands, her own way.

Davis' performance in *Beyond the Forest,* as a kind of female W. C. Fields, and Vidor's commitment to her, are astonishing. Even though she is contrasted with a "good woman" (Ruth Roman) to show that she is the exception, that all women are not like that (a moralistic pressure that Hollywood is not the only one to exercise—the French government made Godard change the title of *The Married Woman* to *A Married Woman*), the Ruth Roman character has little moral weight or value. As Rosa Moline, Davis creates her own norms, and is driven by motives not likely to appeal to the average audience. She is ready and eager to give up husband, position, security, children (most easily, children), even lover; for what? Not for anything so noble as "independence" in terms of a job, profession, or higher calling, but to be rich and fancy in Chicago! And here is Davis, not beautiful, not sexy, not even young, convincing us that she is all these things—by the vividness of her own self-image, by the vision of herself she projects so fiercely that we have no choice but to accept it. She is smart, though, smarter than everyone around her. She says it for all smart dames when David Brian tells her he no longer loves her, that he's found the "pure" woman of his dreams. "She's a book with none of the pages cut," he says.

"Yeah," Davis replies, "and nothing on them!"

Since she began as a belle and emerged as a tough (in *Beyond the Forest* she is a crack shot and huntress), Davis' evolution from superfemale to superwoman was the most dramatic, but she was by no means the only actress in the forties to undergo such a transformation.* Perhaps reflecting the increased number of working women during the war and their heightened career inclinations, other stars made the transition from figurative hoop skirts to functional shoulder pads, and gained authority without necessarily losing their femininity.

The war was *the* major turning point in the pattern and attitudes of (and toward) working women. From 1900 to 1940, women in the labor force had been mostly young, un-

---

* In a characteristically perverse fashion, Ida Lupino went in the opposite direction, from the superwoman matriarch of *The Man I Love* and *The Hard Way* (1942), in which she channels all of her ambitions into promoting her younger sister, to *The Bigamist* (1953), which she herself directed, and in which she plays Edmund O'Brien's mousy, submissive mistress against Joan Fontaine's aggressive career woman. Although Lupino takes the standard anti–career woman position in her treatment of Fontaine, the film presents a positive case for bigamy, or at least suggests that the binary system—one man, one woman, married for life without loopholes—is not the most flexible or realistic arrangement.

married women in their early twenties who were biding their time until marriage. Suddenly, to fill men's places and aid in the expanded war industries, older, married women were recruited, and from that time to the present (when the typical working woman is forty and married) the median age rose with the percentage of women in the labor force. A poll of working women taken during the war came up with the startling fact that 80 percent wanted to keep their jobs after it was over. After a sharp drop-off following the end of the war—when women were fired with no regard for seniority —married women *did* go back to work, although as late as 1949 it was still frowned upon. This, of course, is the source of the tremendous tension in films of the time, which tried, by ridicule, intimidation, or persuasion, to get women out of the office and back to the home, to get rid of the superwoman and bring back the superfemale.

Rosalind Russell came out of the superfemale closet into superwoman roles fairly early in her career. But in *Craig's Wife,* an adaptation of the George Kelly play, she is not only a superfemale but the definitive superfemale, the housewife who becomes obsessive about her home, the perfectionist housekeeper for whom, finally, nothing else exists. It would be comforting to look upon this film, directed by Dorothy Arzner, as a protest against the mindlessness of housewifery, but, like *The Women,* of which the same claim has been made, it is not so much a satire as an extension, in high relief, of the tics and intellectual tremors of a familiar American type. In *The Women,* as the malicious (and funny and stylish) Mrs. Fowler, Russell is the superfemale par excellence; but in *His Girl Friday,* as the newspaper reporter, in *My Sister Eileen,* as the short-story writer, and in *Take a Letter, Darling,* as the business executive, she begins pulling her own weight in a man's world, risks making enemies and losing lovers, becomes, that is, a superwoman.

In *Take a Letter, Darling,* she is the partner in an advertising firm where she began as a secretary. She runs the operation while Robert Benchley, the titular head of the firm, plays miniature golf in his office. He is, to Russell, the kind of benign father figure that Charles Coburn was to Jean Arthur and Irene Dunne. Not in the least bitter at Russell's success, he is quite happy to have been "kicked upstairs" and gives her support and advice whenever she comes to him. At one point, he complains that her competitors—all men, of course—don't understand her :

> "They don't know the difference between a woman and a . . ."
> "A what?" Russell asks.
> "I don't know," Benchley replies, "there's no name for you."

In *My Sister Eileen,* Russell plays the writer-sister trying to sell her stories to a prestigious national magazine. Although the stories concern the escapades of her pretty and popular sister, Russell steals the show as the cerebral one, and gets editor Brian Aherne, too. (The difference in attitudes between the forties and fifties can be seen in the shift of emphasis in the musical remake of *My Sister Eileen* in 1955, in which Betty Garrett retains little dignity as the intellectual sister, but is overshadowed—and shamed—by the popularity of the sister played by Janet Leigh.)*

Katharine Hepburn made the transition from superfemale to superwoman most easily and most successfully of all—perhaps because she was already halfway there to begin with. In her second film, Dorothy Arzner's *Christopher Strong,*

---

* If Columbia had used the Bernstein musical, with Rosalind Russell retaining her stage role, the movie might have been better but no less sexist, with its rousing point-by-point denunciation of feminism : "100 Ways to Lose a Man."

she played an aviatrix torn between her profession and her man. Flying presents an appropriately extreme metaphor for the freedom of the single woman that has to be surrendered once the idea of a family becomes a concrete reality. Torn apart by these conflicting pulls, Hepburn finally dies in a plane crash—that is, she propels herself, like the dancer in *The Red Shoes,* into the abyss between love and career. In both cases, the ending is not just a cautionary warning to deflect women from careers, but a true reflection of the dynamics of the situation: A woman has only so much energy, so much "self" to give; is there enough for profession (especially if it is a dangerous or demanding one), lover, and children? *Christopher Strong* raises these questions, but doesn't really pursue them, and as a consequence it is a less interesting film than it should be, less interesting than Arzner's more "feminist" film, *Dance, Girl, Dance.* But, for all its weaknesses, *Christopher Strong* leaves us with a blazingly electric image of Katharine Hepburn unlike that of any other film: a woman in a silver lamé body-stocking which covers everything but her face—and suggests the chrysalis of the superwoman of the future.

Hepburn, like most tomboy actresses, played Jo in *Little Women,* and shortly thereafter played the eponymous "transvestite" of *Sylvia Scarlett,* one of George Cukor's most enchanting and least-known films. Disguised as a boy, she accompanies her father, a crook on the lam, through the hills of Cornwall. They join forces with a troupe of wandering actors, led by Cary Grant, and embark on a free, magical, oneiric adventure, giving plays in the moonlight. Cukor's feeling for the conventions of theater, where he began his career, leads him into a world halfway between theater and life, a world in which disguises are often worn more easily and more "honestly" than native hues. The milieu and the story of *Sylvia Scarlett* have a Shakespearian feel to them, harking back to an age and a theatrical convention in which sex-exchange was permissible. This is Cukor's first film (and last for a while) in which he dared to challenge, in a lyrical stage whisper, our traditional assumptions about male-female roles.

The delicate equilibrium between a man and a woman and between a woman's need to distinguish herself and the social demands on her become the explicit theme of Cukor's great films of the late forties and early fifties, specifically the Judy Holliday films and Hepburn–Tracy vehicles written by the husband-and-wife team of Ruth Gordon and Garson Kanin. Gordon and Kanin wrote a series of seven screenplays for Cukor, three of which dealt, comically and sublimely, with the problems and the chemistry of the couple.

Almost as a parody of the extraordinary individuals represented by Hepburn and Tracy in *Adam's Rib* and *Pat and Mike,* Aldo Ray and Judy Holliday were a typical, dumb, middle-class, well-meaning, ordinary married couple in Cukor's *The Marrying Kind.* Almost a parody, but not quite. For it is one of the glories of the film that the two characters, without ever being patronized and at the same time without ever being lifted above the class and the cliché in which they are rooted, are intensely moving. Ray and Holliday, on the brink of divorce, have come to a woman judge (who, in her relationship with her male assistant, shows both authority and warmth). Through a series of flashbacks reconstructing their marriage we, and they, come to realize that together they are something they never were apart: a unit, a whole. Two ordinary, less-than-complete individuals who have grown into each other to the point where they can be defined only by the word "couple" have no right to divorce. Separately, they are two more swallowers of the American myth, two more victims of its fraudulence; but together, with their children, they add up to something full and affirmative. In losing their child, they are at first destroyed—their "meaning" evaporates. But in that nothingness, old roles dissolve and they must rediscover themselves. Cukor, Gordon, and Kanin are very much aware of the sexual insecurities that arise from too rigid a concept of male-female roles, and suggest, in the visual and verbal motifs of these "companion" films, that through some kind of "merger" of identities, through a free exchange of traits (as when Holliday, in defiance of the law whereby it is the man who "storms out" of the house in a fight, throws herself into the night), a truer sense of the self may emerge.

In the growing isolation of the New York cultural elite from the rest of America in the sixties, this is the side of marriage and the middle class that has been lost to us. We seem to be able to approach middle-America only through giggles of derision (*The Graduate, Sticks and Bones,* "All in the Family"); and, in dismissing the housewife as a lower form of life, women's lib confirms that the real gap is cultural and economic rather than sexual. In the difference between the couple in *The Marrying Kind* and *Adam's Rib,* Cukor and company acknowledge the most fundamental intellectual, spiritual, and economic inequality between the educated elite and the less privileged and less imaginative members of lower-middle-class America; but they never deprive them of their dignity, or deny them joys and sorrows and a capacity to feel as great as the poets of the earth. The true emotional oppression—the oppression of blacks by whites, of housewives by working women, is pity. For in such lessons in life as we get from suffering, degrees are granted without reference to class or sex. Finally, most honestly, Holliday's Florence and Ray's Chet are the sheep of the world rather than its shepherds: They are the victims of emotions they haven't the words to express, the tools of a mechanical-industrial society they haven't the knowledge to resist. Their greatest defense against its monolithic oppressiveness, against being overwhelmed by routine, inhumanity, and their "proletarian" identity, is each other, is their identity as a couple. In the final, quite noble strength we feel in them as a couple, they confirm the theory Cukor, Gordon, and Kanin seem to be endorsing: that marriage is an institution ideally suited to the people at both the bottom and the top—the truly ordinary and the truly extraordinary, those who are preserved and protected by it, and those who can bend it to their will.

Hepburn and Tracy were nothing if not extraordinary. While preserving their individuality, they united to form a whole greater than the sum of its parts. As Tracy says to Hepburn in *Pat and Mike,* in a line that could have been written by Kanin–Gordon, Cukor, or Tracy himself and that finally tapers off into infinity, "What's good for you is good for me is good for you. . . ."

This was true of them professionally. They came together at a time when their careers were foundering; misfits in the Hollywood mold, they were not in any way typical romantic leads. Hepburn had grown older, the face that once blushed in gracious concession to femininity now betrayed in no uncertain terms the recalcitrant New England spirit. And Tracy, too short and dumpy for conventional leading roles, hadn't found the woman who could lure him from the rugged, masculine world he inhabited. Out of their complementary incongruities, they created one of the most romantic couples the cinema has ever known. His virility acts as a buffer to her intelligence; she is tempered by him just as he is sharpened by her, and their self-confidence is increased, rather than eroded, by their need for each other.

Adam's Rib, that *rara avis,* a commercial "feminist" film, was many years ahead of its time when it appeared in 1949, and, alas, still is. Even the slightly coy happy ending testifies to the fact that the film strikes deeper into the question of sexual roles than its comic surface would indicate and raises more questions than it can possibly answer.

Tracy and Hepburn play a couple of married lawyers who find themselves on opposite sides of a case; he is the prosecuting attorney, and she, seizing upon the crime and its implications, takes it upon herself to defend the accused. A dopey young wife—Judy Holliday, in her first major movie role—has shot, but not killed, her husband (Tom Ewell) over another woman. Hepburn, reading an account in the newspaper, is outraged by the certainty that the woman will be dealt with harshly while a man in that position would be acquitted by the courts and vindicated by society. Hepburn goes to visit Holliday at the woman's prison, and, in a long, lovely single-take scene, Holliday spills out her story, revealing, comically and pathetically, her exceptionally low consciousness. One of the constant and most relevant sources of comedy in the film is the lack of rapport between Hepburn's militant lawyer, constructing her case on feminist principles, and Holliday's housewife, contrite and idiotically eager to accept guilt. The film raises the means-and-end dilemma which has long been the philosophical thorn in the side of our thinking about the rights and reparations of minority groups. Hepburn marshals evidence of women's accomplishments to prove their equality with men, even to the point of having a lady wrestler lift Tracy onto her shoulders and make a laughingstock of him. She goes *too* far and humiliates him, while he remains a gentleman. She stoops to unscrupulous methods while he maintains strict honor and decorum. But, then, he can afford to, since the law was created by and for him.

Even down to his animal magnetism, Tracy wears the spoiled complacency of the man, but Hepburn, ambitious and intelligent, scrapes the nerves of male authority. An acute sense of the way male supremacy is institutionalized in the "games people play" occurs in two contrasting situations of one-upmanship: Hepburn, fiery about the case she is about to take, is describing it to Tracy on the telephone; Tracy, in a familiar male (or marital) riposte, effectively cuts her off by teasing, "I love you when you get caus-y." This is greeted with delight by audiences, who usually disapprove of Hepburn's "emasculation" of Tracy in court, a more obvious but perhaps a less damaging tactic of bad faith. Cukor gives Hepburn an ally in the Cole Porter–type composer played by David Wayne, a character who seems to stand, at least partially, for Cukor himself. He identifies with Hepburn and, in marital feuds, takes her side against the virile, meat-and-potatoes "straight" played by Tracy. Thus the neutral or homosexual character, when he is sympathetic, can help to restore some of the balance in the woman's favor. But as soon as the Hepburn–Wayne collusion becomes devious or bitchy, the balance shifts, and our sympathy goes, as it should, to Tracy.

The film brilliantly counterpoints and reconciles two basic assumptions: (1) that there are certain "male" qualities—stability, stoicism, fairness, dullness—possessed by Tracy, and that there are certain "female" qualities—volatility, brilliance, intuition, duplicity—possessed by Hepburn; and (2) that each can, and must, exchange these qualities like trading cards. It is important for Hepburn to be ethical, just as it is important for Tracy to be able to concede defeat gracefully, and if she can be a bastard, he can fake tears. If each can do everything the other can do, just where, we begin to wonder, are the boundaries between male and female? The question mark is established most pointedly and uncomfortably when, during the courtroom session, the faces of Holliday and Ewell are transposed, each becoming the other.

But Hepburn and Tracy are not quite so interchangeable, and the success of their union derives from the preservation of their individuality, not rigidly but through a fluctuating balance of concession and assertion. Tracy can be humiliated and still rebound without (too much) loss of ego. Hepburn occasionally can defer to him and still not lose her identity. A purely political-feminist logic would demand that she be given Tracy's head, in unqualified triumph (an ending that some small part of us would like to see), rather than make an equivocal, "feminine" concession to his masculinity. But marriage and love do not flourish according to such logic. Their love is the admission of their incompleteness, of their need and willingness to listen to each other, and their marriage is the certification—indeed, the celebration—of that compromise.

This finally is the greatness of Hepburn's superwoman, and Davis' and Russell's too—that she is able to achieve her ends in a man's world, to insist on her intelligence, to insist on using it, and yet be able to "dwindle," like Millamant in *The Way of the World,* "into marriage," but only after an equal bargain has been struck of conditions mutually agreed on. It is with just such a bargain, and a contract, that Cukor's great Tracy–Hepburn film of the fifties, *Pat and Mike,* is concerned.

For the most part, the superwoman, with her angular personality and acute, even abrasive, intelligence, begins to disappear in the fifties. The bad-girl is whitewashed, or blown up into some pneumatic technicolor parody of herself. Breast fetishism, a wartime fixation of the G.I.'s, came in in the fifties. (Its screen vogue was possibly retarded by the delay in releasing Howard Hughes' *The Outlaw,* introducing Jane Russell's pair to the world.) But even amidst the mostly vulgar fumblings toward sensuality, Cukor was there—with Ava Gardner in *Bhowani Junction* and Sophia Loren in *Heller in Pink Tights*—to give some dignity to the sex goddesses and, in films like *The Actress* and *Born Yesterday,* to pay tribute to the enterprising woman.

THE FIFTIES

In 1950, Margaret Sullavan made her last film, *No Sad Songs for Me*. In the same year, Mitzi Gaynor and Piper Laurie made their first films. A year later, Audrey Hepburn and Grace Kelly would make their screen debuts; a year earlier, Nicholas Ray had made his as a director. In 1950, Gloria Swanson made *Sunset Boulevard*, her first film in nine years, and also her last. And in 1950, *All About Eve*, with Bette Davis, Anne Baxter, and Celeste Holm as the triumvirate of theater women, won the Academy Award as best picture. (The same film offered a very young Marilyn Monroe in a small part.) Judy Holliday won the Best Actress Award for *Born Yesterday*. And the eleven films of 1950 considered worthy of inclusion in *The New York Times'* collected reviews were: *Born Yesterday, Father of the Bride, Destination Moon, The Titan—Story of Michelangelo, The Men, 12 O'Clock High, Trio, Ways of Love, Sunset Boulevard, All About Eve*, and *The Asphalt Jungle*. The eleven top films of 1950 listed by Andrew Sarris in *The American Cinema* included the last three plus *Wagonmaster, The Third Man, In a Lonely Place, The Lawless, Winchester '73, Where the Sidewalk Ends, Panic in the Streets,* and *Stage Fright.*

The two lists have in common only a heavy preponderance of male films: the liberal, urban, and big-production type favored by the *Times'* critic, Bosley Crowther, and the Western and action genres favored by the auteurist critic, Sarris.

Meanwhile, there were a lot of films that made no lists. In 1950, Doris Day and Natalie Wood made four films apiece; Debbie Reynolds and Elizabeth Taylor each made three. June Allyson, Teresa Wright, Jane Wyman, Dorothy Malone, Esther Williams, Deborah Kerr, Hedy Lamarr, Jeanne Crain, and Joan Crawford all made two films apiece. And this was a normal year, not distinguished by any more or less activity than others. Actresses would be averaging about the same the next year, and the following year. But then the effect of television would begin to be felt. The defection of mass audiences would take its toll, removing the cornerstone of the studio system and initiating its collapse. By the late sixties there would be nothing left but a vacant lot here, a partially occupied office building there, and some second- and third-generation moguls, with producers, directors, writers, actors, and actresses jockeying for first position and all negotiating separate "packages" and contracts.

The disintegration of Hollywood in the traditional sense came from within as well as without. Thematically as well as technologically, the death of Hollywood was an idea whose time had come, and the sense of alienation from a destructive system formed the basis of such films as *The Goddess, The Big Knife, The Barefoot Contessa,* and *Sunset Boulevard.* These films could hardly be called radical critiques of the system: They were made within the industry, with movie stars, and grossed enough to soften the sting. A movie with real sting was likely to have to bypass the industry completely, and be bypassed, in turn, by distributors, exhibitors, even reviewers (and consequently the public) so that it had little chance of finding even the small audience for which it was destined. Such a film, extraordinary for any time and especially in the light of women's liberation, was *Salt of the Earth*. Directed by Herbert J. Biberman and filmed in New Mexico, mostly with nonprofessionals, it dealt with a copper union strike not only from a Stalinist, but from a feminist point of view. In the course of prolonged picketing, the women take responsibility and prevail, directly challenging the men for their sexist attitudes and delivering vigorous lectures on the subject. This film deserves a footnote as a rarity not only among American films, but among political ones. Hollywood has provided an easy target for feminist outrage, but if anything, it is the political filmmakers, brothers under the skin of oppressed minorities, who have been most negligent in promoting the cause of women. Politics remains the most heavily—and jealously—masculine area, and the left-wing film has its own sexual mythology, preferring a vision of the peasant or laborer, in heroic silhouette, backed up—a little ways down the hill—by the patiently enduring wife.

The decline of the feudal system was by no means an unalloyed blessing. With the dismantling of the studios it was not only the bosses who disappeared, it was also the phalanx of pros, technicians, publicists, contract writers, and bit players who had been available for the most routine projects. Actresses who had finally gained the freedom to choose their parts found there were fewer and fewer parts to choose from. Now they made a movie a year: Soon they would be lucky to do one every three years.

The 1950s also ushered in the split between movies as "entertainment" and movies as "art," though the division would not be officially acknowledged until the sixties. Meanwhile, the facade was as glossy as ever and movie people were pretending everything was still copasetic. But the color was too bright, the makeup too garish, the smile a little forced. The facade was beginning to crack.

For in robbing movies of their mass audience, television had stolen more than bodies and box-office figures. It had destroyed the faith: that belief in their fictions and fables by which the movies touched base with millions of viewers and had the authority of received religion. In a land of many churches and no Church, this mystical bond constituted the only national religion America had ever known (what Patria is for England, the Church for Spain, Mother for Italy), and the only "realism" film has ever known. With the best dreams that money could buy, filmmakers created a reality that was far more real for most people than the world they lived in. But then one realism gave way to another, claiming itself (as it does at least once in every decade, and for every aesthetic school) as the one and only. The dream machine began to creak as soon as audiences became more sophisticated, better traveled, more fragmented, and more demanding. Technology and sociology converged in a new aesthetic of realism (which was itself modified by CinemaScope in the mid-fifties, into an epic cinema that never took over as the main vehicle of narrative film).

The tendency toward smaller crews, location shooting, nonactors, cynical stories with flat or nonendings, even a few stabs at explicit sexuality (which were more like mutilations) seemed calculated to dispel our childish fantasies and topple our false gods and goddesses. These various trends didn't really combine with any significance until the late fifties and early sixties, but the groundwork was being laid.

It was as if the whole period of the fifties was a front, the topsoil that protected the seed of rebellion that was germinating below. The cultural disorientation had begun, but it had yet to be acknowledged. By the sixties, the break would be official and the divorce a quickie. The word "alienation" would be adopted to express the new alignment of "us" against "them"; the culturally disaffected—and enlightened—belonged, if not to America, then at least to one another.

But in the fifties we were still floating. The decade, and the stars who stood out from it in papier-mâché relief— Jerry Lewis and Elvis Presley, Marilyn Monroe and Doris Day—had an unreal quality, images at once bland and tortured. They were all *about* sex, but *without* sex. The fabulous fifties were a box of Cracker Jacks without a prize; or with the prize distorted into a forty-inch bust, a forty-year-old virgin. Society was in a postwar phase, as in the twenties, and the time was ripe for a swing toward sexual freedom. In the forties, this impulse had been drowned in sentimentality; now it was deflected into a joke. With the Production Code to support its native instincts, America was once again able to avoid outright sin and protect its innocence. But innocence, at this advanced age, was no longer charming. It was beginning to look a little unhealthy, what with breast fetishism combining with Lolita lechery in the one ultimate sweater girl/daddy's girl, Marilyn Monroe.

But Marilyn, even Marilyn, was only one of many—stars, trends, moods—and to raise her like some monolith presiding over the decade would be as false as to ignore her completely. Marilyn belonged, the efforts of Arthur Miller and Paula Strasberg notwithstanding, to Hollywood, to movies, and to the mystique of "screen presence," an attribute that was always being compared unfavorably to "real acting," to The Theatah. The division between West Coast and East Coast, between movies and The Theatah, had existed for as long as writers had needed the Hollywood myth to explain their failures and Faustian sellouts, or actors had needed to do a Broadway "hairshirt" stint in penance for their five-figure salaries and kidney-shaped pools. But in the fifties the division between personalities and real actresses became more explicit, and was even exploited by those directors like Elia Kazan, Joseph Mankiewicz, and Billy Wilder who had bridged the cultural gap. The differences were magnified, or enhanced, by technicolor and wide screen, innovations by which Hollywood became more itself than ever before, even as it was dying. Thus, there were the movie-movie stars in living technicolor: Doris Day, Debbie Reynolds, Marilyn Monroe, Jane Russell, Elizabeth Taylor, Kim Novak, Grace Kelly, Lana Turner, Jane Wyman, Ava Gardner, Shirley MacLaine, Cyd Charisse, Virginia Mayo, Debra Paget. And there were the serious-artist actresses in black and white: Anne Bancroft, Julie Harris, Kim Stanley, Jean Simmons, Teresa Wright, Shelley Winters, Patricia Neal, Joanne Woodward, and Barbara Bel Geddes. Then there were the amphibians, women like Janet Leigh, Audrey Hepburn, Anne Baxter, and Judy Holliday, whom one visualizes in black and white with color around the edges.

The distinctions are more difficult to make when one goes back to the films of the early fifties, partly because many stars, like Swanson and Bette Davis, were a carry-over from a time when all movies were in black and white and partly because, as usual, the early part of one decade is a continuation of the preceding one. Jean Simmons was a transitional figure for the forties/fifties as Ann Sheridan was for the thirties/forties. Even when she was playing glib, wise-cracking standby roles in the thirties, Sheridan had an arresting, serious quality that grew into passionate intelligence in the forties' heroines she played. Early fifties' films were still honoring the superwoman and the *femme fatale*, and Jean Simmons, playing both kinds of parts, seemed to combine the predatory strength of the forties' sorceress with the ingenuous gamine quality of the fifties' virgin.

In Preminger's *Angel Face* she plays a bad-girl reminiscent of the forties, but in the peculiar quality of her deceptive facade, the glazed, innocent stare of the angel face, she becomes one of the distinctively Premingerian heroines so characteristic of the fifties. Or, we might say, one of the distinctively fifties' heroines so characteristic of Preminger. Robert Mitchum, an honest ambulance driver on the way up, is the fly she catches in her web: a plot to kill her stepmother (with Mitchum, as chauffeur, at the wheel) in order to have her father (Herbert Marshall) all to herself. In this, she provides another instance of the anti-Lawrentian American woman, preferring the elegant and effete father figure to the lower-class symbol of virility. And she never changes. The plan backfires when Marshall on the spur of the moment decides to accompany his wife, and meets his death with her. At this moment, the audience knows what is happening but Simmons doesn't. She continues playing the piano with a completely expressionless face; the mask is all we ever know of her, and of her remorseless "self." If she is entirely venal and bent on destruction (she finally drives herself and Mitchum backward off a cliff in an ending anticipatory of *Jules and Jim*) she is also exciting in the obsessiveness and implacability Preminger gives her. Nor does he suggest that she is a symbol of destructive womanhood, but rather her opacity raises a limit to our understanding and prevents her from sliding comfortably into the dark-woman stereotype. The chilling flatness of the ending, which by duplicating the previous accident evokes the association of Simmons' impassive face, betrays no emotion and allows none.

There is a hint of insanity here, a consciencelessness that suggests frigidity—a deep freeze of the senses, particularly of sexuality, that may be a clue to Preminger's heroines. Obliged to maintain a romantic image of themselves, they contract under the strain, or take on that anomie that we know from the mad-housewife heroines of contemporary women's films. At the moment when Simmons stares mysteriously, blankly at nothing (or into her own inner space) she is iconographic sister to Tierney (*Laura*), Crawford (*Daisy Kenyon*), Joan Bennett (*Margin for Error*), and such later Preminger heroines as Jean Seberg (*Bonjour Tristesse*) and Carol Lynley (*Bunny Lake Is Missing*), all of whom suggest, with their fixed, enigmatic gazes, framed portraits no less impenetrable than the actual portrait of Laura. But if the women are guilty in sitting still for the portrait, in allowing themselves to be trapped, it is men who worship the portrait, who prefer the romantic image to the real one.

In Preminger's *Whirlpool,* Richard Conte plays a psychiatrist whose unwavering vision of his wife (Gene Tierney) as a beautiful, normal woman blinds him to signs of a psychic disorder (kleptomania) until it is too late. The symptoms have obviously arisen in an unconscious reaction both to his neglect and to his idealization of her. Afraid to tell him, she puts herself in the hands of an unsavory hypnotist (José Ferrer), hoping to "cure" herself. The hold she allows Ferrer to gain over her suggests a sublimated sexual need, and the success of her caper suggests the ease with which a woman can deceive a man who clings to a fictitious image of her. Like so many "normal" marriages, theirs is based on the preservation of mutually understood, fixed identities. They are together, for better or worse—as long as the wife doesn't take her husband by surprise with some unexpected and possibly neurotic needs of her own (he's got enough problems to worry about, she's meant to be the harbor, not the stormy sea). This common conception of marriage contains a built-in hostility to new revelations, to unsuspected personality traits, in other words, to growth and change. Conte, like many husbands, takes Tierney's outbursts of anger or suspicion as expressions of an "alien" personality ("That's not like you, darling") rather than as revelations of a true self he has refused to recognize, or of an anger that has taken refuge in neurosis.

The criteria by which a man judges women and types them as good or bad in the name of morality are often mere safeguards of his own security. Preminger deals with the same theme in *River of No Return,* a Western in which Robert Mitchum must confront and overcome his preconceived notions about Marilyn Monroe's dance-hall entertainer. She proves that she can not only pull her own weight in a trek through the wilds, but can act with more generosity and moral freedom because she is concerned with saving skin rather than saving face. Again, Preminger not only confronts social stereotypes, but subverts them: Monroe's apparent wickedness is as misleading as Simmons' apparent virtue.

Jean Simmons' more positive fifties' powers were exploited in *The Actress,* a film directed by George Cukor from Ruth Gordon's adaptation of her autobiographical play, *Years Ago.* In a small New England town at the turn of the century, a young girl battles with her parents (Teresa Wright and Spencer Tracy) over her desire to become an actress. Her struggle ends in triumph: as the film ends, she is leaving for New York. But the victory of the "career woman" is somewhat adulterated by the fact that it is the story of a *real* person (Ruth Gordon) a biographical woman of the kind Hollywood has always felt more comfortable with than aggressive fictional characters. (And even then there are historical Amazons, like Isadora Duncan, that

Hollywood wouldn't touch, or touch up, with a ten-foot pole of fictionalization.) The film is also weakened, from a feminist point of view, by the nature of the actress herself. Stemming, perhaps, from an unconscious desire to take away the sting (to family, to society) of her victory, she is made to seem silly and problematical—at best, starry-eyed, at worst, untalented. Indeed, Tracy's misgivings about her career seem well founded. Nevertheless, she does break through, and, in the absence of real encouragement, her determination becomes even more heroic.

The story and period milieu, and perhaps the fusion of Ruth Gordon's and Simmons' "elfin" sensibilities, give the film a patronizing quaintness the other Cukor–Gordon–Kanin collaborations do not have. In *Pat and Mike,* Katharine Hepburn is a gym teacher caught between her enthusiasm for sports and a growing sense of pressure to marry and become a "woman." Indecision increases her guilt and lack of self-esteem. The situation crystallizes when, during a golf tournament (and again, later, at a tennis match) her fiancé (William Ching) appears. And what a brilliant conception he is—a bland, comic-horror figure, the "eternal male" as woman's nemesis, society's emissary on a mission to deflate woman before she can find out, and gain confidence in her true powers. Alternately whispering to his companions or beaming at Hepburn with a fatuous grin, he is overconfident, insensitive, hearty, and, through it all, apparently harmless, mystified by her self-doubts, wanting "only the best" for the little lady. The moment he arrives on the scene, her confidence evaporates and her game falls apart. But from another shadow of the male spectrum comes Spencer Tracy, a Brooklynese sports promoter with dubious connections and a vocabulary studded wid dems and dose. He first tries to make her throw a golf match (and even at that his dishonesty is cleaner and more open than Ching's "honor"), but then, realizing she is incorruptible, signs her up as one of his three most valuable properties, along with a racehorse and Aldo Ray. Tracy puts her through her paces (and we are treated to displays of Hepburn's real-life skill at golf and tennis), and enters her in professional competition. It is by gaining Tracy's respect and—in the film's most delightful irony—by becoming a commercial "property," that Hepburn is free to become herself. The support Tracy gives her is not the flattery or adoration of the lover —they don't kiss once in the whole movie—but the admiration of the pro, directed at her skill rather than her sex. Love follows, of course, but without compromising their professional relationship, and in that sense, because of the terms (professional *preceding* marital) and fit (manager-performer) of their "contract," theirs is a less competitive, more congenial relationship than in *Adam's Rib*. In *Pat and Mike*, Hepburn demonstrates with strength and reflex what in *Adam's Rib* she proved with her brains: that women can easily get along without men. Thus, we see her vanquishing, with little more than a flick of a wrist, three crooks who have assailed Tracy. But then, she seems to say as she defers to him in some other way, "Who wants to get along without men?"—especially if the relationship is and always will be, as Tracy says, "Five-oh, five-oh."

As Hepburn was smart, Judy Holliday was "dumb," as Hepburn was assertive, Holliday was shrinking, and yet the suffusing glow and impact of her personality belie her dumbness and diffidence. In *Adam's Rib, Born Yesterday, It Should Happen to You*, and *Bells Are Ringing*, she stretches the stereotype of the dumb blonde into her own doughy shape. She was hardly such stuff, as Harry Cohn was quick to note, as Hollywood dreams are made on. She comes on slowly, with her beady eyes and poker face, and builds gradually into something that lights up the screen.

Staunch and fluffy as a muffin, pigheaded, suspicious, with an oh-ho-you're-not-going-to-fool-me laugh, she listens intently and then comes out with a remark from left field that is sublimely logical to her. She is moony and mulish, hardly the image of glamour or female supremacy. And yet she not only made it in Hollywood, but, in her own militantly sheeplike way, was as much and as invincibly her own person as any crusading feminist. Her realness was not that of the "real people" of the sixties, but a realness of volume and mass and heart.

As the Miss Nobody of *It Should Happen to You* who buys space on a billboard in Columbus Circle to advertise herself, she satirizes, while she attenuates, the instant-celebrity insanity of the decade to come. If only she had remained with us, to redeem and perhaps lend a little poetic dignity to the media-mad exhibitionists, to the letting-it-all-hang-out talk-show artists and the desperate fifteen-second celebrities. For hers was a real innocence and if, in her zeal, she was the first and most outrageous of the unabashed self-promoters, her style was never to be repeated.

As Dean Martin's answering service in *Bells Are Ringing* (her last film, made in 1960), her professional invisibility is a metaphor for the romantic invisibility of the ungainly woman. But her actual concealment enables her to flower. Freed from the anxiety of a "live" confrontation, she is able to open her heart and give without fear of rejection.

The actress—whether as literal thespian (as in *The Actress*) or as a symbol for role-playing woman—is a key female figure throughout film history, but is particularly in evidence in the fifties, when the split between woman and persona became thematically central. The actress legend took various forms: the mystique of the actress, the myth of the movie star, the mystique of the actress versus the myth of the movie star.

In one sense, the actress merely extends the role-playing dimension of woman, emphasizing what she already is. By film tradition, there were two occupations by which a woman "went professional," that is, got paid for doing what she already did: prostitution, in which she is remunerated for giving sexual pleasure, and acting, a variant on natural role-playing. A woman plays roles naturally in self-defense: As the sought-after rather than the seeker, she is placed on the defensive. She adopts masks and plays roles that will enable her to stall for time, stand back, watch, intuit, react. But she also plays roles, adapts to others, "aims to please," because of the central place of love in her life and the need to have her value confirmed by affection and attention.

For all the opprobrium heaped upon "role-playing," acting is also a basic and thoroughly healthy human impulse. Among both sexes, the desire to be other people, to experience other identities, begins in childhood. And whereas prostitution carries with it the mark of the victim, acting is taken up freely and independently. There is Katharine Hepburn, for example, in *Morning Glory,* a little silly, yes, but proud and finally overwhelming. And there is Carole Lombard in *Twentieth Century* and *To Be or Not to Be,* heroic and comical, with a talent she has the opportunity to prove. But with Gloria Swanson in *Sunset Boulevard* and Bette Davis in *All About Eve,* we get not the burning zeal of the actress but the burnt-out candle. All that is left is the vanity of woman.

Thus, there comes to be, in the very association of acting and women, in the choice of the actress as a metaphor for women, an insidious implication. The idea that acting is quintessentially "feminine" carries with it a barely perceptible sneer, a suggestion that it is not the noblest or most dignified of professions. Acting is role-playing, role-playing is lying, and lying is a woman's game. (In *Dangerous,*

Franchot Tone compliments Davis on telling the truth "like a gentleman," and Davis replies, "Perhaps I'm not lady enough to lie.") Despite the fact that men constitute at least half of the acting profession, they are rarely—unless they die dramatically or drink spectacularly—the subject of films. Role-playing and the seeking of approval are narcissistic, vain, devious; they go against the straightforward image man has of himself. (The idea that ego without vanity can motivate a woman to become an actress appears conceivable only to Europeans—to Renoir, to Ophuls, to Bergman; but then, acting and actors are different in Europe.)

The actress becomes, then, for certain directors like Mankiewicz and Wilder what the woman is for certain homosexuals like Tennessee Williams and Edward Albee: not just the symbol of woman but the repository of certain repellent qualities which he would like to disavow. He projects onto her the narcissism, the vanity, the fear of growing old which he is horrified to find festering within himself. A grotesque mirror image of his own insecurity, the actress becomes the painting to the director's Dorian Gray. He loudly hawks the myth that women are more devastated by aging and by the idea of aging than men, but he knows, as recent studies of "menopause" in men show, that it can be just as convulsive for him. By seeing the grotesque side or by exaggerating the degree to which women are affected by age—always in the guise of sympathy—or by focusing on those kinds of women who dread aging most, men add fuel to the myth, and to women's misery, and transubstantiate their own. If the age of forty is traumatic for a woman, it is, for different reasons and not least because he is so little prepared for it, just as traumatic for a man.

Which brings us to *Sunset Boulevard* and *All About Eve,* brilliant films that, as sensitive as they are to a woman's concerns, are also veiled expressions of the anxieties of the directors, Billy Wilder and Joseph Mankiewicz, who were, respectively, forty-four and forty-one when they made them. With Swanson's Norma Desmond and Bette Davis' Margo Channing we are given (in the former more than the latter) the negative side of the positive actress image represented by Hepburn, Lombard, and even Jean Simmons. It is not just that Swanson and Davis are "old" (that is, middle-aged) where Hepburn, Lombard, and Simmons were young; it is that the emphasis is on their age rather than on their talents, their careers. We are concerned with those externals so important to the camera (and for this reason Margo Channing is closer to being a movie star than a stage actress), with women whose success has been based on looks more than on acting ability and for whom age, therefore, is more catastrophic. Margo Channing's career is over at forty; Norma Desmond's slightly later. Yet, in contradiction of these mythic and lugubrious deaths, actresses' careers often outlast those of actors, though not necessarily as romantic leads.

It is ironic that in *All About Eve* Davis is declared obsolete by standards of glamour in a sweepstakes that she of all people had never entered. The importance of the physical, then, is in part a projection of the directors themselves. The heroines are figures of ridicule only in the terms—physical and ephemeral—that the films endorse. By terminating these women's careers so precipitously and implausibly, the directors make us see them as women first rather than as actresses. There is no attempt—through flashbacks, or commemoration—to evoke the past of their glory except as a subjective, and therefore possibly distorted, memory haunting the present. And finally, because the source of their misery is merely "growing old," because their predicament is the stuff of vanity rather than tragedy, they are reduced and trivialized. Lola Montes, who must answer the most intimate audience questions in a traveling carnival, suffers but is never truly humiliated. Margo Channing and Norma Desmond, on the other hand, are humiliated without really suffering: Norma Desmond is a brilliant creation but archetypally unreal, a human vampire; Margo comes closer, through Davis' humanity, to suffering, but her stature is reduced by the general bitchiness of the milieu and of Mankiewicz' attitude toward it. The difference between Ophuls and Wilder–Mankiewicz is the difference between the profound insights of great art and the more pinched ones of camp, or rather between art that implicates the self in the free communion between the conscious and the unconscious, and art in which the link is misshapen, so that self-hatred is disguised and projected onto another, in this case a woman.

Certainly both films abound with talent and wit, and with insight as well. Otherwise they wouldn't be the "classics" they are. Who of even the most fractious feminists would want to erase Gloria Swanson's ex-glamour queen, reigning over her waxworks mansion with all the grace and dignity of a weasel in heat, sinking her claws into William Holden's writer-gigolo in the hopes of making a comeback? There's nothing reprehensible in showing an older woman in love with a younger man and growing old ungracefully. Women do it all the time. But so do men! Yet where are the male grotesques, except in an occasional Sidney Greenstreet performance or a minor-character situation. In Billy Wilder's *Love in the Afternoon,* Gary Cooper plays (admittedly, somewhat awkwardly) an Adolphe Menjou-type "older man" in love with a girl (Audrey Hepburn) half his age. Not only are his feelings reciprocated in full, but his passion is seen as heroic and exciting, whereas Swanson's is not only unreciprocated, but ugly and embarrassing as well. As a gargoyle of vanity and manipulation, she crystallizes the most artificial aspects of her screen persona into an image that has become hers for posterity. Just as the Marion Davies of *The Patsy* and *Show People* was usurped by the caricature of her in *Citizen Kane,* Gloria Swanson, the comic sport of the early silents, has been supplanted by the campy vamp of *Sunset Boulevard.*

Davis is a less sordid and more acceptable neurotic in *All About Eve.* She is anxious but unsuspicious, neither an opportunist like Anne Baxter's cat, clawing its way up the theater curtain, nor the vile-hearted termagant of her former vehicles. She is closer to the self-effacing sacrificial Davis of *The Great Lie* and *Old Acquaintance,* in which she gave Mary Astor and Miriam Hopkins their showy roles.

Margo's second source of anxiety (like Norma Desmond's) is her attachment to a younger man—the director-husband (played by Gary Merrill, whom Davis subsequently married and, ten years later, divorced), who is eight years younger than she. Once again, the older woman–younger man relationship is shown one-sidedly, with the emphasis on all the insecurities it produces (these in the woman only), and with none of the mutual advantages. Mankiewicz is not one to challenge female stereotypes if they are useful (*vide* his exploitation in the film of Marilyn Monroe's dumb-blonde image). The writer-director also follows Ingmar Bergman's footsteps in making the men in *All About Eve* (except Addison) patsies and weaklings. "They'll do as they're told," says the Celeste Holm character. But will they really? And would they be worth all the commotion if they did? Perhaps that is the final catch: It is the worthlessness of the men that makes a mockery of the women's love problems and delivers them, narcissistic camp queens talking to their own reflection, to the effeminists who appreciate them.

In both *All About Eve* and *A Letter to Three Wives,* Mankiewicz used an elaborate flashback technique and multiple viewpoints to suggest and expose the essentially feminine nature of facades and role-playing and acting. Men, that is, *real* men as opposed to actors and feminine men, are incapable of the kind of backbiting jealousy, cattiness, and triviality of the women in *A Letter to Three Wives*. And yet it is a man who so perfectly rendered (and understood?) these "typically feminine" emotions, leading us to the inevitable conclusion that there is more overlap between the sexes than is generally conceded. Even giving Vera Caspary some credit in the screenplay of *Letter,* it is largely overshadowed by Mankiewicz's massive, unmistakable impress: the structure, the dialogue, and the witty, but not always generous, classification of the human beast into subspecies. The highest approval, and our warmest response, goes to the most "feminine" character in the movie, Linda Darnell. Ann Sothern is subtly ridiculed as a successful television writer, and she is made to seem responsible for the problems besetting her marriage to Kirk Douglas. Sexism and cultural snobbery converge in the negative association of a woman and television writing. A "real writer" wouldn't waste his time or corrode his soul by writing for television, just as a "real man" wouldn't trivialize himself by going into acting. Perhaps the guilt of the "oldest whore on the block," as Mankiewicz jovially calls himself, was once again being slyly visited on a female character. But many of film's most exciting women have been given us by misogynists, by paranoids (Nicholas Ray) and by directors (Visconti) who wouldn't be caught dead in bed with them. Mankiewicz gets great performances from women. Ava Gardner, as legend, rebel, and expansive human being in *The Barefoot Contessa,* is one of his sublime creations. But Mankiewicz boasts of his love for women while denying or disguising his affinity for them. Hence, sometimes he speaks through his women, sometimes against them, and sometimes the two are confused.

In the case of Tennessee Williams' women, there is little

confusion. His hothouse, hot-blooded "earth mothers" and drag queens—Blanche Dubois, Serafina, Maggie, and Alexandra Del Lago—are as unmistakably a product of the fifties as they are of his own baroquely transvestized homosexual fantasies. By no stretch of the imagination can they be called "real" women, but they have a theatrical-emotional truth: they are composites, hermaphrodites of two strains—the putative anxiety and frustration of the spinster, and the palpable fear and self-pity, guts and bravura of the aging homosexual. It is from the male in them that the women acquire their hyperactive libidos—and Williams' women are much sexier than Wilder's and Mankiewicz's—precisely because the drives they express are not women's. The scenes between Swanson and Holden, and their embraces, for all their (one-sided) ferocity, are not sexual or even sensual; they are sensory, more like fingernails scratching across a blackboard. The scenes between Paul Newman and Geraldine Page in *Sweet Bird of Youth,* on the other hand, or between Marlon Brando and Vivien Leigh in *A Streetcar Named Desire* are powerfully sexual, in the flexing, posturing fascination of homosexual pornography for a repressed or "closet" seductee. The feelings expressed by Geraldine Page, Vivien Leigh, Anna Magnani for the studs played by Newman, Brando, and Burt Lancaster are of lust, not love, a desire not for souls but for beautiful bodies; but it is lust pierced with bitterer emotions—with the pathos and vulnerability and the self-exposure of the woman/homosexual past her/his prime. The other undercurrent in these tortured relationships is the ambivalence, even self-hatred, of the cultured homosexual who is bound to be spurned by the mindless young stud he is compelled, often masochistically and against his "taste," to love.

The women reveal their male orientation primarily in their physicality; they are not looking for a "total" relationship but for self-validation through a physical one. Whether it is innate or learned, men in real life continue to, and women continue not to, respond to nudity per se, that is, nudity isolated from the romantic values of psychology and context, or to parts of the body isolated from the whole. In this respect, body art, from pinups (male and female) to nudie magazines, is designed to appeal to homosexual and heterosexual men rather than to either type of woman. To excite women, pornography must be couched in different terms, less bald, more ingratiating, and geared to women's rather than men's fantasies. Generally it must build from a narrative basis, continuing from a slow start through resistance to seduction. The erotic lies in the "idea" rather than the graphic presentation of genitals, in that free play of the imagination to which most pornography is utterly alien.

In the sixties we came to realize that the figure of the stud (the gamekeeper, the "macho" Latin, the gigolo) is, like the sex-starved woman, largely a figment of male homosexual fantasy. But in the fifties they were presented in the guise of realism. Thus in William Inge's *Picnic,* made into a film in 1956 by Joshua Logan, Kim Novak's sexually repressed small-town beauty needs only William Holden's gleaming masculinity to bring her to life, and Rosalind Russel's caricature spinster schoolteacher must beg a man to marry her—and then stick her tongue out at the school as she drives away. And in *The Roman Spring of Mrs. Stone,* Mrs. Stone (Vivien Leigh) needs only Paolo's (Warren Beatty's) casual virility to know Life. In a twist on this, *Splendor in the Grass* (appearing in 1961 but belonging in spirit to the fifties), with its suggestion that sexual deprivation—the direct result of social hypocrisy—can lead to madness, suicide, and holocaust, has Beatty needing Natalie Wood in the back seat of his car. The Inge screenplay for *Splendor* promoted an idea once used as a ploy among high school lotharios who tried to get girls to "go all the way." But even in the benighted fifties, among non-sex-educated teen-agers, few fell for it.

The repressiveness of the fifties both enabled and forced the homosexual writer to disguise himself. For him, the frustrated woman who purported to express heterosexual desire was really a cover, an alter ego, a pretext and outlet for themes and feelings he was forced to hide. But homosexual writers through the ages have been able to express, and express themselves in, heterosexual fables. In terms of sexual permissiveness, the fifties offered too much and not enough. The problem was that sexuality itself was becoming central. The indeterminate sensibilities of the artists of the past were no longer possible, but the overt labeling of the sixties had not yet come into effect. The homosexual writer came halfway out of the closet, but disguised in women's clothes that bulged in the wrong places. Whether characters, women characters, are created by hetero- or homosexuals doesn't necessarily matter unless sex itself, that is, sexual desire, is introduced as a component of their nature, and they become a "front" for homosexual feelings. Gays complain that they never had identification figures in the movies, that the only couples the screen provided were heterosexual. But the irony is that if they weren't homosexual couples (or triangles, as in *Breakfast at Tiffany's*) they weren't exactly heterosexual either; and if the women weren't men, they sure weren't women.

Williams' women can be amusing company if we aren't asked to take them too seriously or too tragically. As the Coke-drinking, barefoot, bleached-out flower of the Old South, Baby Doll has her moments in the film that was denounced from the pulpit of Saint Patrick's Cathedral. But generally, under Kazan's direction (or Richard Brooks' in *Sweet Bird of Youth*), they were played as some kind of breakthrough in screen realism (what Kazan has described as a blend of naturalism and supernaturalism). Their life-blood is theatrical and histrionic, playfully and sometimes portentously erotic, and their final effect, with Kazan's viscerality added to Williams' feverish poetry, is an alternation of lyricism and caricature—sexy, yes, but also a little silly.

When Kazan is on his own without Williams, his women are not at all like this. The men have a physical force and even (what Williams' men can never have) a physical camaraderie. But the women are shy, inhibited, tentative, soulful, overshadowed by the agonies of tough-sensitive or tough-tough men. In one of his earliest films, *Panic in the Streets,* the contrast is thematically apposite. Richard Widmark is a federal health officer trying to track down the carrier of a plague, which is in danger of infesting New Orleans. We see Jack Palance, a villain whose henchman is the carrier, constantly making body contact in an aggressive, proprietary way with his subordinates. There is a feeling that the whole male world contaminates, and thus we feel a sharp poignancy when Widmark, having returned home tired and insecure, is lying down and Barbara Bel Geddes starts to touch him and he pulls back. The refusal is overpowering.

Similarly, Kazan's post-Williams heroines—Julie Harris' faithful tomboy pal in *East of Eden,* Patricia Neal's sensitive Sarah Lawrence graduate in *A Face in the Crowd,* Eva Marie Saint's pale urban princess in *On the Waterfront*—are all sexually shy and passive, waiting for the man to come to them. But this is partly because there is some other central concern with which the hero is preoccupied and to which they are only tangential. Unlike Williams' women (who are, after all, extensions of the author) Kazan's are reflections on the men, revealing their psychology through sexual preference, or sometimes, as in *Wild River,* showing up their weaknesses by a greater single-mindedness. The story is generally a man's story, and the conflicts Oedipal or fraternal, but the impact of the shy, subtle woman is all the more significant for the sense of contrast and the lack of histrionics.

Kazan's and Williams' women are perhaps opposite sides of a coin, one expressing the timidity, the other the bravura, of the decade. It was a time of conformity, of rigid standards of "in"ness and "out"ness, of shnooks like Judy Holliday and Jack Lemmon and Shiley MacLaine who were hopelessly "out" of it, and Elizabeth Taylor and Grace Kelly who were "in." Anti-intellectualism, never far from the surface in America, reigned supreme in the fifties' emphasis on popularity. The need to be loved by everybody (the Willy Loman complex), is an American fixation which becomes an obsession.

In the code of behavior governing the popularity contest, there were certain requirements, roughly the same for girls as for boys: It was mandatory to be a "good guy"—fun, witty but not intellectual, superior, neither a hard worker (a "grind") nor a sensualist ("fast"). Implied in this was the fear, for a man, of commitment; for a woman, it was more complex: fear of losing both her identity in a man's, and her "market value." And these fears were reflected in movie star tastes and distastes. Jennifer Jones, Ava Gardner, and Marilyn Monroe were "out"—too voluptuous and sexy. Doris Day and Debbie Reynolds were all right—a trifle corny, but cute and fun. Elizabeth Taylor was the supreme identification figure of all tomboy horse-lovers in *National Velvet,* but she lost their loyalty when she grew intolerably voluptuous. Finally, Grace Kelly and Audrey Hepburn were dead-center "in," boyish and invulnerable, aristocratic and independent. They never swallowed their pride, exploited their sexuality, or made fools of themselves over men. Marilyn did, and she aroused our jealousy and contempt.

Our feelings about Marilyn Monroe have been so colored by her death and not simply, as the uncharitable would have us think, because she is no longer an irritation or a threat, but because her suicide, as suicides do, casts a retrospective light on her life. Her "ending" gives her a beginning and middle, turns her into a work of art with a message and a meaning.

Women, particularly, have become contrite over their previous hostility to Monroe, canonizing her as a martyr to male chauvinism, which in most ways she was. But at the time, women couldn't identify with her and didn't support her. They allowed her to be turned into a figure of ridicule, as they allowed Ingrid Bergman to be crucified by the press. They blamed these stars for acting disadvantageously, whereas they sympathized with Rita Hayworth and Elizabeth Taylor for moving (in the words applied to *That Hamilton Woman*) "lower and lower but always up and up." At the same time, in their defense, women hated Marilyn for catering so shamelessly to a false, regressive, childish, and detached idea of sexuality.

What was she, this breathless, blonde, supplicating symbol of sexuality, the lips anxiously offering themselves as the surrogate orifice, the whisper unconsciouly expressing trepidation? And who made her what she was? She was partly a hypothesis, a pinup fantasy of the other woman as she might be drawn in the marital cartoon fantasies of Maggie and Jiggs, or Blondie and Dagwood, and thus an outgrowth, once again, of misogamy. She was the woman that every wife fears seeing with her husband in a convertible (Hawks' *Monkey Business*) or even in conversation, and that every emasculated or superfluous husband would like to think his wife lives in constant fear of. She was the masturbatory fantasy that gave satisfaction and demanded nothing in return; the wolfbait, the eye-stopper that men exchanged glances over; the erotic sex-and-glamour symbol to Easterners like Arthur Miller turned on by the Hollywood vulgarity the way Nabokov was by that temple of philistinism, the American motel.

The times being what they were, if she hadn't existed we would have had to invent her, and we did, in a way. She was the fifties' fiction, the lie that a woman has no sexual needs, that she is there to cater to, or enhance, a man's needs. She was the living embodiment of half of one of the more grotesque and familiar pseudo-couples—the old man and the "showgirl," immortalized in *Esquire* and *Playboy* cartoons.

The difference between Monroe and the archetypal brassy blonde is the difference between Monroe and Jayne Mansfield, the real cartoon of overblown sex appeal, the fifties' synecdoche (with the part, or rather pair, standing for the whole whose comic grotesqueness was exploited, with complementary male absurdities, by Frank Tashlin in *Will Success Spoil Rock Hunter?* and *The Girl Can't Help It.* Unlike Mansfield, Monroe's heart wasn't in it; they—the cartoon blondes—are hard but she was soft.

She catered to these fantasies and played these roles because she was afraid that if she stopped—which she did once and for all with sleeping pills—there would turn out to be nothing there, and therefore nothing to love. She was never permitted to mature into a warm, vibrant woman, or fully use her gifts for comedy, despite the signals and flares she kept sending up. Instead, she was turned into a figure of mockery in the parts she played and to the men she played with. In *The Asphalt Jungle* and *All About Eve,* she was a sex object and nincompoop. In *How to Marry a Millionaire, We're Not Married, The Seven Year Itch,* and *Niagara,* she was paired with sexless leading men (David Wayne, David Wayne, Tom Ewell, Joseph Cotten) while the other women (Bacall and Grable in *How to Marry,* for example) were given reasonable partners. In *Bus Stop,* with its covertly homosexual patterns, she played a parody earth mother to Don Murray's innocent stud. In Hawks' *Monkey Business* and *Gentlemen Prefer Blondes* she played a tootsie who is most comfortable with older men (Charles Coburn in both) and little boys (Cary Grant as a regressed scientist and George Winslow as a real youngster). In *Some Like It Hot,* her leading man—Tony Curtis—did a Cary Grant imitation, and was thus a "bogus" romantic lead. In her "serious" roles, in *Don't Bother to Knock* and *Niagara,* she was a psychopath, while Anne Bancroft and Jean Peters played the normal women. When she finally played an ex-saloon singer with brains and feelings who *evolves* emotionally (Preminger's *River of No Return,* opposite Robert Mitchum), the film was a flop: Audiences wouldn't accept her as a real woman. In *Let's Make Love,* she played a silly Cinderella to Yves Montand's millionaire. And in *The Prince and the Showgirl* and *The Misfits,* playing opposite Olivier and Gable, her image as sexpot and/or psychopath, as it had already evolved from her Fox films, was treated almost in the abstract, that is, was accepted, unquestioned, as her identity.

And yet, throughout her career, she was giving more to idiotic parts than they called for—more feeling, more warmth, more anguish; and, as a result, her films have a richer tone than they deserve. The best ones, which is to say, the best she could get under the circumstances, are the films that suggest the discrepancy between the woman (and young girl) and the sexpot, even as their directors (Wilder and Hawks) exploit the image, through exaggeration, more than they have to—though still more gently than other directors.

In Billy Wilder's *Some Like It Hot,* Tony Curtis and Jack Lemmon are musicians who, dressed as women, flee Chicago with an all-girl orchestra to escape the mob, as they have inadvertently witnessed a gangland rubout. Their "transvestism" or sexual inversion matches Marilyn's excesses, on the one hand, and Joe E. Brown's "recesses" on the other. Too blonde and buxom, Marilyn is as much "in drag" as they are, a child playing the monumentally daffy, all-American blonde tootsie. She finds in Lemmon her soulmate —a little girl like herself playing grown-up; but in Curtis she finds the sexual casualty (the would-be leading man to match her would-be leading lady) whose strengths match her weaknesses and weaknesses her strengths. They become "lovers" after their own fashion, while, in a parody of Marilyn's usual film fate, Lemmon plays sugar daughter to Joe E. Brown's sugar daddy, and one relationship is no more "heterosexual" or even sexual than the other. And yet, for all the "adult sexuality" they miss and the inadequacies they parade, their relationships are full of feeling, a lost paradise of innocence that, in less charming form, is the temptation of eternal retrogression. They offer a heightened comic understanding of the priorities and evasions of American society and sexual relations, as childhood, extended into middle age, passes into second childhood without so much as a pause or interruption for adulthood. For once, Wilder has found the perfect vehicle and tone for his mixed feelings about America, and there is no covert nastiness or cheap cynicism. The American Dream, male and female versions, with all its materialism and adolescent exuberance, goes through perversion and comes out the other side. And Marilyn, the little girl playing in her mamma's falsies, the sex symbol of America, is right there where the dream turns into a cartoon and back into a dream again.

As the gold digger in *Gentlemen Prefer Blondes*— Hawks' considerably reworked version of the Anita Loos' play and musical—Marilyn consciously exploits the sex-bomb image that men, with their lascivious glances, have forced on her, and gets her revenge in spades . . . or, rather, diamonds. In this spoof of ooh-la-la, it is not women but men who are exposed and humiliated, and the two girls, strutting their wares, command awe much like two renowned gunfighters. The setting, an ocean liner, is deliberately garish, with pinks and reds clashing unmercifully; and the males, usually seen in groups, consist of a little boy, an old man, a suitor who turns out to be a spy, and a group of athletes so intent on toning up their bodies that they fail to observe Jane Russell in their midst. Here Marilyn has accepted her image, and will go one better: She is determined to get paid for it. In the long run, what makes her attractive to men—to a particular kind of man—will wither, while they turn to younger and younger versions of her. She must, therefore, shore up something for her old age, and diamonds are better security than love on marriage. Russell, the champion of love and marriage, is soon disillusioned and joins Marilyn in common cause. Opting for diamonds over *a* diamond, she dons a blonde wig in imitation of Marilyn, in cynical deference to the preference of gentlemen.

Monroe's career, with her death, became a *fait accompli*. It is no longer possible to separate the woman from her image, or to know if it was alterable or not. We can regret all the missed opportunities, but can we wish away the sex "hype" on which Marilyn's career was built and her soul strung out? What if Marilyn had been, as the saying goes, "herself"? Would anyone have gone to the movies to see a sexless and childlike young woman, with dirty blonde hair, a soft voice, ambition, and an inferiority complex? And would we, or she, have been better off if Marilyn had never been born, and if Norma Jean, sitting on the front porch of some Southern California rest home, or even surrounded by a brood of children, were rocking her way into oblivion? All we can say is that she has told us, through her stardom and abuse, more about ourselves than we would have known without her.

The one thing in Marilyn that we can never forget, and perhaps never forgive, is the painful, naked, and embarrassing need for love. This is the quality captured by Paddy Chayevsky in his script for *The Goddess,* the film, directed by John Cromwell, based loosely on the Monroe myth. Here the need for love is given a plausible, and dramatically effective, explanation in the relationship between the small-town girl (Kim Stanley) and her Baptist stepmother, a figure of righteous piety, a stone from which nothing—no amount of accomplishment or money—can squeeze love. Their tortuous relationship suggests something gaping and unfillable that drives a woman to stardom or drink or suicide, or all three. It is a terrible paradox that ambition in a woman goes against her normal or conditioned social instincts and role, and is fed by the neurosis stemming from lack of love, while ambition, as the right and proper way of a man, is fed and augmented by love. And perhaps that very mother-love that gives him the confidence to proceed, has been withheld from the girl, who as "only a girl" is thought to have less need of it. Mothers, revealing their lack of esteem for their own sex (themselves) place their faith and greater love (and greater expectations) in their sons. The boy is generally the white hope of the family, the custodian of its name, while the girl, at best, will share and adorn someone else's. Thus, her desperation and anxiety—the need to secure the love of a man whose property she will become, and to recover the impossible—the love withheld her by her own family.

In most respects—as the plain Jane from the wrong side of the tracks, making out with boys just to get dates, grabbing the first chance to get out of the hellhole she lives in—Kim Stanley's Emily Ann seems closer to Norma Jean than to the sex goddess, whose charisma we must take on faith. And, despite its subject, *The Goddess* really belongs, by virtue of its script, director, actress, and look, to the New York school of realism. Kim Stanley, a black-and-white actress, plays Marilyn Monroe, a technicolor star (even if most of her films were in black and white). Stanley, Shelley Winters, Colleen Dewhurst, Geraldine Page, Julie Harris—these were the women who intimidated Marilyn Monroe, women who were the toasts and talents of the Actors Studio and the Broadway stage, places where Marilyn's credentials were practically useless. But if she, as Arthur Miller's wife, was a back-door Jennie at the Actors Studio, she had them all beat by a mile on the screen where she was a natural, and where even the seam between the shy little girl and the sensual blonde was so transparent that it was, for all intents and purposes, seamless. On the screen, the others were "slumming." They made movies the way the East Siders used to go to Harlem, and you could, more often than not, see the wheels clicking. You could see the strenuously subdued effects building up into "sloppy naturalism," or "sleazy decadence," or "suppressed hysteria": Kim Stanley's too knowing (and too adult) small-townishness in the early scenes of *The Goddess*; Shelley Winters' startled wistfulness becoming, after *A Place in the Sun* a broken (or unbroken) record of pathos.

Meanwhile, Marilyn was not exactly winning popularity contests and setting styles on her home ground. Many stars—Doris Day and Debbie Reynolds, Audrey Hepburn and Grace Kelly—materialized in conscious or unconscious opposition to her and the type she represented. Of the fleshier females with whom she might be thought to share something, Jane Russell was considered largely a joke. Ava Gardner's combination of sensuality and aesthetic appeal, a presence that overwhelmed dramatic shortcomings, made her into something larger than life, too exotic to be an American woman, and as a result she was always playing half-castes (*Bhowani Junction*), outcasts (*The Barefoot Contessa, The Killers*), and revenant redeemers (*Pandora and the Flying Dutchman*).

Left: William Holden as fifties superstud and Kim Novak as the prettiest nice girl in town in a publicity still from *Picnic*. This particular, and peculiarly fifties, notion of sexual affinities was a heterosexualized projection of homosexual tastes.

Elizabeth Taylor as the jockey of *National Velvet* (*top right*) and the idol of horse-lovers and tomboys everywhere grows up—and out—to become the intolerably voluptuous Maggie the Cat in *Cat on a Hot Tin Roof* (*bottom right*).

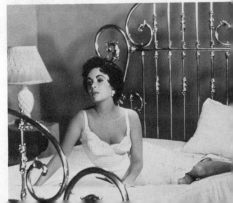

Below: In *Some Like It Hot,* Billy Wilder captures, with more charm than acidity, the infantile nature of American sexual morality, as personified in Marilyn Monroe. Here she creates a doll house on a pullman with innocently inverted playmate Jack Lemmon.

Facing page (*top*): Margo Channing (Bette Davis) congratulates Eve Harrington (Anne Baxter) in the great cat-clawing confrontation of all time, in *All About Eve,* as Bill Sampson (Gary Merrill) and Addison de Witt (George Sanders) look on: ". . . nice speech, Eve. But I wouldn't worry too much about your heart. You can always put that award where your heart ought to be." *Bottom:* Gloria Swanson as aging ex-star Norma Desmond and William Holden as her "house guest" prepare, over after-dinner smokes and old movies, for Norma's comeback, in *Sunset Boulevard.*

Facing page (top): What's wrong with the picture? or transsexual masquerade. In *Breakfast at Tiffany's,* from the Truman Capote novel, Audrey Hepburn's Holly Golightly regards with some suspicion the transaction between George Peppard's stud-lover and Patricia Neal as his guardian. (The legend on the taxi door reads "Take your property.") The story makes more sense if Patricia Neal is seen as an aging queen who has to pay for it and Hepburn as a young fairy princess who doesn't. *Bottom:* Micheline Presle and Gerard Philipe as the classic older woman–younger man in *Devil and the Flesh.* (She will die giving birth to his baby, which he will lack the courage to claim.)

Ingrid Bergman *(top)* in Rossellini's *Stromboli,* as the modern, alienated woman who prefigures Monica Vitti *(middle)*, as used by Antonioni in *L'Avventura* to express a similar cosmic and womanly ennui. *Bottom:* In *Persona,* Bibi Andersson and Liv Ullmann look into a mirror, as their identities seem to merge.

Anna Magnani as the prima donna of the troupe of commedia dell' arte players traveling through South America in *The Golden Coach.* Through the institution that, historically, first employed women as professional actresses, Renoir expresses his reverence for women and theater in one glorious, dynamic, endlessly self-creating image of "authentic" role-playing.

In his early films Bergman goes "behind the scenes." Here, Annalisa Ericson is in the foreground and Mai-Britt Nilsson in the background of the film *Summer Interlude,* in which Nilsson, through a reliving of the past, comes to terms with aging, performing, the death of an idyllic love, and the beginning of a less than perfect one.

Left: Jeanne Moreau in Truffaut's *Jules and Jim,* a Nietzschean superwoman, apparently free and yet fated to be the vehicle of men's fantasies. She is a creature of impulse and desire for the first half of the film, and of doom and destruction for the second.

Top right: Jimmy Stewart suggests a murderer rather than a man determined to refashion an ordinary girl (Kim Novak as Judy) into the replica of the woman (Kim Novak as Madeleine) he has fallen in love with and allowed—he thinks— to die, in Hitchcock's *Vertigo. Bottom right:* Jean-Louis Trintignant's fastidious Catholic bachelor is engaged, by the vibrant Maud (Françoise Fabian), in an all-night binge of conversation, confession, sensual openings (by Maud), and evasions (by Trintignant) in Eric Rohmer's *My Night at Maud's.*

Above: Catherine Deneuve, as the *soignée,* upper-middle-class housewife in the morning and "Belle de Jour" in the afternoon, poses with her colleagues chez Madame Anais (Genevieve Page) in Bunuel's *Belle de Jour.* *Left:* Jane Fonda as the prostitute in *Klute,* who hangs on to her identity by charging men for what other women give out free.

As for Elizabeth Taylor, she was a beautiful package, perfectly fashioned, but without a breath of idiosyncrasy. She grew up in movies and was not, like Kim Novak, brought in and tailored to a certain image (in her case, Rita Hayworth's). Elizabeth Taylor's voice, like that of her less interesting successor, Raquel Welch, had a finishing-school flavorlessness. She was letting it all hang out—but what was it? There was a suggestion of fragility under her beauty and, like Marilyn, she seemed more comfortable with the sweet, sensitive men (Montgomery Clift and James Dean) than the supposedly rugged ones. But she had the ego to survive and become a power. In the beginning, her beauty was enough to carry her through and make any picture she was in worth looking at. She was a "man's woman": in *Giant,* she breaks a southern taboo by straying from the ladies' conversation to join the men. (But she is no rebel; on incurring Rock Hudson's displeasure she pursues the matter no further.) In her apparent sexuality, she was a perfect Tennessee Williams' heroine, sex being the inducement (blatantly spelled out in *Suddenly, Last Summer*) that would attract men like flypaper, and in *Cat on a Hot Tin Roof* she turned Maggie into a garish, musical-comedy idea of sensuality.

Elizabeth Taylor bridged the gap between the "sexy" stars—Monroe, Gardner—and their opposites, and between the letter and the spirit of musical comedy. For it is that spirit—that uniquely American hybrid of high style and greeting-card philosophy, expertise and evasion, artistry and sentimentality—that pervaded the fifties' love stories and comedies that either were, or might as well have been, musicals. Stars like Debbie Reynolds, Doris Day, and Shirley MacLaine belong to the musical-comedy ethic: championing the sunny over the sultry, the romantic over the sexual, and personality over glamour. Theirs are the happy, freckled faces of childhood—still happy and freckled into maturity; simple, uncomplicated, all-American flowers, beaming daisies rather than furled roses or decadent orchids. Song is the natural idiom for their voices and their optimism, for their loves that can't be kept secret, and we feel the presence of song, or the possibility of it, even in nonmusicals, even in un-American roles, like Shirley MacLaine's happy hooker in *Irma la Douce* (actually a nonmusical adaptation of a stage musical) or her less happy hooker in Minnelli's *Some Came Running*. But MacLaine was different from Reynolds and Day. Like Stella Stevens, or like her European counterpart, Giulietta Masina, she was and is tougher and more battered, and more of a doormat. In any case, she was less a mythic figure than the other two, whose naturalness and "girl next door" personalities made them the fifties' successors to the twenties' "personality" types—Colleen Moore, Marion Davies—who represented the hometown team against European phoniness and big-city glamour.

Day and Reynolds represented not just naturalness, but naturalness as a convention, as a reaction to something else, the way producers of commericals use nonactors, "real" housewives and balding men, to counter the hype and falsehood of the message itself. Doris Day was the antithesis of Marilyn Monroe, an opposition made explicit in a 1962 comedy, *The Thrill of It All*. A fresh, ingenuous housewife, she and husband James Garner are dining at the home of a big soap manufacturer. They come in just as he, watching a commerical for his soap, is expressing disgust at the blonde starlet who slithers out of a bubble bath and gives her pitch in a panting, provocative style obviously redolent of Monroe. When Doris Day recounts a funny, "true" story of how she got her children to use the soap, the enchanted executive hires her on the spot to replace the sex symbol. And when she does the commercial live, her fumbling, improvised performance charms the televiewers. But in satirizing the artificiality of most of television through a Monroe look-alike, scriptwriter Carl Reiner is also implicating Monroe in its plastic prepackaging methods.

If anyone seems to have been prepackaged, it is Debbie Reynolds; for where Marilyn was false to her sexuality in only the most innocent way, Reynolds was false to her innocence in the most calculating way. In all her roles—as Tammy, as Sinatra's nemesis in *The Tender Trap*—she was tough as nails, the perpetual ingenue as aggressor. She was, like the ingenue in *The Moon Is Blue* (whether played by Maggie McNamara or, on the stage, by Barbara Bel Geddes), a phenomenon of the fifties—a professional virgin, and the final retribution for the polarization of women into good girls and bad. Reynolds' charmlessness seems almost intentional. Spiky, intrusive, a chatterer, she is the visitation on man of those nightmare fantasies of adorable girls who look enchanting from afar but ruin everything when they open their mouths. She is, once again, the sweetheart as preview of the wife, the justification, with her sexless, domineering ways, for misogamy before the fact. She is the embodiment of all the mistrust and hypocrisy legislated into the Production Code and frozen into a smile, the tease whose every romantic ploy is directed toward marriage and security. It is not her mercenary streak that is offensive—for every woman needs to protect her interests—but her pretense at guilelessness that most irritates. She is nevertheless a talented comedienne, with an unrelenting energy that is a show in itself. When her ruthlessness is exposed rather than concealed, as in the character of the materialistic Southern California wife in *Divorce, American Style*, she can be extremely effective.

Doris Day shared with Debbie Reynolds a certain enterprising spirit and wholesomeness. Both were brash and bold, yet not unemotional, and neither was a helpless, panting female or a recumbent Camille. But here the similarity ends, for Day was a good deal more giving and vulnerable, and she was willing to commit herself emotionally to a degree that has been both overlooked and misunderstood. Debbie Reynolds reminds one of a wretchedly precocious child who even at three was "the little lady," perfecting her dimples and dancing eyes for the day when they would come in handy. Doris Day, on the other hand, begins as a tomboy resisting the frills and appurtenances of being a lady just as later she will resist the frills and facade, but not the emotional reality, of sexual commitment. A good example is a 1951 musical, *On Moonlight Bay,* in which she played a prewar bobby-soxer who, when the family moves to a new neighborhood, staggers and embarrasses the boys with her ball-playing ability. When she meets and falls in love with Gordon Mac-Rae, she willingly but painfully undergoes the training program—dress, dancing lessons—through which she will be transformed into a lady.

When she grows up, she often has a career, about which she is serious, even obsessive. In *My Dream Is Yours,* she is a young widow who comes to Hollywood, under Jack Carson's managerial auspices, in the hope of becoming a professional singer. Her determination is counterpointed comically, a little maliciously, by Eve Arden's sarcasm as Day moves, lock, stock, dog, and child, into Arden's small apartment, oblivious to the inconvenience she is causing. (Once again Arden's superior sensibility and humor are presented as factors inhibiting her success with men and her career.) Day's ambition will not even give way when it is apparent that her success will destroy the relationship with the man she loves. The son becomes a substitute for the lover, and the receptacle, also, for the impetus of displaced ambition. She sings a torch song as a lullaby to him and their rapport brings to mind a similar sequence in Alfred Hitchcock's *The Man Who Knew Too Much,* in which the intensity of her attachment to the son bordered on hysteria. In that film, Hitchcock made it clear that, in forcing her to give up her stage career to marry him, Jimmy Stewart's doctor is responsible for her frustration, her dependence on pills, and her neurosis. In both films, her excesses as a mother—her oversolicitousness and emotionalism—lead us to suspect that she may be playing a false role, covering up for a lack of maternal feelings and a reluctance to be a mother at all.

From the series of comedies produced by Stanley Shapiro in the late fifties and early sixties—*Pillow Talk, Lover, Come Back,* and *That Touch of Mink*—the image of Doris Day we have somehow accepted is that of a forty-year-old virgin defending her maidenhead into a ripe old age. On the contrary, though she begins, usually, as a sexually backward young woman, she overcomes inhibitions and covers light-years in sex education. Unabashedly puritanical, she usually hails from some midwestern town and eschews (but does not condemn) drink and dirty words. And yet, she is ready to give herself to the man she loves. What prevents her is not her coyness but the plot's, not the sacred cherry, but the plot's machinations, which always intervene at the eleventh hour.

In *Lover Come Back,* she is an account executive (once again, she has a job which she takes seriously and obviously enjoys) in a Madison Avenue advertising firm. News has leaked out about a secret product soon to be launched by the rival firm, a product that Rock Hudson has simply fabricated as an expense account dodge. When Day sets out to woo the inventor of the product, Hudson, caught at a scientist's lab (for he has now been forced to come up with something) poses as the bashful scientist and allows Day to wine him, dine him, and provide him with ingenious ideas for advertising the product. Day retains her good faith to the end; it is Hudson, a notorious womanizer and wastrel, who practices the deceit. But the duplicity allows each of them to uncover his or her true identity. As the scientist Hudson becomes repressed and passive, forcing Day to take the initiative (at first professionally) and finally overcome her ingrained prudishness and bring him out as a lover. While he is lying in the spare room, supposedly too shy to make a pass, she quaffs a glass of champagne, dons a negligee, and is about to give herself to him, when the phone rings. It is her boss, informing her of the hoax.

As things work out, her integrity surpasses that of Hudson and his colleagues (Madison Avenue not being notoriously rich in this commodity). They wind up, following a series of comic contrivances, in a motel, the memory of their marriage obliterated by the drunken state they were in when the ceremony was performed. Day awakens beside Hudson and is horrified. "It's all right—you're my wife," he says, naturally assuming that it is the idea of illicit sex that appalls her. But Day, more concerned with his character than with her virginity, is not so easily mollified, and she has the marriage annulled immediately. She leaves town and the next scene occurs months later. She is in a hospital, about to go through with having Hudson's baby when he arrives, chastened and reformed, and becomes her husband again just in time to make the baby legitimate.

There is something here beneath the plot contrivances, and something in Doris Day, that is truer to the American reality than most critics would like to admit. They extol Jeanne Moreau's decadent caprices and Simone Signoret's sultry passion as "realistic," while they find Doris Day's virginity and innocence a superhygienic cotton-candy fable fed to gullible audiences. Actually, it is the comic obstacle course of Doris Day's life, her lack of instinctive knowledge about "being a woman," and the concomitant drive, ambition, and energy that are closer to the American reality than the libidinous concentration of Jeanne Moreau or the metaphysical purity, uncomplicated by the little details of life, of Ingmar Bergman's screen women. (One can hardly imagine Doris Day saying, as Jeanne Moreau once said in an interview—and says implicitly in all her films—that the man should always be master. And we see Day exercising, consciously or unconsciously, a right denied most European, and particularly Bergman's, women: the right not to be a mother.)

The "reassuring qualities" Dwight Macdonald attributes to her in his essay "The Doris Day Syndrome" to explain her appeal to women refer, presumably, to a surface glamorlessness that makes her less threatening to women in the audience. (And why shouldn't women want occasionally to be represented by someone less dazzling than Dietrich or Garbo?) But actually this assumption gives a false impression of Day's character, for not only is she not reassuring, but she makes us uncomfortable. Unlike Grace Kelly, she is not safe, not invulnerable, but, beneath the cheerfulness of the extrovert, she is uncertain, a little shaky. Because she doesn't have the European woman's sense of sexual identity and social place, she is more alone, and more American. And because she doesn't have the model good looks and grace of the American beauty, she must exert herself to achieve. A home-grown existential female lifted into the modern world with a few fundamental moral guidelines, she creates herself. Out of the assorted impulses of ambition and love she becomes someone and tries, with plenty of odds against her, to find out where she belongs and what she can do.

Where Audrey Hepburn and Grace Kelly have only to lift a finger or an eyebrow, Doris Day must work hard, and for a happiness that seems more often than not to hang by a thread. Thus it is not Doris Day, but Audrey Hepburn, whom most mothers want their daughters to grow up to be like and in whom they see their own (real or imagined) poised and protected youth. And it is with Audrey Hepburn and Grace Kelly that young girls, anxious about their sexuality, most strongly identify. Hepburn and Kelly seem safe from the kind of humiliation to which Marilyn Monroe and Jennifer Jones submit. With their slender, reedy grace and boyish figures, they evoke the freedom of adolescence, the androgynous state where a girl identifies with her father as much as with her mother. It is the time before the body has sprouted those features designed so explicitly to imprison her in her role as woman and mother. The menstrual period, the indoctrination into sex, the embarrassment over breasts (unseemly protrusions some would like to have bound tight the way the Chinese women bind their feet), the fear of pregnancy, all leave scars that not even the efforts of Masters and Johnson are always able to heal. In the fifties, through such stars as Hepburn, Kelly, and Day, who escaped the chains of motherhood in their films, the tomboy in woman seemed to cling longer than usual to its prerogatives, and there was a delay in the full flowering (or resigned) acceptance of the maternal role.

But the apparent self-sufficiency of Audrey Hepburn and Grace Kelly got them into trouble. On the one hand, Audrey Hepburn's poise and elfin (a) sexuality, like Kelly's blonde imperturbability, insured her against mistreatment and against striking an unequal (that is, masochistic) bargain. On the other hand, this very superiority aroused resentment. In *Roman Holiday,* Gregory Peck, returning from a night of cards with the boys, is more irritated than delighted to find a beautiful girl in his path. Kelly's cool, which protects her in most cases, served as a pique to Alfred Hitchcock, whose films with her—*To Catch a Thief, Rear Window*—are as much critiques as displays of her effortless star radiance. In *To Catch a Thief,* she is (somewhat autobiographically?) the daughter of a *nouveau riche* millionairess (the father has died, the mother, played by Jessie Royce Landis, is earthy and wonderful), and her rough edges have been polished off too successfully by finishing school. She is spoiled (though fearful underneath that men want her only for her money); she plays with feelings perversely (she is tantalized by the idea of Grant as a cat burglar—until she thinks he has robbed her mother; unlike her mother, she has no instinctive trust or intuitions by which to sense his honesty). In *Rear Window,* she is more committed to their relationship than is Jimmy Stewart, but there is not much in her chic vacuous personality to commit. Like all the heroines Hitchcock wants to shake from real, or imagined, complacency, she is exposed to mortal danger. In both films, she passes the test—for she does have physical courage—with flying colors, but there is a dangling question mark, as the film ends, as to whether she has really changed, or only gotten what she wanted.

Behind a woman's defensive "game" there is the very real fear—a fear to which some directors seem more sympathetic than others—of losing herself in marriage, of losing her identity along with her name. This theme becomes the explicit subject of one of John Ford's loveliest (and from this point of view, most surprising) films, *The Quiet Man.* In marrying John Wayne, the American who has come back to live in Ireland, Maureen O'Hara's redhead Irish firebrand insists on recovering her dowry from her father: a £350 "fortune" and her furniture. Wayne is indignant. In characteristic American fashion, he feels his masculinity and ability to provide for her impugned, until she finally makes him understand that it isn't the money, but what it stands for: The dowry and furniture are her identity, her independence. The furniture, particularly, is part of her personality —like a maiden name—and the money enables her not to be completely dependent on her husband and "absorbed" by him. When she finally does recover the money, she throws it into a furnace.

The dowry is a European custom and this suggests that they understand better than we do the imbalance institutionalized in marriage; of course, it also compensates for the fact that their women enter into marriage with even fewer rights and protections than ours. On the one hand, marriage is a woman's protection, on the other, it legalizes and reinforces her dependency. The point is made rather unusually in a Raoul Walsh film, *The Lawless Breed*. Rock Hudson has fallen in love, and begun living, with the "tough broad" played by Julie Adams—a choice consistent, as critic William Paul has pointed out, with the Walshian hero's eventual preference for the smart, tough woman (the soulmate) over the nice-girl. Adams, however, has suddenly fallen into a state of demoralized inertia (not unlike Ann-Margret's depression in *Carnal Knowledge*). When the couple confront the problem, she tells him she feels he has not really committed himself to her, that he has an out and she does not. He has his "consciousness raised." One evening he returns, without warning her, with the preacher. Their marriage, a crazy, impromptu ceremony, preserves their unique flavor in a union which at the same time provides an underlying security.

Generally, when a woman "acted up"—and her claims to power and liberation would always be considered erratic by the standards of a man's world and peace of mind—the man would either try to tame her, Rhett Butler and Petruchio style, or, failing that, would retreat into indifference with a cool "I don't give a damn." Directors followed the same policy, and in the fifties there were not only fewer films about emancipated women than in the thirties or forties, but there were fewer films about women. Wilder and Mankiewicz are exceptions, as are the two Ford and Walsh films. The big, important pictures as well as the little, cultist ones were practically all male-oriented: tall (weatherbeaten) tales of the last (boxer/Western hero/gangster/gunfighter/you-name-it). What were the big films? *Bridge on the River Kwai, Shane, High Noon, Viva Zapata, The Asphalt Jungle, Stalag 17, The Killing, Somebody Up There Likes Me, Twelve Angry Men,* and so on and so on. No less monolithically male were films by such cultist favorites as Samuel Fuller, Anthony Mann, Robert Aldrich, Don Siegel, and, round the horizon with their six-shooters ready, Budd Boetticher and Sam Peckinpah. With the emergence of neurotically personal, anti-Hollywood types like Nicholas Ray, Joseph Losey, and John Frankenheimer, relations between men and women on film were beginning to look increasingly bleak, not to say paranoid. The distance between Gloria Grahame and Humphrey Bogart at the end of Ray's *In a Lonely Place,* set the tone of impossibility for heterosexual romance, but, wide as the gap was, it was about as close in mutual understanding as Ray's men and women would ever get.

The women's market and the woman's film were disappearing just as the genre's crowning glories—Leo McCarey's *An Affair to Remember,* Douglas Sirk's whole *oeuvre*—were being released to critical apathy or, as usual, condescension. Television was taking over the soap opera function of the woman's film, whose acceptance depended, like the war film, on a universal belief in its causes and premises and an unqualified surrender to its emotional pull. But while the war film somehow managed to survive in one form or another, the woman's film went under, though not, fortunately, without such glorious—and subversive—last gasps as Sirk's *The Tarnished Angels, Take Me to Town, Written on the Wind, Imitation of Life,* and *All That Heaven Allows.* Sirk, a European intellectual, captured as well as anyone the paradox—the energy, the vulgarity, the poverty of values, the gleaming surfaces and soulless lives, the sickness of delusion, the occasional healthy burst of desire—of America, of the fifties, of the cinema itself. Working for the most commercial of producers, Ross Hunter, whose America was one of picturesque landscapes, drowsy mornings, intrigue-ridden afternoons, and happy endings, Sirk managed to use these elements (to bring them, in fact, to a stylish apotheosis), in order to expose them from within. The staples of middle-class life—handsome houses, lavish decors, fast cars, busy social lives, spoiled, demanding children—were the bars of the prison. The mirrors and frames that are Sirk's visual trademark, reflect, among other things, both the frozen, artificial quality and the illusory nature of these creature comforts. Sirk's women all seem to come to us from some glossy-magazine spread, harried, but perfectly coiffed, housewives in a two-dimensional world from which some escape while others remain flattened and embalmed. His films express different needs and different degrees of yearning complacency: Joan Bennett, the quintessential mother in *There's Always Tomorrow* opposite Barbara Stanwyck's uncertain career woman; Dorothy Malone, the reckless bad-girl heroine of *Written on the Wind*; Lana Turner, the glazed, self-centered actress-mother of *Imitation of Life*; and JaneWyman, the mature and delicately sensitive heroine of *All That Heaven Allows* and *Magnificent Obsession*. And in each case, the mirrors suggest, in Sirkian fashion, different orders of self-consciousness: Lana Turner's vacant narcissism, which gives the impression she is looking at herself in a mirror even when she is not; or, in contrast, Jane Wyman's introspective and extroverted self-awareness, her sense of herself and her social position pitted against the urgings of her heart.

Salvation for Sirk's heroines, contrary to the practice of most women's films, is not in the sacrifice of oneself to children or social codes, but in the refusal to make that sacrifice. And his children, far from being the beribboned darlings of so many films, are often monsters of selfishness and unconcern. The two children in *There's Always Tomorrow,* treat their mother (Joan Bennett) like a helpless child and their father (Fred MacMurray) like an interloper. Having sacrificed herself totally to her children, she now reaps the dubious rewards of having them turn the tables in a sick charade of their relationship, excluding the father just as she had. He, in turn, has probably encouraged the separation of home and business, cherishing the dream of a former love (Barbara Stanwyck) whom he is too weak-minded to follow when she reappears in his life. The "noble" sacrifices are, in every case including Stanwyck's, absolutely wrong choices made according to notions of duty and happiness that go against not only self-interest, but the interests of everyone else involved.

In *All That Heaven Allows,* a film uncannily ahead of its time, Jane Wyman plays a well-heeled and respected widow, with two grown children—a boy at Princeton and a girl (a rapt Freudian) who does social work in New York. Enter Rock Hudson, who has come to prune Wyman's trees. She is a respectable bourgeoise and he is a loner, living off in the woods. She is some years older than he. (At one point in the movie, her friend Agnes Moorehead perfectly expresses society's view when she says that at forty a man wouldn't be happy with any woman over twenty.) The arguments against their love have been laid out. Wyman has a socially acceptable alternative—a man she occasionally goes out with, a widower and old friend, a hypochondriac twice her age in spirit, who groans and complains about his liver, but of whom her children and friends wholeheartedly approve. When, in one scene, she comes downstairs dressed in an elegant, low-cut evening gown, her shocked son shatters her confidence with a sarcastic remark. Her daughter, who pretends to espouse progressive ideas, quotes Freud: "When we reach a certain age sex becomes incongruous."

And yet it is quite apparent that Wyman wants not only

love, but sex. Love blossoms between her and Hudson. (He has never been more appealing; his sweet passivity and her gentle, motherly concern are perfect complements.) When it comes time to break the news to children and friends, the issue is less the age difference than the difference in their life styles. The children behave, needless to say, far worse than one would have thought possible. They say such a marriage would embarrass them, would ruin their lives, and yet, once they have forced her to give up Hudson, they disappear completely, following their own destinies. But not before giving her the television she had never wanted and leaving her, in a sublime, ironic Sirkian image, to look at her own reflection in the screen, to see in the image of her loneliness her pointless sacrifice projected into the infinity of old age. This time, however, it is not too late. She hesitates, transfixed for a moment by the proud, erect "public" Jane Wyman she had seen on the screen, then acts, taking the initiative that leads to a reconciliation.

Sirk was not a stylistically timid director, and he withheld nothing—magical coincidences, heavenly choirs, Christmas card landscapes, roaring fires, and sparkling eyes—to evoke the inner light that draws his characters to their individual destinies. Some people may prefer the more discreet Sirk in *There's Always Tomorrow* or even in the more skeptical *Imitation of Life,* with its quartet of women embodying the complete spectrum of female relationships: mother and daughter, black and white, servant and master, career woman and family, and rivals in love. But even here the black girl's agonizing quest for her identity is not seen from her point of view as much as it is mockingly reflected in the fun house mirrors of the culture from which she is hopelessly alienated.

Hudson's "little log cabin" in the woods, with its fourteen-square-foot plate glass window at which deer nuzzle amiably, is hardly a picture of the rugged life, and it is not as if Wyman were marrying a black. But in the terms of middle-class security and conditioning with which Sirk makes us understand her, her choice could not be more radical, far more so, for example, than the cute miscegenation of *Guess Who's Coming to Dinner*. For Jane Wyman is not a young woman with her life ahead of her (whose "testing" of her family is really a way of letting them display their tolerance), but a mature woman for whom the community blessing and self-pity afforded by sacrifice would be more comfortable. And she is making the decision not in the first flush of romance but later, when she must go after Hudson and risk rejection, taking full responsibility for choosing—not the whole world, but the greater happiness over the lesser happiness.

Like Cukor, Sirk suggested—in the stars he used and the alternation of trapped and entrapping men and women—that "male" and "female" characteristics must occasionally be released and allowed to flow freely between bipolar extremes. At one point, Wyman is questioning Hudson on the source of his strength, trying to muster courage to break the news of their engagement. "You want me to be a man?" she asks. "Only in that one way," he replies. And in such flexibility, we feel, lies the true fulfillment of the woman and the man, as human beings and together, as well as the realization of the woman's film as the man-woman's film. *All That Heaven Allows* is as advanced and, without an explicit word or image, as sexually aware as any film made since. It presents an "older woman" who is neither ridiculed (in the American fashion) nor (in the European) revered as a "maturing" experience for and by a young man who would never dream of marrying her.

For with all her vaunted sensuality and the reverence she inspires, the European woman is bound by a tradition of sexism even older than America's; bound, too, by a far more rigid social stratification. She is less free to "start over" than Jane Wyman's deceptively proper and upright lady, or Doris Day's tomboy career girl from the Midwest, or Katharine Hepburn's wizard athlete, or Judy Holliday's dumb blonde diehard, or Jean Simmons' dauntless actress. And Marilyn, even Marilyn, got the love she wanted—in the never-ending waves that have followed her death—and eluded the grasp of time and the dirty old men.

THE EUROPEANS

Because woman did not fight back, man quickly took the advantage and made her the scapegoat for all his vices and fears.

He was abashed that his penis moved, unbidden, when he looked at Eve, and so he invented penis envy.

He was terrified by the prospect of his own demise, and so he invented God and His Son to resurrect and redeem him.

He was resentful that another man had preceded him and made love to his mother, so he invented the Virgin Birth and vasectomized his father.

He was intimidated by woman's sexual desire, and so he invented the mutually exclusive virgin and the whore.

He was worried lest woman, resenting his freedom, should want to live and work as he did, and so he invented and ordained the mother in honored vassalage to him.

He was ashamed of growing old and ugly, and even more ashamed of being ashamed, and so he invented female vanity to exorcise and account for these fears.

Woman's image of herself is so entwined in the tangle of myths and inventions made by man that it is hard to look at it straight. It is even harder in Europe, where centuries of tradition and all the forces of culture have reinforced these myths. In Europe, a woman is chained to her throne. Sensitive artists, sons, and lovers come to worship at her feet. If she breaks free, their pilgrimage fails; if her light goes out, so does theirs. In America, men and women are not so closely and inextricably, emotionally and ideologically, bound. A woman can more easily invent herself—not easily, but more easily. And she is proportionately less venerated.

The difference between the two is not unlike the difference between the European actress and the American star. The European actress, suggesting (and generally playing) a recognizable social type, fits into a realistic context as the European film more closely follows the "documentary" tradition of pioneer Louis Lumière, while the American star, natural heiress to the magic of co-pioneer Georges Méliès, leaps out of her social environment, free of its interdictions. What are female "movie stars," after all, but supreme inventions, self-contained women, without mothers and fathers, without children, without dishes, and with lovers (either literally or in serial marriage) instead of husbands? They stand out in bold relief from their culture, rather than fading into it. Their power, both on and off the screen, is the mark of their victory over social taboos. Often they "play" themselves and, in a sense, pay for their privileges, as when, like a goddess or royalty, the movie star (Ginger Rogers in *In Person*) yearns to be "just a woman," and so, in disguise, comes down among the people and enjoys simple pleasures and cooks simple meals. In a sense, every performance of an American movie star imitates this action, as, Christ-like, the "immortal" becomes mortal in the historical time of the film. The European actress, on the other hand, recedes into a concrete and precise period and class (Maria Schell as the washerwoman Gervaise) while at the same time she seems to stand implicitly, like most European women, for the "eternal feminine." A paradigmatic example: Anna Magnani in *The Miracle* is at once a poor, self-deluded peasant woman and the Virgin Mary.

European actresses rarely become international "stars," a word that already suggests a slight dislocation or transcendence, a separation from context which would jar with their identities. Of the French, only Brigitte Bardot had, for a time, the kind of mythic identity we associate with stardom. The roster of French male stars is slightly longer: Jean Gabin and Jean-Paul Belmondo; Alain Delon, Yves Montand, and Jean-Louis Trintignant; Charles Boyer and Maurice Chevalier as "movie Frenchmen." But French actresses are so rooted in their environment that they rarely "travel well." Most have at one time or another tried their luck in English-language films: Danielle Darrieux, Michèle Morgan, Micheline Presle, Jeanne Moreau, Simone Simon, Simone Signoret, Cecile Aubrey, Mylène Demongeot, Brigitte Bardot, and Catherine Deneuve; only Signoret emerged with any distinction, and even then, it was as a character-actress, not a star. In *The Cat People,* Simone Simon acquitted herself well in what was, after all, a very French, soft and catlike, role. And Darrieux in translation abandoned her elegant and refined image and became a French sex kitten, a spitfire, but to neither great loss nor great gain. As for the rest, in English they all managed to sound like parodies of themselves. The actresses in Bergman's repertory, so sublime in his films, have done little better in America. Of course, this is partly because the projects were not suited for them, or directors were insensitive to their subtleties. But it suggests how enormously European actresses are dependent not just on context but on their director.

International art film favorites like Anna Magnani, Jeanne Moreau, Monica Vitti, and whichever of Bergman's women happens to be in the ascendancy are real women first and celebrities second. This is the fascination they have for most Americans. Abstracting from them we conclude that women in European films are more interesting, more sensual, more complex. But in the first place we see less of them than their American counterparts, and see them always at their best. We assume they are more versatile, but actually, if Garbo is always Garbo, is Magnani ever not Magnani? The comparison becomes more invidious when we consider that these women are special cases even on their home ground, and are no more representative—in their sexual "abandonment" or passion—of the average European woman than Jane Fonda is of the American housewife.

Magnani, Moreau, Vitti, and their colleagues are women who have been sponsored, some of them half "created," by important directors. We see their films, the top of the iceberg of modern European cinema, without ever descending to the sludge of eclectic mediocrity, chauvinistic vulgarity, and institutionalized sexism that constitute their national film industries. Against their routine output, our own commercial films stack up favorably—or did until recently. Americans, ever prone to self-hatred, have too readily allowed themselves to be intimidated by European intellectuals. With little experience of the reality of the concept "bourgeois," Americans have nonetheless accepted that its invidious implications apply equally to their own heterogeneous population as to the calcified French middle class. The mind-lessness, the materialism, the violence that come through almost incidentally in most American films seem like healthy urges compared to the pettiness, the chauvinism, and the unspeakable complacency of the average French *boulevard* film and the vision of life it embraces. Most of them don't come up to the level of Claude Sautet's *The Things of Life* and *Cesar and Rosalie,* superficially pretty films in which a feeling of the smug rightness of bourgeois life embraces everything from objects (including woman) to jobs to art to relationships and bathes them in that undifferentiated glow of self-satisfaction that is the deadliest quality of French culture.

In *Playtime* Jacques Tati satirizes the fixation of his middle-aged American women tourists on the gadgets being demonstrated in his omnifunctional modern building, but it is the French (and Tati himself) who are obsessed with such items. The heroine of most contemporary French com-edies is not far from the fatuously frenetic eager-beaver heroine of the *cinéma-publicité* commercials, passionately embracing some new *truc* for the enhancement of the happy bourgeois home, like the fanatical floor-shiner in the weakest segment of Jean Renoir's *Le Petit Théâtre de Jean Renoir.*

The woman that we know through the superior Euro-pean movies is in one way an elitist figure—though she can be aristocrat or proletarian—as a result of the "higher" sen-sibility projected onto her by her director. And to the extent that her image proceeds from one man, she does not reflect the problems of her society so much as the explicit preoccu-pations of the artist. Rarely does she go behind his back and emit the signals of a collective unconscious, as her American counterparts do, but she presents, almost nakedly, the inten-tions of her cinematic sculptor.

We are, perhaps, overfamiliar with these intentions, with

the treatment of women in, say, Antonioni or Truffaut, in which theme and method are one and are more easily extracted from context and defined than attitudes toward women in an American film. We know all the gossip related to the European women and their directors, the details of their relationships, whether they lived together or were married and for how long, and how this has affected the portraits that evolved. We know that they were loved, their careers promoted, their interests, so long as they coincided with their masters', served. We can only speculate, as we reexamine the themes of certain directors, what kind of love this was: whether it liberated, imprisoned, or did both; whether a director allowed the women he loved to shape his vision of women, or whether, conversely, he imposed his views, as preconceptions, on the women he directed.

Thus Ingmar Bergman's women may be definitive women, but only according to definitions and evolutionary patterns provided by Bergman himself, and in relationships over which he plays God, forever interposing his love of woman's "true nature" as he, rather than she, sees it. The women in European movies may be more "real" and "better understood" than their American equivalents, but it is in terms of a vision of realism advanced by men, a vision the women tacitly support in return for preferential treatment. The European woman "knows her place" and expresses herself (as an ordinary woman or superfemale) within her society, while the American woman strikes back. To the Europeans, Joan of Arc was a martyr, and it is on her death that the films of Robert Bresson and Carl Dreyer concentrate. To the Anglo-Saxons, she was a rebel, a woman of action, and this is the side of her that interests Shaw and Otto Preminger.

I will never take a husband [says Shaw's Joan matter-of-factly]. A man in Toul took an action against me for breach of promise; but I never promised him. I am a soldier; I do not want to be thought of as a woman. I will not dress as a woman. I do not care for the things women care for. They dream of lovers, and of money. I dream of leading a charge. . . .

It is this—Joan's repudiation of her femininity, turning her self into a superwoman—and not her mystical vision, that would constitute heresy for the European woman.

In the characters of Anna and Kitty (based on his own wife) in *Anna Karenina,* Tolstoy gave us two basic kinds of European women—dissatisfied and tragic, stupid and happy —and they haven't changed much to this day. In so doing, Tolstoy summed up at once the most enlightened and the most constricting aspects of the European attitude toward women. Kitty is the "womanly woman," a child in whom nature and society are reconciled. She is docile, sure, and instinctive, a natural meeting place of religious faith, family feeling, and feminine intuition. Her husband, Levin, visiting his dying brother, is awestruck when she goes straight to the sick man's bed and is able to console him. Later, Levin is tortured by religious doubts and metaphysical problems that, certain she wouldn't understand, he can't or won't divulge to her. To him, the wife is a thing apart, at one with her cycles and her children and her biological destiny. This mystical, fundamentalist view of women does not fade with the nineteenth century, but conditions the thinking of most Europeans, including the foremost "woman's director" Ingmar Bergman.

But then, as a counterbalance to Kitty, there is Anna Karenina, who for all her womanly instincts has an intellectual faculty as well. (And if Bergman has his Kittys, he has his Annas too: Mai-Britt Nilsson in *Summer Interlude*; Bibi Andersson in *The Touch*; Eva Dahlbeck in everything. Lola Montes is Ophuls' equivalent, while for Dreyer she can

be found in *Gertrud* and for Renoir in *The Golden Coach.*)
The Anna-type is capable of analyzing love while being in
its throes; in the variousness of her love, we see the narrow-
ness of men's. Thus when Anna, having taken in a little
English girl, is chided by her brother who fears she will
come to love the adopted child more than her own, she
answers, "There a man speaks. In love there's no more nor
less. I love my daughter with one love, and her with another."

The same applies to a woman's love of men, to her ability
to love more than one and to love in different ways, as
Bergman shows in *The Touch,* Dreyer in *Gertrud,* Renoir
in *The Golden Coach.* This is a fundamental truth of
woman's nature that most men are too egocentric to admit,
and that women themselves have been inhibited from expressing. The myth of exclusive love has held sway more
tyrannically in America than anywhere, probably as an outgrowth of a woman's need to feel secure. But in the widening
of sexual (and professional) horizons for women, we may
have cheapened the value of intercourse without reapprais-
ing, and upgrading, sensual experience. The oppressive labeling of sexes and sexual identities is more of a straitjacket
than the most stifling impositions of monogamy, and the
emphasis on orgasmic bliss has brought about a sexual
methodology that bypasses all the different kinds of love
and sees intimacy almost exclusively as "foreplay." It is
here that we are indebted to the Europeans. If they are re-
miss, even myopic, when it comes to women of action,
women without men, they are microscopic when it comes
to women in love. And if their artists have generally failed
to envisage woman as adventurer and seeker after knowledge for its own sake, they have succeeded in exploring the
more sophisticated avenues of her sensual existence. The
products of a more feminized culture to begin with, European

directors are at ease in what American artists disparagingly dismiss as a "woman's world." As a running antidote to Hollywood in its more repressive phases, European films and filmmakers suggested that there was more sensuality between heaven and earth than was contained in the films that passed the Hollywood censor.

In the early days, there were the Europeans in exile—Stroheim, Ophuls, Sternberg, Lubitsch, and the Scandinavians Stiller and Seastrom—who heretically intimated that the blood continues to beat after marriage, that life goes on though not necessarily happily ever after, and that women not only have sexual desires but can conceivably be found desirable by the opposite sex. From the thirties on, with a break for the war, the sophisticated, big-city audiences in America had a steady supply of European art films: the Pagnol trilogy (*César, Fanny, Marius*), *Pépé le Moko, Children of Paradise,* the René Clair musicals, the films of Jean Renoir's middle period, the Italian neorealist films (*Open City, The Bicycle Thief*), the steamy dockside tragedies of Marcel Carné and Julien Duvivier, the anarchic-lyric poems of Jean Vigo, the Gallic-camaraderie celebrations of Jacques Becker, and the taut melodramas of Henri-Georges Clouzot. The foreign film supply and demand peaked in the fifties and sixties, and the abundance and legitimacy of the sex shown on the screen—its "redeeming artistic value"—made it impossible for American movies to go on mincing images. (Now, of course, America has come through and out the other side without ever learning Old World pleasures. It is the pornographic capital of the world, with a monopoly on sexual utilities—like massage parlors and blue movies—having bypassed "Go" to go directly to "Come.") Even with a few strategic cuts and euphemistic subtitles for the innocents at home, such foreign films of the late fifties and early sixties as *Diabolique, The Lovers, And God Created Woman,* and *Hiroshima, Mon Amour* went a lot farther in décolleté and depravity than the home product. Pillars of communities large enough to have an art house could enjoy glimpses of bare breasts and entwined bodies in the name of high culture.

The images of women in European films came not just from society (the types Jacques Siclier enumerates in his study of French actresses, *Le Myth de la Femme dans le Cinéma Français,* but from literature as well. Thus we get the *bien-elevée* upper-middle-class heroine (in movies, Danielle Darrieux is her quintessence); the whore (and variations in between from French society); and, from nineteenth-century fiction, such staples as the older woman, the mother, the woman who gives up all for love. In French cinema of the sixties, we come upon a new kind of heroine, reflected in (and perhaps drawn from) twentieth-century French fiction, although her prototype begins with Mme Bovary. This is the discontented, spiritually and/or sexually hungry woman, often adrift in a world from which she feels estranged. This "alien" is further subdivided into the intellectual-moral heroines of Mauriac, Resnais, Duras, and, in Italy, Rossellini and Antonioni, and the amoral, nonintrospective, spoiled, drifting heroines of Sagan, Godard, Rohmer, Tanner, Vadim.

Integral to the French tradition of the "well-made film" (the tradition against which Truffaut, Godard, Chabrol, Rohmer, and their colleagues were reacting, first as critics for *Cahiers du Cinéma,* then as the pioneers of the "new wave") were those time-honored images of woman—as mistress, actress, whore, older woman—images sanctioned by culture and society. The older woman is a far more respected figure in European fiction than in our own, where, when she exists at all, she is depicted as a grotesque. In France, she is a required course in a young man's coming of age (in a sentimental-education system tailored to men), but heaven help either of them if they should contemplate marriage. The older woman is a surrogate mother and, as in any good transference, enables the boy-man to live through and "cure" his maternal fixation. Films like *Devil in the Flesh* with Micheline Presle and Gerard Philippe, and *The Game of Love* with Edwige Feuillère as the older, Nicole Berger as the younger woman, deal with wise and sensitive older women and their feckless young lovers; his passion spent, the young man will be on his way, while the older woman has only her memories to keep her warm.

If the love affair has been successful for the young man, it will allow him to resolve the conflicting sexual and spiritual sides of his mother image into a unified picture of woman, a picture not split, as it so often is for men, between the virgin and the whore. Then, unlike the prototypical Italian male, who never reconciles the two, the Frenchman will be in a healthy position to fall in love with a woman who is his equal. But at what a price. Thus, the older woman is provided by society, and reflected in film, as an instrument of psychotherapy. And the more honored and glorified she is, the more sensitive and "superior" she is seen to be, the further she is from being considered a possible partner for life. Whether the young man renounces the older woman, or tragedy conveniently intervenes to separate them, the impossibility of their love is a foregone conclusion. Being a perfectly safe arrangement, there is some complacency and nostalgia in the frequency with which it is depicted and the period context in which it is generally placed. Almost all of Claude Autant-Lara's older woman–younger man films— *Devil in the Flesh, The Red and the Black, Le Bois des Amants*—are set in the past, while the one film he made about an older man–younger woman, *En Cas de Malheur*, takes place squarely in the present.

With *Murmur of the Heart,* Louis Malle brought the young man–older woman relationship out of the genteel, romantic nineteenth-century tradition and into the twentieth century by altering it from the unconsciously to the consciously Oedipal, that is, by making the older woman not a surrogate but a real mother. But it is difficult to accept lovemaking between a mother (however "naturally" Lea Massari plays her) and her son as quite the joyous, companionable, and harmless thing Malle makes it appear. For it is precisely the surrogate nature of the traditional older woman–mistress that enables the young man to resolve his conflicts. Intercourse with a real mother would be less likely to liberate into happy heterosexuality; more likely, it would stunt Malle's sexually confused, sensitive adolescent forever.

There was another reason for returning to the romantic era, a period for which Max Ophuls, particularly, had a deep feeling and stylistic affinity. It was only within and against the rigid codes of a traditional society that the liberated gestures of certain women could take on the heroic aspect that we find, for instance, in Stendhal's great women—the militarists of love whose passions do not preclude political intelligence. These are real women, like Madame de Sevigné, Ninon de Lenclos, women of high birth and ambition who presided over salons, women of low birth and ambition who became courtesans, who braved ambiguous positions within a conventional society to wield influence over men and world events.

It is not Autant-Lara, who filmed *The Red and the Black,* but Ophuls who is the true heir to Stendhal, though he would never have dreamed of adapting for another medium the author he loved most. Ophuls, like Stendhal, is the student of love, in all its shapes and permutations. If life is the battlefield and love, the central conflict, then the women are the generalissima. Lola Montes, Madame de, Lisa (in

Letter from an Unknown Woman) begin as ordinary women who are carried, by the inexorable momentum of love, over vast emotional terrain: Lola Montes' sweep through history from kingdom to carnival; the chain of events that Madame de, in pawning her earrings, sets into motion and that is consummated by her death. Life is motion, the motion of tracking and circular camera movements, which the director uses with a dizzying and ever-deepening effect, like themes in a Mozart opera. Ophuls' deceptively effervescent style has made him an easy target for the serious critics, who charge that he has betrayed the cynical "realism" of his sources in *Liebelei, Letter from an Unknown Woman, La Ronde.* On the contrary, such a one-sided and misogynous view of human nature is cheap. Ophuls provides the hope, but not the certainty, of romantic redemption. He does this by pitting hope against time, by suggesting, within the whirls of *mise en scène,* the even more tragic view of movement as an inescapable progression toward death. Even the opposition of movement and stasis is not a simple one. Each contains internal contradictions: Ophuls' view of society as an institution at once frivolous and solid, superficial and intractable; and his view of the obsessive love that dares oppose society as at once foolish and magnificent. Danielle Darrieux's Madame de begins by asking too little of life and ends by asking too much of men whose concept of love is bound by codes of honor, codes she at first betrays and then moves beyond. Like the artist or madman, she moves outside the bounds of conventional society. Anyone who misunderstands her death misunderstands her life; her love is as "selfish" in a sense as her previous frivolity. Being obsessive and absolute, it finally goes beyond its object—Vittorio de Sica—and consumes her.

The other passionate heroines of the famous love films —Michèle Morgan (*Les Grandes Manoeuvres, La Sympho-*

nie Pastorale, Port of Shadows), Simone Signoret (*Casque d'Or, Thérèse Raquin*), pale beside Ophuls' vision of Darrieux, the "typical Frenchwoman" transformed by her love and suffering into a pale, gaunt penitent. By the end, even before she dies, she is no longer a "real woman," the substance of men's fantasies, but already the shadow of a saint. Although created entirely within the framework of a romantic "woman's film," Madame de is more truly radical than her modern counterparts. It is a curious phenomenon this: that many of the great dramatic heroines are to be found in works of art produced within the most reactionary and antifeminist societies. It suggests an inverse ratio not just between political and artistic radicalism, but also between women's rights and women's representation in art: Electra, Medea, Antigone, Clytemnestra came at a time in the history of drama when women were rigorously excluded from public events, and may not even have been permitted to attend plays, much less perform in them. Women had greater latitude in the society of classical Rome, but they were not well represented by the drama. Nor have the outstanding heroines of film and literature come from the political Left—from the revolutionary cinema of Eisenstein, the polemics of neorealism, Marxist, or Third World cinema. They have come instead from the ranks of the upper-middle classes, the "decadents." These are the "haves" rather than the "have-nots," those with the luxury of choice.

Ophuls is one of the few directors, indeed few artists, of any nationality to treat woman, in Simone de Beauvoir's terminology, as "subject" rather than "object," as an absolute rather than a contingent being. She takes a path entirely of her own choosing; and even if that path is through love, her "natural vocation," it becomes unnatural when carried to the extreme. Jean Renoir envisions women within a more traditional and conventional prism of stereotypes, of virgins and whores, but his women, always distinctive and rarely "glamorous," become increasingly complex and autonomous as he goes along. At first, his women are unmistakably allied with evil; it is they who give such films as *Toni* and *The Human Beast* a dark, brooding quality. Celia Montalvan in *Toni* and Simone Simon in *The Human Beast* bring men to their destruction. It seems a characteristic of young men (cf. Hawks), perhaps a sign of lingering adolescence, to see women as malignant. Woman represents the grown-up world, the dividing line between youth and maturity, the "disillusionment" of innocence. The young man sees her, before he has had a chance to really experience and enjoy heterosexual love, only as a disruptive influence, a break with the simple unity of the past. But Renoir's women evolve to the point where they are not so easily classified, and where his love for them becomes an instrument of *their* self-determination. His expansiveness and generosity of vision extend to his taste in women, which is so instinctively and magnanimously *not* that of conventional cinema (or sexist) aesthetics that it has automatically narrowed his potential audience. In his choice of women, perhaps more than in any other area, he resembles his father, whose taste for the round, the thick, and the palpable, he inherited, and he shares with Godard a liking for the awkward vitality of the foreign (non-French) woman.

Renoir's reverence for life leads ultimately, and with sublime circularity, to a reverence for art, specifically for the acting that constitutes the essence of life, and some of his most memorable women are actresses: the roseate Ingrid Bergman of *Elena et les Hommes,* and the gloriously histrionic Anna Magnani as the commedia dell'arte prima donna of *The Golden Coach.* Both approach their roles as actresses so exuberantly that they go "overboard": Bergman dashing about Paris in a fervor of patriotism, Magnani playing to her lovers onstage, in the arena, and on the throne, exude an excess of womanliness that no one who wants women kept in their places—or actresses in their roles—could create or even countenance.

For Renoir's Elena, love is her eventual and natural destiny, but love raised to a supreme power of the universe. Elena's determination to make some great sacrifice for her country is faintly ridiculous, but no more so than the business of politics itself. After trying and shedding several ill-fitting roles, she finally slides into the one, as Mel Ferrer's beloved, for which she seems to have been created.

For Renoir, the power to which even love bows, and in which it supremely partakes, is the theater, which finally is another, more expressive form, and art, of life. Jean Gabin, the impresario of *The French Can-Can,* and Magnani in *The Golden Coach*—director and actress—inspire but can never be consumed by love, since their art, an overriding affair with life, encompasses it. Like the earlier prima donnas of the commedia dell'arte, Magnani knows certain texts and can embellish and embroider, adapt to her audience, and almost certainly captivate them. For three men to fall at her feet is only natural; and the three who do—the archduke, the bullfighter, and the actor—embody three stereotypically male attitudes toward woman. She embraces them all, disinfecting their egomania with her humor, perhaps favors the archduke but must bid good-bye to him, too. For she is the center, dividing and unifying, creating and endlessly recreating the figure of herself as theater. And, yes, she will be a little lonely.

Role-playing, as seen by Renoir, does not have the invidious connotation the term acquired, in the sixties, from French existential philosophy. It is not, for Renoir, a splintering and disintegrating act, but an exploratory and creative one. His women are not playing out a Sartrian "unauthentic" charade, but are working their way through layers of the self, trying on different images, and constantly creating "scenes" to contain them. Ingrid Bergman, converting her inability to play comedy into an asset, plunges farther into the folly and artifice by which she will finally be shaken to her senses. Magnani, carrying her proscenium arch wherever she goes, has no division between "art" and "life."

Renoir, like most Europeans, is less concerned with woman's point of view, or with her creative possibilities, than with her re-creative and mediational power, and the effect she has on the world around her. She is inspirational: the source of clashing and destructive feelings in his early films, of passions that reveal and heal in his later ones. And if she is not the seeker, neither is she condemned for the havoc she causes.

Fritz Lang shares the bleak, black-and-white view of women of the early Renoir. Both men made different versions of the same two films. *The Human Beast* and *La Chienne,* Renoir's originals, have a foggy, fatalistic atmosphere that envelops the men and women in a psycho-drama of mutual destruction. Lang's American remakes—*Human Desire* and *Scarlet Street* (both subject to the pressures of the Production Code)—have a more mechanistic fatalism. In both of Lang's films, the woman is the bitch-betrayer. The Glenn Ford character in *Human Desire* is portrayed as a complete innocent, rather than Jean Gabin's crazily jealous lover who commits a *crime de passion* in *The Human Beast.* The Joan Bennett wench in *Scarlet Street,* euphemized up the employment scale from the whore of *La Chienne,* seems more, rather than less, cruel and arbitrary.

Lang's vision of the world, like his view of women, is more schematic than Renoir's. He sees good and evil almost as live forces, and the world as a chessboard susceptible at any moment to disruption by some greater force of evil, chaos, or the unconscious. *Kriemhild's Revenge* (the second part of Lang's silent film of *Die Nibelungen*) presents, in Margarete Schon's monumental performance, a frightening spectacle of revenge gone berserk. At the peak of her fury, she is transformed by her passion into some supernatural force, neither man nor woman.

Lang's women are generally Madonnas or Mary Magdalens, and their interest lies not in their psychological complexity, but in the strange conjunction of the archetypal and the idiosyncratic. In *The Big Heat,* the opposing principles —Jocelyn Brando's Madonna (wife of Glenn Ford and mother of his child) and Gloria Grahame's whore (to Lee Marvin's gangster)—gradually merge and, with the death of the former and the atonement of the latter, are symbolically fused. Grahame's face is disfigured—in one of the most brutal images on film—by the scalding coffee Lee Marvin throws at her. The mutilation is itself symbolic—the ultimate payback of a John to his whore. Later, as she lies dying from a gun wound, Ford turns the scarred side of her face against the pillow, thus figuratively erasing it.

In a similar situation transposed to a Western, Marlene Dietrich is a sacrificial figure in Lang's *Rancho Notorious,* the *femme fatale* at the other pole from the dead, innocent wife. Throughout, Lang's sensibility remained split between virgin and whore.

The modern twentieth-century French heroine is no less a product of a director or writer's sensibility, though she may seem more culturally liberated than her nineteenth-century predecessor, and while she may participate more directly in the *Zeitgeist* of the modern world, she is generally seen in no less a romantic context. There are occasional career women in French films: a doctor in Jean Gremillon's *The Love of a Woman* and again in André Cayatte's *Justice*

Is Done. But in neither of these is the career anything other than a ploy to advance the melodrama. Frenchmen can accept working women more easily than we can because there are so few of them, and they exist almost as a separate category. But it is the feminine women who are the heroines of love stories, even the antiromantic, modern variation in which the heroine, Bovary-like, is well provided for, a disconsolate bourgeoise, yearning far more than seeking. She is the victim of ennui, that peculiarly and oppressively French version of boredom: a mood of restlessness that is more than just casting about for something to do but that falls short of metaphysical despair. It is, by nature, a feminine mood in its combination of desire and frustration, the urge to do or feel more powerfully, and the lack of outlets or opportunities to express these feelings. Ironically, it is the Italians, so archaic in their attitudes toward women in most ways, who—in the Monica Vitti and Ingrid Bergman characters created by Antonioni and Rossellini—give us an ennui that, in its suggestion of material surfeit surrounding a spiritual void, is closest to the metaphysical *angst*.

For the Frenchwoman, who is every bit as pragmatic as her countrymen at heart, there is usually some concrete answer to her hunger. If her needs appear vague, it is only because she hasn't found the answer that would enable her to state the question. The answer, generally, is some form of passion—the antidote to ennui and to the dreary connubial love and imprisoning security of the modern French heroine. In *The Lovers,* Jeanne Moreau finds in one night of passion sufficient justification for leaving her husband and children (a situation American audiences could not accept and, despite its extraordinary scenes of sexuality, the film was a box-office flop). Or perhaps the passion is of another and, again, peculiarly French kind: the passion for the city over the provinces. In *Thérèse Desqueroux,* Emmanuelle Riva's bored chatelaine finally abandons the country, the husband, and all those trees for the Paris traffic and the taste of a *café noir* at a sidewalk café. Resnais' heroines—Emmanuelle Riva in *Hiroshima, Mon Amour* and Delphine Seyrig in *Muriel*—are trying, unsuccessfully, to resolve the fragments of their lives into some new whole. But they are unable either to release themselves from the images of the past or to settle with these images and learn to live with some new reordering of them.

There are wandering heroines, unburdened by either ennui or *angst,* young women without ties—or values—to shed. They are the counterpart of the American male protagonist who "hits the road" in search of himself, is generally cast adrift in an urban setting that suggests the impersonal nature of modern civilization. Agnes Varda's *Cleo from 5 to 7* uses this framework to explore a theme that has become crucial to the feminist "coming to consciousness" : a woman's sense of herself as the figment of men's fantasies. The film concerns an afternoon in the life of a young singer who is waiting for the results of a biopsy. As she wanders through Paris, she gazes inward for the first time and discovers a void. Realizing that if she were sick, the men who "love" her would soon disappear, she perceives that the fabric of her personality designed to charm them would disintegrate too. Like Alice Adams, she had willingly fashioned herself according to the instructions in their eyes; she had created a human doll who didn't exist without them.

A more self-defined waif is the sensualist, the Brigitte Bardot rebel-voluptuary, the well-heeled but barefoot sybarites of Françoise Sagan. But if she is the antithesis of the *angst*-ridden, intellectual heroine (the distinction James makes in *The Bostonians* between people who "take things easy" and people who "take things hard"), she stands as no less of a reproach to bourgeois society and male prurience. Bardot is to Emmanuelle Riva as the Hollywood technicolor star is to the black-and-white Method actress. Bardot is sensual where Riva is cerebral, intuitive where she is analytical, active where she is reflective, and yet both embody a critical attitude toward their society and, implicitly, toward the proprietary interests of men. Both resist being "used," both confront with their own integrity the false roles in which men would cast and dominate them. Bardot's appeal, and the unfortunate evanescence of that appeal, lies in her purely sexual nature. She is a waif and a nymphet, a woman of the world and a child of nature. By being frankly and freely sexual, she is no longer a sex object, that is, she cannot be bought or bartered. She cannot be loved for her exterior only because the outside is the inside, or loved just for her body, because her body is her soul. But, tragically, this is true only so long as she is young, and, therefore, in a larger, cosmic sense she is being used. The revenge of Humbert Humbert on the Lolita who snags him is that her appeal is only good for a couple of years, a magnetic dot in the universe. The nymphet has a shorter career expectation than anyone, and Bardot is considered lucky to have had seven or eight years in the limelight.

Her successors in the Sagan-sensualist line, being less sensational and less inimitably childlike, may prove to be more enduring. Jane Asher in Skolimowski's *Deep End* and the blonde Yugoslav actress in his earlier film *Barriera*; Haydee Politoff in Eric Rohmer's *La Collectioneuse*; Bulle Ogier in Alain Tanner's *La Salamandre* (she is closer to the intellectual heroine in Jacques Rivette's *L'Amour Fou*), and some of Godard's early women, including Bardot herself in *Contempt,* all express a kind of sexual knowledge and spiritual innocence that defies the sexual and romantic categories constructed by men.

These women refuse to be idealized or patronized. They

are alike in being all of a piece, sensual, impulsive, amoral . . . or perhaps just realistic. In *Deep End,* one of the most underrated films of 1971, Jane Asher is an attendant in a sordid public bath in East London, a place that becomes a metaphor for some of the squalid, mercenary accommodations to life that she has had to make. She is engaged to one man, and having an affair with another. John Moulder Brown, a fresh-faced adolescent, comes to work as her assistant, falls in love with her, and obsessively refuses to see her as anything less than the Snow White of his dreams. In a wild finale, he tries and fails to make love to her in the bottom of an empty pool, and he repays her for his own humiliation by killing her. His sexual failure is a direct—and poetic—outgrowth of his refusal to abandon his romantic illusion, an illusion that, as Skolimowski makes clear, is more flattering to the sensibility of the beholder than to the beheld. And so Asher dies, a martyr to the male ego, and to a militant purity far more evil than any compromise she has made with life.

In Alain Tanner's *La Salamandre,* two men are collaborating on a television script that describes the alleged attempt of a young factory worker, Rosemonde (Bulle Ogier), to kill her uncle. They have already embarked on their version of the story, sociologically causal and complete, when they meet Rosemonde, begin talking to her, and fall into her weird rhythm. At every point their imaginative re-creation of the story bogs down in the mire of her unyielding, irreducible reality. They are disarmed of their intellectual equipment, just as Patrick Bauchau's dandy is disarmed of his in *La Collectioneuse.* Their knowledge of women, their morality, their logic—all instruments of their own protection—are useless when they are confronted with women who do not want or need them.

The two men in *La Salamandre* consider themselves political revolutionaries, but it is Rosemonde who is truly radical in her offhand delinquency. She quits the sausage factory (where, in a comically phallic image, Tanner has shown her stuffing sausages with an insolence that should be as disquieting to men as the tales of castration among ancient matriarchies), works in a shoe store, steals, is rebellious, sloppy, uncooperative. She feels suffocated by the stifling atmosphere of her environment and yet is without a glimmer of true moral refinement. She is unyieldingly unaesthetic whereas most of her prototypes, in the films of Truffaut and Godard which have influenced Tanner, are beautiful enigmas who reflect, and are a product of, the sensibilities of their chroniclers.

One of the earliest and most important of these enigmatic heroines was Jean Seberg in Jean-Luc Godard's *Breathless*. Godard was influenced, in turn, by Seberg's portrayal of Cecile in Preminger's film of the Sagan novel, *Bonjour Tristesse*. In *Breathless,* Seberg becomes the perfect expression and focus of Godard's ambivalence toward women, a mixture of idealism and misogyny as intense as Chaplin's. At the end of *Bonjour Tristesse,* Seberg, having caused the death of the woman her father loved, sits staring at her image in the mirror, seeing and feeling nothing. At the end of *Breathless,* standing beside her dying gangster-lover (Jean-Paul Belmondo), whose whereabouts she betrayed to the police, she looks into space, seeing and feeling nothing. Sexually, she is a whore; emotionally, a virgin. Something is missing: a conscience, a soul? Like the women played by Anna Karina, Godard's then-wife, in *Le Petit Soldat, Pierrot le Fou,* and *Bande à Part,* she teases the hero with her seeming wholeness, and does so ingenuously, leading him to his destruction. Her soul is a *tabula rasa* with a slick surface: nothing adheres. She is not even malevolent. Her cruelty lies in her indifference, in the equal ease with which she can make a life-or-death phone call to the police—or not make one.

Godard's feelings for women are remarkably similar to

his feelings toward America—extreme love-hatred. (His feelings toward America, symbolized in the recurrent images, both sensual and repellent, of automobiles, are so personal they might easily be called "misogyny.") His actresses are American, or Americanized. Karina is non-French (Danish, actually), and is given a persona that is an amalgam of American genre heroines—or rather, Godard's affectionate interpretation of American genre heroines—she is gangster's moll, hoofer, singer, virgin, and whore. His relationship with her was tempestuous and masochistic; like Chaplin, he sought out the woman who would make life miserable for him. Far from wanting a "real woman," he wants a child-woman. In *Le Petit Soldat,* Michel Subor states flatly that no woman should ever pass twenty-five.

In *My Life to Live,* which purports to present a woman's point of view, the prostitute played by Karina dies. But her death is justified not by objective social reasons, but by Godard's artistic ones: As his wife-model, he has killed her by turning her into a work of art. This he acknowledges in a reference to Poe's *The Oval Portrait,* in which the subject begins to ail as the painting takes shape, and dies when the likeness is complete.

The title of *A Woman Is a Woman* is enough to suggest the European male's conception of a woman's rather limited function in life (or that there is some commonly held definition). Her destiny is to make babies, and here Anna Karina is being denied her wish (she wants one right away, like a new dress or a candy bar) by her lover, Jean-Claude Brialy. And yet Godard sympathizes with her, with her insecurity, with her need for a commitment from Brialy; he attacks the double standard which allows Brialy to commit infidelities (for something so minor as fleeting satisfaction) and prohibits her from committing them (for something so major as conceiving a baby).

Those films—*A Married Woman, Two or Three Things I Know About Her*—in which Godard identifies with women's problems of a sociological nature are his least effective; those in which his romantic emotions, however ambivalent, are engaged are his best—*Masculine/Feminine,* and the Karina films. *Contempt,* combining passion and objective analysis, is perhaps his greatest. In it, Bardot plays a tragic projection of her mythic image. She is the wife of an intellectual screenwriter (Michel Piccoli) whose failures and compromises erode and gradually destroy their marriage. The setting in Capri and the sense of grandeur in the characters' spiritual Odyssey justify the classical framework and the conjunction of Homer and Lang as Godard's twin sources. And Godard finally confronts in the Piccoli character the childishness and self-delusions of the male intellectual who had projected his failures onto the betraying woman.

In his political films, Godard's self-hatred, and with it, his misogyny, increase. In *La Chinoise, Weekend, Sympathy for the Devil,* and *Wind from the East,* the sullen, inexpressive, and intolerant figure of Anne Wiazemsky is a projection of, and retribution for, his middle-class guilt: a slogan-spouting radical whose dreary presence becomes a reproach not only to his own backsliding but to all bourgeois (that is, "individual") ideals of life, love, art. His ambivalence toward America reaches a peak in his two most recent films, *Tout Va Bien* and *Letter to Jane.* In the latter, a "structuralist" essay made expressly for the New York Film Festival, he alternately chides and analyzes Jane Fonda for allowing herself to be used for imperialist-media purposes on her trip to North Vietnam; in *Tout Va Bien,* he betrays the ambivalence by which he associates America with "stars" by using Jane Fonda in the lead but by constantly shunting her off to the side so that the "proletarians"—his musical-comedy factory workers—can express themselves.

There is, in both Godard and François Truffaut, a quality of eternal, overgrown adolescence, a purity just too exquisite for this world, that expresses itself in the men they have chosen to represent them on the screen and in the women who excite or betray them. Jean-Pierre Léaud, though functioning as the alter ego of both directors, is indelibly associated with Truffaut, particularly as his surrogate, Antoine Doinel, in the autobiographical films, *The 400 Blows, Stolen Kisses,* and *Bed and Board.* Léaud is the fumbling, eternally innocent male, straightforward and guileless, whose inexperience is no match for the instinctive wisdom and wiles of a woman. In *Stolen Kisses,* Antoine pursues his sweetheart (Claude Jade) but is more at ease with her parents, or with the "older woman" played by Delphine Seyrig. Where Godard's awe of women is tinged with hatred, Truffaut's is all admiration, but one attitude can be as inhibiting in creating a fully rounded portrait as the other. One of Truffaut's most interesting films in its analysis of male egoism, *The Soft Skin,* is nevertheless one of his least engaging, perhaps because the protagonist, a slightly stuffy intellectual played by Jean Desailly, bears so little relation to Truffaut or his alter ego, Antoine Doinel. In this film, both the mistress (Françoise Dorléac) and the wife (Nelly Benedetti) are made to wait in the wings while this most unlikely Don Juan travels here and there, gives lectures, pursues his all-important career.

Like the adolescent heroes of his own and other films, Truffaut's artistic weakness, in refusing to grow up, expresses itself in an insistence on preserving his own innocence and purity—a compulsion to which his women become, very subtly, sacrificial scapegoats. They die or surrender, that innocence may live. There is something hauntingly self-destructive in the women Truffaut chose to be his sacrificial scapegoats, to die so that innocence and purity could live: Françoise Dorléac, who played the hapless mistress in *The*

Soft Skin died several years later in an automobile crash; Nicole Berger, who commits suicide in *Shoot the Piano Player,* died in an automobile crash as well. Jeanne Moreau's hedonism, her bouts with overweight, have undertones of self-destruction. As Catherine, the goddess who kills herself and her lover at the end of *Jules and Jim,* Moreau never looked more beautiful. But that is the point: Something died with her, and in subsequent films and photographs, she looks increasingly tired, world-weary, even decadent. She doesn't "take care of herself," and perhaps that is her glory; she lives and her face shows it, while other actresses embalm themselves so they can come alive on the screen. Moreau is a sensualist and epicure—she eats, drinks, loves, and, like Edith Piaf, allows herself to be used. This is the side of her nature—her gaiety and generosity—that comes through in the first half of *Jules and Jim*; she even allows herself to *become* the image of the statue that Jules and Jim carry in their hearts. If she is a fantasy, she is a glorious fantasy, appealing to both sexes, to men as "eternal mistress," to women as Nietzschean Superwoman; capable of loving two men at once, she is beyond good and evil and monogamy. But in the second half, she becomes a force of evil, a projection of man's desire for exclusivity, for possession. She carelessly destroys her own life and two others, and brings the film down around her with the burden of her guilt. The men cannot, do not, participate in the guilt, just as Truffaut cannot, does not (for most of his career) lead innocence over the divide into experience. It is always death rather than compromise. The marriage between Claude Jade and Jean-Pierre Léaud depicted in *Bed and Board* is worse than death, it is a bourgeois sampler of pseudo-romance arrested and frozen, like the freeze-frame that closes *The 400 Blows.* But then comes *Two English Girls,* based, like *Jules and Jim,* on a novel by Henri-Pierre Roché; arguably, it is Truffaut's greatest film. He is confronting, in a story close to him but not autobiographical, and through two young girls rather than through Léaud (who here is but the witness and catalyst) the terrible struggle to grow up, to surrender innocence without seeing the loss of it as the end of the world. Two young sisters (modeled on Charlotte and Emily Brontë) are living in the English countryside in the early part of the century. Both are chaste and hypersensitive; one, the sculptress, yearns to feel and mold life with a self-conscious Lawrentian zeal; the other, the stay-at-home and diarist, is a neurasthenic suffering an exquisite inner agony of repression and desire. Truffaut is closer here than he has ever been to understanding a woman's point of view. (If only he would make a sequel to this in which we might see Charlotte's thirst for independence, her lonely and, for that time, quite radical journey to a foreign city to teach school and support herself.) The two sisters' pained, lyrically contrasting sensibilities are kept in a continual equilibrium by the young man who makes love to both of them. By placing them within a puritanical period framework, Truffaut can get away with inhibitions and hesitations that are reactionary by today's escalated sexual rhetoric. But the truth is that the girls' fears and uncertainties are as characteristic of contemporary women as of their grandmothers, and their convulsions over being virgins even more so. The melodrama and adolescent fatalism of Truffaut's early films are in this one, but here Truffaut can separate them from himself and observe them with detachment; there is a growth here, a going beyond and coming to terms with the past, an acknowledgment that death is too easy and too unsatisfactory an end to innocence, that make this film and its theme harsh and beautiful.

Without ever violating that proud, delicate privacy that both sisters (Kika Markham and Stacey Tendeter, neither of whom is conventionally "beautiful") cling to, Truffaut gets "inside" them far more effectively than he did with Catherine Deneuve in *Mississippi Mermaid,* which celebrated her beauty and his love. Although Deneuve can without exaggeration be called the most beautiful woman in the world (or in movies or in whatever the contest), there is something bland and static in her beauty. In the flush of her youth, and in the pastel colors of Jacques Demy's *Umbrellas of Cherbourg,* she was the definitive and enchanting musical-comedy ingenue. But once past her extreme youth she had to become a woman and, like so many ingenues, she was not a womanly type. It took Buñuel to suggest, in *Belle de Jour,* that beneath her placid exterior was the seething desire to be degraded that could find satisfaction in a house of prostitution. Buñuel enables us to see Séverine from both a man's and a woman's point of view: As a spectator, a man luxuriates in the peculiarly erotic tension between the fashionable young bourgeoise and the masochistic voluptuary that emerges each afternoon; for the female spectator, she embraces all women who have ever fantasized such anonymous degradation, which is to say, all women. She is both an art-and-sex object and a subject who willingly surrenders herself. Once again, it is from the pedestal of purity on which her husband has raised her that she needs to fall so far and so precipitously. In the end, a tragedy must occur because society (husband, lover, friend) cannot tolerate her dual nature.

Because, until recently, the European filmmaker has been more of a conscious artist than his American counterpart and more often than not has originated the idea and/or the screenplay of his films, women have more explicitly expressed his attitudes. The phenomenon of a filmmaker directing and building a film around the woman he loves introduces additional elements into a situation already loaded with sexual master/subject explosives. Will the director become jealous of the star's leading man and diminish his part, or cut down on his close-ups? It has been known to happen. (Richard Corliss has reported that during the shooting of *Red River,* Howard Hawks became jealous of John Ireland's attentions to Joanne Dru, and reduced Ireland's part accordingly; Ireland lost a good role but won Dru, whom he later married. And George Cukor was reportedly fired from the set of *Gone with the Wind* through the intervention of Clark Gable, who felt that Cukor was paying too much professional attention to Vivien Leigh and Olivia de Havilland and not enough to him. Will the director overidealize the woman, or give her too much freedom, or impose his own ideas on her too rigidly?

Will she come to be so defined by what he has made her (as Vitti has been by Antonioni and Stéphane Audran by Chabrol) that audiences can see her in no other way, and other directors become leery of using her? In this sense at least, European actresses have been far more "imprisoned" by their images than have Americans. Then, too, what a man sees in the woman he loves may not be what audiences see—or want to see. This is particularly true if, as in the cases of Ingrid Bergman and Julie Andrews, their images have already crystallized for the public, which does not want to see the chips in the crystal so lovingly revealed by Roberto Rossellini and Blake Edwards.

When Bergman left Hollywood for Italy and Rossellini, she shed the opalescent skin of the fairy-tale princess to become a real, particular woman—a transformation that delighted neither her fans nor her critics, and which she herself came to regret. Thus her statement, while making *Anastasia* with Anatole Litvak, that she was "glad to be back with the pros." Though the most spiritual of filmmakers, Rossellini shapes his characters not as the ascetic, otherworldly (though sometimes erotic) loners and reprobates of Bresson but as composites of earth and spirit, occasionally divided against themselves. Under Rossellini, Bergman actually becomes the first of the middle-class, alienated heroines. She goes from the Hollywood image of a serene, vaguely worldly lady who discovers a storybook passion on a sea of shimmering close-ups, to become a woman who is spiritually lost, out of touch with, but trying to get back to, her senses. In movies like *Stromboli* and *The Strangers* (or *Voyage in Italy*), as the baffled, drifting heroine, she prefigures the *angst*-ridden women of Antonioni. But people weren't ready for her, and little credit was given to Rossellini for his prescience.

With Rossellini, there is always the hope of recovering one's balance. With Antonioni, the emotional and social wastelands are commensurate and complete, the emptiness of one reflecting the emptiness of the other like two mirrors face to face. Monica Vitti is the perfect high priestess of nihilism, a beauty who will reflect the emptiness without impairing it, who will convey a sense of loss without a concomitant (and energizing) sense of hope.

As the existential French heroine can be vaguely traced to Françoise Sagan, the Italian heroine appears in outline in Cesar Pavese's novels, one of which formed the basis of *Le Amiche,* an early Antonioni film. Vitti provides her with finishing touches—chic but disheveled, listless, intelligent, actively passive (unlike the sexually aggressive Bardot heroine), a figure who expresses the bleakness of the modern soulscape. In this sense, Antonioni "uses" Vitti aesthetically; she is active or passive, stationary or mobile according to his whim, and her usefulness lies in her willingness not to obtrude, but to be content to echo his despair. Denied the medium of speech—woman's most powerful tool of definition —she becomes one more mirror in Antonioni's glacial vision, reflecting a view of society that, unlike Rossellini's, is political and social rather than moral and psychological, and that sees redemption collectively rather than individually. (In his new love, the People's Republic of China, Antonioni has apparently found a landscape unblemished by even so pliable an emblem of individualism as Monica Vitti.)

Yet even as she carried out Antonioni's mission, Vitti evoked, in her muteness, a state of mind that women responded to, particularly in the early sixties. The search for Anna at the beginning of *L'Avventura* had to be abandoned. Woman had lost something—a part of herself, perhaps—and the emptiness was deafening. Like other more recent anesthetized heroines, Vitti is the dead end of feeling, of relationships lived the old, complacent way; the end of the race of women as chattel and romantic fantasies. But this is the death that had to be reached before women could begin to be reborn.

In their sensitivity to the plight of modern women, Rossellini and Antonioni are exceptional, particularly among Italians, who even at their most enlightened usually think of woman in terms of the awesome and all-powerful mother. More than in France, there is an unspoken understanding: Through their position in the family women run society (if Italian society can be said to be run, and while allowing men titular supremacy) but only so long as they keep to their special province. In France, women are central to culture and the arts, which in turn are central to the nation. In Italy women are the power of the family; the family, in turn, is the mainstay of the country and the only cohesive force among an anarchic and decentralized race.

In Italy, the idea of a professional woman is either inconceivable or intrinsically comic, as in *The Honorable Angelina,* where Anna Magnani plays a Bella Abzug–type congresswoman. Italians are all actors and buffoons, and comedy is instinctive to their cinema, as composition is to the Japanese cinema, or a sense of dialectic to the French.

The humor is rarely subversive, and the average Italian comedy merely reinforces Italian chauvinism and complacency. Films will quite happily satirize the inequities of the Italian family structure, the patriarchy (or what Luigi Barzini argues is a "crypto-matriarchy"), the divorce laws, the Catholic Church, antiquated ideas about women, the laziness and lechery of the Italian male—without the least intent of changing them. They merely, and merrily, hold up a mirror in which the nation can look fondly at its own idiosyncrasies, and try to preserve them from attack by outsiders in a changing world.

Naturally there is a tendency to develop busty, maternal-type actresses. Who would have thought, between her earth mother roles and the later comic mistress and mamma stereotypes perpetrated in the de Sica films (*Yesterday, Today, and Tomorrow*; *Marriage, Italian Style*), that Sophia Loren could play the airy comedienne of Cukor's *Heller in Pink Tights*, of *Houseboat* (where she held her own with Cary Grant), and of Sidney Lumet's *That Kind of Woman*. In *Heller*, as a member of a troupe of actors touring the American West in pioneer times, she is no longer the statuesque but too-too solid earth goddess whose humor comes from the mining of familiarly Italian situations, but an adaptable star who generates comedy slyly and brilliantly on her own. In these films she appeals to women as well as men, whereas in her Italian, or Italian-type roles, her sexual lusciousness is directed to "men only."

The other two in Italy's quartet of great directors—Federico Fellini and Luchino Visconti—share, perhaps more than Antonioni and Rossellini, traits of the Italian temperament, but like all great artists they transcend national boundaries (although Fellini seems to be getting more, rather than less, parochial). Fear and awe of women is raised to a high C of operatic intensity in the films of Luchino Visconti, under whose direction the specter of female malignancy has taken cover in some extravagantly memorable women's parts: Alida Valli's voracious countess in *Senso,* Annie Girardot's catalyst of destruction in *Rocco and His Brothers,* Anna Magnani's monstrous and sublime stage-mother in *Bellissima,* and Maria Schell's fiercely wistful young woman in *White Nights.* One might compare the cold, almost necrophiliac eroticism of Isabel Weingarten in Robert Bresson's *Four Nights of a Dreamer* with Visconti's histrionic treatment of Schell in his version of the Dostoevsky short story. Visconti's vision of women is as neurotic and baroque as Fellini's—both visions spring from the same deep fears and psychic resistances—but while Fellini's wariness occasionally spills over into contempt, Visconti's often soars into awe. His women are monsters but on a grand scale, rarely the gargoyles, glimpsed in passing, of Fellini, but rather tall, statuesque, matriarchal types who are plugged into some mysterious cosmic energy, frightening in its intensity and greed. Compare the severe, proud, aristocratic presence of Sylvana Mangano in *Death in Venice* with the fussily feminine apparition of Sandra Milo in *Juliet of the Spirits.* But Visconti's all-out theatricalism becomes dangerously manipulative as it sometimes redeems, but often clouds, his misogyny.

Giulietta Masina is representative of Fellini's women only insofar as none of Fellini's women are representative of real women. And they become increasingly grotesque— bloated emanations of his sexual fears—as the films slip farther from the observed life or narrative moorings of his early period into the stylized, repetitious fantasy of his later films. The women are quintessentially Italian in that they conform to the either/or rubrics of demoness harpie (the whore in *8½*) or virgin apparition (the diaphanous "White Rock girl" in *8½*); the oversexed sex goddess (Anita Ekberg in *La Dolce Vita*) or the undersexed and equally un-desirable wife (a bespectacled Anouk Aimée in *8½*).

Until she became the (undesirable) wife figure in *Juliet of the Spirits,* Masina belonged to none of these groups. She was sexually neutral, a sprite, a life force that happened to inhabit the body of a woman. As the eternally optimistic, eternally wounded, and eternally resilient tramp of *Variety Lights, La Strada,* and *Nights of Cabiria,* she is the female counterpart of Chaplin—except that, in her relations with the opposite sex, she is even more craven and pathetic, since her devotion is without the cruel streak that saved Chaplin's tramp from unrelieved pathos, or the dignity that saved Verdoux. Masina is willing to become a doormat for the man she loves, but even then she can't make a sale. The door-mat is found to be threadbare and is discarded. But up it flips, ready for a new day, and a new foot in its face.

As studies and celebrations of an actress, her films are brilliant. If we accept her not as a "prostitute" or a Christ figure, but as the ultimate actress, we can better appreciate the dazzling repertory of facial expressions, the irrepressible exuberance, the ability to retire for the night in the depths of despondency and awaken, the previous misery forgotten, recompose her face into a grin, and start over. And finally, after the repertory has been run through several times and is about to start again, it is not to her versatility that we respond, but to her tenacity.

So intimately is Masina's persona bound to that of a performer that when Fellini tries, in *Juliet of the Spirits,* to expand her biography and turn her into a real woman, we feel—particularly in the kind of woman she becomes—a falsification and a reduction of her screen character. She is no longer the self-renewing actress, doing a one-woman roadshow production of herself, but a mousy little housewife, the object of Fellini's guilt and pity. What might have been an admirable study of a woman in the throes of a kind of spiritual change of life seems more a hook for Fellini to hang his own inventions on. She hasn't got a fantasy she can call her own, but must experience an array of hallucinations straight from the lending library of Fellini's imagination. Magnani seems to know what she is doing when, in *Fellini-Roma,* she shuts the door on the director saying, "I don't trust you."

Fellini has more comic genius than Rossellini, Visconti, and Antonioni put together, and it is lamentable that he abandoned the intimately satirical vein of his early films for excursions into a self that is fast depleting itself. The humor of *I Vittelloni, The White Sheik,* and *The Miracle* (for which Fellini wrote the screenplay and played Saint Joseph), is often savage. There is something mournful and uncompromising (and ultimately more honest and genuinely introspective) in the portraits of Italian masculinity offered in *I Vittelloni, The White Sheik,* and the character of Zampano in *La Strada,* than in the solipsistic worlds of his later films.

Some of this mordant humor comes through in directors of the younger generation, particularly Marco Bellocchio, who with his contemporary, Bernardo Bertolucci, feels the tensions of the family as more neurotic than ever. Sisters predominate over sweethearts, and mothers (or mother figures) over mistresses, whether it is in the self-abuse and desuetude of Bellocchio's *China Is Near* or the rumblings of incest and insanity in his *Fist in His Pocket* or the love affair with the young aunt (Adrianna Asti) in Bertolucci's *Before the Revolution.* The combination of intense family ties and an authoritarian religion monitoring a repressive society leads to covertly erotic family relationships, or such psychopathic sexual deviation as the inspector's whore fetishism in *Investigation of a Citizen Above Suspicion.*

It is difficult to separate the virtues of Bertolucci's

Last Tango in Paris from all the pandemonium surrounding it, or even from its own serious flaws and gross calculations. Also, a film so heavily dependent on, and about, eroticism will naturally elicit as many divergent responses (turning off as many as it turns on) as there are sexual preferences. Being concerned not just with the "de-repression" of a woman through anonymous and abusive sexual acts, but with the de-repression of a specific woman—Maria Schneider—by a specific and overpoweringly significant man, Marlon Brando, it is this *idea* that is important, and that makes it erotic for women. Beginning with the first "no-name" seduction in an empty Paris apartment, and in the alternation of the romantic feelings and sexual desire in which the partners are never quite in sync (she goes from love to desire to indifference, he from casual domination to love), Bertolucci brings together the necessary and sometimes contradictory elements in eroticism for women. For if he is saying that the "sex-only" affair is doomed, he suggests that it is also necessary. In surrendering her body "without strings," without receiving any assurances of emotional involvement, without making any claims for the spirit, she has a better chance of freeing her mind from its enslavement to the body (whether from over- or under-valuation), and of freeing herself from that emotional dependency, the compulsion to suffering, that is so often a product of fear rather than freedom. Schneider's journey under Brando's instructions into her own entrails is a terrifying one, but if she emerges she will be in such possession of herself that she won't have to hold on for dear life anymore. In the same film, Jean-Pierre Léaud, who plays a filmmaker-lover recalling Godard and Truffaut, is the romantic suitor. He wants to capture and frame his idol, at a different ratio but with the same deathly effect as the oval portrait. Léaud uses her, freezes her; Brando, turning her inside out, releases her.

The film can be faulted for its pretensions, for an unwarranted melodramatic ending, for various borrowings and lapses, even for the casting of Maria Schneider who seems too perverse and knowing for her fate, too sexually advanced for an Oedipal fixation. But Bertolucci seems to know, as so few filmmakers do, what kind of sexual fantasies appeal to women. There are no genital close-ups of the kind that are the stock-in-trade of hard-core pornographic movies, and, though we come away with the impression of having witnessed detailed sexual activity, the film is far more verbally than visually explicit. That we turn invariably from their bodies to look at their faces is at once the glory and the defeat of the erotic, which is at its most intense just as it is turning into its opposite, the spiritual and romantic. This is a woman's eroticism, involving as it does the spirit in endless conflict with the senses, merging and separating. *Last Tango* enables women to surrender to their sexual fantasies and emerge with their souls intact. Brando's conversion to the role of a proper suitor comes too late; he has brought his subject too close to the death principle and it is she who takes him over the edge. In an ending consciously echoing Jean Seberg's blank stare at the close of *Breathless,* Schneider stares off into the space of nothingness, profoundly touched and yet untouched.

What Bertolucci shows us in the contrasting relationships of Schneider with Brando the lover and with Léaud the observer/worshipper, suggests that the more a woman is made to sustain a director's romantic and intellectual/artistic and sexual fantasies, the less "free" she will be to discover her own—and reach other women. Bardot belongs to no man, whereas Karina is Godard's "property." This is borne out in the women of Ingmar Bergman, and in their evolution from the free, sensual, intelligent, and highly individualized creatures of his early career, to the tortured, stifled women, increasingly imprisoned by the images Bergman has given them, of his later career. In *Cries and Whispers* we are a long way from the wild, autonomous Harriett Andersson of *Summer with Monika* or the self-defining Mai-Britt Nilsson of *Summer Interlude,* or even the range and diversity of women in *Waiting Women, Journey into Autumn, Smiles of a Summer Night,* and *Brink of Life.* In his latest film, Bergman seems to have turned Harriett Andersson, Liv Ullmann, and Ingrid Thulin into parody-composites of their previous selves (or personae) in a setting that rigorously and pretentiously excludes all signs of idiosyncratic life. And Bergman the artist controls them like puppets, abusing them for being what he has made them: Thulin—neurotic, intellectual, and repressed; Ullmann—beautiful, vain, sensual; and frustrating any attempts at interrelationships by silencing their conversation and aborting sensual overtures between them. The early Bergman heroines had a kind of separation from the director; they communed more with one another and were seen often in medium shot, surrounded by family and friends. Their world was fuller, and they were less central, less suffocatingly *present.* The later women are so close to Bergman as to be projections of his soul (as well as his sexual vanity), and it is a soul to which we should pay homage. Any criticism of Bergman must be prefaced with the understanding that he, more than any other director and in movies that were a revelation for their time, took women seriously, looked with curiosity and respect at every facet of their lives, domestic, sexual, reproductive (though honoring some more than others), never thought of them as "second-class citizens" (the reverse, if anything), and, by not fastening on one single woman as his Galatea, watched over the film-birth and blossoming and development of one extraordinary woman after another. He has provided us with an array of women characters as rich and complex as those of any novelist, male or female.

Bergman's career is totally entwined with the women who

served as his actresses and with the actresses who served as his wives and mistresses; and since his work is also a progressive burrowing into the self, it follows that as he becomes older and more despairing (and less sexually vital) his women will suffer the consequences. From the very beginning, woman has been something sacred to Bergman, something to live up to; and if he has given us some of the most complex and sensually intelligent women of cinema, he has also placed them on a pedestal. For Bergman, woman's love, originating in the life-giving and nurturing power of procreation, is spontaneous and complete; his men are often pale shadows—spineless intellectuals, temporizing lovers, doubters, and compromisers.

Bergman seems to have become even more mystical about childbearing as he grows older, as he grows farther away from that faith with which he was locked in struggle in the early films, and whose loss, in the course of filming *Winter Light,* provided (he has told interviewers) the turning point in his life. Harriett Andersson, the wild girl (and delinquent prototype for such pouty waifs as Bardot and Bulle Ogier) of *Summer with Monika* rejects motherhood completely and is not treated unsympathetically. Bibi Andersson, in *Brink of Life,* rages against but is finally reconciled to her pregnancy, while the supermother represented by Eva Dahlbeck has an unconscious reaction against the masquerade of her super maternalism and loses the baby. In his later films, woman is often split in two, both incomplete: the "natural," sensual, unthinking woman (Gunnel Lindblom in *The Silence,* Bibi Andersson in *Persona*) and the desiccated, intellectual woman (Ingrid Thulin in *The Silence,* Liv Ullmann in *Persona*). But whether it is renounced, or—as it most often is—accepted, childbearing is the consummate experience of a woman's life; for a mystic and anti-intellectual like Bergman, it is the consummate experience of all life. The artist, often played by Max von Sydow, is a figure of dubious achievement, a weak, vacillating character. Like Tolstoy's Levin, but with less positive connotations, he is the tormented thinker, the wanderer, the seeker, while his wife (for example, Liv Ullmann in *Hour of the Wolf*) is the strong, intuitive, and enduring one. Man's metaphysical quest leads to the demons and fantasies of his unconscious, while woman's metaphysical quest leads, as in *Persona,* to withdrawal and silence.

With the exception of *Persona,* in which the idea of two women exchanging identities and the half-conscious power struggle between them is brilliantly realized, some of Bergman's lighter and more homely films tell more about women than his more metaphysical ones. One of his most penetrating character studies is that of Mai-Britt Nilsson as the ballerina in *Summer Interlude* who relives the ecstasies of a youthful love while coming to terms with the impurities of a present one. Eva Dahlbeck, the tall, blonde comedienne of some of his early films, is one of Bergman's greatest and least appreciated actresses, precisely because she is not a Bergman "type" and seems to have eluded his vampirish possession. She is not the smoldering, sensual earth mother that men respond to; rather, like Rosalind Russell, she is a sparklingly witty, self-possessed woman whose comic timing is a sign of her intelligence. As the aristocratic wife of Gunnar Bjornstrand (her perfect match and Bergman's loveliest actor) in *A Lesson in Love,* as the perspicacious mistress in *Journey into Autumn,* and as the brilliantly regal actress in *Smiles of a Summer Night,* she is always her own person, a kind of Restoration comedienne, a woman of high style for whom motherhood is by no means the automatic and instinctive choice it is for Bergman's other women.

The Touch, with Bibi Andersson and Elliot Gould, was panned universally by the critics (largely zeroing in on

Gould's abrasive performance); yet it is one of Bergman's most profound and least pretentious studies of a woman—here a perfectly ordinary housewife whose life becomes radically different after the death of her mother. (The death of a parent, so crucial to male literature and a man's sense of his own evolution, is rarely treated with such respect as a major stage in a woman's life. Without spelling out any of the precise effects the mother's death has had on Andersson, Bergman suggests many things about the woman: with the autumn coloring, her own impending middle age; the shattering of the family hierarchy in which she was both mother and child; the absence of the authority figure to "keep her in line"; and, simply, the gap, the loss of a central person to love and be loved by. All of these in conjunction, perhaps, with the oppressive security of her life, lead her into an intense, almost psychotic, affair with Gould. He is unbalanced, sometimes maniacal, but his strange love stirs dormant feelings both motherly and womanly, normal and perverse. In her wholesome, antiseptic, normal married life with von Sydow, she has suppressed those rude and bloody passions that secrete an odor of death and bring one to an awareness of life. Not that she ceases to love her husband. And here Bergman understands what Tolstoy understood and what both as they grew older ceased to have the largeness of spirit to admit: that a woman can love more than one man at the same time. It is, perhaps, a woman's protection against heartbreak, against the danger of loving only one person and having him reject her. Von Sydow gives her the traditional face-saving ultimatum: She must leave him or see Gould no more. She leaves; but, when things don't work out with Gould, she returns home, pregnant. Bergman never shows us von Sydow's reaction—that would be too humiliating—but he has taken her back and learned to accept compromise in the process. For that, of course, is what life is all about—

which is not to say that ecstasy, ugliness, madness, high comedy are not important or should not be sought with fervor. The affair with Gould is over, and Bergman allows, not for the first time, a trace of humor to appear as we see Andersson leaving Gould forever, her Italian primer in her hand, on her way to the adult education class which will fill the gap he has left.

In European cinema, no less than in the American, the more heroic images of women come from the past. Throughout his career from the twenties on, the Danish filmmaker Carl Dreyer instinctively felt for the plight of women even at the relatively esoteric level of his style and the splendid isolation of his milieu. *Gertrud,* his last and one of his greatest films, pictured a woman who asked too much not only of the men in her life, but apparently of the members of the audience, who walked out in droves from the film when it was released in 1965. Part superfemale, part superwoman, Gertrud was an artist at love, for which she had both an appetite and a vocation. But her lovers had neither her staying power nor her honesty, neither her commitment to sustain an affair, nor her courage to break it off when the time came.

Falconetti, the woman Dreyer chose to play the title role in *Joan of Arc,* is one of the most memorable women of the screen. In the rough texture of her skin and parched lips we feel the spirit made palpable through the senses, and in the alternation of weakness, bewilderment, and courage, the fusion of the heroic and the womanly. As he could reduce a saint to human dimensions, he could see holiness in the most humble circumstances, and so naturally, for Dreyer, the home was as worthy a place as the cross to view the conflicts of the human soul, and another of his remarkable characters was the mother in *Ordet,* a woman whose gift of love was as casual as it was capacious, infinite and yet unsmothering. And in one of his most "relevant" films, *Master of the House,*

Dreyer prompted what is essentially a women's lib critique *avant la lettre* of the roles in marriage by which male supremacy is sanctified and perpetuated.

The same year (1926) saw the release in Russia of one of the most extraordinary feminist films of that or any other time, Abram Room's *Bed and Sofa*. This film, with its remarkably unhysterical treatment of abortion, is practically unknown, having been glossed over in film histories. In it, Ludmilla Semyonova, a sophisticated and sensual woman who obviously demands more than her husband, a hail-fellow–type (Nikolai Batalov) can give her, becomes the center of a *ménage à trois* that has as its ostensible *raison d'être* the Moscow housing shortage. Batalov's old friend (Vladimir Fogel) arrives in the city for a job and, unable to find lodgings, comes to live with them. While Batalov is away on a business trip, Fogel and the wife fall in love and have an affair. When the husband returns and discovers what has happened he is appropriately enraged, but then relents (the housing shortage being what it is) and insists his friend stay on. Not only is the initial awkwardness quickly dissipated, but the two men relax into a living arrangement, playing chess each evening, telling stories, and being waited on hand and foot. They have—in what is not an alteration but merely a multiplication of the usual domestic setup— succeeded in transforming the wife-mistress into a mother and in reverting quite happily to infancy.

Semyonova, thoroughly exasperated, now discovers she is pregnant, whereupon she goes to an abortion clinic, a step that is treated with as little fanfare and emotionalism as a visit to a dentist (perhaps with less). While waiting in the antechamber, she hears a baby crying on the street and abruptly changes her mind, a reversal that has been viewed as a palliative to producers, but that can be viewed more charitably as an understandable change of heart. The denouement is certainly uncompromising enough, as she goes home, packs her things, and is last seen, a vision of lonely, moral triumph, on board a train riding off into the unknown— preferring the one baby in her belly to the two grown ones left behind.

Old women, ugly women, and women directors have perhaps fared better in Europe than in America, but the gap between them is not as great as one would assume. There was lovely Sylvie in René Allio's *The Shameless Old Lady,* but what greater portrait of cantankerous and victimized old age is there than Beulah Bondi and Victor Moore in Leo McCarey's *There's Always Tomorrow,* or Henrietta Crosman in Ford's *Pilgrimage?* There will perhaps be a new wave of feminist films from Europe, led by such directors as Mai Zetterling (*The Girls*) and Vera Chytilova, whose *Something Different* showed, on parallel tracks, the different life styles and frustrations of two women carving out their own lives: an Olympic gymnast and a middle-class housewife.

For the most part, European women in films have been, for better or worse, the creation of their directors, most of whom have been men. Roger Vadim had a distinctively and erotically liberating influence on the women he loved and shaped, a voyeur's appreciation of otherness, as opposed to the increasingly claustrophobic control Bergman has had over his women. Brigitte Bardot, Catherine Deneuve, and Jane Fonda were all launched and "liberated" by Vadim, and each went beyond the tutelage of the director to become a star, representing only herself. The romantic idols of Godard, Antonioni, and Bergman, however, remain identified with the directors whose property, and pawns, they have become. The difference suggests the contrasting attitudes and effect of the two men in *Last Tango in Paris,* and the necessity for woman to emerge, through whatever the means of her liberation, as her own invented self. For if everyone, to some extent, kills the thing he loves, how much more cruelly, yet more gloriously, does the artist, the director—by fixing her, freezing her into the image he wants to preserve, by suppressing some of her qualities, emphasizing others, and finally by not allowing her to grow old, by keeping her "forever young, forever fair."

Thus it is by virtue of those very qualities we respond to —their complex "female" psychology, their sensuality—that European heroines are bound ever more tightly to their "natural" roles, enthralled by (and in thrall to) a vision of the world articulated by men, in which their place is ultimately grander and mystically nobler than his, but more limited and more boring on earth. Even their most archetypal roles—the waif, the rebel, the discreet bourgeoise, the older woman, and the whore—can be seen to emanate not from their own desires, but from those of the men who both worship and fear them.

THE SIXTIES

From a woman's point of view, the ten years from, say, 1962 or 1963 to 1973 have been the most disheartening in screen history. In the roles and prominence accorded women, the decade began unpromisingly, grew steadily worse, and at present shows no signs of improving. Directors who in 1962 were guilty only of covert misogyny (Stanley Kubrick's *Lolita*) or kindly indifference (Sam Peckinpah's *Ride the High Country*) became overt in 1972 with the violent abuse and brutalization of *A Clockwork Orange* and *Straw Dogs*. The growing strength and demands of women in real life, spearheaded by women's liberation, obviously provoked a backlash in commercial film: a redoubling of Godfather-like machismo to beef up man's eroding virility or, alternately, an escape into the all-male world of the buddy films from *Easy Rider* to *Scarecrow*. With the substitution of violence and sexuality (a poor second) for romance, there was less need for exciting and interesting women; any bouncing nymphet whose curves looked good in catsup would do.

With the collapse of the star system, women lost much of their economic leverage. We have ample evidence of the fakery that went into creating the stars' facades, of the misery that went on behind these, and of the tyranny of studio despots who insisted on the image at the expense of the human being underneath. All of which inevitably raises the question of whether it is possible to be both a star and a human being. If it isn't, how many would have traded in stardom for pale humanity?

The sixties, which witnessed the disappearance of the studios and the phony glamour industry, gave the stars a chance to find out, as they receded and "real" human beings took over (showing their "authenticity" by scorning lipstick for eyeshadow and dresses for jeans). But somehow it wasn't the great love-and-reality trip it was supposed to be. Even with the screen thrown wide open to nudity and to love-making positions in tune with the wildest dreams of sexologists, there was still nothing as eye-openingly erotic as the rising and ebbing tide of bubbles on Claudette Colbert's breasts in the milkbath scenes in 1932's *The Sign of the Cross*. Or the casual plunging necklines and glittering body-fitting dresses of the early thirties. Or the love-hate-suspicion relationships of the forties. Or the sudden outbursts of Grace Kelly's snooty, repressed heroines in Hitchcock's films of the puritanical fifties. Somehow Colbert's top parts, Ginger Rogers' camisole, Shearer's cleavage, Harlow's sheaths, and Kelly's kiss were more exciting. Not just because the partially revealed is more alluring than the totally revealed, but because Colbert, and Shearer, and Harlow, and Kelly were "stars." We *knew* them. They were familiar, important, vaguely respectable. When they did something daring, we shivered. The star had power, which included the power of withholding—a power that, like sex itself, was her trump card in a country where men and women had never learned to like each other very much. But as the sixties opened, the Production Code was relaxing, inch by inch. With successive revelations on the screen, the decade progressed like a stripper, though awkwardly—like a novice in a hurry to get off the stage.

In the sixties, they didn't make films like they used to. Once again, economic and aesthetic factors converged to change film history. With the collapse of the studio system as a result of the inroads made by television, fewer and fewer films were being made, and those that were were taking longer and longer to make. Distribution became increasingly erratic as the cost of merely opening a film went up. An actress might be seen in one film and then not again for several years. She couldn't redeem a poor performance or a lousy picture with a better one six months later.

Even the "hottest" actresses—Julie Christie and Julie Andrews at the beginning of the decade, Barbra Streisand and Jane Fonda at the end—were lucky to make a film a year, and some of the appealing but lesser-known ones—Joan Hackett and her colleagues in *The Group,* for example, and Billie Whitelaw, Honor Blackman, Anne Heywood—have long been lost from sight or mired in unrewarding projects. Actresses like Vanessa Redgrave and Julie Christie, Jane Fonda and Mia Farrow, were no longer mythic idols. They were women whose images changed constantly with their roles, and their offscreen antics had to be downright revolutionary to do so much as raise an eyebrow. In deliberately refusing to marry the fathers of their children, Mia Farrow and Vanessa Redgrave were applauded, or ignored, for doing what Ingrid Bergman had been ostracized for only ten years before.

The impulse to become a star and the studio machinery

to create and sustain stars were dead. F. Scott Fitzgerald's comical account of the Metro party where all the stars spoke their own lines instead of those provided them by screenwriters ("Powell was facetious without wit—Shearer was heavy without emotion") came true. Now actors and actresses went on talk shows complete or incomplete with the personalities they'd been born with, or rather the personalities, perhaps no less artificial than the old glamour images, they had nurtured as concerned, "real people."

The absence of the image-manufacturing apparatus gave the actresses greater freedom, but as nonstars they had less power. The growing self-consciousness of film worked to actresses' disadvantage. With the rise of the director as superartist they were at his mercy not only for their employment but for their images, images that were ever less rounded and more peripheral as directors became ever more subjective and self-indulgent.

Major filmmakers seemed to fall into two factions: the neurotic and talented *auteurs* (Wilder, Losey, Penn, Ray, Kubrick, Peckinpah, Nichols, Frankenheimer, Edwards, Aldrich, and Schlesinger), whose sexual anxieties spilled over into their treatment of women, and relatively neutral directors (Zinnemann, Wyler, Wise, Lean, Cukor), whose prestige projects (*A Man for All Seasons, Dr. Zhivago, West Side Story, Justine, The Children's Hour, Lawrence of Arabia*) and star vehicles (*The Sound of Music, My Fair Lady, Funny Girl*) all seemed overstuffed with self-importance or "production values" and undernourished. Even the most obvious of the star vehicles of the past had been less obvious, had worked harder to integrate the star into the narrative framework and to adapt it to her, than did these extravaganzas made after the collapse of the star system.

There were some memorable women's performances: Shirley Jones and Jean Simmons in *Elmer Gantry*; Shirley

MacLaine in *The Apartment*; Piper Laurie in *The Hustler*; Geraldine Page in *Sweet Bird of Youth*; Lee Remick in *Wild River* and *Days of Wine and Roses*; Judy Holliday in *Bells Are Ringing*; Ruby Dee and Ellen Holly in *Take a Giant Step* (in which black women came into their own briefly, not to reemerge until the seventies) ; Lola Albright in *A Cold Wind in August*; the women (Claire Bloom, Shelley Winters, Glynis Johns, and Jane Fonda) in *The Chapman Report*; Rita Tushingham in *A Taste of Honey*; Eva Marie Saint in *All Fall Down*; Dolores Dorn in *Underworld USA*; Tuesday Weld in *Bachelor Flat* and *Soldier in the Rain*; Anne Bancroft in *The Pumpkin Eater, Seven Women,* and, with Patty Duke, *The Miracle Worker*; Joanne Woodward in *The Stripper* and *Rachel, Rachel*; Julie Andrews in *The Americanization of Emily*; Kim Stanley in *Seance on a Wet Afternoon*; Julie Christie in *Darling* and, with Shirley Knight, *Petulia*; Joan Hackett in *The Group*; Jane Fonda in *They Shoot Horses, Don't They?* and *Klute*; Natalie Wood in *Inside Daisy Clover*; Sandy Dennis and Ellen O'Mara in *Up the Down Staircase*; Vanessa Redgrave in *Morgan* and *Isadora*; Audrey Hepburn in *Two for the Road*; Faye Dunaway in *Bonnie and Clyde*; Viva in *The Nude Restaurant*; Maggie Smith in *The Prime of Miss Jean Brodie*; Dyan Cannon in *Bob and Carol and Ted and Alice* and *Such Good Friends*; Lynn Carlin in *Faces*; Glenda Jackson in *Women in Love*; Ellen Burstyn in *Alex in Wonderland* and *The Last Picture Show*; Cybill Shepherd in *The Last Picture Show* and *The Heartbreak Kid*; Cloris Leachman in *The Last Picture Show*; Barbara Loden in *Splendor in the Grass* and *Wanda*.

But even these, the great women's roles of the decade, what are they for the most part? Whores, quasi-whores, jilted mistresses, emotional cripples, drunks. Daffy ingenues, Lolitas, kooks, sex-starved spinsters, psychotics. Icebergs, zombies, and ballbreakers. That's what little girls of the sixties and seventies are made of.

For all the isolated brilliance of these performances, they don't really add up to anything. There was no consistent buildup, no ebb and flow within the films, between the sexes, or through the decade. All the prizes (even from the patriotic Academy of Motion Picture Arts and Sciences) seemed to go to the Europeans. It was the decade when Joan Crawford and Bette Davis were turned into complete travesties of themselves in *What Ever Happened to Baby Jane?* as were Davis and de Havilland in *Hush, Hush, Sweet Charlotte,* the decade when Katharine Hepburn was debased into a Broadway-cute Eleanor of Aquitaine in *The Lion in Winter* and a Stanley Kramer liberal in *Guess Who's Coming to Dinner.* And Elizabeth Taylor bounced back and forth from heterosexual fantasy to homosexual nightmare, from hussy (*Butterfield 8*) to hustler-bait (*Suddenly, Last Summer*) to harridan (*Who's Afraid of Virginia Woolf?*) to hoyden (*The Taming of the Shrew*) to hypochondriac (*Boom*).

The few older-woman characters were grotesques (in the Davis camp category), villains (Anne Bancroft in *The Graduate*), mummies (Merle Oberon in a vanity production called *Interval,* in which Merle's marvels were applauded at the expense of "silly girls"), and utter mistakes (the double humiliation of frumping up thirty-four-year-old Liv Ullmann, in *Forty Carats,* into an "older woman" of forty—forty! Can you imagine an "older man" of forty!—in a "May–December" affair which, if you switched the sexes, would be considered May–June). The new liberated woman was nowhere in sight, and what were we offered as the "strong woman" of the seventies? Raquel Welch as travesty-male, a pinup as gunfighter or roller-derby queen. In every case, we got not only less than we might have expected and hoped for, but less than ever before: women who were less intelligent, less sensual, less humorous, and altogether less extraordinary than women in the twenties, the thirties, the forties, or even the poor, pallid, uptight fifties. There were no working women on the screen, no sassy or smart-talking women, no mature women, and no goddesses either. There were, instead, amoral pinup girls, molls taking guff from their gangsters that would have made their predecessors gag, and thirty-year-olds reduced to playing undergraduates. At the other extreme, as a sort of cartoon reversal of the damsel in distress and of the supermacho black and kung fu hero, the action heroine popped up in one or two Chinese martial arts films and black superwoman epics, *Cleopatra Jones* and *Coffy,* that were the tail end of the blaxploitation genre. A sort of revival of the old Pearl White tradition, these were women who could function in a violent way, but compared to the magnetic Shaft, they were more superbland than superblack. None of them could hold a candle to the glorious and humanly efficient Diana Rigg on "The Avengers."

Apart from the violent genre movies, however, the fate of black women in film is a reversal of the downward drift of women in general. Whereas the portrayal of blacks from the silents to the sixties is one extended blot on the white conscience, with Hattie McDaniel and her ilk playing maids and happy darkies, the recent story of black women—Cicely Tyson in *Sounder* and *The Autobiography of Miss Jane Pittman,* Diahann Carroll in *Claudine,* Ellen Holly and Vonetta McGee as reflective genre heroines—is more optimistic. They have benefited not just from the socially conscious impulse behind films like *Sounder* but from the fact that blacks have taken over those romantic conventions, more congenial to the spirited woman, that whites have abandoned.

The ideal white woman of the sixties and seventies was not a woman at all, but a girl, an ingenue, a mail-order cover girl: regular featured, generally a brunette, whose "real person" credentials were proved by her inability to convey any emotion beyond shock or embarrassment and an inarticulateness that was meant to prove her "sincerity." Directors scanned the ladies' magazines for models they could mold, girls whose brows—and psyches—wouldn't be lined with anything more than the concern to appear beautiful. (The ladies' magazines, in turn, in particular the fashion magazines, had to prove their seriousness by presenting models no longer as anonymous clotheshorses, but as real women, with names and personalities and down-to-earth habits like washing their faces with soap and sometimes even cooking their own meals.)

Even the good women's parts were, by and large, subordinated to, or upstaged by, the men's, and most (a far larger proportion than in the fifties) of the films were men's films. From covert misogyny to overt antagonism, from *Lawrence of Arabia* and *Psycho* to *The French Connection, Dirty Harry,* and *Straw Dogs,* from Crowtherism to cultism, whichever way and from whatever end you looked at things, it was a man's decade in the movies.

Without anyone ever quite realizing it at the time, the pattern had been established in the fifties. The baroque anguish and pessimism with which directors like Nicholas Ray, John Frankenheimer, Joseph Losey, Billy Wilder, and Stanley Kubrick had treated men and women in the fifties came to dominate the sixties. Films that had then seemed curiously eccentric—as different from each other as each was from the Hollywood film—can in retrospect be seen to have shared a worm's-eye view of life that would become the official point of view of the sixties. These directors were able to emerge as artists and dominate as they did because film itself was passing from a popular entertainment to a fine art, from the classical, narrative framework and team product to the creation of the single artist. The "modern" director acquired (or brought with him) the aesthetic and temperamental problems assailing modern artists in other fields. Just as the twentieth-century (in comparison to the nineteenth-century) novelist suffers from a fragmented, incomplete vision of the world, so the modernist filmmaker was similarly "cut off" from society, and from the studio microcosm, that had nourished the classical filmmaker. It was an artistic decision that he *made* as inevitably as he breathed the *Zeitgeist,* but that was also partially made for him by the collapse of the studios.

His tendency, like that of the modernist in the other arts, has been to go into himself rather than outward into the world, and his characters suffer the anemia of being extensions of his ego rather than wholly autonomous beings. No longer is there a "normal" world, as there is in Dickens or Tolstoy or even in the films of the thirties, against which the central characters' dilemmas unfold; instead, the artist's self-projections *are* the world. His demons, like invading body-snatchers or Martians, people the real world and turn it into a neurotic reflection of himself.

There is a deliberately claustrophobic quality to films like *The Servant, The Collector, Who's Afraid of Virginia Woolf?, The Graduate,* and *Midnight Cowboy,* where society is brought in only in a stylized way and often as a kind of prison, and where women are reduced to men's jailors or passing fantasies. If *Hiroshima, Mon Amour, Breathless,* and *La Dolce Vita* (all released in 1960 and 1961) were the major stylistic influences of the decade, the English cinema —swinging-mod and kitchen-sink—established a certain cynical, derisive, and crypto-homosexual attitude toward men and women. Rita Tushingham's "ugly girl," (to be succeeded in the seventies by Liza Minnelli and Jeannie Berlin), the pregnant fag-hag waif in *A Taste of Honey,* teams up with a homosexual to have her child. In *The Knack* she plays a "bird" of such negative sex appeal that she can safely share a flat with four swinging lotharios (whose preening is rightly seen by playwright Ann Jellicoe as a mating dance performed more for each other than for women). The homosexual theme finally becomes explicit in Sidney J. Furie's *The Leather Boys,* where poor Rita Tushingham is enough to drive her young husband from their marriage bed onto the back seat of another fellow's motorcycle.

Another English male image by which women could be properly put in their place was the peacock and his "birds." Both *Alfie* and the James Bond pictures present men brandishing their masculinity through the exploitation of women, but in the very act of turning women into sex objects, they cheapen their own value and their own triumphs. Sexual strutting, generally identified with a non-U background, often got by as a form of social criticism. The lower-class rebels—rock stars, rugby players, victims—the antiheroes of *The Loneliness of the Long-Distance Runner, Look Back in Anger, Billy Liar, Saturday Night and Sunday Morning, Room at the Top, This Sporting Life, Help!, If,* and *A Hard Day's Night* (or the antihero turned arriviste of *O Lucky Man!*) are all male, and the women, when not shrill mothers or coarse wenches, are merely bystanders. John Schlesinger's *A Kind of Loving* is typical of the slightly patronizing "lower-class" study which sees its hero (Alan Bates) as trapped, in this case by a girl he has made pregnant and for whom he has absolutely no feeling. Although the Bates character is made to grow up and accept responsibility, the reconciliation is phony, and the prospect of happiness with the girl as she has been presented seems very dim.

Because of their alibi as social discontents, the most swinish antiheroes—Alfie, and Bill Maitland in Osborne's *Inadmissible Evidence*—are heroic compared to those around them. Even Laurence Harvey's ruthless climber in *Room at the Top* is made out to be an exonerable victim of class prejudice, although Simone Signoret is an effective counter.

His female counterpart is Julie Christie's Darling, who, in John Schlesinger's 1965 film, put swinging London's most cynical export item on the market. She is the Anglo-

Saxon equivalent of Sagan's amoral heroines, but with more disguised ambition and less real sensuality. Like Harvey in *Room at the Top,* she uses two (actually three, but the Italian nobleman barely figures) members of the opposite sex as her stairs to the top. Also like Harvey, she is upstaged by one of them. Just as Simone Signoret outshines Harvey in *Room at the Top* not only with her acting but with her humanity, so, in *Darling,* Dirk Bogarde has the same twin advantage over Christie, and makes the same point for morality. With this movie, Christie ushered in, or perhaps crystallized in female form, a sixties' aura—in much the same way that Joan Crawford's go-go girl in *Our Dancing Daughters,* exactly forty years before, gave the definitive flapper to an era already in full swing to her tune. The films were alike in other ways: They both made stars of heroines who, with their ruthless insistence on having a good time, were the very embodiment of a spirit that was more the way an age liked—or feared—to see itself than the way it actually was.

Being so spectacularly contemporary, these were not films, or even performances, for the ages. Besides, Christie's petulant, paper-thin model on the make is really just a centerpiece for the men. Her later, underrated "kook" portrayal in Richard Lester's *Petulia,* is, by contrast, a rich and moving performance. In *Petulia,* the combination of "woman's film" material and Lester's pop pyrotechnics (razzle-dazzle footage of the contemporary San Francisco "scene") conspired to conceal the film's true value from critics ever on the alert for (or against) relevance but deaf and dumb to romance. This, not the synthetic *Love Story,* was the love film of the sixties, a double bonus coming when it did and from a director like Lester, whose films were becoming more political and tendentious. Even here, the "important subject" syndrome is apparent in Lester's compulsion to jazz up the film with topical references, a typical socially conscious reflex of embarrassment over emotional material. He lacked the confidence to let the story stand on its own.

The story is, as one sympathetic critic pointed out, straight out of an old Carole Lombard movie. Girl married to a rich, inexplicably weak husband (Richard Chamberlain) who is controlled by his father (Joseph Cotten) falls in love with a soulful and slightly cynical surgeon (George C. Scott) who has sort of broken off with his wife (Shirley Knight). The performances are extraordinary: particularly those of George C. Scott as the middle-aged man who has one more chance at love and can't quite go through with it; Christie as the apparently wild, spiritually chaste young woman; and Shirley Knight as Scott's taut, crazier-than-Christie (in a less obvious way) ex-wife who is about to remarry and will probably make the same mistakes all over again. Lester's fireworks conceal, perhaps deliberately, the fact that there is nothing in the film that couldn't have passed the censor ten years ago: Petulia's immorality is only apparent; the doctor could take advantage of her but falls in love; in the end—but wait, there's the difference. In the end, nobody is punished or saved. Nobody gets what he wants. Lester gives us neither the happy ending nor the noble, sacrificial one. Scott doesn't go with Christie, but he doesn't go back to his wife either. He just doesn't go at all, he stays where he is, in the weary name of compromise, of playing it safe, of surrender. The older generation has lost the capacity to live by pure feeling, while the new one lashes itself into a frenzy trying. And in the split, in the loss of connective tissue between man and woman, between one generation and another, they all lose the power to regenerate.

The focus of the English and American films of the period is generally on the male protagonist, often the director's alter ego, as an alienated spirit, the antihero as the principal victim of the cruelties of modern life. The sterility and inhumanity of his existence is seen to be attributable to work, marriage, or success. (When the angry young man marries the upper-class bitch, or makes it financially, he is more miserable than ever, for it is crucial to the artist's poetic self-image to see himself as outsider and victim.) The antihero is a loser, a madman, or an outlaw. That a woman might not be entirely satisfied with her lot in life, or might want to let go with a little insanity of her own, never occurs to these protagonists, or to their creators, who fancy they have the monopoly on *angst*. Some more sympathetic than others, they are the refugees from middle-class life, the only idealists in a world of cynics and opportunists: Jack Lemmon in Billy Wilder's films (*The Apartment* and *The Fortune Cookie*) and Ray Walston in Wilder's *Kiss Me, Stupid*; the failed and frustrated heroes of Irvin Kershner's films (Robert Shaw in *The Luck of Ginger Coffey,* Sean Connery in *A Fine Madness,* and George Segal in *Loving*); James Mason's addict schoolteacher in Nicholas Ray's *Bigger Than Life*; David Warner's loony with an ape complex in Karel Reisz's *Morgan*; the eternally neurotic Warren Beatty as the oversensitive (or oversexed) young man of *Splendor in the Grass,* the Byronic wastrel in John Frankenheimer's *All Fall Down,* the impotent gangster in Arthur Penn's *Bonnie and Clyde,* or the hipster on the run in Penn's *Mickey One,* and the lonely, baffled idealist in Robert Altman's *McCabe and Mrs. Miller*; Dustin Hoffman's pubescent waif in Mike Nichols' *The Graduate* and the Camille-like Ratso Rizzo in Schlesinger's *Midnight Cowboy*; Rock Hudson's escapee from suburbia in Frankenheimer's *Seconds*; the trio of Peter Falk, Ben Gazzara, and John Cassavetes in the latter's *Husbands*; Albert Finney's fatigued and dispirited writer in *Charley Bubbles*; Robert Redford's alienated skier in *Downhill Racer* and virginal politician in *The Candidate*; Michael Sacks' time-tripping hero in the film version of Vonnegut's *Slaughterhouse-Five*; the ultimate disillusioned-heroes-in-flight, the Fonda–Hopper motorcycle duo in *Easy Rider*; Jack Nicholson's wrinkled "boy genius" dropout in *Five Easy Pieces*; and Gene Hackman and Al Pacino as the mice-and-mendicants of *Scarecrow*.

There is also a whole subgenre of "road" films in which a young hero—not so young as he would like to be—takes off in a car, plane (*Zabriskie Point*), or motorcycle to escape the clutches of America (generally symbolized by his parents or the law), and finds himself somewhere between the desert flowers and the sagebrush, a symbol of Nowhereman. Sometimes he has visions and head-trips. The hero of *Vanishing Point* sees a nude girl on a motorcycle who, unfortunately, does not turn out to be a mirage. In the road films, the women are lucky to be mere bodies, way stations where the heroes can relieve themselves and resume their journey. For in the more "civilized" antihero films, the woman is generally a villainess, a conformist waiting patiently or clutching impatiently to bring the hero back into the fold, to reintegrate him into the hypocritical society whose emissary she is. Within this negative range, the wives vary from the monstrous (in *Husbands* and *Slaughterhouse-Five*) to the ineffectually beautiful blondes of Kershner's films (Mary Ure, Jean Seberg, Eva Marie Saint) to the sympathetic if subordinated Vanessa Redgrave and Billie Whitelaw of *Morgan* and *Charley Bubbles*. Rarely is a woman, let alone a wife, permitted to explode against the inequities of her situation or embark on her own journey of liberation. Even in the neo-woman's films of the seventies—*Diary of a Mad Housewife, Klute, Such Good Friends, Sunday, Bloody Sunday, Play It As It Lays*—her rebellion is defensive, and her victory often pyrrhic. Before these new, quasi-women's lib pictures, there were actually a few films that dealt with a woman's discontent: Richard Brooks' *Happy Ending,* with Jean Simmons as the disillusioned wife, was, purely and simply, a failure. Francis Ford Coppola's *The Rain People* was an erratic, pretentious, but often interesting effort, with Shirley Knight as a housewife on the run. But her cross-country quest eventually belongs less to her than to the men she meets, to James Caan's pickup and Robert Duvall's cop. An aesthetically rich but psychologically obscure madness gripped Susannah York in Robert Altman's *Images.*

One "woman's film" that seems to have been overlooked in the hysteria of the decade is *Rachel, Rachel,* starring Joanne Woodward (under Paul Newman's direction) as the thirty-five-year-old virgin schoolteacher who stands uneasily at the threshhold of the second half of her life. *Rachel, Rachel* is one of a small group of films, including Altman's *A Cold Day in the Park,* Cassavetes' *Faces,* and *The Prime of Miss Jean Brodie,* that deal sympathetically, and for purposes other than sheer melodrama, with the problems of a repressed and unglamorous woman. (*The Killing of Sister George* might have deserved more points for tackling unpleasant truths if it hadn't tackled them with such relish and sensationalism.) The melodramatic aspect of *A Cold Day in the Park* never overwhelms the character of Sandy Dennis' repressed, Victorian-Canadian heroine, whose dormant sexual curiosity allows her to become the prisoner of a malignantly charming hippie. Altman counterposes traditional and countercultures much as John Cassavetes does in *Faces,* with Seymour Cassel's free spirit finally releasing Lynn Carlin's uptight housewife. In *Rachel, Rachel,* after surviving a skirmish with revivalism, a lesbian overture from her best friend (Estelle Parsons), a heterosexual affair, and her mother's overdependency, Woodward takes her life in her hands and goes off alone. Her story is all the more triumphant, in terms of its own fiction and of movie commercialism, because she is not only unglamorous, but unexceptional in every other way. She is a very ordinary person, with no ultimate salvation—sexual liberation, economic advancement, drugs, encounter therapy, or even love—in store for her. And yet, perhaps for these very reasons, she engages us completely. As played by

Woodward, she has, in her developing sense of self, enormous dignity, which makes her life worth our attention.

In *The Prime of Miss Jean Brodie,* Maggie Smith's attractive Scottish schoolteacher reveals herself to be a pernicious, even murderous influence, as she sublimates her lust for life in her pupils and drives them to the loves and deaths she hasn't the guts to risk herself. This traditional view of the schoolteacher as a suppressed hysteric coincides with the literary conception of the governess, who was to nineteenth-century fiction (and life) what the teacher was to the early twentieth century. This was the only respectable profession for an unmarried woman, a woman who was, it was understood, without economic support but of a certain class and education. The governess, like the schoolteacher after her, was "incomplete," was sexually deprived, which in turn led to her behavioral neuroses. Mark Schorer diagnoses Jane Eyre as a hysteric and the governess in Henry James' *The Turn of the Screw* a psychotic. But where Jane Eyre comes through with the fire of her intellectual and moral energy to assert her own values, in the more romantic domain of movies, the schoolteacher is generally seen—and generally sees herself—as a pitiable figure, synonymous with "old maid." Rosalind Russell (*Picnic*) Katharine Hepburn (*Summertime*), even Katherine Ross (*Butch Cassidy and the Sundance Kid*), all flee at the first opportunity, and with the first man that gives them a nod, an occupation that by society's lights is a fate worse than death. As spinsters, or spinster-types, Woodward and Smith are more believable, sophisticated, even more dignified than the old Kazan–Williams–Inge maudlin marms, but they suffer from the same problem: sexual malnutrition. It does indeed seem weird, not to say astonishing, that this privation, purveyed in fiction as the chief cause of misery among women, never seems to plague men, although if we are to believe their protestations of sexual need, legislated into the double standard, they are biologically more sex-driven than women, and, it should follow, more anguished by the frustration of that need.

And yet, if a man—in film or literature—is deprived of sex (for example, Warren Beatty in *Splendor in the Grass*) there is no slur or reflection on his sex appeal: Generally, he either chooses abstinence or it is chosen for him by society, and he doesn't look the worse for the wear (or nonwear). A woman, on the other hand, must look as pinched and bloodless as a prune, the objective correlative of her unlubricated vagina. It is rare that a frigid woman is permitted, like Hedda Gabler, to be beautiful and vital, but even Hedda is destructive, incomplete, and almost homicidal. The vision of the virginal woman as some kind of freak (a vision no less perverted than the concept of her as sacred) is purveyed not just by conventional heterosexual society, but by militant lesbians as well. *Village Voice* writer Jill Johnston ransacks the lives of deceased artists looking for clues to lesbianism and is concerned when their lesbian potential has gone unfulfilled; her philosophy of life-as-art cannot accept the possibility that the wound of unfulfillment spurred the bow of artistic achievement. The drive to compensate is crucial, as the relatively low output of fine art in a totally permissive society seems to prove. If frigidity drove Hedda Gabler to destroy (or was at least part of the compound of drives and frustrations that formed her personality), why can't it have driven Virginia Woolf to create? Thus, while we may deplore Virginia Woolf's sexual trauma, we should also entertain the possibility that it activated the compensating "wholeness" of her novels instead of feeling sorry for her, as Johnston does, for being a "woman who couldn't possibly have enjoyed sex." It is a mistake in any event, and an oversimplification that does great injustice to the female sensibility, to isolate orgasmic sexual fulfillment as the supreme and only form of sexual experience. In this, Johnston and other chauvinistic lesbians merely adopt the imperialistic characteristics of male sexuality that they presumably abhor, and use absolutist labels that exclude a wide range of affective feelings and behavior.

The emphasis on orgasmic sex is masculine in thrust, finding its apotheosis in the phallic philosophy of D. H. Lawrence. The three latest movies based on Lawrence's works—*The Fox, The Virgin and the Gypsy,* and *Women in Love*—were all made, as Pauline Kael suggested in her review of *The Fox,* when it was too late to make them. In the very act of opening itself up to sex, the screen had gone beyond Lawrence; the "new morality" made it possible to show everything—homosexual and heterosexual copulation —without ever coming to terms with the vestiges of repression that lingered in most members of the audience. If one were to accept the screen version, women had been freed from their inhibitions not by some slow, difficult process of building confidence and trust, but overnight, by fiat. There have been no films, except possibly Bertolucci's *Last Tango in Paris,* that have detailed what it is like for a specific woman to overcome the mountainous conditioning against her sexual release. Nor have there been any intermediary stages. There is only sexual liberation or nonliberation, either/or, nudity or full dress. And when women were "liberated" on the screen—that is, exposed and made to be sexually responsive to the males in the vicinity—it was in order to comply with male fantasies or, in the viragoes of Ken Russell or Robert Aldrich, to confirm men's worst fears. Glenda Jackson as Gudrun in *Women in Love,* is even more abrasive and emasculating than her Lawrentian prototype in the novel, who was herself based on Katharine Mansfield: a cruel portrait by any standards. Lawrence was out to savage, in Gudrun and Hermione, the new, twentieth-century intellectual woman. For him, the perfect woman, like Kate in *The Plumed Serpent,* would be intelligent without being intellectual, her repressed sexuality ready to burst forth at the right touch, and eventually to be offered on the altar of male supremacy. According to the myths of modern film and fiction, which are meant to represent an advance over the Victorian ones, it is inconceivable that a woman could live, thrive, even enjoy life without being "laid" at least four times a week. If a man's need for a woman, or for self-validation, is sexual, he doesn't see that a woman's need for him (and for self-validation) is largely psychological. If he's Lawrence, he does perceive the psychological root of the need and wishes to thwart it. Or if he is a mystical "macho" writer like Mailer, he sees his ability to satisfy a sexually hungry woman —a fit companion and competitor in the ring—as a feather in his own cap. Ideally, she shouldn't want sex too much or, above all, too actively; she should just be ready when man the aggressor wants to find a place for his pride and joy. As the poet/prophet of sexual liberation, but also for his own deeper reasons, Lawrence did want sexually demanding women. It was their psychological hunger he mistrusted. As Birkin's ministrations to Ursula show in *Women in Love,* and as Lawrence revealed in his comments on, among others, Hawthorne's women (*Studies in American Literature*), he was afraid that women would unman him as his mother had done; he felt the need to possess was the most primal, and lethal, element in a woman's love. In order to avoid this "corruption," he would deny them intellect altogether— overlooking the fact that their need to possess resulted from a spiritual and intellectual appetite that was largely frustrated by society. In the religion of the phallus, as in the religion of Christ, men and women are meant to rise above their selfish and conditional identities, their petty possessiveness, in a transcendental union of souls. And yet the effect is to reinforce male superiority; the phallus acts as a totem to strike fear and awe in woman (and appease man's fear and awe of the womb), and to distract women from their spiritual quest.

This fear and awe of woman-as-mother, or wife-as-mother, is the prime source of female grotesques in American movies. Preston Sturges' *Hail the Conquering Hero* is one of the bitterest and most scathing satires on momism ever made. Aldrich's *What Ever Happened to Baby Jane?* and *The Killing of Sister George* present women turned in on themselves, a negative image and parody of his all-male worlds. In a way, the very idea of *Baby Jane,* in exploiting, or underlining, the stranglehold power of its two stars on our film consciousness, suggests mothers who can't let their sons go. Much easier to dispose of them by sicking them on each other than try to come to terms with them individually, as women. This is society's final revenge on Davis' and Crawford's star image and on their power: the implication, by the exaggeration of their exaggerations, that they were never real, never women, but were some kind of joke, apart from women and a warning to them. *Sister George* deals with outright monsters, and in its all-female freak show, it opposes itself to Aldrich's male films and the serious heroics of such as *The Dirty Dozen, Flight of the Phoenix,* and *Ulzana's Raid.*

Aldrich also took his turn at the Hollywood show-biz saga, with *The Legend of Lylah Clare,* a baroque, pseudo-Sternberg–Dietrich story with Kim Novak as the irredeemably bland starlet and Peter Finch as the sensitive woebegone director. The difference between the two teams is not the difference between parody and the thing parodied, because Dietrich, like a great work of art, contains elements of self-parody; rather, it is the difference between an original and a plastic facsimile. The joke was on the parodists. The glorious and cruel playpen world of Robert Mulligan's *Inside Daisy Clover* comes closer to the sense of bewilderment and deracination felt by the starlet (Natalie Wood). Here her strongest relationship, her only real and dependable relationship, is with her mother (Ruth Gordon). Natalie Wood's starry-eyed wistfulness has never been more appropriately or sympathetically treated. For the most part, and in other Mulligan films as well, she is less poignant than boring, a perfectly perfect, unchallenging sixties' woman.

Julie Andrews was another perfect, and usually perfectly safe, star, an antidote to the denizens of swinging London. Like a good governess-chaperone, she came along in *Mary Poppins* to counter the bad impression of *The Servant, The Knack, The Collector*. The quintessentially English nanny, she yet seemed more all-American than the all-Americans. Just as Doris Day's dimples battled Marilyn Monroe's curves, and Betty Grable and her jazz-band buddies countered Harlow and her midnight lovers, so Julie Andrews was the clean-living antithesis to swinging London, countering the taste for leather whips and leather boys with raindrops and roses. Still, like some of her earlier counterparts (Day more than Grable), she had the enterprising spirit of the tomboy. She was alert, wide-eyed; she looked, listened, and learned. There is nothing very threatening or exotic or even sexy about her (although in *The Americanization of Emily* she is treated more ambivalently and interestingly), but there is something a little ruthless in her ladylike pursuit of her ambitions. She, too, like the flappers she evokes (and played in *Star!* and *Thoroughly Modern Millie*), is out for a good time, but unlike them, she never really lets go. The wheels are clicking all the time, as Blake Edwards suggests in *Darling Lili*, where Andrews is the ultimate in performing woman: a spy.

Basically, thoroughly modern Millie was the least modern of heroines: she was eager where the others were listless, she was sexless where they were sultry, she was voluble where they were locked in deep Pinter-like silences, and she was off on her own where they were presented as clinging like ticks to the menfolk, sucking the last drops of their innocence. Such, anyway, are the heroines of Losey, Pinter, and Losey–Pinter.

FROM REVERENCE TO RAPE

Vivien Merchant's feline sexuality, carried over from *The Homecoming* to *Accident,* is seen as a dark, destructive force; there is something ancient and unfathomable in her presence, the spirit of a matriarchal goddess living in the present, visiting doom on men's innocence. In *Eva,* Losey turns Jeanne Moreau into a sluttish parody of herself, a voracious earth mother who devours men. In *The Go-Between* a worldly Julie Christie persuades an innocent boy to transmit letters to her farmer lover and is thus responsible, not only for his disillusionment with love, but also—the film and the Hartley novel on which it is based would both have us believe—for his lifelong celibacy. (For once we *do,* if only for a moment, have a "dried-up" bachelor—the boy as an old man at the end of the film—but, typically, his "incompleteness" and chastity are not the result of his being unwanted, as is generally the case with spinsters, but of the destruction by a woman of his faith in love.) In *Accident,* one feels that the two aging professors (Stanley Baker and Dirk Bogarde) are really bound together rather than driven apart by their desire for the blandly evil enigma played by Jacqueline Sassard. *First Love,* Maximilian Schell's overly lyrical adaptation of the Turgenev short story, is yet another film that shows enigmatic woman as the beautiful illusion and destroyer of innocence. Here Dominique Sanda, who not only represents but looks like beautiful death, brings on John Moulder Brown's first palpitations of love and pangs of heartbreak. Although Sanda drifts in and out looking exquisitely malevolent, it is Brown who is the love object, whose Tadzio-like beauty is sought out and lovingly framed by the camera, and whose pinup prettiness suggests a boy who has never been troubled by the pain of love or the awkwardness of adolescence. (In *Deep End,* Jerzy Skolimowski shows a completely different side—literally and figuratively—of the same actor. There, Brown's beauty, which is visually de-emphasized, and his innocence, become cruel and egotistical luxuries. When he is humiliated, he is driven to kill in revenge. Hence, it is not women's worldliness, Skolimowski seems to be saying, but men's innocence, their insistence on purity in an impure world and their need to blame woman when the purity must finally be surrendered, that is truly wicked.)

The built-in sensuality of the film medium presents a permanent dilemma: A director, even with all good intentions, can hardly help turning a beautiful woman into a sex object, and there is always the danger that what starts as an exposé becomes exploitation. The line between the two is precariously thin in *La Mort d'un Bucheron,* a Canadian film by Gilles Carles, which details the coming-to-consciousness of its beautiful (and shapely) backwoods heroine through prolonged stints as a model and dancer-stripper, doing sexy routines in which her anatomy is, from the point of view of *mise en scène,* several emotional degrees more prominent than her anxiety.

A perfect example of this conundrum, of the way cinema can so easily turn exposé into exploitation, is the adaptation of John Fowles' *The Collector* (directed by William Wyler). A work which, like Fowles' other novels, is a critique from within of male possessiveness and ownership, becomes an erotic essay on the object of that possession, in this case Samantha Eggar who, as Terence Stamp's captive, is pinned and mounted like one of his butterflies. The movie, in utter contradiction of the spirit of the book, becomes the ultimate look-but-don't-touch voyeuristic fantasy of the neurotic (or, in this case, psychotic) male. Since the story is told from Stamp's point of view, the audience is led to appreciate Eggar —her russet coloring, her freckles, her legs—the way a lepidopterist would appreciate the markings of a butterfly. The Eggar character, denied a point of view, becomes nearly inanimate, a male possession, an art/love object.

The whole Lolita cult invokes a similar perverse master-object relationship between man and woman. The demands of a nymphet like Shirley Temple, or her more nubile sixties successors—Tuesday Weld, Hayley Mills, Mia Farrow, and Sue Lyon—are easily satisfied; she would rather have toys than boys, and her sexuality is rudimentary enough to be almost interchangeable with a boy's. The screen Lolitas are there to fulfill old men's fantasies as painlessly and covertly as possible. When there is pain and recognition of suffering, as in Nabokov's *Lolita* or Frankenheimer's *I Walk the Line,* the pain turns out to have been inflicted by a child whose innocence is only an illusion, a veil behind which a malevolent minx is waiting to lure a man to his ruin.

Malevolent woman, woman as "destroyer," can lead man to his doom not just aggressively and violently, but passively, and imperceptibly. One of the dominant images of the sixties is the somnambulist—not in the metaphorical sense in which Parker Tyler applied the term to Leigh and Davis—but as a true sleepwalker, whose very passivity allows her to become an agent of evil. She is an extension of the woman as work of art and object of pure contemplation.

In *The Collector,* a relatively impersonal director—Wyler —was not expressing his own obsessions but simply telling a story the most effective (arousing) way he could. For a director like Roman Polanski, on the other hand, the image of the anesthetized woman, the beautiful, inarticulate, and possibly even murderous somnambule is at the core of his work: Catherine Deneuve as the placid, demented heroine of *Repulsion,* Mia Farrow as the frightened, pregnant wife of *Rosemary's Baby,* Sharon Tate as the beautiful, last-minute "convert'" to vampirism in *The Fearless Vampire Killers,* and Francesca Annis as the ultimate sleepwalking heroine, Lady Macbeth, in Polanski's *Macbeth.* To what extent, if any, does Polanski "expose" (that is, criticize) the plight of woman as victim and to what extent capitalize, in fetishistic fashion, on the eroticism of her passivity? Even in *Repulsion*, he doesn't reveal the heroine's madness until the end, and the retroactive sympathy is minimal. In all the other films (and even in *Repulsion*) the chills of diabolism and the titillation of torture are stronger than the bonds of empathy.

In Polanski's tortured, paranoid universe, the woman, simply by being susceptible of "impregnation" by something outside her, is a potential carrier of evil. His blonde heroines all become instruments of the devil and fulfill his fears of evil, just as the lobotomized actresses he chooses to play them fulfill his ideas of women. Polanski is a perfect example of the artist whose vision of women is not formed according to what he sees, but conversely, whose women are chosen as they conform to his preconceptions.

For a male-chauvinist Pygmalion, the lure of the sleep-walker, the child-woman, the butterfly is practically irresistible. In one of the major *oeuvres* of the decade, the sextet of films that includes *My Night at Maud's, La Collectioneuse, Claire's Knee,* and *Chloë in the Afternoon,* Eric Rohmer explores this lure as he falls victim to it. Through his wavering and usually self-deluded protagonists, Rohmer examines the forces in a man—the impulses, the subterfuges—that lead him to respond to and choose one woman over another, often less challenging, woman who is either safer or else inaccessible. In all except the last film, which seems more cynical as a result, the hero pays a price for rejecting the superior woman. In *My Night at Maud's,* Jean-Louis Trintignant musters his Pascalian Catholicism to rationalize the inevitability of choosing a blonde whom he has merely glimpsed in a cathedral over the generous and sensual Maud. Françoise Fabian's glorious Maud is the antithesis of the sleepwalking heroine; she is an intellectual, a free thinker in the best sense of the word, a woman without crutches or prejudices, ready to commit herself. But for all that she is no match for the unknown woman, the blonde to whom Trin-tignant feels himself predestined. When they finally do meet, and she turns out to be suspicious and prudish, this only corroborates the vision of purity with which Trintignant had endowed her.

In *Claire's Knee,* the diplomat (Jean-Claude Brialy) passes up the relationship offered by the poetic and pre-cocious Laura (Beatrice Romand) in favor of the ecstasy of contemplating the knee—a detached "unit" of eroticism—of the blonde, athletic, conventionally beautiful Claire (Lau-rence de Monaghan). Even with her, his involvement is almost purely egocentric. Irritated by her love for a fellow her own age and by their indifference to him, he maliciously causes a rift between them; but even when he has her at his feet, he rejects her, refuses the responsibility that embracing her would entail, and makes preparations to rejoin his fiancée. From what we have seen (in a photograph) and been told of her, she is a mature, capable career woman who will make few demands on him.

Bernard Verley, as the typical French executive in *Chloë in the Afternoon,* is the least likable and the most callow of Rohmer's heroes. Chloë, a drifter and old acquaintance, in-sinuates herself into his life, but the attentions he pays her are halfhearted. He would rather dream a double life than live it, or than live one life fully. The film ends enigmatically; he returns to his wife, there is a scene, she breaks down, they are apparently reconciled. But his flight from Chloë and return to his wife is not a man's return to a woman he now understands and values, but to a wife to whom he is bound by covenant. When he embraces her, it is not with a new sense of commitment, but with relief: She is a refuge from decision and desire and emotional risk. The grounds for a savage critique of a man like Verley are there, but Rohmer does not pursue them, and seems almost, in the end (and this, dismayingly, is the grand finale of his moral tales), to espouse Verley's bankrupt bourgeois "morality" in the name of Pascalian choice.

Rohmer (in *My Night at Maud's* and *Claire's Knee*) draws a dialectic between the blonde and the brunette, using the same moral coordinates as Hitchcock (blonde: conceited, aloof; brunette: warm, responsive), which are, in turn, a fascinating switch of the traditional signals. The sexual connotations of the old iconography remain—blonde: virgin; brunette: whore—but the values are reversed, so that it is the voluptuous brunette who is "good" and the icy blonde who is "bad." For Hitchcock, beginning with Madeleine Carroll in *The 39 Steps* and continuing through Grace Kelly (*To Catch a Thief, Rear Window*), Eva Marie Saint (*North by Northwest*), Janet Leigh (*Psycho*), Tippi Hedren (*The Birds, Marnie*), Kim Novak (in her Madeleine persona in *Vertigo*), Dany Robin (*Topaz*), and Barbara Leigh-Hunt (*Frenzy*), the blonde is reprehensible not because of what she does but because of what she withholds: love, sex, trust. She must be punished, her complacency shattered; and so he submits his heroines to excruciating ordeals, long trips through terror in which they may be raped, violated by birds, killed. The plot itself becomes a mechanism for destroying their icy self-possession, their emotional detachment.

The brunette—Kim Novak (as the "real" Judy, in *Vertigo*), Diane Baker (*Marnie*), Suzanne Pleshette (*The Birds*), and Karen Dor (*Topaz*)—is "good," that is, down to earth, unaffected, adoring, willing to swallow her pride, even maternal. Sometimes too much so. Like Norman Bates' "mother" in *Psycho*, who might, by a stretch of the Oedipal complex, be categorized among the brunettes, they are inclined to be possessive and even a little sticky. They are too available. The grass is greener, the hair blonder (the knee sexier, the image more unattainable), the lure greater on the other side of the fence. The Hitchcock protagonist is attracted to the girl he can't have, and the misogynist in Hitchcock (as in Chaplin, Godard, etc.) invests the character with poisonous personality traits to punish her for rejecting him. She is exquisitely beautiful, but frigid, snooty, uncaring. And part of the fascination, unequivocally sexual, is of Snow White being degraded: Grace Kelly's fashion-plate playgirl exposed to danger in *Rear Window* and *To Catch a Thief*; the alabaster skin of Tippi Hedren's rich-bitch being pecked by birds and spattered with blood.

But what about her, what about the frigid or frightened woman whose cool may be a veneer and whose point of view is rarely articulated? The woman who, as a girl, has been so indoctrinated against sex, against allowing a man to take advantage of her, that she has frozen, perhaps permanently? Hitchcock allows this inference to be drawn from all his blondes, without actually taking their side until *Marnie,* one of his most disturbing and, from a woman's point of view, most important films. Almost a parody of the woman on her way up the professional ladder, Tippi Hedren's Marnie changes her job as well as her wigs regularly, plays up to her employers, and steals from their safes. On one level, this suggests the revenge of the pretty girl who is hired for her legs rather than her skills and is considered "fair game" by her leering employers (who must be repaid for giving her the job she didn't deserve). On the pathological level, Marnie hates men as the result of an early sexual trauma and finds "sexual" release only through horseback riding. Her thefts, like the star's ambition in *The Goddess,* are a desperate, futile attempt to win a mother's love. Once again, the woman is driven in the socially "unnatural" direction of ambition and career to gain the love that has been denied her.

She succeeds in eluding the grasp of most men until she meets Sean Connery (in a brilliant performance), whose appetite is only whetted by her hostility. He is obviously attracted to her because—not in spite—of her kleptomania and her frigidity. By society's standards, he is a kind, considerate husband who takes on the burden of her guilt and tries to help her; by Hitchcock's, he is as perverse and "sick" as she is.

If Hitchcock's women must be tortured and punished, his men are fully implicated in the deed—and the more detached they seem, the more guilty and morally responsible. (Cary Grant's self-righteous sacrifice of Ingrid Bergman in *Notorious* is far more reprehensible than her actual spying; only the "villain" played by Claude Rains has any claim to virtue.) Hitchcock's lovers are rarely "normal"—they proceed not from attraction to trust to mutual love to marriage to happily-ever-after, but from wariness and self-deception to suspicion to prejudice to disapproval to antagonism, etc. They are perverse to begin with, and their reconciliations are often ironic. The flimsiness of the happy ending in *Marnie* indicates not so much that certain perversities are too deep for resolution, but that perversity is the very soul of attraction; that the images we construct and fall in love with are at least as important and "real" as reality.

This theme finds its most sublime expression in *Vertigo*, in which Jimmy Stewart walks out on the wonderfully warm, intelligent Midge (Barbara Bel Geddes) to chase a phantom woman, the blonde Madeleine. His delirious pursuit, her "death," and his terrible disappointment when he sees her "reincarnated" as the crude and vulgar Judy (both parts are played by Kim Novak), form a perfect paradigm of the romantic's cruel and persistent obsession with the ideal over a mixed reality, of Hitchcock's ambivalence to his stars, and of our own. In Stewart's desperate efforts to remake Judy over in Madeleine's image (and our own sympathy with the attempt), Hitchcock exposes the romantic impulse to turn woman into an art object. In our instinctive preference for the elegant, silent, "period" Madeleine to the noisy, everyday, modern Judy we are made aware of both sides of illusionism. For, as Robin Wood pointed out in his book on Hitchcock, there is a sense in which Madeleine *is* more real than Judy, as she gives expression, in her heightened theatricality, to feelings and refinements that are beyond the coarse Judy. In just such a way do the stars symbolize the beauty and romance and independence we seek. The danger is in mistaking them for the reality, in imposing (as Stewart insists on doing) the star image on the stubborn, distinctive faces of real people.

But there is a further sense in which neither Madeleine *nor* Judy is real, and the division of women into such extremes (again, the Verdoux complex) distracts attention from the possibility of a "fusion" woman, as Stewart's quest for the romantic ideal takes him farther and farther away from Bel Geddes.

Hitchcock wouldn't be able to pinpoint, with such precision, our own ambivalence if he didn't feel it even more intensely. As much as it is directed at the beautiful blonde —or the charming bachelor—it is directed at the "star," that luminous creature of the screen who is able to claim our attention, our love, our idolatry with so little effort, while the homely people of the earth—the old, the fat, the plain— must work so hard to win so little. Hitchcock tries to correct the ethical imbalance of screen life by indicating the moral flabbiness of his spoiled heroes and heroines, and by allowing his secondary characters, his villains and victims, a greater range of feeling and depth. But sexual ambivalence creeps in even here. The male villains—Raymond Burr in *Rear Window,* Claude Rains in *Notorious,* Herbert Marshall in *Foreign Correspondent*—are some of the most memorable and sympathetic characters in all of Hitchcock, whereas their female counterparts—Patricia Hitchcock and Laura Elliott in *Strangers on a Train,* Jane Wyman in *Stage Fright,* the Nazi ringleader's daughter in *The 39 Steps*—are equally memorable, but less sympathetic. Hitchcock's instinctive alliance with the outsider gives him an insight into the dilemma of the unattractive woman that is sharp and wonderful. His homely women provide a disturbing challenge to the aristocracy of stardom, and to the supremacy of the "beautiful people." But Hitchcock cannot help punishing the "ugly ducklings" for not being beautiful, perhaps he is punishing his daughter as an extension of himself (as Elaine May did to hers in *The Heartbreak Kid*). And so he lays it on— the spectacles, the beady eyes—a little too thick. Not as thick as the usual Hollywood idea of ugly (and hence their superiority as examples of plain women), but just enough so that they are more appalling than appealing as sexual beings.

In Hitchcock's later films the image of the star gradually recedes, and by the time of *Frenzy,* the dialectic between the beautiful person and the commoner is gone. Like Chaplin in the valedictory *Monsieur Verdoux,* there is no longer any romantic image to sustain Hitchcock. The women that are left—Anna Massey's jaunty bar girl, Barbara Leigh-Hunt's marriage-broker, Vivien Merchant's relentless gourmet—are all "ugly ducklings," and the men incomplete. The "hero," Jon Finch, fades behind the gregarious villain, who leaves as many corpses in his wake as Verdoux. This jauntiest of Hitchcock's films is also the most dismal: The world has turned upside down, and charm has gone completely to the side of villainy.

Frenzy is probably the only movie in which the man is never implicated in the suffering the women are made to undergo, a suffering that, in the early films, is both retribution and reproach: In *Notorious,* Ingrid Bergman pays for Cary Grant's self-righteousness; in *Psycho* Janet Leigh pays for Anthony Perkins' psychosis; in *Vertigo* Kim Novak pays for James Stewart's obsession; just as, analogously, Jane Asher, in Skolimowski's *Deep End,* is made to pay for John Moulder Brown's blind romanticism. There is a distinction between violence done to women in Hitchcock and Skolimowski, and in the work of other seventies' directors: The difference is that Hitchcock and Skolimowski make it clear that their threatened, raped, or murdered heroines are the direct manifestation and indictment of their heroes' smugness or madness, while other directors rape their stars without ever touching them.

Claude Chabrol, who collaborated with Eric Rohmer on a book about Hitchcock, shares the master's Catholic background, his preoccupation with sin and redemption, and his taste for perversion. Chabrol's wife and star, Stéphane Audran, has come to exercise for him the same pull of attraction and repulsion, but in the more social context (Chabrol is sociological where Hitchcock is mythic) of the French bourgeoisie. She is, in its most precise and tasteful incarnation (for example, her definitive madame checking on the *gigot d'agneau* in Buñuel's *The Discreet Charm of the Bourgeoisie*) the modern bourgeoise, gradually benumbed by the "thingness" of civilization. Chabrol hints that she is so jaded that only some taint of primordial evil can stir her. Thus, as the wife in *La Femme Infidèle,* she awakens to her husband's love only after he has killed her lover; and as the schoolteacher of *Le Boucher,* she is simultaneously fascinated and repelled by the homicidal impulses of her butcher-suitor. In *Les Bonnes Femmes,* Chabrol's harrowing and lyrical film about four Parisian shopgirls, their cheap romantic fantasies merge with the sordid violence of life—a violence that in some terrible way becomes their deliverance. This is not only one of Chabrol's great films, but one of the great films about women, as brutal and unglamorous as it is unpatronizing in its treatment of helplessly mediocre girls who are both ennobled and deluded by their ridiculous dreams. We see them in their individual and collective ruts: as they go back and forth to work in an electrical appliance store, under the constant surveillance of their obese, lecherous boss and his authority-designate, a superstitious old woman. Discontented with their lives but unable to imagine or pursue better ones, they "escape" their routine at noisy nightclubs and cheap vaudeville shows. Finally they become the all-too-willing victims of various predators, of melodrama, even of death. The most attractive escort turns out to be a murderer and his girl is ecstatically released, once and for all, from the dreary string of tomorrows and tomorrows and the illusion of love and romance.

Recourse to lesbianism is seen, by even as sophisticated a director as Chabrol (in *Les Biches*), as something provisional and incomplete. Except for Beryl Reid's bull dyke in *The Killing of Sister George,* most of the lesbians in film—Audran and Sassard in *Les Biches,* Anne Heywood and Sandy Dennis in *The Fox,* Dominique Sanda and Stefania Sandrelli in *The Conformist*—are attractive women who cater to male fantasies (after all, until hard-core pornography, most sexploitation movies featured female couples) and who seem merely to be waiting for the "right man" to come along. As lesbianism becomes a more serious threat to the male ego and to heterosexual hegemony, it will probably be shown less rather than more often; it may already have lost its comfortable place as a male turn-on. Bergman's later films, for example, reveal him to be increasingly nervous about the possibility of his girls getting together behind his back and, in a final revenge on their "creator," dispensing with him altogether.

For the most part, unisex and the tendency toward androgyny of the counterculture, though it implied a liberalization and coming together of both sexes, seemed associated only with the male sex. Men were entitled to grow long hair and wear beads and indulge in a kind of polymorphous passivity, and what did women gain in exchange? Pants. Fine, and what else? They got to sit and watch while male unisex—which was less a true "feminization" than a cosmetic, adversary femininity—challenged "macho" sex. *Performance,* made in England by Nicholas Roeg and Donald Cammel, but really Anglo-American in its far-out, trans-Atlantic, transsexual vision of the "scene," was the culmination of certain tendencies of the decade, particularly the insistence on a dialectic that was more journalistic than real. Mick Jagger as the polysexually loose rock star representing the counterculture and James Fox as an uptight, old-time gangster (economically, a capitalist, and aesthetically, a genre figure, tyrannized by beginning, middle, and end) exchange identities. Fox is seduced by the liquid, nonlinear, multisensory style of Jagger's commune; Jagger by the violence of Fox's vendetta. But the film and most of its supporters refused to recognize that Fox is really a Jagger in Fox (square) clothing, and that Jagger, as the sparks generated by his concerts prove, is no innocuous flower child. In other words, they approximate each other to begin with in their sensuality and effeminacy, but they have no existence, no meaning without each other. They would float away without this opposition, a spurious one that reflects the need of Americans to think and pontificate and act in terms of dichotomies, in the absence of either a real ideology, or the combination of moral convictions and flexibility that are the liberal habit of mind at its best.

One extreme exists by the authority of the other, its indispensable opposite. Just as Nixon "Agonistes," as he has been brilliantly dissected by Gary Wills, feeds on self-pity and resentment and on (real or fabricated) enemies, rather than on any positive self-sustaining principle or even pure aggression, so many of his enemies seem to materialize in response to him and feed on his (real or imagined) machismo. Like the red-neck squares vis-à-vis the Third World comrades in *Billy Jack,* the two factions need each other, and are never happier (or funnier) than when in direct confrontation. They activate their mutual adrenalins, a fine device for debate and drama, but what do they do between the acts? Or after the revolution? They must necessarily seek out other extremes, talk in divisive terms (a rhetorical practice at which Nixon is not the only expert) of radicalism and conservatism (both spitting on liberalism), of the under-thirties and the over-thirties, the sadists and the masochists. The ins and outs become, ironically, a totalitarian device used as often in the name of Populism as of law and order. We deplore Madison Avenue lingo and computerese while using labels as sterile and reductive to define ourselves, and our sexual proclivities. Perhaps the we-versus-them habit of thinking proceeds from the original rigid division between male and female, further subdivided into straight and gay, butch and femme. These designations, imposed most furiously by the militant "deviates," refuse to admit the mixed drives in all of us, as if no one, either literally or in fantasy (imagination is not accredited with the faculty of sexual liberation) ever crossed from one category, with its thousand subdivisions, to another.

The labels become the vehicles and channels of our thinking and reacting. Thus "butch" (as the active, "male" sexual posture) or machismo is the hardhat response to "femme": that is, not just to the intrusion of women in all-male domains, but to the intimidating sexual casualness of the "female" male, the flower child, the hippie, and—on an economic level—the spoiled, long-haired young man of the counterculture. The pop/rock star, from Dylan to Donovan to James Taylor and culminating in the histrionic androgyny of Mick Jagger, is the model of the "femme" male, the symbol and commemorator of dropping out as a life style. The rock scene is antifemale not just for the obvious reasons: the exclusion of women as performers, the proliferation of groupies, and the outright chauvinism of most of the lyrics, but because the males have taken over female characteristics. And, as the early rock stars like the Beatles initiated the dropout life style, the later ones initiated the more massive defections from traditional malehood.

Why can't a man be more like a woman? was a question women had always asked themselves (the most popular screen lovers had always been the gentle, sensitive ones, the ones who "understood" them), little suspecting how far things would go. When a woman expressed a preference for the cultured man over the beer-drinking bully, she hadn't anticipated that he would become so soft and sensitive that he would drive her right out of business, and would in his tenderness turn not toward her but toward his own mirror image. If we wonder what happened to all the good women's roles in the sixties and seventies, we might take a look at the films of some of the actors. The first fumbling gestures of androgyny, as an expression of alienation, began with Brando. Phallic drive decreased in such fifties' prototypes as James Dean and Montgomery Clift, and was felt to have all but disappeared in such sensitive sixties' actors as Peter Fonda, Terence Stamp, Paul Newman, David Hemmings, Keir Dullea, Pierre Clementi, Alan Bates, Jean-Pierre Léaud, Marlon Brando, Bob Dylan, Roddy MacDowall, Omar Sharif, Richard Chamberlain, Michael York, James Fox, Jack Nicholson, Art Garfunkel, Jeff Bridges, Beau Bridges, Robert Redford, Dirk Bogarde, Tom Courtenay, Arlo Guthrie, Jean-Louis Trintignant, Ryan O'Neal, John Moulder Brown, Al Pacino, and Bruce Dern.

This is, obviously, a heterogeneous list; not all of them have long hair or are card-carrying members of the counter-culture or are under thirty (though most retain honorary status). They may not have such obvious feminine quali-ties as long eyelashes, full lips, baby faces, an air of helpless-ness, or whatever. But aesthetically or morally, they have appropriated characteristics that once attached to movie hero-ines: the glamour, the sensitivity, the coyness, the narcissism, the purity, the passivity, the self-pity. (Everything, that is, except the toughness and resiliency, the energy and ambition.) Often they are paired with women less attractive than they, or presented with the star focus, filters, and lighting once reserved for women, while their leading ladies are given the warts-and-all treatment—for example, David Hemmings and Vanessa Redgrave in *Blow-Up,* or Peter Fonda and Verna Bloom in *The Hired Hand.*

Occasionally, the idea of a relationship between a young man and an older and/or less attractive woman suggests a new kind of mutual responsiveness, a workable if unconven-tional fit—for instance, that of Ruth Gordon and Bud Cort in *Harold and Maud,* and Jane Wyman and Rock Hudson in the movies they made together. But this is all too rare. It is not that there weren't beautiful men in films past: Gary Cooper was more beautiful than any woman except Garbo (in fact, Ernst Lubitsch started the rumor that they were the same person: "After all," the director proposed mischie-vously, "have you ever seen them in a movie together?"). Tyrone Power, Leslie Howard, Errol Flynn, Robert Taylor, Douglas Fairbanks, Jr., were beautiful, but they played men, grown-ups, nonetheless. They wore suits and ties and, once over twenty-one, had their adulthoods to maintain; they weren't expected to act like eternal undergraduates, and they didn't have the luxury—or perhaps the *burden*—of emotional and occupational freedom in a pressureless society. We can only assume that Gary Cooper would have been permanently demystified had he been caught with his psyche unzipped in an encounter session, or in an all-male consciousness-raising group. Nor can one imagine Errol Flynn leaping through the air only to land in a massage parlor, in the well-paid hands of a professional masturbator. Indeed, *Carnal Knowledge* might stand as the quintessential "now" film in its distortion (by simultaneously magnifying and degrading it) of the sex principle (male erection-and-single-orgasm sex) as the only bond between men and women, and the wedge that inevitably drives them apart. Unhappily, the view presented is also a true distortion, a vision of sex as an adolescent competition that, with many Americans, persists well into middle age. The women are seen in terms of (generally ugly or castrating) sexual fantasies; the one intelligent-romantic woman of that film, Candice Bergen, cannot be envisioned beyond the moment she outlives her romantic usefulness to the men, and so disappears from the movie. Ann-Margret's splendid and original characterization of a woman increasingly demoralized by marriage, letting herself go, inch by added inch, into catatonia, is the marvel of the film. But even she is presented as a harridan so that Nicholson can emerge with more dignity and sympathy than he deserves. We get an image that purports to indict the men but that insidiously defends them, not least through the satisfaction they take in degrading the women. In the relation between the filmmakers (Nichols and Feiffer) and their protagonist, we get the indulgent view of the artist toward his creation, the mother toward her child. Thus Nicholson is a bad but charming boy, whose "bad"ness, when it is not an asset, is a product of wicked society and evil women, while his charm is all his own. And finally, for all his problems, he is a typical "neat guy," and as such, he scores with the men if not with the women. Just as sexual achievement is often a matter of showing off for other men (sleeping with a woman who slept with Jack Kennedy—ten points; with one who slept with Kissinger—four), so is filmmaking, and *Carnal Knowledge* is and remains closer to the locker room than to the bedroom.

At the other extreme of the feminine heroes and the lyrical, all-male love poems is the "hardhat" film, one being a sort of reverse mirror image of the other. This response to the passive hero, and to women's liberation as well, shows up toward the end of the decade in violent, machismo films like *Straw Dogs, A Clockwork Orange,* and *The Godfather,* and neo-machismo films (that is, getting the kicks but feigning mockery) like *High-Plains Drifter* and *Dillinger.* The sudden public obsession with books and films about the Mafia and the Nazis, both celebrating male power and male authority figures at their most violent and sexist, suggests a backlash in which middle-class men, fearful of their eroding masculinity, take refuge in the supermale fantasies of Don Corleone and Dr. Goebbels. The cult of violence concided perfectly with artistic freedom and directorial "demigoddery," and with the instincts of directors who, as Americans, continue to be poets of violence and remedial readers in the language of love.

Stanley Kubrick, with women as the prime target of his hostility or indifference, has managed to be both youth-oriented and hardhat at the same time. The young—the "new morality" to the contrary—are generally both intolerant and nonsensual, preferring the mechanical world of cartoons and science fiction, or the ascetic world of political activism and, for entertainment, the passive, drifting-in-space sensation of "head" films, to the demands of anything closer to home. Thus, Kubrick was made to order for the under-thirties, with his derisive humor and holocaust wit (*Dr. Strangelove*), his cynical shock endings (*The Killing*), and his seductive science-fiction epic, *2001, A Space Odyssey.* *2001* expressed not the horror or the fear of the sterile technological future that its partisans claimed it did, but a voluptuous surrender to clean, nonhuman efficiency. Kubrick is a misanthropist and particularly a misogynist; but his hatred of women is not the visceral explosion of a deep Swiftian disgust but a fashionable and fastidious distaste. Even in the rapes in *A Clockwork Orange* (by Alex, who is a perfect, violent synthesis of the chic antagonists of *Performance*), one is struck by the absence of real dread or loathing that comes from the depths of one's being. Instead, the images of the two grotesque women, and the reasons for extinguishing them, are all "intellectual" and aesthetic. In their poses, their faces, their attire and coloring, their pneumatic figures, the women are merely pasteboard props in the pop-art scheme of the film, pinballs to be toppled in Kubrick's nasty bowling ballet. It would be preferable—cleaner, more honest—if Kubrick hated them more. As it is, they are merely ugly peripheral figures in a color-magazine spread, executed by a man whose strongest emotion is a slight aversion to the human race.

To this, one must prefer even the lugubrious self-pity of the "odd couple" films: the all-male love (or like) stories such as *M*A*S*H**, *Easy Rider, The Odd Couple, Butch Cassidy and the Sundance Kid, Husbands, Midnight Cowboy, Wild Rovers, Bad Company, A Separate Peace, Pat Garrett and Billy the Kid,* ad infinitum, or the all-male big-city melodramas of *Dirty Harry* and *The French Connection.* (The buddy-films, or the chemistry of certain pairings, are so popular that they have already spawned sequels.) Not only in film but in plays such as *The Championship Season* and *The Changing Room,* the sixties and particularly the seventies may go down as the time when men, released from their stoical pose of laconic self-possession by the "confessional" impulse and style of the times, discovered each other. They were able to give voice, or lyrical vision, to feelings for each other they had been keeping under their Stetson hats. They could now live out relationships and feelings that had remained below the surface. Thus, the difference between Don Siegel's *Madigan* (1968) and his *Dirty Harry* (1971), or producer Phil D'Antoni's *Bullitt* (1968) and *The French Connection* (1971) is that the earlier films have token women and the latter ones exclude them (except in the most marginal contexts), thereby confirming what was latent in earlier genre films—that all the feeling and rapport are between the men, between a cop and his superior, a cop and his sidekick, or a cop and his Nemesis, the criminal. When a woman is introduced—and Inger Stevens' wife in *Madigan* is one of the more sympathetic of the species—she must play second fiddle to her husband's work, making the wife of the gumshoe truly the Stepin Fetchit of women's roles. This kind of tokenism women can do without.

The closer women come to claiming their rights and achieving independence in real life, the more loudly and stridently films tell us it's a man's world. As Dirty Harry pummels his victim—a gurgly and girlish psychopath—with a multiple-orgasm splatter of bullets that sends the audience into groans of ecstasy. As the new Godfather (played by Al Pacino) closes the door on his wife and on any further important communication between them. As Susan George, in *Straw Dogs,* struts around like Daisy Mae before the brier-patch yokels, and then gets it once, twice, and again for the little tease she is. The provocative, sex-obsessed bitch is one of the great male-chauvinist (and apparently, territorialist) fantasies, along with the fantasy that she is constantly fantasizing rape. As Peckinpah said, in a *Playboy* interview, "There are women and there's pussy," a statement that not only overlooks the fact that there's a little of both, like the virgin and whore, in all women, but that misrepresents Peckinpah's feelings, so viscerally apparent in film after film, that all women, way down deep, are pussy. For all his vitality, he can't inject life into Ali MacGraw, the romantic heroine of *The Getaway* (although admittedly he does not have much to work with), while he obviously gets—and gives—his kicks in the relationship between the sluttish wife (Sally Struthers) and the sadistic villain (Al Lettieri), whose combined antics drive her husband to suicide. It's as implausible as anything in *Straw Dogs,* but, like Susan George's shenanigans (and unlike Kubrick's malicious mayhem), it has the dubious virtue of being an authentic gut fantasy. The anti-intellectual theme of *Straw Dogs,* whereby Dustin Hoffman's mathematician has to "prove his manhood" by ingeniously murdering a gang of cretins, is, on the other hand, a phony fantasy, an impulse Peckinpah doesn't really feel, possibly because only a real intellectual is capable of working up a good steam of intellectual self-hatred. This impulse is very much the springboard of such man-against-the-wilderness parables as *Deliverance,* made from James Dickey's novel, in which an unfit and unlikely foursome pit their flabby hulks and flabbier characters against the rapids, and *Jeremiah Johnson,* in which Robert Redford tests his mettle against Bruno and other forms of wildlife that are far from the single swinger's and city-slicker's experience.

Violence, which the Supreme Court doesn't deem as injurious to public morality as sex, is the indispensable staple of male pornography, expressing itself in apocalyptic allegories of male virility. What is alarming is not that an old geezer like Sam Peckinpah should wish to bathe his twilight years in the blood of "macho" fantasies like *Pat Garrett and Billy the Kid,* but that young college-grad writers like Rudolph Wurlitzer (*Pat Garrett*) and John Milius (screenwriter of *Jeremiah Johnson,* director-writer of *Dillinger*), who are even farther removed from the myths of the Old West and the "pioneer" mentality, should take up the sexist cudgel so enthusiastically and set themselves to inventing new tough-guy and man-to-man fables that are no less pernicious for being comic or self-conscious.

As men have resorted to greater and greater violence, women have withdrawn into a numbness which is in many ways more disheartening—but which may prove in the long run a more honest, and productive, response. As for their "sexual awakening," movies went from prudery to pornography with very little in between. The "new morality" film feasted on love objects of an ephemeral, disposable nature : chicks, kooks, and groupies, cartoon pinup girls, houri of Bond-like superstuds (avenged if not redeemed by the Amazon antics of Modesty Blaise and Barbarella). The camp and homosexual sensibilities merged to create the silicone seductresses of pulp film like Raquel Welch (the female Burt Reynolds), nonwomen like Twiggy and Goldie Hawn, and the male and female drag goddesses of the Warhol–Morrissey factory, from Candy Darling to Sylvia Miles. Odd but talented actresses like Barbra Streisand and Liza Minnelli were miscast and promoted, to fill a vacuum, into all-purpose stars.

One of the few exciting women's roles was, as usual, provided by a historical figure—Isadora Duncan, as played by Vanessa Redgrave—but the film was cut in half and eviscerated before it was released. In both Karel Reisz's *The Loves of Isadora* and Ken Russell's television version starring Vivian Pickles, Isadora is played, however brilliantly, by an Englishwoman. Where is the American actress who could suggest the forces that fused in the making of Isadora, the poetry of Whitman, the spaces of Southern California, and the exuberance of a uniquely American feminism?

The only indigenous woman's role with any life or feeling during the past decade was, curiously, the rural heroine, in both ingenue and mother versions ; it was as if to suggest

that only with a complete lack of sophistication, of awareness, could a woman be happy, or at least continue to feel.
But even these heroines have usually been doomed to disappointment: Pat Quinn is swallowed up by the emotional
demands of the young habitués of *Alice's Restaurant*; Faye
Dunaway writes poetry and rides for destruction in *Bonnie
and Clyde*; Tuesday Weld's hillbilly seductress in *I Walk
the Line* is destined to grow up into the used and dissipated
heroine of *Play It As It Lays*; Verna Bloom plays the mother-
bride to Peter Fonda's cowboy in *The Hired Hand* and second fiddle to his buddy, Warren Oates; Ellen Burstyn and
Cloris Leachman in *The Last Picture Show* have their last
flings at passion before they disappear into the sexual vale of
the over-forty woman. Then comes Barbara Loden's *Wanda*
to tell us that country bumpkins are no better off than city
slickers. The ignorant West Virginia hillbetty is just as
susceptible to anomie as the big-city heroines of *Klute, Diary
of a Mad Housewife, Such Good Friends, Thank You All
Very Much, Sunday, Bloody Sunday,* and *Play It As It Lays*.
In all of these there is a "coming to consciousness," a sense
of women played false by the old relationships—marriage,
procreation, love affairs—that are always conducted on a
man's terms: Committing herself totally, she leaves herself
wide open, while he squeezes her in among the various
options of his life and, when it is all over, moves on. The
heroines respond to this dilemma, or to its possibility, in
different ways: Jane Fonda, in *Klute,* becomes a prostitute
—partly to exercise her acting ability but mostly to keep
control of her life and her emotions, to avoid for as long
as she can the trap of "falling in love"; in *Sunday, Bloody
Sunday,* Glenda Jackson continues to insist on the "total"
relationship her bisexual lover can never give her; Carrie
Snodgress in *Diary* has a brief, unsatisfactory affair and
winds up in group therapy; Sandy Dennis, in *Thank You*

All Very Much, goes ahead and has her illegitimate baby without informing its father; the wife in *Such Good Friends* tries to grasp, even experience, the pleasures of infidelity practiced by her late husband and fails miserably; Bibi Andersson in *The Touch* has a heart-wrenching affair with Elliot Gould; and Tuesday Weld, in *Play It As It Lays,* as the thirtyish model and star of her ex-husband's *cinéma-vérité* movies, has given up trying altogether. But in their very numbness and destitution, and in their desperate flight from love, these women attest to its continued importance in their lives. As women, they had been "groomed for love," conditioned to think of romance and marriage and child-bearing as the central facts in their lives, and they feel that without these "natural" roles, they are nothing; without love, on however masochistic a basis, they are only half-alive. But having arrived at nothing, they can go one step farther: They can say that nothing is better than a false something.

This despair, which some have mistaken for feminism's negative sin, is actually a more honest reflection of the spirit of the age than the violence that is its antidote and escape. As expressed by women writers like Paula Fox and Joan Didion and Doris Lessing, it is a reaction not just to their oppression as women, but to the world around them—to the surplus of material things and (though it is not fashionable to say so) of people; the constant threat to body and soul, and to security; the scarcity of time; the tiny spot each of us has been allocated, in eternity and among the multitude, to make our mark, and the increased pressure to do so; the corruption of morals on a vast scale, the terminal disease of capitalist "growth," and the inevitable conclusion that men, as the powers that have brought us to where we are, have made a botch of it.

Thus the confusion as to whether movies like *Desperate Characters* and *Up the Sandbox* (both inferior adaptations of the novels of Fox and Ann Roiphe) are about women's liberation or about the world; and the tendency to overlook the importance of class—the fact that both are expressions of that very confusion by women (upper-middle class, educated) who enjoy a greater freedom of choice than they have ever had before. And the confusion as to what is true and what conditioned in a woman's (or a man's) nature, how much we can and want to change ourselves while preserving some of the values of sexual difference and opposition; what, finally, will be the consequences and the by-products of the mutations we seek.

So the question of love is still central to the "woman's film," but perhaps it may undergo mutations of its own. Love, the masochistic love in which most of these heroines found themselves, was an addiction whose cure—withdrawal into loneliness—was as painful as the mutilations of love itself. If adjustment and compromise (the acceptance of a less than total love that Glenda Jackson's mother in *Sunday, Bloody Sunday* advocates in the wisdom of experience) is the ultimate solution, then it must be achieved on more equal terms. To lay the groundwork, withdrawal—temporary or permanent—is necessary for a woman. The discipline, solitude, renewed acquaintance with oneself in a mirrorless interior—this is the path to self-love, love of one's own sex, and finally, but not necessarily, love of the opposite sex. It becomes imperative for woman to reinvent herself, to create an identity that is not just an inoculation against "falling in love" but that exists transcendentally for its own sake, and that will eventually enable her to go beyond herself to the world at large, to an interest in its history which she at last will have a hand in shaping.

These heroines are still the dead end of the old order, turning everything—the anger, the guilt, and the despair—inward and substituting a new masochism for the old one.

In *Sunday, Bloody Sunday,* Glenda Jackson gives up her job and luxuriates in the hopelessness of a one-sided affair; the wife in *Such Good Friends* feeds perversely on bitterness and hatred; the wife in *Diary* is caught between the self-hatred of the spoiled housewife and the urge, so long suppressed it may even have atrophied, to *do* something; Maria Wyeth of *Play It As It Lays* has drained the love out of her body, as well as the ambition, and can't think of any good reason for getting a transfusion. The ending of *Klute* is ambiguous: Fonda goes off with Sutherland, but hints that she may occasionally return to New York, where she feels her real identity—fragile and negative as it is—to be.

The new "woman's films" are more sophisticated than the old ones, but more despairing too. The relegation of men —cads, caricatures, and pretty-boy lovers—to the shadows seemed in the old women's films a dubious but understandable convention. Now, as a glance at the films of the last decade will show, this shadowiness seems a reflection of reality, of a separation of the sexes more radical than at any previous point in our history. There may be hope for reconciliation (of the sexes, of *all* the sexes), but the overtures must proceed from a mutual commitment, and they must be gestures that are open and exploratory rather than proscriptive and judgmental.

Gestures must be backed up by law. Unions must be opened to women, and women's professionalism accepted not only by men but by women themselves. There are so many habits we have to unlearn—the constant need, for example, to be sexually validated by the opposite sex—and so many reflexes to overcome: men, their distrust and fear of the professional woman, women, their dislike and distrust of their own sex. It is not by living out every option but by tolerating them that we may reach the state of flexibility which is the only true source of sexual, and emotional, security. Perhaps, then, the vacant, freeze-frame faces of the heroines of *Diary* and *Play It As It Lays* are not the signal of a final, but of an intermediate, death—death to the "woman's film" and woman's concerns as separate and secondary.

But surely the recent pain and struggle of woman's self-exploration has yielded more fruit and taken her farther than those feeble overtures offered by the film industry would have us believe and this is the real scandal. At present, the industry, such as it is, is giving women the same treatment that it gave blacks for the half-century after *Birth of a Nation*: a kick in the face or a cold shoulder. And whether it is tokenism or the "final solution," it is, as minorities everywhere have discovered, no solution at all. Only outside the industry, in independent filmmaking (or in Europe), is there anything that could call itself a woman's cinema. In documentaries like Nell Cox's *A to B,* Kate Millet's *Three Lives,* Claudia Weill's *Joyce at 34,* Amalie Rothschild's *It Happened to Us,* Julia Reichert and Jim Klein's *Growing Up Female,* and a host of others, women are exploring the "inner space" of their conditioning, discovering long-suppressed anger, contending with the conflicting demands of their lives as mothers and professionals, and finding relief and moral support in a shared experience.

But when will women really come into their own power, or when will the evidence of this power be felt? Where is the mechanism for turning autobiography into the new myths, the new narrative forms? How will women break through the barriers of a commercial cinema more truly monolithic in its sexism than it ever was in the old days of Hollywood? Where are the women to create new fictions, to go beyond the inner space—as women are doing every day in real life —into the outer world of invention, action, imagination? The women involved in the creative end of commercial films, as novelists, screenwriters, directors, are an illustrious handful—Susan Sontag, Penelope Gilliatt, Eleanor Perry, Barbara Loden, Elaine May, Jay Presson Allen, Adrien Joyce, Joan Didion, Joan Silver, Lois Gould, Karen Sperling, Edna O'Brien, Margaret Drabble, Ann Roiphe. (Add for good measure, European directors like Vera Chytilova, Nelly Kaplan, Marguerite Duras, Mai Zetterling, Agnes Varda, Liliana Cavani, Lina Wertmuller.) And still, what a tiny squadron against the armies of men. And where are the actresses, the Jean Arthurs, the Bette Davises, the Rosalind Russells, the Carole Lombards, the Ida Lupinos, the Veda Ann Borgs, to play the parts they will write and direct? And where are the audiences, the women as well as the men? At *The Godfather*. At *Deep Throat*. At *Deliverance*. And where are the women's groups, in colleges and out? Attacking male chauvinism in movies and crawling all over the male chauvinists, paying them thousand-dollar lecture fees to come and account for themselves.

Where, oh where, is the camaraderie, the much-vaunted mutual support among women? It was there, without advertising itself, in the twenties: among Griffith's women, with Clara Bow and her college pals; in the thirties, among the gold diggers, with Kay Francis and Aline MacMahon and Eve Arden, and in the advice and support of older women like Binnie Barnes and Billie Burke; in the forties, with Bette Davis and her female costars; even in the fifties, with Marilyn Monroe and her millionaire-hunting friends. But where, in the movies and out, are their modern equivalents?

1974–1987

THE AGE OF AMBIVALENCE

The treatment of women in the movies over the last ten years is the story of an absence, followed by a fragmented, schizophrenic, but oddly hopeful presence. After a period (the mid- to late seventies) during which grown-up women were as rare as fireflies in January, they began to return to cinema, but not with a collective voice or cohesive pattern, and certainly not in roles that could be held up as blueprints for budding feminists. There were tigresses and super-women, of course: Sissy Spacek as Marie Ragghianti (in *Marie*), the woman who blew the whistle on state corruption in Tennessee while remaining a maternal paragon to three small children; Sigourney Weaver as the tough-but-not-unfeminine jock space captain of *Alien* and its sequel; Kate Nelligan as Nicholas Cage's awesomely self-sacrificing mother in *Eleni*; Jessica Lange, Spacek, and Sally Field as country women who wear spunk the way Sylvester Stallone sports muscles; and Meryl Streep as a composite of striking roles and a symbol of Artistic Integrity, as an actress who is typecast as an actress who is not typecast. But these women were candidates for canonization, superior to everyone else on the screen and remote from most of us. On the flip side of the superwoman coin—and its most fascinating contradiction—were the crazy women. In this, the most significant development of the eighties, movies have served up an endlessly expanding category of neurotics, murderers, *femmes fatales,* vamps, punks, misfits, and free-floating loonies whose very existence was an affront, not only to the old, sexist definitions of pliant women (or even categorizable psychotics), but also to the upbeat rhetoric of the women's movement. The violence unleashed ranged from the homicidal (the women shoppers in Marleen Gorris's *A Question of Silence:* the rape victim turned murderer in *Ms 45;* Martha Henry as the worm-turned husband-killer in the Canadian film *Dancing in the Dark;* Chantal Akerman's powerful study of housewifely anomie, *Jeanne Dielman;* and Theresa Russell's greedy disposer-of-men in *Black Widow*); to the adamantly depraved (the very contemporary *femmes fatales* of *Blue Velvet* and *Something Wild*); to the obstreperous slapstick antics of Kim Basinger in *Blind Date* and Bette Midler in *Ruthless People* and *Outrageous Fortune;* to the sexually anarchic (the angelic tart in the British film *Wish You Were Here* and the crazy waif in *Betty Blue*) to the merely (comically, lyrically, or suicidally) depressed heroines of Margarethe von Trotta, Beth Henley, Woody Allen, Eric Rohmer.

In a curious way, even when the anger was turned inward, these women were symbols of defiance, of a refusal—or inability—to live by the old rules, accompanied by the doubts and confusion that any such shift must necessarily bring. And they resonated with a good many women who weren't convinced by the rosier picture painted elsewhere. There was an ever-widening gap between the avant-garde and the mass media: how did you reconcile the anguished heroines of Margarethe von Trotta and the manically deconstructed feminine prototypes of Chantal Akerman with the perky doctors and lawyers on television?

Whether the films were made by men or by women, the "crazies" weren't the sultry (and diabolical) *femmes fatales* of traditional male fantasy, those silky icons of the *film noir* whose self-possession represented a force beyond man's control and who were responsible for his "fall," but postfeminist types whose moves were orchestrated less by male needs than by some mysterious promptings of their own. They could be liberating as well as destructive, and even if they didn't break free of the romantic/sexual bond, they threw normal courting rules to the wind. They largely escaped the punitive resolution of the *film noir;* the endings they produced were untidy and their power wasn't neutralized by the end of the film.

The appearance of these women, with their strange, scattered impact but cumulative fascination, is of recent vintage. If a visitor from outer space had landed on Planet Earth in the late seventies and looked to movies as a cultural indicator, he (she, it?) would have known that women were up to something only by their absence. For ten years, the top box-office stars were men: Sylvester Stallone, Clint Eastwood, Charles Bronson, and Chuck Norris doing the honors in the action roles; Robert de Niro, Al Pacino, and Dustin Hoffman in the soulful ethnic parts; Jack Nicholson as the all-around lovable bastard and Redford and Newman as the male pin-ups, to be joined by such resplendent youth idols as John Travolta, Richard Gere, Tom Cruise, Don Johnson, Rob Lowe, and Mel Gibson, all of whom were delighted to assume the sex-object roles abandoned by women. For a very long time, Barbra Streisand was the only "bankable" female—possibly because she had the high profile ethnic definition of an old-fashioned star and was easy to write for, unlike such interestingly anomalous actresses as Ellen Burstyn, Susan Anspach, and Cloris Leachman. And even she ran out of credibility when she produced, directed, and starred in *Yentl*, to be charged with chutzpah for doing what had only added to Warren Beatty's renaissance credentials. (The real arrogance of *Yentl* was not in Streisand's assuming the directorial reins, but in imposing her torchy star persona on an otherwise absorbing feminist fable.)

The trickle of feminist-inspired movies of the mid-seventies—*A Woman under the Influence, Alice Doesn't Live Here Anymore*, and *An Unmarried Woman*—had led us to anticipate, if not a revolution, at least a gaggle of films that would chart our evolution as emerging feminists. The women's movement was at its crest and anything was possible: women would begin making mainstream films, entering the industry as decision-makers, starring in movies about the momentous changes in their lives. The independent cinema would continue as a haven for "small" films, autobiographical and avant-garde cinema, while those who had shown an aptitude for narrative (Joan Micklin Silver, with *Hester Street,* or Claudia Weill with *Girlfriends*) would be tapped by studio heads eager to cash in on the great drama of the mid-twentieth century. As stars, women would disengage themselves from the "gaze," the male perspective that, according to the psychoanalytic theories of British feminist structuralists, had frozen women in postures that catered to male needs and anxieties rather than allowing them to express their own desires.

Instead, women virtually disappeared from the screen, as sex objects or as anything else, for over a decade. Our oratory of hope and protest was greeted with a yawn of

indifference, as the multinational executives and deal pack-
agers of the "New Hollywood" panted after the youth market, abandoning—and being abandoned by—the adult audience in the process. The Hollywood producer was never one
to rush into the breach and embrace revolutionary ideas and
emblems, especially if the carriers of the disease were
women. F. Scott Fitzgerald noted the cultural lag back in
1931, writing in "Echoes of the Jazz Age": "The social attitude of the producers was timid, behind the times and ba-
nal—the Jazz Age was almost middle-aged by the time Hollywood acknowledged it and even then faintly, fitfully and
superficially." But if the moguls were reluctant to confront
the flapper, they were ostriches when it came to feminists.
And there was no network, no "club" to receive and support
those few women lucky enough to acquire power. After
Streisand, Jane Fonda and Goldie Hawn were the only two
actresses able to convert box office clout into behind-the-
scenes control. They've produced most of their movies over
the last decade, while at a slightly lower rung of bankability,
Jessica Lange and Sissy Spacek have been able to initiate
and develop smaller projects. Elaine May persists (or per-
sisted; the returns on *Ishtar* are not in) as an anomaly: a
brilliant script doctor with "connections" that got her directorial assignments when women (and men) of more proven
talent were going begging. Whether one finds *A New Leaf*
and her frenzied and only intermittently funny buddy films,
Mikey and Nicky and *Ishtar* lyrically dopey (the view of her
cult) or just plain sloppy, they unarguably contain some of
the most gratuitously nasty images of women to appear in
the last ten years.

Whether in the feminist camp, partly in it, or defiantly
male-oriented, these female power brokers, along with the
rare woman producer (Sherry Lansing, Marsha Lassiter)

were less a solid phalanx than a shaky lineup of individuals who were likely to have to swallow the urge to protest and adapt to commercial fashion just to stay in business. And the Young Turks who might have been expected to ally themselves with women—Martin Scorsese, Brian De Palma, Francis Coppola, Paul Schrader, George Lucas, Steven Spielberg—burrowed into violent male-centered melodramas or retreated into a no less fantastic world of eternal adolescence.

The fact is, movies no longer reflected our lives, and we (or those of us who still went to movies) no longer expected them to, nor looked for heroines who worked, married, divorced, thrashed out the conflicts between home and career. As the medium of photography had taken over the realistic function of nineteenth century painting, so television had taken over the sociological role that movies once played. But with two remarkable exceptions, those sturdily endearing testaments to women's solidarity, *Cagney and Lacey* and *Kate and Allie,* the vision of working woman was hollow and formulaic. Nothing in movies came close to conveying the special quality of women's relationships on a day-to-day working, or living, basis as did those remarkable series and the endlessly fresh performances of Tyne Daly and Sharon Gless as policewomen and Jane Curtin and Susan St. James as divorced mothers.

Oh, yes, we finally did get a couple of mainstream feminist films. One, about the three-ring circus, familiar to working women, of trying to hold down a job, raise a kid and run a household all at the same time, and who got the role? Dustin Hoffman, in *Kramer versus Kramer.* And the other, the story of a woman "of a certain age" and homeliness struggling to make her way, and fight off harrassment, in a man's world. And what was it? *Tootsie,* with (yet again)

Dustin Hoffman as the actor who has his consciousness raised and his sexual complacency punctured, in the course of his travails as a very plain woman.

The scenes in which Jessica Lange and Hoffman become friends, then intimates—those moments in which two very different kinds of women discover a bond in their mutual vulnerability—set off with infinite grace the image of "sisterhood" that we expected to be the grand theme of the decade.

Instead, the feminist theme, when feminism appeared at all, was of conflict. In those early "mad housewife" movies, cinematic echoes of *The Feminine Mystique,* women were torn between the mind-numbing and soul-destroying confines of domestic duty, on the one hand, and that exhilarating call to independence. Frank and Eleanor Perry's early adaptation of the Sue Kaufman novel, *Diary of a Mad Housewife; A Woman under the Influence,* John Cassavetes's harrowingly loony family drama starring wife Gena Rowlands as a housewife driven mad by baby talk; Martin Scorsese's *Alice Doesn't Live Here Anymore,* with Ellen Burstyn, a songbird sprung from domesticity by her husband's death, as the liberated, middle-American merry widow of the seventies; and Paul Mazursky's *An Unmarried Woman,* the enchanting sad-funny parable of a woman (Jill Clayburgh) left in the lurch by a philandering husband: these were the first *cris de coeur* from the bottomless depths of marital misery. These movies are not without flaws: in their brief against society's insensitive husbands, *Alice* and *A Woman* both lapse into a shrill, accusatory tone, turning Burstyn and Rowlands into fashionably helpless symbols of martyrdom that deny the spunk and resourcefulness they radiate as women. Yet (as I can testify, having lectured with both films around the country), housewives responded intensely to these characters, identified with their superiority to their boorish and blue-collar husbands, even felt that Ellen

Burstyn had suffered so grandly that she deserved (and they could overlook the improbability of her receiving) the ultimate in Hollywood having-it-all fantasy. As Mr. Right and Liberation, too, Kris Kristofferson's sexy, laid-back rancher, he of the nonmacho style, the secure ego and the even more secure bank account, was the *beau ideal* of the atavistic romantic in all feminists.

Women reacted less charitably toward Paul Mazursky's *An Unmarried Woman,* both toward Jill Clayburgh herself as an Upper East Side housewife left in the lurch by her philandering husband, and to her decision to forgo a trip to Vermont with irresistible Alan Bates in order to stick by her new job in an art gallery. Actually, as the sort of upper middle class woman who was raised on fifties notions of fidelity and the indissolubility of marriage, and who is thrown back on the minimal resources with which upper-crust schooling and a taste for the arts have provided her, Clayburgh would seem more in need of compassion than women who have proved themselves professionally, who have a job and a modicum of self-esteem to fall back on. But somehow—was it the apartment overlooking the East River? Clayburgh's skinny thighs? or her relative stoicism?—women didn't seem to feel that Clayburgh suffered enough and refused her their sympathy. Nor would they buy her turning down the impossibly attractive Alan Bates, witty, gorgeous and successful, whose work was hanging in the Museum of Modern Art! Women were of fiercely mixed minds: on the one hand, she didn't deserve him; on the other hand, as long as he was there, she'd jolly well better snap him up! How dare she pass up a trip to Vermont with the guy just to consolidate her position at that paltry art gallery. The very same women who had issued manifestoes on the need for self-reliance and an independent income to face those statistically probable years of solitude found themselves gnashing their teeth at

Clayburgh's missed opportunity. (And missed Mazursky's most telling revelation, when Bates tells Clayburgh he "approves" of her working, thus summing up centuries of condescension whereby men have whipped women's self-confidence more effectively than if they had beaten them.)

The sticking point, of course, is star chemistry, the way two paragons act as magnets not only for each other but for all of our hopes and fantasies of True Love. The tidal wave of attraction that enlists us in the devout wish for their consummation was inscribed into the very syntax of star cinema. We absorbed the cinema's lessons in love willingly and greedily during our growing-up years to the point where we salivate like Pavlov's dogs for the happy ending, the "forever" union of two perfect creatures that corresponds to our own drugged fantasies of love. And no wonder; for here was a convention, the courtship duet, conducted on *neutral* turf and culminating in marriage, that exalted woman, holding her as equal to the male, even as women in society were still regarded and treated as inferiors. In a sense, we created the stars and then they created us; that is, we made them into embodiments of an ideal, *equal* love which we were then doomed to yearn for, to dream of, to try and duplicate, and to comb the earth in search of in a state of perpetual disappointment, blaming Hollywood for our failure to achieve similarly glittering romantic destinies. There's a group of "realistic" women in *An Unmarried Woman,* Clayburgh's slightly dumpy careerwoman friends, all of whom are in the throes of various messy romantic entanglements; but do we identify with them? Do we accept this homelier version of the war between the sexes? No, no more than *these* women, poring nostalgically over pictures of the old stars, identify with Eve Arden instead of Joan Crawford, Thelma Ritter instead of Grace Kelly! In the bickering, bitter marriages endured by character actors, Hollywood had always offered ample clues of the thorny path ahead. But these were warnings no one chose to hear.

Nor did women accept the ending of the Australian film *My Brilliant Career*, about a would-be writer (Judy Davis) who forces herself to refuse the well-nigh irresistible offer of marriage from the gentleman farmer played by Sam Neill. Gillian Armstrong's movie is about a writer's realization that comfort and domestic bliss are the enemy, solitude and anguish the necessary soil out of which the author develops her literary consciousness. But women, chucking their own feminist principles in a collective longing for Mr. Right, yearned for the happy ending and were furious at Judy Davis for not working out some compromise modus vivendi (a log cabin out back with a padlock on the door?). If the screen lover "completes" the woman, whose vocation is romance, so their union seduces and fulfills *us*.

The very strength (we might say stranglehold) of romance lies in its fusion of two powerful strands: the desire for love, that noblest urge to transcend the boundaries of the self (and gender) on one hand and, on the other, the narcotic of fantasy—an addiction all the more powerful because, unlike other addictions, it can be prolonged and replayed indefinitely in the imagination. The seductiveness of this combination suggests both the difficulties in wresting ourselves from so powerful a drug, and the degree to which we have a vested interest in our own "subjugation." In leaning so heavily on the unilateral notion of male oppression, a good many feminists ignored the other half of the equation, the active role of women in permitting, encouraging, and *controlling* scenarios of dominance and submission. As habitual (and not unwilling) exhibitionists, we're entitled—and compelled—to acknowledge a certain complicity in the shadowy delights of male voyeurism. In denying this complicity, in insisting on the thesis of victimization, feminists not only deprived women of a collaborative autonomy in the imagining of love stories, but of a secret pleasure in the dark side of sex, those delirious (and politically "incorrect") fantasies of dominance and submission which it was the function of sexual liberation to allow us to express.

The most provocative and sophisticated challenge came from British feminist structuralists Laura Mulvey and Claire Johnston, who, using the heavy artillery of French semioticians like Barthes and Derrida, deconstructed the Hollywood cinema with the psychoanalytic theories (chiefly those dealing with castration) of Freud and Lacan. Hitchcock and von Sternberg were taken to task, at great theoretical length, for the ways in which their women (Dietrich for Sternberg, Hitchcock's icy blondes) "produced meaning" and catered to male narcissism by not being women at all, but phallus substitutes, "nonmales" whose function was to reassure men as to their own unchallenged supremacy in the world. It was by means of the "gaze"—characterized by Mulvey as a three-way process involving the camera and the other actors on the screen, both acting as surrogates for the male viewer—that woman was deprived of her own subjective desires and converted into this symbol of male desire.

The structuralist approach, with its seductive methodology, has recently extended its influence beyond academe and the quarterlies, where it has held tyrannical sway for the last ten years, to become part of the jargon of "serious" criticism throughout the country. But the doubts as to its viability (other than as a provocative starting point) remain. Not the least interesting question was why these self-proclaimed radicals would spend so much time and energy on obsolete, bourgeois artists (hardly representative, at that!) rather than attending to the progressive and politically acceptable cinema of feminists and the avant-garde. (When Mulvey and Peter Wollen began making films, it was with a highly theoretical work like *Penthiselea,* and for a coterie audience.) Moreover, Mulvey and Johnston neglected the context in which the films they studied were made and seen, that tremendous audience diversity, that lack of consensus, which is such a thorn in the side of sociologists and theoreticians. For example, what about female audiences? Are men the only ones who "gaze," and even appropriate and convert the object-woman into their own fantasy worlds? There's reason to believe that Dietrich was considerably more popular with, and intriguing to, women (and homosexuals) than men, who as a general rule preferred less exotic women—Betty Grable and other "girl next door" types rather than such extreme types as Marilyn Monroe (too sexy and too needy), Audrey Hepburn (too precious), Katharine Hepburn (too arrogant).

One is inclined to respond, as one does to *Ways of Seeing,* John Berger's ingenious Marxist dissection of woman-as-commodity in nineteenth century painting (1977), that the theory simply doesn't tally with our visual (and, with movies, aural) experience, our sense of women as far more complex, secretive, autonomous, far more "their own persons"— and also, more threatening—than the one-sided account allows for. In Hitchcock, particularly, a major theme, and one in which the director himself is implicated, is the sexual terror and the ignominy of the voyeur: the most conspicuous but by no means the only example being Jimmy Stewart's "impotent" (because incapacitated) window-gazer in *Rear Window,* retreating in panic from Grace Kelly's lusciously aggressive predator. In denying the other half of the equation, women's willing participation in arraying themselves for the male gaze, the British ignored Freud's own insights into the tremendous energy and displacement that goes into female narcissism—an energy that could, by implication, be channeled into a more direct acquisition of power, more open forms of desire. These were objectives that women were moving toward—but by no means in a straight line, and by no means in the solid phalanx apotheosized in feminist rhetoric.

Directors to whom the gaze theory might be more usefully applied—but whose films also expose its inadequacies—are Brian De Palma, whose *Dressed to Kill* turned Angie Dickinson into a neurotic, sexually insatiable "older woman," then pummeled and bloodied her for her "desires." And David Lynch, who in his retro-Hitchcockian reverie, *Blue Velvet,* revisits the virgin-whore fantasy from the point of view of a fifties adolescent plunked down in an eighties *Walpurgisnacht* setting. Blonde "good girl" (Laura Dern) is held in (mock) wholesome pristine opposition to the libidinous Isabella Rossellini, whose debauches with superkink Dennis Hopper provide sensational keyhole "gazing" for Lynch's surrogate. But in the messy here-and-now, with audiences (and feminists) divided over both films, there is—mercifully—no consensus, no last word as to what is a correct, what a demeaning portrait of woman, and certainly no one has given the theoreticians a mandate to speak for all of us. Admittedly both women are the projections of male fantasy, depraved "cases" whose sexual appetites are rendered gratuitously, without the complicity of the male "voyeur" (as opposed to the Kim Basinger character in *Blind Date,* whose rampage is provoked by the drinks Bruce Willis has carelessly—or intentionally—given her). Still, it might also be argued that both "heroines"—Isabella Rossellini, at least—elude the efforts of The Male to understand or "save" them.

And so does Melanie Griffith as the square-baiting hellion in Jonathan Demme's *Something Wild.* In this very eighties sunny-noir excursion into middle America, Griffith's *femme fatale* kidnaps and "liberates" a repressed businessman (Jeff Daniels), drives off into the unknown with him, and, in a show of strength, ties him to a motel bed and has her way with him. In *Street Smart,* in a genuinely erotic woman-initiated seduction scene, Kathy Baker's appealingly worldly prostitute firmly leads a robotlike Christopher Reeve in an act of love which is somehow all the sexier for his pliancy.

Isabella Rossellini, speaking for the decadent in all of us, admitted to being attracted to the role, and there is a sense that both actresses—Rossellini and Griffith—are doing just what they want to do, confusing and perhaps disarming their voyeur-saviors in the process. Moreover, in both films it is the young man, the super-square, who is the real virgin, and it is the woman who has her choice between the punk and the Galahad. Whatever one may think of either movie (I think both directors' earlier films—Lynch's low-rent *Eraserhead* and Demme's *Swing Shift*—are more satisfying), the wildly aggressive Griffith and the sultry Rossellini are no mere "objects"; and their failure to satisfy male fantasies or alleviate their own anxieties is largely what the movies are about.

Within the given of a male perspective, there were often some subversive wrinkles and teasing asides, challenges by women stars and directors that delicately pierced the heart of the sexist matter. Director Amy Heckerling took a teen coming-of-age project conceived from a male point of view, *Fast Times at Ridgemont High,* and gave it a radical twist by showing the pathos, reluctance, and painful disenchantment of the supposedly ecstatic (for the male) First Time through the eyes of the girl initiate. And Kathleen Turner blazed forth as a revolutionary combination of old-fashioned, I-know-who-and-where-I-am star confidence, and the casual antiglitter approach of an 80s "real person." She has tackled an audacious variety of roles with a no-nonsense intelligence and sensuality, from the soap opera seductress of *Body Heat* and the slovenly writer transmogrified in *Romancing the Stone* to the gangster's moll in John Huston's *Prizzi's Honor,* the prostitute in *Crimes of Passion,* and the anti-sentimental bitch-wife (alternating with the sweet cerebrum) opposite Steve Martin in *The Man with Two Brains.* (Martin, one of whose many appealing qualities is a preference for smart women, was also paired with Lily Tomlin in her best movie role, that of the female half of Steve Martin's androgynous clown in *All of Me.*)

If it had had the courage of its lurid inspiration, *9 ½ Weeks,* the movie based on a woman's fantasy (or memoir?) of an obsessional sadomasochistic sex binge, might have been a disturbing and exhilarating trip rather than the timid, glossy, catered affair it turned out to be. Women, like the writer of *9 ½ Weeks,* understand the degree to which the masochist—usually the woman in fantasies of dominance-submission—controls the proceedings, allows brutality up to a certain point, yet secretly wants to be taken over the edge; the titillation comes from suspense as to when that point will be crossed. Fantasies of brutal sex can be seen as a woman's way of exorcising her very real fear of rape, and of situations in which she is pure victim. In fantasies, she tames male power by eroticizing it and conforming it to her wishes. The desire for control (and, by implication, role reversal) takes various forms: dramas of retaliation, as in *Ms 45,* Abel Ferrara's harrowing, funky, low-budget X-rated tale of revenge in which a rape victim, a mute garment-district worker, prowls through the streets and annihilates her attacker in a bloody finale.

In the heroine-as-prostitute movies—*Klute,* Lizzie Borden's *Working Girls,* and Marleen Gorris's *Broken Mirrors*—women reverse their roles as love's slaves and acquire a temporary, dubious power by selling sex (or rather, the use of their bodies), remaining aloof while feigning the delirium that men expect and allow themselves to be fooled by. Sex, particularly in Borden's movie, is deeroticized by the ho-hum just-another-job treatment of the workplace (a pricey

Manhattan bordello), the johns, the negotiations, and the purchasing and disposal of condoms. And the hooker heroines are less turned on by the risk of danger than by the idea of controlling their lives, saying yes or no to a john, faking pleasure and thus remaining detached. Talking, getting personally involved with a client is more strenuous (because emotionally draining) than the kinkiest activity on the sexual menu. The spectacle of a prostitute sneaking a peak at her watch (Fonda in *Klute*) or disposing of a used condom (Louise Smith in *Working Girls*) deals a death blow to male fantasies of mutual ecstasy (and other myths, like the golden-hearted prostitute of movie tradition and the emotionally frigid whore of sociopathology), but it enacts a new feminist fantasy, that of a miraculous immunity. Women will somehow emerge from these tired and unloving transactions with their souls intact, their inner selves magically untainted by a "profession" that they, having been raised in a society that regards prostitution with contempt and horror, must surely recoil from. Like a good many prostitutes, Louise Smith's Molly is a lesbian. While this makes her detachment more plausible, Borden's efforts to make her a figure of sympathy to an upscale audience—she is a Yale graduate and a professional photographer—only force us to wonder why such a highly-qualified woman would become a prostitute in the first place.

There's an echo here of that rationalization popular in women's circles in the early seventies: hookers were somehow morally "cleaner" in getting paid for what wives were dishing out for free, or in the devious hope of an emerald pin or an eleven-speed dishwasher. In a society in which women are exploited as unpaid homemakers and childraisers (goes the argument), whores at least engage in an aboveboard transaction. This is a rationale dreamt up by educated women and nonhookers, by women who, like these films, refuse to acknowledge the toll taken by prostitution, the damage to the self, the warping of a woman's belief in and capacity for loving. So be it, these films (and women) would probably say; love is invariably a sexist enterprise. But is aping men the way to change it? In trying to hang onto control, salvage her self-esteem, isn't the prostitute-heroine in danger of losing control and her soul to boot? *Working Girls,* interesting as a feminist (and leftist) take on the sexual commodity market, is finally more depressing than straight porn. The combination of cheap caricature (the materialistic madam), amateurish acting (except for the superb Smith), and a theme that requires a deadening of the responses— theirs and ours—in order to be accepted, leaves a sordid aftertaste. The movie means, like Borden's other work, to be a parable of the exploiters and the exploited in a capitalist society (a theme for which female garment workers or Mexican grapepickers might have served better, if less commercially), but it is really the story of different degrees of powerlessness. In effect, the johns here are really metaphors: they, like the prostitutes, are losers enacting a defensive ritual against those in power: men who don't have to pay for sex, and women (the smaller group) who get what they want without it.

Nevertheless, the spirit of *Working Girls* was in keeping with the depressing note struck by most women in movies about sex. From the fascinating but darkly morbid sisterhood dramas of von Trotta to *Smooth Talk,* Joyce Chopra's disturbing young-woman-coming-of-age film (from a short story by Joyce Carol Oates), sex, male sex, was a menace to body and soul. Was it perhaps a new feminist twist on sexual Puritanism? For nowhere was there a glimpse of the life-affirming, passionately erotic female to which the women's movement and the sexual revolution were meant to give license. Nowhere a sense of that glorious sexually complete woman to which early twentieth century writers like Colette and Lou Andreas Salome pointed the way in their life and art. Lou Salome, though not a feminist, was a passionate supporter of women's superior capacity for love. The extraordinary life-affirming intellectual who enraptured the leading geniuses of her day (Nietzsche, Rilke, and Freud being only the most famous) traced woman's sexual glory to her ability to give with her whole body and soul, as opposed to man's partial and spiritually neutral participation. Erotic passion, which was an anomaly for a man, was normal and continual for a woman, and could open her up to her innermost self.

But like shell-shocked veterans of love's wars, women were in retreat, emulating rather than rejecting men's compartmentalization of sex. Prostitution was the perfect way of beating men at their own game by imitating them, and the climax to this hostile power play was not fornication but murder. A film that worked its way mesmerizingly from one to the other was Belgian director Chantal Akerman's *Jeanne Dielman, #23 Quai du Commerce, 1080 Bruxelles* (1975), a three-and-a-half hour long avant-garde film about the compulsive orderliness of a bourgeois housewife-cum-prostitute (Delphine Seyrig). Like the title, the movie followed, at a systematic snail's pace, every domestic detail of the woman's life, from chopping onions, skinning potatoes, and scrubbing the tub (minute by tedious minute) to disappearing into the bedroom, with clockwork predictability, for her no-less-solemnly conducted afternoon tryst. We wait, in horrified anticipation, for that tiny break—an accident, an unforeseen disruption—that will trigger madness, breakdown, and the violence we've been dreading and waiting for. It comes: she takes a kitchen knife to her john. Dutch director Marleen Gorris imagines a similarly savage, similarly ice-cold *crime passionel* in *A Question of Silence* (1983), the shocking film in which three women shoppers, strangers, suddenly and without consultation kill a store manager who has been guilty of nothing more than smug condescension. Like the murder of her husband by Martha Henry in the Canadian mad-house-wife film, *Dancing in the Dark,* these are—ostensibly—*actes gratuites,* arbitrary killings enacted under chillingly rational circumstances. The crime by the trio of Dutchwomen reaches beyond the immediate victim to the whole male race, the "good guys" (complacent liberals who "understand" women's hysteria) as much as, perhaps more than, the out-and-out misogynists. Similarly, when Martha Henry as an equally manic and obsessed housewife kills her husband with a kitchen knife, her revenge is directed not so much at the single infidelity that he has confessed to at a "festive" birthday dinner, as at the lifetime of obtuseness contained in this crowning insensitivity. In this adaptation (by Leon Marr) of Joan Barfoot's intriguing madwoman novel, the heroine speaks her piece from an institution, and Martha Henry even more than Delphine Seyrig has the squashed (but often darkly funny) movements of a somnambulist, a woman who has been brainwashed (in effect, lobotomized) by the "good housekeeping" approach to marriage. Seyrig bears her own incandescence, a spiritual quality that is somehow at odds with the domestic robot she is meant to portray. If her elegance contradicts the filmmaker's intentions, she is also what gives the film its hypnotic quality—something lacking in Akerman's later films, arch, snooze-inducing musicals in which the dreams of romantic shopgirls are deconstructed in song and dance.

The portrait of domesticity as hell on earth was not confined to the art cinema: even commercial movies had caught up with the enormously increased percentage of working women/wives, so that where earlier movies had forced women to abandon their careers in favor of marriage, the newer movies, like the Bancroft-MacLaine *The Turning Point,* took the side of the career woman.

Still, it wasn't a clean break. Claudia Weill's *Girlfriends* was perhaps one of the first "feminist" films to suggest the divergence between women (best friends) when one (Melanie Mayron's photographer) took the "high road" of career, the other the "low road" to suburbia. In Herbert Ross's *The Turning Point* MacLaine as the suburban housewife was forced to acknowledge that she may have made a mistake, that Bancroft had done the right thing in forsaking marriage for dance, eventually becoming a prima ballerina with the American Ballet Theatre. But the question then arose: why was this woman (Bancroft) so unhappy? Why was she made to feel shriveled and incomplete, half a woman at the end of her illustrious career? The myth of motherhood as womanhood, i.e., that only in giving birth (and caring for her young) does woman become truly "herself" dies hard, and no one was more energetic in keeping it alive than Swedish director Ingmar Bergman. His *Autumn Sonata* features Ingrid Bergman as a once-famous concert pianist who is made to wallow in guilt for past negligence toward her daughter, the now grown Liv Ullmann. In neither movie is there any suggestion that for some women, the pleasure in art, or in any obsessional vocation, might be equal to or greater than childrearing. And these were not simply male visions of women's dilemma, but movies heavily influenced by the sensibilities of the women involved: Nora Kaye, the dancer-wife of Herbert Ross, *The Turning Point*'s director; and Ullman and Bergman, who participated in the writing of the script of *Autumn Sonata*. This was also, along with the lugubriously reactionary *Terms of Endearment,* one of the few films to deal with mothers and daughters, the subject that of all the issues of the decade most obsessed women, and struck at the heart of our investigations into the conflict between freedom and a biological/cultural determinism.

In *Violets Are Blue,* a lovely, underrated "woman's film" starring Sissy Spacek, Kevin Kline, and Bonnie Bedelia, the career woman (Spacek), now a successful photojournalist, tries to return and reclaim her former lover . . . as well as the idyllic small-town life on the Maryland Shore that goes with him. It doesn't work, and in the final shot, as Spacek returns to her globetrotting career, the movie acknowledges that the kind of woman who loves her independence, her bachelor digs, her job, her travel, is not the one to put down roots, make bouillabaise, and find ultimate satisfaction in a wholesome small-town community.

There was a split; the seventies were turning into the Age of Ambivalence. Even if Hollywood hadn't ignored us, we would have been hard-put to find a consensus as to just what we wanted to see on the screen: did we want women to be shown, dismally and realistically, as victims; or progressively, as vanquishers of mighty odds? In the dust-settling period of feminism, a few home truths were in order: equality hadn't been achieved overnight; men had proved singularly unreliable at housework (the domesticated daddies of the male parenting movies notwithstanding); and "having it all" was a privilege reserved for a very few, very rich, very energetic women. Those who had gotten to the top were suddenly suffering from a malady called "Superwoman Burnout." And recently, in conjunction with the media-encouraged epidemic of babymania among the upper middle classes, there's been the horrifying spectacle of "radical housewives," women who've turned in their declarations of independence and returned to childbearing, childrearing, and homemaking with the single-minded zeal of born-again converts. There arose the suspicion that those old Hollywood movies in which women had been forced to choose between home and career (in favor of home) weren't just propaganda on the part of a male conspiracy. The conflict—now resolved in favor of career—reflected a deep polarity within women themselves. There was, at the very least, a

THE AGE OF AMBIVALENCE

sense that options are limited for women (as they are for
men) by energy, temperament, time; and that there were
mutually exclusive choices, say, between a life of mobility,
an all-consuming career or sexual adventure, on the one
hand, and the devotion to family on the other (and that even
within the family there might be unhappy conflicts between
husband and children).

A friend told me that when she and her husband were
married in the forties they inherited an air conditioner with
only two speeds, On and Off. They lived and slept in com-
parative peace and comfort, there being no alternative.
Then, some years later they bought a shiny new model with
ten speeds. From then on, their night life was a misery, with
each one arising in secret to set the dial for his comfort, only
to have the other creep up minutes later to readjust it. What
more apt metaphor for women in the 1980s, besotted with
ten options instead of two! Twenty years ago, a woman was
either married or she wasn't; if she was, she had children; if
she wasn't, she was a "spinster." Now the spectrum of
choices and gradations is endless and woman is in a bewildering world of constantly shifting alliances: she may be
heterosexual, homosexual, bisexual, repressed, or un-
determined; she may be married with children and a job,
but does she see herself as a working mother or as a career
woman with family? There's at least a 50 percent chance
she's without a mate, but is it temporary and how does she
feel about her state of aloneness? Weak or strong? She may
be living with a Significant Other or with an Insignificant
Other. Where do her loyalties lie? Victoria Jackson, playing
a female "reporter" on Saturday Night Live's newscast, was
watching a tape of herself making a shambles of an on-cam-
era assignment in Alaska while trying to cope with her
manic small baby. "Wait a minute," she whined furiously, in
response to criticism that she should have left the kid at

home, "First I'm a mother, *then* a wife-slash-lover-slash-best friend, *then* a homemaker and *then* a reporter!"

Women seemed to be racing back and forth between the poles of two insane ideals, the perfect Wife/Mother and the Successful Professional, unable to feel adequate on either count yet unwilling to forfeit one for the other or even to accept falling below the mark. It was almost as if we were unconsciously *nurturing* a sense of imperfection, pulling back, retreating into that comfortable sense of inadequacy from the mountaintop where, for a moment, we had glimpsed our own awesome strength. This was the one thing we couldn't quite bring ourselves to acknowledge—our ability to go it alone or in unorthodox combinations—as if such an admission would blow the world away, demolishing forever the myth of male superiority.

Men became alarmed nonetheless. One has to see, in the obsessionally male-oriented cinema of these years, a backlash to the threat that women posed. Robert Altman's eerily memorable *Three Women* and Federico Fellini's *City of Women* were the only works of art by men to take seriously, and with courageously admitted anxiety, the possibility of women abandoning men and forming a society of their own. For the most part, the backlash took the form of nymphetmania (the cycle of movies drooling over precocious and nubile teen stars like Brooke Shields, Tatum O'Neal, Kristy McNichol, and Jodie Foster), male rites-of-passage movies, and that most curious of late-seventies phenomena, the male parenting movie. From the emotional and domestic realms presided over by Dustin Hoffman (*Kramer versus Kramer*), Jon Voight (*Table for Five* and *The Champ*), Al Pacino (*Author! Author!*), Donald Sutherland (*Ordinary People*), Michael Keaton (*Mr. Mom*), and Martin Sheen (*Man, Woman and Child*), women are expelled to the wings or banished altogether, having shown their unfitness for the task—mothering—now to be performed by men. In man-child paradises, crusty fathers emerge from their masculine carapaces and learn to love, a trend that has to be seen as a monumental (if covert) act of compensation on the part of the male power elite of Hollywood, producers and directors thrice divorced, exorcising their guilt over abandoned children, or perhaps (an even more devious scenario) providing ammunition for the custody fights which fathers stood an increasing likelihood of winning. An obvious backlash against the women's movement, the misogyny in these movies, the venom directed against the "career women" in, say, *Tender Mercies* or *Terms of Endearment,* and the defense of the old-fashioned wife, was far more vituperative than the anti-working woman bias in the old studio films. In these, uppity women executives might be reduced to tears, Katharine Hepburn might be ridiculed for not being able to scramble eggs, but this was only so that, upon repentance, the prodigal housewives might be welcomed back into the fold. Now there was a real sense of separatism, perhaps because men realized that the stakes were changing, that although some women were more comfortable with the myth of male superiority, others were demanding power openly and less deviously, and were not prepared to bolster men in return for a now-mythical security, that of the strong and loyal "oak-tree" male.

The move toward separateness in the seventies, the attempt of women to reclaim a central position for themselves and break the bonds of dependency—on men, on Hollywood—was something one felt as an undercurrent rather than as anything resembling an articulated program or even a conscious theme. In the two-steps-forward-one-step-back rhythm of social change, women began making their way back into movies in the eighties, with a subtly new consciousness. However opposed—or indifferent—anyone might be to the themes of feminism, they were there none-theless, as often in the absence of women as in their presence.

In most cases, the surge was coming from outside Holly-wood, and with a variety that defied ideology and was im-possible to chart along a positive-negative curve. Susan Sei-delman's man-crazy heroines in thrift-shop couture, like Dorris Dorrie's stranded sixties men, were postfeminist. *Entre Nous,* Diane Kurys' entrancing memoir of her mother's intense relationship with another woman, like Donna Deitch's outright lesbian tale, *Desert Hearts,* were unmis-takably the work of eighties women's sensibility, but with-out being overtly political. By contrast, the Argentine Maria Luisa Bemberg intermingled feminist and left wing protest in *Camilla* and *Miss Mary,* women-oriented portraits of her country's oppressive aristocracy. The stubbornly idiosyn-cratic heroines of Eric Rohmer, the ignorant peasant girl in *Hour of the Star* (1987), Suzana Amaral's funny, mystical Brazilian fable, or Sandrine Bonnaire as the fierce lost soul in Agnes Varda's *Vagabond* are hardly "role models," but they are marginal women who become beacons of intensity in the hands of compassionate directors.

When Seidelman, Borden, Bette Gordon, and the rest of the new generation of American independent woman directors, less explicitly feminist and more postfeminist punk, burst on the scene, they followed in the path, if not the footsteps, of groundbreaking directors like Claudia Weill, Joan Micklin Silver, Martha Coolidge (who made a dubious transition from feminist documentaries to Hollywood Valley-Girl and kidfilm projects). And for all their presumed liberation, the new generation had many of the same conflicts as their predecessors. In *Des-perately Seeking Susan,* Seidelman shows us women di-vided in two, between the free-wheeling alleycat pose of Madonna's New Woman and the more timid housekitten, Rosanna Arquette; and her *Making Mr. Right* presents a variety of women, all in the throes of romantic obsession, one woman (the heroine, played by Ann Magnuson) determined to have some say in the conditioning of the male lover of the future.

Old forms and types were transformed to suit the eighties. There was a new toughness in the *femme fatale*—Kathleen Turner in *Body Heat,* Theresa Russell in *Black Widow,* Melanie Griffith in *Something Wild,* Jane Fonda in *The Morning After.* "All right," women were saying, "You want to use us as sex objects, then pay the price." If men weren't going to take women seriously, then women would take their relationships for what they could get out of them. There was a hard-nosed realism here, reflecting the fact that there are very few Prince Charmings able to marry and support a woman. The rise in the cost of living, the rarity of available men, the narcissism and selfishness of the male yuppie create a mutual suspicion that goes beyond the sexual hostilities of the forties *film noir.* In the forties, there were more Cinderella stories, more grounds for believing in a fairy tale ending, partly because sexual and social coercion still existed: once upon a time, a man had to marry the hatcheck girl if he'd gotten her with child. Now, everyone was willing to settle for less in matters of permanence and fidelity.

It remains to be seen whether the well-publicized perils of promiscuity may rein in the permissive themes of the eighties and bring back romance, but one has to wonder how we will regain the sense of trust (never very deep, perhaps) that was based on fixed roles. There have been few "normal" love stories recently, and the great love stories of the last three years? *Children of a Lesser God* (between a deaf girl and a teacher of the deaf); *Room with a View* (period);

The Fly (what happens to a couple when one changes and the other doesn't); and the gay love stories: *Kiss of the Spider Woman, My Beautiful Laundrette,* and *Desert Hearts.*

Instead of redemption waiting at the end of the new "love" stories, there was increasing fragmentation and mobility. Even our personalities seemed discontinuous; we were reinventing ourselves every decade. A woman gets on a plane—who knows where she is going, what she is doing, who she will *be* when she arrives! We want to try on other roles for size.

The appeal of *Black Widow* and *Outrageous Fortune* was in two contrasting women taking each other's measure, identifying with their opposites, mentally trying on each other's personality for size. In a movie written by a woman, Leslie Dixon, Shelley Long and Bette Midler brought their comic personae into glorious collision as the first female "buddy team." In *Black Widow,* Theresa Russell as a slyly mocking murderer and Debra Winger as a workaholic drone are more intrigued by and attracted to each other than either is to the men in their lives. The movie is about two different kinds of women who are, perhaps, two sides of the same person—woman as workaholic and woman as greedy hedonist.

The sudden emergence of "bankable" stars like Streep, Lange, Spacek, Keaton, and Goldie Hawn not only filled the vacuum created by the endless cycle of "boys" films—kiddie movies and special effects superspectacles—but may have come about because of it. The rites-of-passage movies featuring stars like Tom Cruise, Michael J. Fox, and the infamous "brat pack" were dedicated to the sexual initiation of boys, and were invariably the work of grown men revisiting and refashioning their teenage years, seeing their exploits in a more favorable light. For women, unlike men, adolescence is not the time of the awakening, the moment of crossing the threshhold into womanhood. Sex is more a terror than an opportunity (witness the huge popularity with girls of the slasher, *Halloween/Friday the 13th* films, in which the tartish "fast" girl is violently punished); it is not until a young woman goes out into the world, leaves the "womb" of friends and family, marries (or gets a job) and has her wings clipped, discovers the split between the nurturing woman and the free spirit, that her consciousness is stricken—and raised! Until then, she believes she can have it all—hence the natural gulf between adult women who have cut their feminist teeth on the world, and the next generation, their daughters and friends, who take feminism's gains for granted.

At the other end of the age spectrum, perhaps one of the major and most subtle accomplishments is the changing view of aging women and women alone. The solitary woman is no longer a figure of pathos or ridicule, as in that venerable figure of the fifties, the Repressed Schoolteacher waiting to be liberated by a Stud. And some of the most interesting movies have featured two women: *Julia,* the tantalizing but too slavishly faithful rendering of the Lillian Hellman memoir starring Jane Fonda and Vanessa Redgrave; Diane Kurys's *Entre Nous; Loyalties,* the Canadian film (by Anne Wheeler) about a bond between two women that transcends racial barriers; and Margarethe von Trotta's powerful fables of sisterhood, especially *Marianne and Juliane,* the haunting story of a terrorist and her more conventional sister. Women are not afraid of assuming more masculine qualities, of showing their skills and trying on different roles for size. Bette Midler, Cher, Angelica Huston, and Helen Shaver have played weird or sexually daring roles that only a more liberated cinema could accommodate. Jessica Lange's Patsy Cline (in *Sweet Dreams*) was a lusty broad, finally defeated by death and a soap opera plot. Most significantly of all, women's careers—perhaps later getting started without studios to back them up—are lasting longer.

Women in their thirties and forties, who would have been pushed into mother/grandmother roles or forced into retirement in an earlier era, are playing vital, sexually active women. Jane Fonda, as a "has-been" star in *The Morning After,* makes glorious fun of being past her prime, and the trio of actresses in *Crimes of the Heart* are almost a decade older than the girls of Beth Henley's play. But while capturing the youthful scattiness of the sisters, Lange, Spacek, and Keaton create a sense of pathos and time gone by. Mental agility and physical fitness, the eternal quest for self-discovery, keep us young.

The same goes for the restless forty-ish women in Woody Allen's films: Mia Farrow, Barbara Hershey, and Dianne Wiest, in *Hannah and Her Sisters* seek answers in different places and with varying degrees of success; they've been through the wars, yet (therefore?) they are all irresistibly sensual. Even the "old-fashioned" women in Allen's *Radio Days,* his mother (Julie Kavner) and aunt (Dianne Wiest) are endowed with richly dimensional natures and a sensuality one doesn't usually find in a son's recollections of his parents' generation. It's the kind of empathy we're more likely to find in European cinema: we're used to seeing Jeanne Moreau take on the years gallantly, her lovers, her disappointments, her *petits péchés* etching gorgeous lifelines on her temptress's face. But who would have thought that actresses so defined by their youth as waiflike Mia Farrow or Barbara Hershey, the flaky sixties flower-child, could make the passage into womanhood so triumphantly, be more interesting without the little girl mannerisms.

There's an inevitable element of sexual narcissism and of the ringmaster in all of this, as Allen and his taste-in-women are the centrifugal force, even when he's playing a marginal role. These are *his* women, his discoveries, and without his sponsorship, where would they be? They'd have fallen through the cracks in a film industry dominated by men.

What's remarkable is that so many women have finally made their way to the top without the studio system to support them, and that the struggle itself has given substance to their style. A whole generation of women didn't really hit their stride until their thirties, and in the meantime, these were not women who sat around "doing publicity" and waiting for the next picture, or whose lives revolved around "the industry." That sense of lives lived richly and apart from movies and of having succeeded on their own is part of their strength and attractiveness as performers. They came to maturity without ever passing through the "ingenue" phase, making us realize, as they did so, that we were no longer interested in dewy-eyed innocents, or blonde bombshells. Harlow was at her peak when she died at 25, Marilyn Monroe over the hill at 35. They—their types—had no place to go. By contrast, Cybill Shepherd made a splash as an ingenue, went out like a light, and in earlier times that might have been the end of it. Instead, in her mid-thirties, giving the impression that she could take it or leave it, she returned in triumph. What's especially interesting about her role as Maddie, the cool and capable head of the Blue Moon Detective Agency, is that her ice-queen executive has none of the nasty undertones that went with the turf when stars like Rosalind Russell and Joan Crawford played "boss ladies" in the forties, and movies were trying to show women what wasn't good for them.

What the picture shows—especially outside the Hollywood mainstream—is a diversity of women working, and in such numbers that a festival devoted exclusively to women's films is no longer thinkable. The numbers mean that there will be less, rather than more, political uniformity, and little chance of there being a single political "line" that directors, actors, critics can agree on. There is very little common ground among the films, say, of Penelope Spheeris, Agnieszka Holland, Yvonne Rainer, Marta Meszaros, Doris Dorrie, Micheline Lanctot, Lee Grant, Valie Export, Lina Wertmuller, and Jill Godmilow. Likewise, in the range of roles portrayed, women will be victims and avengers, reckless, sexy, puritans, radicals, and up-tight bitches, dippy dames and morose modernists, their very diversity a guarantee against stereotype.

For every stereotype there's a counter-stereotype and the story of women can no longer be reduced to a recitation of evils. As a younger, less hidebound and less conflicted generation emerges, it becomes easier for all of us to speak with our own voices and just assume that someone will be listening, to go against the grain of male desires and definitions, to be strange, loud, impolite, enigmatic, baroque, beautiful, ugly, vengeful, funny. We want nothing less, on or off the screen, than the wide variety and dazzling diversity of male options.

INDEX

INDEX

INDEX

INDEX

INDEX

INDEX

INDEX

INDEX

INDEX

INDEX

INDEX

INDEX

INDEX